In the Face of
Diversity

CHINA AND THE WEST IN THE MODERN WORLD

William Christie, Series Editor

China and the West in the Modern World publishes original, peer-reviewed research on relations between China and the West from the accession of the Manchu Qing dynasty in 1644 to the present. The series brings into play different national and disciplinary perspectives to achieve a more thorough and cross-culturally nuanced understanding of the political, economic, and cultural background to the negotiations and realignments currently underway between China and Western nations.

The Poison of Polygamy
Wong Shee Ping, translated by Ely Finch

South Flows the Pearl: Chinese Australian Voices
Mavis Gock Yen, edited by Siaoman Yen and Richard Horsburgh

Tribute and Trade: China and Global Modernity, 1784–1935
Edited by William Christie, Angela Dunstan and Q.S. Tong

Made in Chinatown: Chinese Australian Furniture Factories, 1880–1930
Peter Charles Gibson

The Flip Side: Old China Hands and the American Popular Imagination, 1935–1985
Stuart Christie

In the Face of Diversity: A History of Chinese Australian Community Organisations, 1970s–2020s
Nathan D. Gardner Molina

In the Face of Diversity

A History of Chinese Australian Community Organisations, 1970s–2020s

Nathan D. Gardner Molina

SYDNEY UNIVERSITY PRESS

First published by Sydney University Press
© Nathan D. Gardner Molina 2025
© Sydney University Press 2025

Reproduction and communication for other purposes
Except as permitted under Australia's *Copyright Act 1968*, no part of this edition may be reproduced, stored in a retrieval system, or communicated in any form or by any means without prior written permission. All requests for reproduction or communication should be made to Sydney University Press at the address below:

Sydney University Press
Gadigal Country
Fisher Library F03
University of Sydney NSW 2006
Australia
sup.info@sydney.edu.au
sydneyuniversitypress.com

 A catalogue record for this book is available from the National Library of Australia.

ISBN 9781743329986 paperback
ISBN 9781761540004 epub
ISBN 9781743329993 pdf

Cover image: Banner and lion dancers of the Sydney Chinese Support Committee for Olympics 2000. Taken by King Fong at Dixon St., Haymarket, July 1993.

We acknowledge the traditional owners of the lands on which Sydney University Press is located, the Gadigal people of the Eora Nation, and we pay our respects to the knowledge embedded forever within the Aboriginal Custodianship of Country.

Some quotations from historical sources may contain terms or views that are culturally sensitive, outdated, or racist, and do not reflect current understanding or contemporary values. The wording in these quotes does not reflect the views of Sydney University Press or the author. The use of Chinese scripts (simplified or traditional) in this book reflects the scripts used in the original materials.

Acknowledgements

As this book is based upon my doctoral thesis, I first must thank my PhD supervisors, Prof Antonia Finnane and Prof Sean Scalmer, for their advice, encouragement and patience. I was extremely lucky to have them as mentors and I hope I can one day pay forward the generosity they have shown me. I am especially grateful to Antonia for her influence on my attitudes toward writing, scholarship and the importance of history.

Furthermore, I gratefully acknowledge that my PhD research was enabled by some academic awards. I will always be thankful to Jane Hansen for creating the Hansen PhD Scholarship in History. I was honoured to be the inaugural recipient of the prize and it changed my life in no small way. Additionally, the Victorian Government's Hamer Scholarship enabled me to undertake a year of intensive language study at Nanjing University, without which I would not possess the language ability to undertake this study. During my PhD, I was also fortunate to receive a Norman McCann Summer Scholarship at the National Library of Australia. The six weeks spent with the library's expert staff and trove of oral histories and English- and Chinese-language materials was invaluable for this book. The transformation of my thesis into a book was helped by generous funding from the Australian Academy of the Humanities through its Publication Subsidy Scheme. I am also grateful to the Academy for inviting me to deliver the 2024 Hancock Lecture where I could publicly share some of this research.

I will always treasure the time shared with my interviewees and other members of those Chinese Australian community organisations who were enthusiastic about my research and willing to share their time, their opinions and their memories. You were all fonts of historical information, but also instructive about the past condition of Australia's multiculturalism and how we should ensure its future. In this regard, I especially want to mention an afternoon spent with the late Tsebin Tchen. His vision of multicultural Australia left a lasting impression on me. I hope he would have approved of this work.

I was helped through this journey by the friendship and advice of PhD and early career researcher colleagues. I thank Bernard Keo, Jiyuan "Luke" Yin, Sam Watts, Beth Marsden, Sofie Onorato, Antonia Smyth, Daniel Dunne and Shan Windscript for reading drafts and making comments, checking my translations, helping me with applications and opportunities, and for inspiring me to keep going. I thank the examiners of my thesis, Ien Ang and Liangni Liu, for encouraging me to turn it into a book. I am grateful to Will Christie and the editors at Sydney University Press, especially Naomi van Groll, for their patience and feedback on the manuscript. In this regard, I also want to thank Kerry Brown, Jayne Persian, John Fitzgerald, Kate Bagnall, Pookong Kee and Ien Ang who provided comments, suggestions and endorsements. A special thank you to Sophie Loy-Wilson whose advice and example has greatly motivated me over the past year. I also acknowledge all of my comrades at the National Tertiary Education Union at the University of Melbourne whose solidarity and staunchness through trying times has been inspiring.

My deepest gratitude is for my wife, Tini. You are always the first and last source of advice. I wouldn't have got here without the trust you put in me. *Te amo.*

Contents

Acknowledgements	v
List of plates	ix
Abbreviations	xiii
Preface	xv
Introduction	1
1 Chinese Australian community organisations from White Australia to multiculturalism	25
2 Early optimism and challenges	65
3 The "Blainey debate"	103
4 The Tiananmen Massacre and the "89ers"	139
Plates	176
5 The "Hanson debate"	197
6 Community organisations in the "Chinese century"	235
7 The "China influence" debate	271
The Chimera: Chasing unity in the face of diversity	307
Bibliography	319
Appendix 1	359
Appendix 2	363
Index	383

List of plates

Plates 1–3 These three images depict the rise, fall and rise again of the See Yup Temple in Melbourne.   176–177

Plate 4 On 12 October 1910, Lieutenant Governor Sir Edward Stone laid the foundation stone for the CWA's community hall, where it still stands on James Street in Northbridge, Perth.   178

Plate 5 William Fong took this photo in the 1960s, likely part of a Chung Wah Society Chinese new year celebration. Blending the old and new, the procession leaders in traditional garb rode on the back of a truck and marching girls accompanied the lion dancers.   179

Plate 6 With the advent of multiculturalism, parades and festivals became important expressions of community identity and fostered inter-ethnic familiarity. Here, some children are being drawn into the Chinese New Year celebrations.   180

Plate 7 A member of the Chinese Fellowship of Victoria cooks spring rolls as part of Chinese New Year festivities.   181

Plate 8 As multiculturalism became more accepted as part of Australia's national identity, the country's ethnic diversity was often displayed in its public celebrations, such as in this Australia Day parade in Canberra in 1987.   182

In the Face of Diversity

Plate 9 Professor Geoffrey Blainey had been the inaugural president of the Australia China Council, a body intended to promote understanding and cultural exchanges between the two nations. Here, Blainey and fellow ACC member Tom Keneally flank Mr Liu Gengyin, Vice-President of the Chinese People's Association for Friendship with Foreign Countries, during his visit to Australia in June 1983. 183

Plate 10 The Blainey debate stoked anti-Asian sentiments and emboldened racist organisations. National Action was one such racist organisation that increased its activities at the time. Reproduced here is a page from the October 1984 newsletter of the Chung Wah Association, alerting its membership to the circulation of these materials in Perth neighbourhoods. 184

Plate 11 The Australian Chinese Forum was formed to increase interest and participation in Australian politics among Chinese Australians. One of its methods to do so was to invite politicians and community leaders to speak at its functions. Al Grassby, the commissioner for community relations and "godfather" of Australian multiculturalism, was a recurring guest at such functions. Here he is speaking at ACF's annual dinner in 1986. 185

Plate 12 In the wake of the Tiananmen Massacre, Chinese students sought to stay in Australia and eventually became the country's largest single intake of asylum seekers. Here, a student leader adresses a crowd at the Australian National University. 186

Plate 13 At a rally in front of the PRC Consul General's residence in Toorak, protestors "indignantly condemn" China's government for the "savage massacre" (quoting English and Chinese text shown on the banners). 187

Plate 14 Protesters at the rally in Toorak seemed to come from many walks of life, representing both the diversity of Chinese communities and the unanimity in condemning the massacre. 188

Plates 15–16 Pauline Hanson's politics represented a great threat to multiculturalism in Australia. 189

Plate 17 Hanson's divisive politics also had the contrary effect of bringing marginalised communities together. 190

List of plates

Plate 18 The rise of One Nation prompted many Chinese Australians to take more interest in politics, with some even deciding to run for election. In the 1998 federal election, past president of the Chinese Association of Victoria, Dr Ka-Sing Chua, ran with the Unity Party, a multiculturalist party that formed to oppose Pauline Hanson.   191

Plate 19 Around the turn of the century, it was relatively easy to embrace both Chinese and Australian identities. Here, Michael Xu dons a cork hat and raises a glass of beer after becoming an Australian citizen in 1997.   192

Plate 20 John Howard had a fraught relationship with Chinese Australian communities during his prime ministership, due largely to the perceptions of his light touch towards Pauline Hanson, his retreat from multiculturalism, and his alignment with Geoffrey Blainey during the 1980s.   193

Plate 21 In its early days, the Chinese Youth League was a target of ASIO surveillance for its communist leanings (when the Chinese Communist Party finally won the civil war in 1949, members of CYL paraded through the streets of Sydney with a homemade flag of the People's Republic).   194

Plate 22 The "Glory and Dream" concerts planned for the Sydney and Melbourne town halls prompted the formation of the Australian Values Alliance.   195

Plate 23 A spike in Sinophobic abuse and assaults followed in the wake of the COVID-19 pandemic; other Australians were also targeted owing to their East Asian appearance. The Chinese Australian Forum stepped forward to spearhead the "Chinese Australian response" to the problem, appealing to the public and politicians for support in multiple ways.   196

Abbreviations

89ers	Chinese students who sought permanent residency in Australia as a result of the 1989 Tiananmen Massacre
ACCA	Australian Chinese Community Association (of New South Wales) 澳華公會
ACF	Australian Chinese Forum (later CAF) 澳華論壇
ACTCAA	Australian Capital Territory Chinese Australian Association 堪培拉澳华会
ACWA	Australian Chinese Workers Association 澳洲华人总工会
AKMT	Australasian KMT (see KMT below)
AVA	Australian Values Alliance 澳洲价值守护联盟
ASIO	Australian Security Intelligence Organisation
CAF	Chinese Australian Forum (previously ACF) 澳華論壇
CASA	Chinese Association of South Australia 南澳中華會館
CASS	Chinese Australian Services Society 華人服務社 (later stopped referring to the acronym to be known simply as "CASS", which became the forerunner organisation to CASSCare)

CAV	Chinese Association of Victoria 維多利亞省華人協會
CCP	Chinese Communist Party 中国共产党
CFV	Chinese Fellowship of Victoria 維省僑友社
CWA	Chung Wah Association (Perth, Western Australia) 中華會館
CWS	Chung Wah Society (Darwin, Northern Territory) 中華會
CYL	Chinese Youth League 澳洲僑青社
DIEA	Department of Immigration and Ethnic Affairs (Dec 1975 – Jul 1987)
ELICOS	English Language Intensive Courses for Overseas Students
FCA	Federation of Chinese Associations (Victoria) 維省華人社團聯合會
ICECAV	Indo-China Ethnic Chinese Association of Victoria 澳洲維省印支華人相濟會
KMT	Kuomintang (The Chinese Nationalist Party) 国民党
PLA	People's Liberation Army 人民解放军
PRC	People's Republic of China 中华人民共和国
QCF	Queensland Chinese Forum 昆士蘭華人論壇
RSL	Returned and Services League of Australia
ROC	Republic of China (Taiwan) 中華民國
SYS	See Yup Society (Melbourne) 四邑會館

Preface

In the 1980s, Jennifer Cushman challenged historians to move beyond a "one-dimensional" understanding of Chinese in Australia as gold miners or sojourners. An ever-growing body of scholarship about Chinese residents covering roughly 50 years either side of Australia's Federation has met this challenge well.[1] However, scholarship about Chinese Australian history in the post-war period is much less common and histories of Chinese Australians since the end of the White Australia period even more so. To attend to this deficit, *In the Face of Diversity* breaks new ground by tracing the history and diversity of Chinese Australian communities in the post-White Australia era and offers the first sustained, nation-wide account of the manifold community organisations that have emerged since the advent of "multicultural Australia". It draws on Chinese- and English-language materials as well as interviews with past and current "community leaders" to create a comparative study of the most influential community organisations and their formations, participation in society, political actions, mutual cooperation and, sometimes, competition. The book is a response to the persistent conceptualisations of a single "Chinese Australian community" in Australian society and the

---

1   Keir Reeves and Tseen Khoo, "Dragon Tails: Re-Interpreting Chinese Australian History", *Australian Historical Studies* 42, no. 1 (2011): 8.

homogenisation of Chinese Australians. An imagined "Chinese vote" at election time or attacks on people of East Asian appearance during the recent COVID-19 pandemic for "bringing the disease from China" are a couple of examples of the essentialisation of Chinese Australians and their communities that are perhaps most familiar at present. There is, however, a much longer history of such conceptualisations from both inside and outside Chinese Australian communities. So, while the present dearth of historical studies in this field warrants the writing of this book, the true impetus for constructing this comparative history is to test the persistent notion of a single, cohesive or united Chinese Australian community.

In the Face of Diversity owes much to three seminal works of Chinese Australian history: C.F. Yong's *The New Gold Mountain: The Chinese in Australia, 1901–1921* (1977); John Fitzgerald's *Big White Lie: Chinese Australians in White Australia* (2007); and Mei-fen Kuo's *Making Chinese Australia: Urban Elites, Newspapers and the Formation of Chinese-Australian Identity, 1892–1912* (2013). Each used a national scope in their analyses of Chinese Australian history and community formation and each relied on Chinese-language materials to construct their histories. Fitzgerald's *Big White Lie* is especially influential because it effectively responded to the contemporary national debate about the legacy of the White Australia policy at the time of its publication. *In the Face of Diversity* attempts to offer a similarly authoritative account of Chinese Australian communities that complements previous scholarship by drawing our attention from the late 19th and early 20th centuries to the late 20th and early 21st. Moreover, the book should offer something to current discussions around Australia's national sovereignty, its social cohesion, and the future of migration.

One of the more prominent national debates in Australia today centres on China's alleged influence or political interference in Australia. Though it is an over-simplification to describe it as such, the debate can be divided into camps that either raise the alarm about China's present danger toward Australia or advise Australia to be watchful of China's rising power without necessarily being fearful. Recent books that warn of China's nefarious meddling in Australia include Clive Hamilton's *Silent Invasion: China's Influence in Australia* (2018) and Peter Hartcher's *Red Zone: China's Challenge and Australia's*

Preface

Future (2021). On the other side are recent books that encourage Australia to view the present debate soberly and reflect on the country's own insecurities (notably its history of Sinophobia). David Brophy's *China Panic: Australia's Alternative to Paranoia and Pandering* (2021) and James Curran's *Australia's China Odyssey: From Euphoria to Fear* (2022) are notable examples. The increasing number of publications entering the debate reflect the growing preoccupations about this topic among academic and general readerships alike.

Whereas these books contain concerns about Sino-Australian relations from the "Australian point of view" (be that the political view from Canberra or a more generalised attitude from Australian society), *In the Face of Diversity* stands out by bringing to the fore Chinese Australian communities' own views about the present debate and the histories that inform them. It is important to include the views of Chinese Australians in this debate because they are often implicated (willingly or not) on racial grounds. It is also important to listen to Chinese Australians rather than just talk about them. Naturally, the opinions they present are informed by understandings of the past. As such, Chinese Australian perspectives offer not just a more nuanced view of the present Sino-Australian relationship and its local implications, but also fresh insights into more established interpretations of recent Australian history as well.

In the Face of Diversity also engages with the current movement to include more non-English accounts of Australian history by drawing on materials written in other languages or produced by ethnic communities other than the dominant Anglo-Celtic one. In addition to those of Yong, Kuo and Fitzgerald mentioned above, other noteworthy studies of this type include Sophie Loy-Wilson's *Australians in Shanghai: Race, Rights and Nation in Treaty Port China* (2017); Samia Khatun's *Australianama: The South Asian Odyssey in Australia* (2019); and Mavis Gock Yen's posthumously released *South Flows the Pearl: Chinese Australian Voices* (2023). As Khatun describes, such works help to break down the "monolingualism" of Australian history and reconstruct a less Euro-centric framework for understanding the country's past. *In the Face of Diversity* follows a path inspired by Khatun, and with luck it has arrived somewhere near her work and others like it.

In the Face of Diversity

Because *In the Face of Diversity* touches upon many important moments in Australia's recent past, fragments of this history have been encountered in scholarship concerned with different questions. There have been many studies about the making of White Australia, its slow dismantling and its eventual transformation into multicultural Australia. Marilyn Lake and Henry Reynolds' *Drawing the Global Colour Line* (2008); Gwenda Tavan's *The Long Slow Death of White Australia* (2005); James Jupp's *From White Australia to Woomera: The Story of Australian Immigration* (2007); and Mark Lopez's *The Origins of Multiculturalism in Australian Politics 1945-1975* (2000) are notable for pioneering new understandings in this area. Each uses different analytical lenses – be that as transnational, social, policy and political histories – to view Australian society holistically. Prominent moments in recent Australian history, like the Blainey and Hanson debates, have provoked a lot of passionate responses and sober reflections about Australian society and its internal race relations. For this book, some relevant examples include Andrew Markus and M.C. Riklefs' *Surrender Australia? Essays in the Study and Uses of History: Geoffrey Blainey and Asian Immigration* (1985); Ghassan Hage's *White Nation: Fantasies of White Supremacy in a Multicultural Society* (2000); and Laksiri Jayasuriya and Pookong Kee's *The Asianisation of Australia?: Some Facts about the Myths* (1999). The sustained defence of socially pluralistic ideals in these works, and at times their provocative critiques of Australian society, are choice examples of humanitarian scholars working as the conscience of the nation. Though *In the Face of Diversity* does not claim the same level of prestige as these scholars or their works, it nevertheless offers a view of Australian society that, although particular to Chinese Australian communities, is holistic enough to provide fresh food for thought for all Australians.

Of course, this book is not limited to an Australian audience, as much of its subject matter is inherently transnational in character. Scholarship about the Chinese diasporas has become an important subset of Chinese studies, as indicated by the creation of the *Journal of Chinese Overseas* and the growing amount of academic interest in Chinese diasporas – including the diaspora in Australia. Many of these are collected works: Khun Eng Kuah-Pierce and Evelyn Hu-Dehart's *Voluntary Organizations in the Chinese Diaspora* (2006); Khun Eng

Preface

Kuah-Pierce and Andrew P. Davidson's *At Home in the Chinese Diaspora* (2008); and Julia Kuehn, Kam Louie and David M. Pomfret's *Diasporic Chineseness after the Rise of China: Communities and Cultural Production* (2014). Important monographs to specifically examine the Chinese Australian experiences include Jan Ryan's *Chinese Women and the Global Village: An Australian Site* (2003); Lucille Lok-Sun Ngan and Chan Kwok-bun's *The Chinese Face in Australia: Multi-Generational Ethnicity Among Australian-Born Chinese* (2012); Jia Gao's *Chinese Activism of a Different Kind: The Chinese Students' Campaign to Stay in Australia* (2013); and *Locating Chinese Women: Historical Mobility between China and Australia* (2021) by Kate Bagnall and Julia Martínez. Jan Ryan's research into Chinese Australian women covers a similar period to *In the Face of Diversity* and even touches upon women's involvement in community organisations. It is an excellent study on women's personal histories and their complex local and transnational networks. Because Chinese peoples have a long presence in many parts of the world, the field of study of Chinese diasporas is broad. Scholars writing about Chinese Australian history therefore often find themselves writing for two audiences: one interested in local or national history and another interested in the development and character of Chinese diasporic communities. The comparative study of Chinese Australian communities in this book gives something novel to both audiences, and its incorporation of transnational histories and current trends in Chinese studies means it also remains relevant to local and international scholars of Chinese diasporas.

In the Face of Diversity offers a study that is quite distinct from the abovementioned works. No other monograph analyses the history of Chinese Australian communities and their representative organisations in contemporary times, let alone uses this history to test the assumptions about a singular, unitary Chinese Australian community. For those interested in Australian and Chinese Australian history, the book provides detailed accounts of Chinese Australian responses to significant moments in Australia's recent history and puts those responses into a longer historical context. For those interested in Chinese diaspora communities and migration, it traces the development of diverse communities and organisations across the last five decades and the span of the Australian continent. And, rather than paint them as targets of White racism or external nationalist machinations, *In the Face of Diversity* depicts Chinese Australians as important actors in Australia's multicultural history.

In the course of writing this book, I have read hundreds of community newsletters, dozens of commemorative booklets and scores of media releases, as well as analysed petitions, speeches, photographs and other ephemera. Of course, community organisations appear in newspapers and government documents, too. These materials were in both English and Chinese scripts – some even hand-written – and held in the libraries and archives of the University of Melbourne, the Australian National University, Monash University and the University of New South Wales, as well as the Australian Institute of Criminology, the State Libraries of New South Wales and Victoria, and the National Archives of Australia. By far, the largest collection of materials is held by the National Library of Australia (NLA). The defunct websites of community organisations and pages that had otherwise been removed were found through the *Wayback Machine* and the NLA's *Pandora* websites. Other materials were sourced or copied from the private collections of individuals.

While there is much material to work with, gaps in the record still exist – even in the collections of community organisations. Like any other work of history, this study is restricted by the sources that are available, and which community or organisation is covered at any particular point in the study is influenced by the availability of relevant materials. There are also sometimes inaccuracies within community organisations' own accounts or records. The special commemorative booklets made by community organisations to mark important anniversaries sometimes reflect opinions more of the present-day than those of the past. Many are tinged with their latter-day editors' feelings of nostalgia or a (well-deserved) sense of achievement. The study thus draws on newspapers, government documents and census data to corroborate some of the history.

Interviews with past and present members of community organisations provide opportunities to fill gaps in the historical record and further clarify facts (or at least gain another subjective view of them). The pragmatic goal of using interviews to fill gaps in knowledge has been combined with the scholarly responsibility to give voice to

Preface

the subjects of this study: the existence of "living sources" is not just a historical boon because their inclusion is imperative to the creation of socially conscious historical work. The study includes interviews with 10 individuals from Melbourne, Sydney and Brisbane who were or continue to be leading members of Chinese Australian communities and organisations. Interviews were conducted in person, digitally recorded and lasted between two and four hours. They were targeted at the interviewees' personal experiences in community organisations during the historical episodes relevant to this study. Nevertheless, the interviews' conversational style meant that discussion inevitably digressed to other facets of the interviewees' lives. Allowing interviewees to speak as they wished before returning to the main questions was treated as ceding some control to interviewees and seen as part of the collaborative process.[2] A de-identified list of sample interview questions is reproduced in Appendix 1.

The difference in ethnicity between the interviewer (that is, the author) and interviewee is recognised as one potential influence on the interview, but so are other factors like differences in age, the location of interviews and the language (English) in which the interviews were conducted. Another influential factor was that interviewees spoke anonymously. While this has precluded the attribution of quotes to particular speakers, the anonymous format allowed the interviewees to speak freely and candidly.[3]

In addition to my own interviews, other oral history interviews with prominent Chinese Australians held by the NLA have informed this study. These largely come from two projects undertaken by Diane Giese; the Post-War Chinese Australians Oral History Project (1992–1998) and the Chinese Australian Oral History Partnership Project (1999–2002). More than 50 of these interviews were analysed

---

2 James Holstein and Jaber Gubrium, *The Active Interview* (Thousand Oaks, California: SAGE Publications, 1995), 15, https://doi.org/10.4135/9781412986120.
3 Kevin Bradley and Anisa Puri, "Creating an Oral History Archive: Digital Opportunities and Ethical Issues", in *Oral History and Australian Generations*, eds Katie Holmes and Alistair Thomson (Oxon, UK, Routledge, 2017), 75–91.

for the book and more than 20 interviewees' reflections on their involvement in community organisations feature here.[4]

A final and important note is that throughout my research I try to maintain an awareness that a White Australian writing a history of Chinese Australian communities is necessarily in a position separate from the focus of the research. Additionally, I must maintain an awareness that the multicultural and migration history recorded in this book took place on (and continues) in the context of Aboriginal and Torres Strait Islander dispossession.[5] This awareness is informed by Edward Said's argument that ideas, cultures and histories cannot be studied without also studying the configurations of power in which they exist, as well as the awareness of the author's own position within those same configurations.[6] My use of sources created by community organisations, in both English and Chinese, and interviews with past and present members is my attempt to use a methodology that cedes as much agency to its historical subjects as possible by letting them speak for themselves. While acknowledging the historical and current forces that impose racial and cultural domination over non-White peoples, I approach my study as a history of Australia and Australians – because Australia is, ideally and in fact, multi-ethnic and multicultural.

4　Diana Giese, Post-War Chinese Australians Oral History Project, sound recording, 1992, National Library of Australia; Diana Giese, Chinese Australian Oral History Partnership, sound recording, 1999, National Library of Australia.
5　While I acknowledge that referring to the individual nations or language groups is best practice, the contexts discussed in the book typically compel me to use more collective terms like Aboriginal and Torres Strait Islander peoples or historically used terms like Aboriginal Australians. I referred to the following source to inform my use of terms: Australian Institute of Aboriginal and Torres Strait Islander Studies, "Indigenous Australians: Aboriginal and Torres Strait Islander People", 7 December 2020, https://tinyurl.com/3pm7dypm.
6　Edward Said, *Orientalism*, 5th ed. (London: Penguin, 2003), 5–12.

Introduction

In 2020, at a Senate Inquiry into Issues Facing Diaspora Communities in Australia, Senator Eric Abetz asked three Chinese Australians to denounce the Chinese Communist Party (CCP). Other individuals speaking to issues regarding Chinese Australian communities were not asked the same question. The only discernible reason for Abetz to single out these three was that they were Han Chinese – the ethnic group that makes up 90 per cent of the population of the People's Republic of China (PRC) and the overwhelming majority of CCP membership.[1] Against a backdrop of concerns about the CCP's influence in Australia, Abetz's targeted questioning is one example of the racial essentialism and ethnic homogenisation of Chinese Australians that has grown more prevalent in recent years.[2] There are other examples. Journalist Peter Hartcher warned the readers of his latest book *Red Zone* that "Australia has built a Chinese community of 1.3 million without really understanding it or its consequences".[3] Hartcher points out this dubious

---

1 John Fitzgerald, "Eric Abetz's War on Chinese Australians Has Beijing Rubbing Its Hands", News, *Crikey*, 7 February 2021, https://tinyurl.com/2zhepyp5.
2 Jason Om, "'We're Not Panda-Hugging Spies': What It's Like to Be a Chinese-Australian Voter", *ABC News*, 8 May 2019, https://tinyurl.com/3m4rwusb.
3 Peter Hartcher, *Red Zone: China's Challenge and Australia's Future* (Melbourne: Schwartz Publishing 2021), 174.

and monolithic "Chinese community" now in the country's midst not to demystify it, but to reveal the naivety of (non-Chinese?) Australians. Concerns about China's political influence in Australian society are highly contemporary, but the characterisation of Chinese Australians as an undifferentiated "Chinese diaspora" or "Chinese community" – united, coherent or "one" – is not.

In many instances, collective terms have been used aspirationally by Chinese Australians themselves. In January 1984, community activist Katie Young wrote an article for the newsletter for the Chinese Fellowship of Victoria (CFV) entitled, "All Chinese in Australia 'Unite and Advance', for Peace on Earth, Good Will in Mankind". In it, she expressed her hope that through the establishment of a national Chinese-language newspaper, the *Sing Tao Daily*, community divisions would narrow and "eventually disappear".[4] Just over two years later, at the National Conference of the Australian Chinese Community, she spoke of her wish for the leaders gathered there to "communicate as one big family" and create a peak national body through which the community might speak "with one voice".[5]

From past to present, the references to "unity" and "one-ness" suggest a unitary Chinese Australian community as latent and inevitable, if not already a fact. However, an analysis of the materials created by community organisations reveals a diversity of histories, ambitions, values and needs that seem unlikely to be the purview of a single community. If there are current desires, as Hartcher suggests, to understand the "Chinese [Australian] community of 1.3 million", how it was "built" and its potential "consequences", then understanding the diversity of Chinese Australian *communities* is paramount.

In this book, the concept of a unitary "Chinese Australian community" is explored by analysing and comparing Chinese Australian community organisations from the beginnings of official multiculturalism in the 1970s to present times, focusing on the

---

4 CFV, "Newsletter January 1984" (Chinese Fellowship of Victoria, January 1984), 9, State Library of Victoria.
5 Katie Young and Gim Wah Yeo, eds, *National Conference of the Australian Chinese Community Sydney, November 28–30, 1986* (National Conference of the Australian Chinese Community, Sydney: The Conference, 1986), 5.

Introduction

organisations' articulations of belonging, a (trans)national identity and multicultural ideals over this period. By drawing on the materials created by these organisations and from interviews with past and present community leaders, it becomes clear that a unitary, unified or united Chinese Australian community is a recurring chimera in the socio-cultural space shared by Chinese Australians. As history shows, community organisations adopted different positions on a spectrum of possible relationships to their Australian and ancestral homes. Political developments in either or both could compel unity or division among them. It is a history that shows Chinese Australian community organisations practising a highly participatory style of multiculturalism over the decades, albeit with adjustments to fit the ever dynamic and manifold imaginings of what constituted a "Chinese Australian community".

The book is divided into seven chapters with each covering a historical moment that galvanised the political and social activity of Chinese Australian community organisations. They give us insights into the various ideas, values and objectives that motivated Chinese Australian communities and organisations, as well as demonstrate the kinds of issues that bring them together and drive them apart. The episodes are:

1. the repeal of racially discriminatory immigration policy;
2. Australia's turn to multiculturalism in the early to mid-1970s;
3. the 1984 "Blainey debate";
4. the Tiananmen Massacre and students' campaign for permanent residency in Australia, 1989–93;
5. the "Hanson debate", 1996–98;
6. the advent of the so-called "Chinese century" in the early 2000s; and
7. the rise of the "China influence debate" in Australia from the 2010s until today.

Together, these episodes traverse periods of great demographic, social and political change in Australia and abroad.

The current conversation

The inspiration for this book came to me in August 2016. As I sat waiting at a Melbourne tram stop, I was puzzled to see Mao Zedong smiling at me from across the tracks. It was, in fact, a portrait of him on the front page of *The Age*. The headline exclaimed "Controversial Chairman Mao Tribute Concerts Sharpen Chinese Community Divide".[6] Finding the article online, I learned that two Chinese Australian organisations were at the centre of the brouhaha: one known for staging patriotic celebrations of the People's Republic of China; and the other founded specifically to combat expressions of PRC nationalism. The article suggested this "widening schism" among Chinese Australians was a recent phenomenon, although the impassioned statements issued by each organisation suggested that their divisions ran further into the past. Moreover, the prospect that these two organisations (or any others) could encapsulate all Chinese Australians of the "local diaspora" was dubious. Nonetheless, my chance encounter with Mao at the tram stop was the perfect inspiration to dig deeper into contemporary Chinese Australian history.

In much of what has been recently written, contemporary Chinese Australian communities have been drawn into scholarly, political or popular discussions as potential vectors of PRC influence or victims of White Australian racism. In their own ways, both of these discourses erode the multicultural fortitude of Australian society and the agency of Chinese Australian communities. The prevalence of these views in recent national debates makes a modern historical account of Chinese Australian communities all the more timely.

With regard to PRC influence, Peter Hartcher's abovementioned *Red Zone* is a more recent example, however Clive Hamilton's *Silent Invasion* is the seminal work. As a social scientist, Hamilton is principally concerned with the CCP's nefarious intentions for Australian democracy and its influence in Australian society. As part of his investigation of the PRC's reach into Australian political and

---

6 Philip Wen, "Controversial Chairman Mao Tribute Concerts Sharpen Chinese Community Divide", *The Age*, 22 August 2016, https://tinyurl.com/36z6fcbw.

social institutions, Hamilton examines various Chinese Australians, their communities and their organisations. He finds many to be sycophants for the PRC or, at worst, fifth columnists. Luridly, he closes his book with conjectures about the percentages of Chinese Australians loyal to China before Australia:

> Remembering that there are over one million people of Chinese heritage in Australia, we could expect some, citizens and non-citizens alike, to take to the streets to express their loyalty to Beijing – in other words, to Australia's enemy. This could create ongoing and potentially severe civil strife, unrest that would be orchestrated by the Chinese embassy in Canberra. The prospect of civil discord is not mere speculation.[7]

It is worrying to consider how the above logic might lead to indiscriminate harm toward Chinese Australians (like the spike in racist violence and abuse toward Chinese Australians and other Australians of East Asian appearance documented during the COVID-19 pandemic). It is unfortunate, but Hamilton accepts that loyal Chinese Australians "may have to take some collateral damage to win the larger battle" against the PRC's political interference in Australia.[8] While Hamilton is right to be vigilant about the PRC's political interference in Australia, scholars must ensure that "collateral damage" is *not* inflicted indiscriminately upon any Australians rather than accept it as the price of our work.

On the other side of the debate, modern China historian David Brophy has criticised Hamilton's "muscular language of loyalty" as an example of (White) Australia's expectation for Chinese Australians to become Australian chauvinists: any perceived scrutiny or hesitancy to embrace "Australian values" on their part becomes evidence of disloyalty to Australia.[9] In his book *China Panic*, Brophy insists Australia's hardening stance toward the PRC is more a product of its

---

7   Clive Hamilton, *Silent Invasion: China's Influence in Australia* (Melbourne: Hardie Grant Publishing, 2018), 280.
8   Clive Hamilton, "Why Do We Keep Turning a Blind Eye to Chinese Political Interference?", *The Conversation*, 4 April 2018, https://tinyurl.com/9a8tcnrv.

own history of xenophobia than of China as a real geopolitical threat. Brophy fits the recent negative treatment of Chinese Australians into this frame. For example, Brophy insists many commentators "missed the point" when condemning Senator Abetz's demand for Chinese Australians to denounce the CCP:

> Some said he was wrong to do what he did because Chinese Australians who condemn the CCP risk endangering family members in China; others pointed out that his approach might compromise Australia's security by alienating the Chinese-Australian community. Well intentioned though these talking points might have been, they nevertheless had the effect of shifting an overdue and uncomfortable conversation about Australian attitudes back to the more familiar terrain of the big, bad CCP.[10]

Throughout his book, Brophy reveals the racism often hiding behind Australia's stated national concerns. However, these "uncomfortable conversations" about Australian racism are not novel. White Australian racism is infamous and well-studied at home and abroad. What is truly unfortunate is how little the conversation has progressed or how much of it is repeated. Perhaps we should collectively take a different tack. In contemporary Australian history, Chinese Australian community organisations have consistently pursued discussions about racism, belonging and identity with the wider Australian public – often to good effect – and today many Chinese Australian communities are again engaging with the present discourse about "the big, bad CCP". Instead of further centring discussions about White Australia and Australians then, this book does something that is patently overdue, yet refreshingly simple. It bases the scholarly discussion of contemporary Chinese Australian communities on a study of contemporary Chinese Australian history and does so by drawing on the materials produced and the opinions voiced by these communities themselves.

---

9   David Brophy, *China Panic: Australia's Alternative to Paranoia and Pandering* (Melbourne: Black Inc., 2021), 146.
10 Brophy, 151–2.

Introduction

According to historian Sophie Loy-Wilson, it has long been time for Chinese Australian history to be accepted as Australian history. In Loy-Wilson's view, this will only happen when Australian historians begin studying Chinese Australian history as Australian history rather than an offshoot of Sinology or diaspora studies. In this same vein, there is a growing movement to write Australian history using sources in languages other than English. Samia Khatun "challenges the suffocating monolingualism" of Australian history through the writings of 19th-century South Asian Muslims: people who opened Australia's vast outback for European colonisation but who were themselves colonised subjects of the British Empire.[11] Khatun acknowledges that the precedent for including non-English sources to tell Australian history comes from Indigenous histories – she points to Minoru Hokari's work as an example; Khatun also mentions Loy-Wilson's use of Chinese texts to shed new light on Australia's history of trade with China.[12] These works diversify the chorus of Australia's historical voices and challenge the premise of Australia's overwhelmingly Anglo-Celtic, English-speaking history.

Who is "Chinese"?

Understanding that not all "Chinese" Australians come from China is fundamental to this book.

Table 0.1 reflects many aspects of Australia's history of Chinese immigration during and after the White Australia policy. The large dip in the number of people born in China points to the legacy of early Chinese Australian migrants and the curtailment of further migration under the *Immigration Restriction Act*. Between 1976 and 1981, a dramatic increase in numbers of people born in Vietnam, Laos and

---

11 Samia Khatun, *Australianama: The South Asian Odyssey in Australia* (Brisbane: University of Queensland Press, 2019), 4.
12 Minoru Hokari, *Gurindji Journey: A Japanese Historian in the Outback* (Kensington, NSW: University of New South Wales Press, 2011); Sophie Loy-Wilson, *Australians in Shanghai: Race, Rights and Nation in Treaty Port China* (London: Routledge, 2017), https://doi.org/10.4324/9781315756998.

Table 0.1 Australian residents born in source areas of ethnically Chinese migrants. Data compiled from Australian censuses. Note, these figures capture residents of other ethnicities, not just Chinese.

*Cambodia, Laos and Vietnam were combined for the 1971 census and not specified for the 1966 census. PRC and Taiwan were combined as "China" for the 1971 and 1966 censuses. Malaysia includes the Federated States of Malaya, and Singapore includes Straits Settlements – the former and latter were combined in the 1933 and 1947 censuses.

Year	Cambodia	Hong Kong	Laos	Malaysia	China	Singapore	Taiwan	Vietnam
1911	N.A.	413	N.A.	100	20,775	701	N.A.	N.A.
1921	N.A.	255	N.A.	143	14,859	330	N.A.	N.A.
1933	N.A.	236	N.A.	866*	8,579	866*	N.A.	N.A.
1947	N.A.	762	N.A.	1,768*	6,404	1,768*	N.A.	N.A.
1954	N.A.	1,554	N.A.	2,279	10,277	1,127	N.A.	N.A.
1961	N.A.	2,474	N.A.	3,905	9,153	1,744	N.A.	N.A.
1966	N.A.	4,206	N.A.	9,179	17,390*	3,641	17,390*	N.A.
1971	717*	5,583	717*	14,945	17,601*	5,532	17,601*	717*
1976	496	8,818	454	19,880	19,542	8,989	431	2,427
1981	3,589	15,717	5,352	31,598	25,883	11,990	877	41,097

Introduction

Cambodia points to the number of refugees Australia accepted from war-ravaged Indochina. The table also shows the effects of Australia's other domestic and foreign policies. The steady growth of numbers of people born in Malaysia and Singapore points to the flow of students who came to Australia through tertiary education initiatives like the Colombo Plan. Indeed, the jump in numbers for Malaysia and Hong Kong between 1976 and 1981 is partly explained by the relaxation of family reunion visa conditions as many students pursued careers in Australia and brought their families to join them.

During this 1972–82 period, Malaysia had been a source country for an especially large number of *huayi* Chinese Australians – ethnic Chinese who descended from earlier immigrants to non-Chinese lands.[13] The *huayi* are an important demonstration that not all "Chinese" come directly from China to Australia. Ethnic Han or Hakka Chinese made up a large proportion of the refugees arriving in Australia from war-torn Vietnam, Cambodia and Laos.[14] Beginning in the mid-1960s – before the end of the White Australia policy – the number of people in Australia who were born in countries that were sources of Chinese migrants increased. This change reversed the decades-long attrition of the "Chinese Australian population".[15]

Of course, this table does not show the actual number of Australians who would identify themselves in some way as Chinese. As pointed out by Pookong Kee – himself a Chinese Malaysian Australian – place of birth does not necessarily match ethnicity. We can only estimate how many ethnic Chinese were among emigrant students from Malaysia or refugees from Vietnam. Moreover, Australian-born Chinese Australians do not appear in the figures. Using census records of "race", C.F. Yong calculated that in 1921 there were "3,458 Australia-born Chinese who regarded Australia as their home" including "mixed-blood" peoples.[16] Another way Chineseness can be

---

13   Gungwu Wang, "Among Non-Chinese", *Daedalus* 120, no. 2 (Spring 1991): 135–57.
14   Pookong Kee, *Chinese Immigrants in Australia: Construction of a Socio-Economic Profile*, IAESR Working Paper, no. 13/1988 (Melbourne: Institute of Applied Economic & Social Research, 1988), 7.
15   Kee, 10–14.

captured by the census is by recording the languages most spoken at home. In 1976, there were 4,212 local-born Chinese Australians who "regularly used Chinese", compared to 25,690 overseas-born. Of course, this is not a perfect measure either: Ien Ang powerfully questions the ability of language to necessarily reflect ethnicity in *On Not Speaking Chinese*.[17] Someone like Ang, born in Indonesia and speaking English, Dutch and Bahasa Indonesia but *not* Chinese, would fall through the census' metric for Chineseness. People in Ang's position would have to wait until the Australian census began asking questions about "ancestry" to record their Chineseness – which itself is subjective.

Nevertheless, the census captures the heterogeneity of Chinese Australian communities in Australia, especially in this early period of multiculturalism. Based on the above considerations, it would be reasonably safe to conclude that at least half of the "Chinese in Australia" were not "Chinese" in the strict "Mainland China" sense.[18] Kee himself points out patterns of settlement by different cohorts: Malaysian Chinese in Melbourne, Singaporean Chinese in Perth and Hong Kong Chinese in Sydney.[19] Moreover, ethnic Chinese migrants from these places were typically wealthier, more highly educated and had a greater command of English, which enabled a smooth transition into Australian society. Ethnic Chinese refugees from Indochina, on the other hand, largely lacked these resources and abilities and their transition into Australian society was more difficult as a result.[20] Some of these differences manifested themselves in the community organisations established by these different cohorts.

---

16 C.F. Yong, *The New Gold Mountain: The Chinese in Australia, 1901–1921* (Adelaide: Raphael Arts, 1977), 5.
17 Ien Ang, *On Not Speaking Chinese: Living Between Asia and the West* (London, UK: Taylor & Francis Group, 2001).
18 Kee, *Chinese Immigrants in Australia*, 43.
19 Kee, 37.
20 Kee, 44.

Introduction

What is "Chinese Australian"?

In the Australian context, Ien Ang's research about the "Chinese diaspora" is arguably the most influential. She has delved into the use of ethnic and national identities by state powers for nation-building purposes, the historical development of identity categories and power hierarchies, as well as the present socio-political circumstances that perpetuate them.[21] The observations and critiques Ang offers are of vital relevance if we are to understand what it means to be "Australian", "Chinese" or "Chinese Australian". From there we can begin to understand the communities or organisations comprised of such individuals.

Ang sits with other scholars who believe that the identities of individuals or groups oscillate between different identity categories (like Chinese, Australian or Chinese Australian) according to the needs of the present moment.[22] As Lucille Lok-Sun Ngan and Kwok-bun Chan argue, it is precisely because identities are social constructs – that is, products of individual action and group interaction at a particular time and place – that they are valuable for scholarship. Though identities might possess problematic expressions (like nationalism), scholars must engage with individual and collective identities because it is a fundamental way by which people describe themselves to others, interpret the values of society, or navigate their own lifepaths.[23] In the case of communities and community

---

21 Ang, *On Not Speaking Chinese*, 11, 17, 34–6; John Fitzgerald, "Diaspora and Discourse: Transnationalism and the Subject of Modern History", in *Re-Examining Chinese Transnationalism in Australia–New Zealand*, ed. Manying Ip (Canberra: Centre for the Study of the Chinese Southern Diaspora, ANU, 2000), 13–24.

22 Ang, *On Not Speaking Chinese*, 34–6; Andrew P. Davidson and Kuah-Pearce Khun Eng, "Introduction: Diasporic Memories and Identities", in *At Home in the Chinese Diaspora: Memories, Identities and Belongings*, eds Kuah-Pearce Khun Eng and Andrew P. Davidson (London: Palgrave Macmillan UK, 2008), 2–3, https://doi.org/10.1057/9780230591622_1; Jen Tsen Kwok, "Asian Australian Citizenship as a Frame of Enactment in the Parliamentary 'First Speech'", *Journal of Intercultural Studies* 27, no. 1–2 (February 2006): 187–8.

23 Lucille Lok-Sun Ngan and Chan Kwok-bun, *The Chinese Face in Australia: Multi-Generational Ethnicity among Australian-Born Chinese* (New York:

organisations, it is a shared identity that brings people together in the first place.

We cannot assume that we all know or share a concept of Chinese identity or "Chineseness"; the concept is as diverse as the peoples who invoke it.[24] In his historiography of the concept "ethnic identity", Gerald Izenberg proposes the following framework:

1. a common proper name that identifies the essence of the community;
2. a myth of ancestry that enables a sense of kinship;
3. shared memories of a common past (including, for example, important events or heroes for commemoration);
4. a common culture including language, customs or religion;
5. a link to a homeland, though not necessarily physical (as is the case with diaspora or migrant communities); and
6. a sense of solidarity among members of the group.[25]

The Chinese Australian community organisations appearing in the following pages display many of the features identified by Izenberg to various degrees, at various times. The aim of this book, however, is not to interrogate the existence of these community organisations' Chinese (Australian) identities – it takes these as a given. Instead, it focuses on how these organisations have articulated, negotiated and differentiated specific collective identities in the historical moment. That is, how do they articulate their Chineseness, their Australianness, or their Chinese Australianness, when and why? Does this or has this changed over time? Ang and Ngan and Kwok-bun have used the term "Chineseness" throughout their works to refer to the various attributes of a Chinese identity such as language ability, connection to community or phenotypical features. As these scholars have pointed out, Chineseness is linked to discussions of Chinese authenticity and the

---

Springer, 2012), 196; Gerald N. Izenberg, *Identity: The Necessity of a Modern Idea*, Intellectual History of the Modern Age (Philadelphia: University of Pennsylvania Press, 2016), 20-2.
24 Ngan and Kwok-bun, *The Chinese Face in Australia*; Khun Eng Kuah-Pearce and Andrew P. Davidson, eds, *At Home in the Chinese Diaspora* (London: Palgrave Macmillan UK, 2008), https://doi.org/10.1057/9780230591622.
25 Izenberg, *Identity*, 206-7.

policing of identity boundaries.[26] In keeping with the convention, Chineseness and other "-ness" terms will regularly appear here.

Social and political forces also police the authenticity and borders of "Australianness" – as seen during the Blainey, Hanson and China influence debates. As these debates have revealed, one major problem with Australianness is whether it is fundamentally a shared civic identity among its multi-ethnic citizens or whether it still depends on being ethnically Anglo-Australian, or at least being White.[27] This dilemma poses a recurring challenge for Chinese Australian communities and organisations to "prove" their Australianness to non-Chinese (namely White) Australians. This underlying tension – between theoretic ethnic equality at odds with the real ethnic hegemony of Anglo-Australians – is a principal animating dynamic in many of the historic episodes covered here.

A further complication lies in the ingrained unconscious assumption of who a "real" Australian is. Regardless of their ethnic background, most Australians assume that Anglo-Australians embody Australianness – both culturally and phenotypically. The problem with this, as Jon Stratton and Ien Ang point out, is that while Anglo-Australians are the self-appointed arbiters of Australianness, they typically do not perceive themselves as an ethnic group.[28] It is rather "ethnic minorities", like Han Chinese, who seem in practice to be the "ethnics" of Australia's multiculturalism; Anglo-Australian ethnicity – its language, institutions, holidays, arts, sports, cuisine and so on – sits apart from the other minority ethnic elements despite (or perhaps

---

26 Ang, *On Not Speaking Chinese*, 21–36; Ngan and Kwok-bun, *The Chinese Face in Australia*, v–xix.
27 Laksiri Jayasuriya, David Walker and Jan Gothard, "Introduction", in *Legacies of White Australia: Race, Culture and Nation*, eds Laksiri Jayasuriya, David Walker and Jan Gothard, 1–7, https://tinyurl.com/3rsxehhb.
28 Jon Stratton and Ien Ang, "Multicultural Imagined Communities: Cultural Difference and National Identity in the USA and Australia", in *Multicultural States: Rethinking Difference and Identity*, ed. David Bennett (London: Taylor & Francis Group, 1998), 157–8, https://tinyurl.com/ybc8pc22; Ien Ang, "Beyond Chinese Groupism: Chinese Australians between Assimilation, Multiculturalism and Diaspora", *Ethnic and Racial Studies* 37, no. 7 (7 June 2014): 1194.

because of) the control Anglo-Australians exert over their tolerance and therefore survival. Ghassan Hage brings this tension into view when he turns questions often asked of "ethnic Australians" back on their White Australian inquisitors:

> Are Whites still good for Australia? Have they been living in ghettoes for too long? Are they dividing Australia? Do we need an assimilation program to help ease them into the multicultural mainstream?[29]

By understanding a "sense of belonging" as a relationship between people and place, we can see what makes this feeling enticing and necessary. This could be the joy, comfort or pride that someone draws from belonging to a transnational or diasporic community or, conversely, the hurt and unease they feel if alienated from the "mainstream".[30]

These metaphysical feelings are connected to the real world because – as the history covered in this book shows – when a community's feeling of belonging is affected by real-world events, it can motivate the community to (re)act. Viewing belonging in this way helps to explain instances when self-interested or materialist motivations for action are not readily apparent.[31] The idea that belonging to a community is important rests upon the idea that the community is itself important. And because a person feels their community is important, that person is motivated to act on behalf of their community.

As Hage argues, it is in the exercising of these rights and responsibilities – in Australia's immigration debates "that we have to have" or "the need for strong borders" – that White belonging is achieved and protected. Perennial immigration debates are thus a society-wide ritual that the White Australian majority performs to reassert exclusive belonging to Australia when they feel that other

---

29 Ghassan Hage, *White Nation: Fantasies of White Supremacy in a Multicultural Society* (New York: Routledge, 2000), 245–7.
30 Ang, *On Not Speaking Chinese*, 11–12, 55.
31 Izenberg, *Identity*, 207–11.

Introduction

ethnic communities have come too far in asserting their own belongings.[32] Again, the Blainey, Hanson and China influence debates offer historical examples.

Hage's argument can usefully be applied the other way around, too. As will be seen, it is in such moments of debate that the need for exercising rights and responsibilities to belong becomes acute for Chinese Australian community organisations: for instance, asserting rights to live without racial prejudice in a multicultural Australia, or assuming community-oriented responsibilities through greater social and political participation. Rhetorical statements from community organisations like "we are Australian" or "Australia is our country, too" deliver the same message in blunter, but by no means less powerful terms.

What is a "Chinese Australian community organisation"?

My decision to use community organisations to interrogate the concept of a "Chinese Australian community" is partly informed by the scholarship of Ien Ang. In April 2011, Ang attended a conference of Chinese Australian community organisations and community leaders entitled "Finding the Chinese Australian Voice". There she heard various speakers discuss the need for organisations to overcome the fragmentation of Chinese communities and to effectively promote group interests. What puzzled Ang, however, was the reasoning behind the pursuit of this need:

> The fact that "ultimately, we are all Chinese" was presented as the natural reason why a united front was not only desirable but logical. Precisely because of the unquestioned prevalence of this presumption, however, conference goers did not manage to develop pertinent answers to their own questions. Notwithstanding being a joyous occasion for social bonding, the conference ended without a clear way forward ... rather than reifying Chineseness as a primordial ethno-cultural substance,

---

32   Hage, *White Nation*, 239–40.

we should examine the ways and contexts within which it is imaginatively produced and reproduced as the salient marker of an ethnic identity.³³

By insisting on a substantive term like "Chinese" to describe themselves, these community organisations, in Ang's view, embraced rather than critiqued the social and political powers behind the Chinese Australian identity. Ang insists we move away from preoccupations with identifying which individuals are Chinese Australian and instead move toward studying where and how notions of a Chinese Australian community emerge, and how they act and react to that reality.³⁴ But how should this be done? If being Chinese Australian is constantly subjectively emerging and contingent, as Ang holds, how can we ever say that any two or more individuals have a similar conceptualisation of what it means to be Chinese Australian and therefore constitute a group or community? Community organisations, despite being the source of Ang's question, also provide an answer.

Notwithstanding the unique, emergent and contingent qualities of everyone who comprises it, a community organisation's membership, by virtue of its voluntary nature, suggests that its constituent individuals share at least some common aspects of identity, aim, ethos, tradition and so on. In other words, members are naturally unique individuals but they share some aspects of identity in part or to a degree that is significant enough to warrant coming together as a group. By extension, it is safe to presume that potential members are personally attracted to what a community organisation represents or feel an affinity with its goals. Members symbolically pledge to uphold the values and objectives enshrined in a community organisation's constitution at the time of registration and reaffirm this bond through membership dues, service to that organisation and participation in its activities.

Forming community organisations, pursuing societal participation and undertaking political interventions are actions that transform political and social ideas about how a society should look or function

---

33 Ang, "Beyond Chinese Groupism", 1188.
34 Ang, 1184–8.

Introduction

into deed and reality. As Jen Tsen Kwok argues, voluntary community organisations are "vehicles for political action" because they embody the political will of their members and let their members substantively express that will within broader cultural, political, economic and social dynamics.[35] This makes community organisations excellent units for examining social and political history. The idiosyncrasies and contingent identities of individual members notwithstanding, the people comprising a membership share not just some identity qualities, but also ideas on how those qualities should motivate actions and reactions to the world around them.

Still, how to define a community organisation, or rather, how to choose which organisations to analyse, is challenging. In May 2020, Victorian Consumer Affairs listed 441 community organisations with the word "Chinese" in their title as registered incorporations (a further 193 are listed with lapsed registrations). Along with those Chinese Australian community organisations of broad interests encountered in this book, the list includes niche interest groups dedicated to bodybuilding, caravanning, oenology, and stroke survivors' support.[36] Many more groups exist under the names of Chinese provinces, districts, language groups or transliterations – the Federation of Chinese Associations (FCA) Victoria counts more than 100 such groups as member organisations.[37] The existence of so many groups necessarily meant taking a selective approach.

In their own research of community organisations, Khun Eng Kuah-Pearce and Evelyn Hu-Dehart focus on entities that:

1. are non-governmental organisations that have voluntary membership, originate out of local or migrant Chinese communities and are controlled by them;

---

35 Jen Tsen Kwok, "An Etymology of "Asian Australian" Through Associational Histories Connecting Australia to Asia", *Journal of Australian Studies* 41, no. 3 (3 July 2017): 351–2, https://doi.org/10.1080/14443058.2017.1346696.
36 Consumer Affairs Victoria, *Search for an Incorporated Association*, 2020, https://tinyurl.com/382h3r5j.
37 FCA, "注册会员团体 zhuce huiyuan tuanti (Registered Member Organisations)", Federation of Chinese Associations – 维省华联会, n.d., https://www.vicfca.org.au/vicfcagroup.

2. serve as ethnic and cultural brokers between the Chinese community(ies) and wider society;
3. actively promote social, cultural, education and other interests to their own members and wider society; and
4. aid in the localisation process of migrants in an adopted country and "mainstream" them.[38]

Because this book is investigating conceptualisations of a united or unitary Chinese Australian community, it further narrows Kuah-Pearce and Hu-Dehart's list to organisations that:

1. exhibited a special interest in political and social issues;
2. undertook cultural maintenance, networking or recreational activities, as a means of propagating the idea of a Chinese Australian community;
3. admitted members on the basis of their desire to be part of, represent or develop a local Chinese Australian community (as opposed to admitting members on the basis of, for example, their place of personal origin or occupation); and
4. addressed social welfare issues and community needs to advance the interests of members and the broader Chinese Australian community.

The community organisations that meet these criteria came from across Australia. They represent communities of diverse backgrounds, and in the course of their existence they have generated ample historical materials for research purposes. The materials are sufficient to trace around 15 community organisations over the 50-year period studied here, with around another 15 organisations appearing regularly in the materials of others. Key organisations include the Chinese Fellowship of Victoria, the Chinese Association of South Australia, the Chung Wah Association of Perth, the Chung Wah Society of Darwin, the Queensland Chinese Forum, the Australian Chinese Community

---

38 Khun Eng Kuah-Pearce and Evelyn Hu-Dehart, "Introduction: The Chinese Diaspora and Voluntary Associations", in *Voluntary Organizations in the Chinese Diaspora*, eds Khun Eng Kuah-Pearce and Evelyn Hu-Dehart (Hong Kong: Hong Kong University Press, 2006), 6, 14, https://www.jstor.org/stable/j.ctt2jc01q.5.

Introduction

Association of NSW, and the ACT Chinese Australian Association. These organisations are introduced throughout the book at the moments where they were particularly active or their materials especially rich.

Chapters

The decision to focus on "historic moments" for Chinese Australian community organisations in recent history was a practical and a conceptual one. It was during the episodes covered in this book that Chinese Australian community organisations were most socially and politically active – and thereby created a wealth of historically valuable materials in the process. In this regard, the book follows the interests of the community organisations themselves. The fact that community organisations from across Australia and from a spectrum of different backgrounds were responding to the same issues shows the need to pay attention to these particular moments. Analysing these moments sequentially also shows how community organisations changed over time, as well as responded immediately to the issues at hand – a way to see both "the forest and the trees", which W.H. Sewell Jr posits sociologists and historians are respectively predisposed toward when viewing "transformative events" like the historical moments investigated here.[39] With the help of community-made or non-English-language resources, as well as Chinese Australian voices, the book re-examines these moments to expand understandings of Australian history.

The main body of the book is divided into seven chapters. The first begins with Australia's turn toward multiculturalism in the 1970s. It sets up how, after a long period of demographic and social atrophy for Chinese Australian communities under racially discriminatory policies, the multicultural turn heralded a renaissance for communities and organisations. Old organisations were revitalised and new

---

39 William H. Sewell, *Logics of History: Social Theory and Social Transformation*, Chicago Studies in Practices of Meaning (Chicago: University of Chicago Press, 2005), 1–23.

organisations came into being. By following the change from "White" to "multicultural Australia", this chapter outlines an underlying pattern among communities and organisations, which is that social pressures tend to negate differences between them and foster cooperation. Conversely, as adversities diminish, diversity increases.

The second chapter continues with the multicultural turn as its backdrop and focuses on the optimism and challenges community organisations encountered in the 1970s. Community organisations showed increasing comfort in asserting Chinese, Australian, and Chinese Australian identities, as well as the confidence to make their own paths into a multicultural future and reconceptualise modes of Chinese Australian unity. Because some sections of society opposed or were incongruous to the country's new multicultural direction, community organisations developed ways of responding to racist organisations and racist content in Australian media.

Chapter 3 introduces one of the first major challenges to multiculturalism: the Blainey debate. In March 1984, Professor Geoffrey Blainey ignited the eponymous debate by criticising Asian immigration, multicultural policy and the "Asianisation" of Australia. Community organisations across Australia were galvanised by concerns that Blainey's public esteem and respectability might enable baser racism to proliferate in society. Many organisations considered "uniting" the Chinese Australian community as a means to respond to the debate; they discussed the prospect of creating a peak representative body at the first National Conference of the Australian Chinese Community in 1986. Though competing ideas about Chinese Australian unity stymied the creation of this peak body, community organisations nonetheless defended the tenets of multiculturalism. Through burgeoning political and societal engagements, they embedded themselves deeper into the fabric of Australia.

Chapter 4 covers community organisations' responses to the 1989 Tiananmen Massacre in three phases. The first was the initial response to the tragedy in which many community organisations reassessed their relationships with the PRC and the CCP in highly emotive terms. The second phase was marked by community organisations' varying support for the Chinese students' campaign for permanent residency in Australia. Here the idea of Chinese Australian unity was again

Introduction

broached as a means to respond to a contemporary issue, but it again failed to materialise due to differences between organisations. The third phase analyses the great demographic repercussions of absorbing 45,000 Chinese students into existing communities, while community organisations began normalising relations with the PRC in the early 1990s.

Chapter 5 examines the years 1996 to 1998 when Pauline Hanson's presence in Australian politics and society engendered fresh debates about multiculturalism and Asian migration. Though a time of great peril for Australia's multiculturalism, it was also a time of great liveliness. Here, an array of Chinese Australian community organisations cohered into a broad movement with each organisation voicing opposition to the "Hanson debate" in its own way. Meanwhile, certain organisations adept at capturing public attention became recognised as "leading voices" of the Chinese Australian community. These community leaders used their voices to decry not just Hanson but also the irresponsible media coverage and the expedient politicking that enhanced her influence.

The sixth chapter looks at the early years of the new millennium that many have called the dawning of the "Chinese century". Following China's ascendant global esteem, many Chinese Australian community organisations expressed their pride in the PRC's achievements – with such expressions being welcomed and even encouraged by the PRC. But this was a period of Australian nation-building, too, with the Sydney Olympics, the Centenary of Federation and the republic referendum also giving community organisations cause to celebrate and ruminate on their Australianness. Despite the competing national chauvinisms, community organisations could nevertheless walk a line between China and Australia, commending and critiquing either more or less as they pleased.

The final chapter covers the hardening of Beijing's soft-power initiatives and Australia's growing alarm at China's influence in its social and political affairs over the last decade. As Sino-Australian relations grew more testing, and with demographic changes underway, Chinese Australian community organisations found themselves less able to enter political and social discourses as they once would have – exemplified by the stifled responses to racism arising from the

COVID-19 pandemic. At the same time, the social and political spaces in which these organisations once participated have become dominated by outspoken, partisan political organisations promulgating competing types of Chinese Australian identity and unity – an example being the public row arising from the *Glory and Dream* concerts planned for Sydney and Melbourne in 2016.

This book hopes to restore historical agency to the community organisations that were directly affected by and responded to these historic moments. In scholarly discussions of Australian multiculturalism or racism, the Blainey or Hanson debates, Beijing's crackdowns or soft-power initiatives, Chinese Australian voices, experiences and perspectives often appear as bit players in supposedly grander historical narratives. By focusing on the responses of Chinese Australian community organisations during these watershed moments, *In the Face of Diversity* positions them as actors who *did* history, rather than groups to whom history *was done*.

Part of this is an aim to highlight the role of Chinese Australian community organisations in the making of multicultural Australia, thereby demonstrating the importance of Chinese Australian history as Australian history. This has determined the geographic scope of the book, which is the whole country rather than one part of it. But this scope is also determined by the topic. Chinese Australian community organisations have been most visible when responding to national and international developments. At the same time, their local interests remain deeply embedded in their responses to such issues. Community organisations thus work as conduits for the localisation of national issues and for local actors to reach the national stage. If the "Chinese Australian community" does exist, it should exist through these organisations.

In the following chapters, I argue that Chinese Australian unity has never *truly* been realised. Granted, if viewed through the lens of a particular issue or at a particular moment, disparate communities and organisations can appear as a single composite body. However, the division of these communities becomes clear when they are viewed at another time or through the lens of another issue. In modern times, the diversity among Chinese Australian communities has been too great for any singular community – as it has been popularly imagined – to exist.

Introduction

This unreached unity notwithstanding, the highly participatory mode of multiculturalism practised by Chinese Australian community organisations has left a lasting impact on Australia's society and politics – and for the better. The actions of these organisations have helped to cumulatively build Australia's present multicultural reality. Moreover, these community organisations demonstrate different ways to make a claim of belonging in a multicultural nation – with themselves belonging to Australia and Australia belonging to them *as* Chinese Australians.

These arguments are significant because they dismantle the myth of a single Chinese Australian community or bloc and rebuild a solid understanding of many diverse communities instead; each with their own aims, needs and participatory capacities. This encourages us to reconsider the structure of Australia's multicultural society and, by encountering non-English sources and interviews, revise Australia's history from non-White perspectives.

1
Chinese Australian community organisations from White Australia to multiculturalism

In 1973, the Whitlam government removed Australia's final piece of racially discriminatory immigration policy. The act marked an official end to the "White Australia policy" and a symbolic end to White Australia. These official and symbolic ends were also a moment of official and symbolic beginnings, as the Whitlam government, through policy and political rhetoric, offered multiculturalism as a new vision for the future.[1] It was a shift that heralded a renaissance for Chinese Australian community organisations. Old organisations that had been dormant during the restrictive immigration and assimilationist program of White Australia became active again. They attracted new members, renovated premises and projected their presence into their local communities once more. New community organisations were also founded by new migrants to Australia, many of them young professionals and families who wanted to maintain their Chinese identity and pass it on to their children. Such organisations shared an eagerness to weave themselves into the social and political fabric of the nation; to embrace and be embraced by the country as it turned toward multiculturalism.

---

1   Anthony Moran, *The Public Life of Australian Multiculturalism* (Cham: Springer International Publishing, 2017), 28–37.

The multicultural turn was not a moment of instant, radical change. As Gwenda Tavan sets out in her aptly named book *The Long, Slow Death of White Australia*, social change is a drawn-out process.[2] In the case of multiculturalism, this process spanned successive governments in the 1970s with antecedent and subsequent policies on either side of that decade. To be successful, multiculturalism also required a shift in Australia's immigration profile and a change in the attitudes toward non-White Australians on the part of White Australians. This took time. Writing decades after the turn, Wang Gungwu noted in his foreword to *Legacies of White Australia* that it was "unrealistic" to expect that all White Australians would give up their desire for a White society so quickly.[3] Likewise, it would take time for some effects of the multicultural turn to become visible in non-White Australian communities and their representative organisations – such as changes in number, size, form and public prominence. But multicultural policies did bring about some immediate changes, including funding for cultural and social activities, incorporation into migrant settlement services, and integration with government bodies.

To grasp the significance of the multicultural turn for Chinese Australian community organisations, it is necessary to understand the histories of the organisations themselves. The first community organisations set up by Chinese were bastions of fraternity and mutual protection in the ambivalent or hostile societies of Australia's 19th-century colonies. After Federation and over the decades, these older organisations adapted to the harsh realities of White Australia. In comparison, community organisations established around the multicultural turn expressed their confidence and belonging relatively free of pernicious social pressures. The differences between the new and old organisations began to reveal the significance of the shift from White to multicultural Australia. From this moment, we started to see the

---

2 Gwenda Tavan, *The Long, Slow Death of White Australia* (Melbourne: Scribe, 2005).
3 David Walker, Jan Gothard and Laksiri Jayasuriya, eds, *Legacies of White Australia: Race, Culture and Nation* (Perth: University of Western Australia Press, 2003), vii–viii.

1 Chinese Australian community organisations

different ways community organisations could "do" multiculturalism, view their Chineseness and claim their Australian belonging.

Shifts of the 1970s

The first challenges to the various policies and laws regarding immigration, naturalisation and assimilation that comprised the White Australia policy came with migration from Eastern and Southern Europe during Australia's post-war period. While Australian fears of racial miscegenation with Chinese or Japanese military might have greatly influenced Australian immigration policies between Federation and the Great War, hierarchies of whiteness had also been incorporated. Some of Australia's early parliamentarians considered the "Greek race" a cautionary example for White Australia – a "degenerate race" whose centuries of interactions with "barbarian" Ottomans had "destroyed or driven out" their "ancient Greek or Roman blood".[4] After the Second World War, Australia's first Minister for Immigration, Arthur Calwell, advanced the "populate or perish" mantra, allowing once "ambiguously white" migrants from Central and Eastern Europe to be gradually welcomed as "New Australians". The Menzies government later cast the immigration net even wider to include Southern Europeans.[5] A slow relaxation of restrictions by successive governments followed until the last vestiges of racially discriminatory immigration legislation were repealed by the Whitlam government's *Australian Citizenship Act 1973*.[6] Soon after, the Whitlam government moved to uphold international agreements relating to race, immigration and naturalisation, including the UN's *International Convention on the Elimination of All Forms of Racial Discrimination*. Al Grassby, then

---

4 Andonis Piperoglou, "'Border Barbarisms', Albury 1902: Greeks and the Ambiguity of Whiteness", *Australian Journal of Politics & History* 64, no. 4 (2018): 535–9, https://doi.org/10.1111/ajph.12518.
5 James Jupp, *From White Australia to Woomera: The Story of Australian Immigration*, 2nd ed. (Cambridge: Cambridge University Press, 2007), 10–13.
6 Tavan, *The Long, Slow Death of White Australia*, 189–99; Jupp, *From White Australia to Woomera*, 8–10; Australian Parliament, *Australian Citizenship Act 1973* (1973).

Whitlam's Minister for Immigration, emphatically declared the White Australia policy to be dead: "give me a shovel and I'll bury it".[7]

Historians have debated the amount of credit owed to Whitlam for shaping multicultural Australia: whether his government had any noticeable impact on non-White immigration and its role in ending discriminatory legislation, and thus the White Australia policy, or whether it was more symbolic than substantive.[8] The origins of multiculturalism do extend beyond the Whitlam government. Since the 1950s, scholars such as Jean Martin and Jerzy Zubrzycki had been advocating a shift from assimilationism to "cultural pluralism", and in the late 1960s a "proto-multiculturalism" began to emerge from the ideas and lobbying of community activists like Walter Lippmann, David Cox and Alan Matheson.[9] Yet officially drawing a line under White Australia and turning to multiculturalism required other steps for which Whitlam and his government deserve some credit.

In many ways, Whitlam's government shepherded an ideological shift in Australian society; providing the language and ideas for future policy to be successful. Though he showed a preference for the phrase "family of the nation", Grassby first officially used the term "multicultural" in the title of a 1973 policy paper that contemplated Australia's future:

> My concept of a society able to sustain growth and change without disintegration is a society based on equal opportunity for all ... I believe by the year 2000 we will need to have perfected ways

---

7 Gwenda Tavan, "Creating Multicultural Australia: Local, Global and Trans-National Contexts for the Creation of a Universal Admissions Scheme, 1945–1983", in *Wanted and Welcome? Policies for Highly Skilled Immigrants in Comparative Perspective*, ed. Triadafilos Triadafilopoulos (New York: Springer, 2013), 39.

8 Jupp, *From White Australia to Woomera*, 41–2; Tavan, *The Long, Slow Death of White Australia*, 201–11.

9 Jayne Persian, *Beautiful Balts: From Displaced Persons to New Australians* (Sydney: NewSouth Publishing, 2017), 183–7; Mark Lopez, *The Origins of Multiculturalism in Australian Politics 1945–1975*, 1st ed. (Melbourne: Melbourne University Press, 2000), 90–130.

of inducing this equality for all, in fact as well as in law, by far-reaching legislative and ameliorative measures.[10]

Not long after, the kind of affirmative action and legislative change that Grassby extolled became a reality. The *Racial Discrimination Act 1975* made it unlawful to discriminate against individuals on the basis of race, ethnicity, colour or place of origin.[11] A Commission for Community Relations was established to implement the Act and other multicultural policies with Grassby, the "godfather of multiculturalism", becoming its first commissioner.[12] The optimism these changes brought for non-White Australians after decades of White Australia was palpable. "In [White Australia's] place was a new vision for Australian society," says Tim Soutphommasane, Australia's former Race Discrimination Commissioner, "a multiculturalism that sought to celebrate ethnic and racial difference rather than suppress it."[13]

Though the racism that characterised White Australia was becoming less publicly acceptable, a monocultural mindset was nonetheless deeply imprinted on the nation's White majority. Consistent policies and political support were necessary to lead (White) public opinion toward greater acceptance of multiculturalism. When Malcolm Fraser became prime minister in 1975, his government maintained the bipartisan support for multiculturalism seen during the Whitlam years and directed multicultural policies toward further nation-building efforts. Emblematic of this support was the Fraser government's immediate re-establishment of a Department of

---

10   Al Grassby, *A Multi-Cultural Society for the Future* (Canberra: Australian Government Publishing Service, 1973).
11   Tim Soutphommasane et al., *I'm Not Racist But ...: 40 Years of the Racial Discrimination Act* (Sydney: NewSouth Publishing, 2015), 49 50, 255–66.
12   Al Grassby, "Commissioner for Community Relations: First Annual Report" (Canberra: Office of the Commissioner for Community Relations, 1976), v; Andrew Jakubowicz, "'Don't Mention It ... ': What Governments Want to Hear and Why about Multicultural Australia", *Cosmopolitan Civil Societies Journal* 6, no. 2 (2014): 4–5; ACF, "ACF Newsletter August 1986" (Australian Chinese Forum, August 1986), 5, State Library of New South Wales; Hage, *White Nation*, 83.
13   Soutphommasane et al., *I'm Not Racist But*, 34.

Immigration and Ethnic Affairs – Whitlam had abolished it in 1974; Grassby had called it "incurably racist".[14] Fraser also instigated the *Report of the Review of Post-Arrival Programs and Services for Migrants*, led by Frank Galbally. The "Galbally Report" found that the assimilationist mission of previous governments had failed due to the reluctance of migrants to abandon all aspects of their former identities and the lingering racial prejudices of many White Australians.[15] Logically, the report concluded, national cohesion could not be achieved if the popular attitudes toward Australia's multi-ethnic reality remained unchanged. It stressed that the right of migrants to maintain their native culture must be protected and mutual respect and understanding for others' cultures must be encouraged.[16] The Galbally Report became a foundational document for Australia's modern multiculturalism.

By accepting all findings of the report in 1978 and acting on them, the Fraser government ensured that Australia's future would be premised on multicultural ideals.[17] Fraser improved visa processes for family reunion, enhanced delivery of English-language education for immigrants and established the Special Broadcasting Service (SBS) in 1978 to cater to Australian audiences from non-English-speaking backgrounds.[18] Jupp points out that Fraser's support for multiculturalism translated to palpable changes in Australia's immigration intake and therefore its demography. Asian countries like the Philippines and Malaysia remained in the top ten immigrant source countries during Fraser's time as national leader. Vietnam and Cambodia appeared in this bracket toward the end of Fraser's prime

---

14 Jupp, *From White Australia to Woomera*, 42.
15 Australian Institute of Multicultural Affairs, *Evaluation of Post-Arrival Programs and Services* (Melbourne, 1982), para 1.1–1.5.
16 Frank Galbally, *Report of the Review of Post-Arrival Programs and Services for Migrants* (Canberra: Migrant Services and Programs, 1978), para 1.1–1.5.
17 Galbally, para 1.7.
18 David R. Cox, *Immigration and Welfare: An Australian Perspective* (Sydney: Prentice Hall, 1987), 185–6; Jupp, *From White Australia to Woomera*, 45; Andrew Jakubowicz, "Days of Our Lives: Multiculturalism, Mainstreaming and 'Special' Broadcasting", *Media Information Australia*, no. 45 (August 1987): 18–19.

ministership, owing largely to his humane treatment of refugees – for which Jupp maintains "the Fraser government is best remembered".[19] Of course, it should also be remembered that Fraser's refugee policy was politically expedient for his government's domestic and international interests – his government's *de jure* recognition of Indonesia's annexation of Timor-Leste and muted response to the humanitarian crisis unfolding there is another example of Cold War politics.[20] As Katrina Stats has suggested, Fraser's "genius" was in using a humanitarian approach to maintain the sanctity of Australia's borders without jeopardising the country's international obligations and standing.[21]

Migration increases under Fraser were highly relevant to Chinese Australian communities, but immigration numbers alone cannot be used to evaluate the "growth" or quality of Australia's multiculturalism. The *Ethnic Communities Directories* published sporadically between 1975 and 1992 by the Department of Immigration and Ethnic Affairs offer further insight. The number of community organisations listed in them can be used to infer the size, type and vitality of ethnic communities active in Australia.[22] Table 1.1 reproduces the number of

---

19　Jupp, *From White Australia to Woomera*, 43.
20　Vannessa Hearman, "Australian News Photography and Contested Images of Famine in Indonesian-Occupied East Timor", *Australian Historical Studies* 54, no. 3 (3 July 2023): 542–4, https://doi.org/10.1080/1031461X.2023.2189275; Peter Job, "The Evolving Narrative of Denial: The Fraser Government and the Timorese Genocide, 1975–1980", *Critical Asian Studies* 50, no. 3 (3 July 2018): 442–66, https://doi.org/10.1080/14672715.2018.1489731.
21　Katrina Stats, "Welcome to Australia? A Reappraisal of the Fraser Government's Approach to Refugees, 1975–83", *Australian Journal of International Affairs* 69, no. 1 (1 February 2015): 83–4, https://tinyurl.com/mb5m4kjw; for further context, see: Claire M. Higgins, *Asylum by Boat: Origins of Australia's Refugee Policy* (Sydney: NewSouth Publishing, 2017), 86–109.
22　The directories have appeared under slightly different titles over the years: *National Groups in Australia: A Directory* (1975); *Directory of National Group Organisations in Australia* (1977); *Directory of Ethnic and National Group Organisations in Australia* (1979); *Ethnic Communities in Australia Directory of Organisations* (1981); *Directory of Ethnic Community Organisations in Australia* (1984–1992).

community organisations that described themselves as "Chinese" in these directories.

Table 1.1 Number of community organisations listed as "Chinese" in Commonwealth *Ethnic Communities Directories*.

*No directory available for Northern Territory in 1975

State | Year	1975	1977	1978-79	1980-81	1984	1987	1989	1992
Australian Capital Territory	0	0	1	1	1	2	4	5
New South Wales	9	17	15	17	30	34	23	28
Victoria	9	13	13	17	22	26	21	23
Queensland	2	4	4	4	6	11	9	13
South Australia	1	1	1	2	3	6	6	3
Western Australia	1	2	2	5	4	7	4	4
Tasmania	0	0	0	1	1	4	2	1
Northern Territory	N/A	1	1	2	2	3	3	3
AUSTRALIA	22	38	37	49	69	93	72	80

Table 1.1 shows that many Chinese Australian community organisations are concentrated in New South Wales and Victoria, which correlates with the cities of Sydney and Melbourne being centres of migration and long having large Chinese Australian communities. Between 1978 and 1987, the number of community organisations in these states increased. This indicates the creation of new organisations, but the appearance of those established prior to the 1970s (such as the Chinese Youth League or the See Yup Society) suggests older organisations saw a benefit in making themselves better known to the public and government. The growth in community organisations in

1 Chinese Australian community organisations

the other states and territories is slightly different. Cities like Adelaide, Perth and Darwin each had only one Chinese Australian community organisation in multiculturalism's early stages. Yet the number of community organisations in these places doubled or tripled over the 1978–87 period. Tasmania, for example, had no community organisations at the beginning of this period and four by the end. The total number in Australia more than doubled. Of course, there were more community organisations again than those listed in the directories. For example, Perth's Chung Wah Association and Adelaide's Chinese Association of South Australia were not listed in the 1975 and 1989 directories respectively despite both organisations still operating and featuring in other editions.

The government's creation of a directory of minority ethnic community organisations itself marked a cultural shift. Whereas ethnic community organisations would once have been treated by Australian governments with indifference or even suspicion – there are many examples of ASIO surveillance of Chinese Australian community organisations for suspected communist activities, for example – they were now recognised as important conduits for migrant welfare provisions and settlement services.[23] Australian governments supported the incorporation of community organisations into services for translation and interpreting, and the recognition of overseas qualifications, as well as their affiliation with Migrant Resource Centres (another initiative of the Galbally Report). Through Grant-in-Aid and other schemes, funding became available for community organisations' social activities as well.[24] Government recognition of and support for community organisations grew their confidence and prestige. The increasing length of the *Ethnic Communities Directories* year on year suggests a growing eagerness of groups to join the pages of this "who's who of ethnic Australia", too.

---

23 Jupp, *From White Australia to Woomera*, 45. The National Archives of Australia includes many documents compiled by the Australian Security Intelligence Agency pertaining to the surveillance of Chinese Australian community organisations. These include files on the Chinese Unity Association (A6122, 1410), the Chinese Youth League of Australia (A6122, 1914–1917) and the Friends of Democratic China (A6122, 320).
24 Cox, *Immigration and Welfare*, 230–43.

Gwenda Tavan argues the Australian government's multicultural momentum was in step with the majority of (White) Australians' sentiments.[25] Indeed, in the early '70s, Australia's road to multiculturalism ran alongside other social justice movements. Movements like the protests against South Africa's Apartheid or support for Aboriginal land rights in Australia brought together groups that had once been more strictly separated by ethnic, class and generational boundaries.[26] Of course, Tavan also shows that the "death" of White Australia was delayed by sections of Australian society who wanted the White status quo to remain. Ghassan Hage describes the lingering "White nation fantasies" of these people – wherein Australian belonging is not equally shared among all Australians and "true" Australianness is reserved for White ethnic groups, with the Anglo-Australian ethnic majority being pre-eminent.[27]

Such works outline what many minority ethnic communities in Australia more or less felt to be true – that the country could not realise its multicultural future without reckoning with its racist past. Historical oppression remained deeply significant to the formation and continuation of long established Chinese Australian communities and the organisations that represented them. As Eugenia Tsoulis states, the struggles for visibility, social justice and equity are still integral to understanding the participation (and protests) of Indigenous and ethnic minority communities in Australian society today.[28] Thus, an awareness of how historical oppression affected Chinese Australian communities and organisations is still instrumental to understanding them after the multicultural turn.

---

25 Tavan, *The Long, Slow Death of White Australia*, 209–11.
26 Mark Peel and Christina Twomey, *A History of Australia*, 2nd ed., Palgrave Essential Histories (London: Palgrave, 2018), 231–46; Frank Bongiorno, *The Eighties: The Decade That Transformed Australia* (Melbourne: Black Inc. Books, 2015), 305; Moran, *The Public Life of Australian Multiculturalism*, 29–36.
27 Hage, *White Nation*.
28 Eugenia Tsoulis, "Hand in Hand: Indigenous Australia and Multiculturalism" in Andrew Jakubowicz and Christina Ho, *"For Those Who've Come across the Seas...": Australian Multicultural Theory, Policy and Practice* (Melbourne: Australian Scholarly Publishing, 2013), 249–50.

1 Chinese Australian community organisations

Survival of early Chinese Australian community organisations

Discriminatory legislation and societal marginalisation compelled early Chinese residents in colonial Australia to form community organisations for moral and material sustenance.[29] Moreover, these organisations advocated an individual's or collective community interests, especially in the face of ambivalent or hostile Anglo-Australian authorities. In response to such pressures and roles, early communities and organisations adapted and reshaped themselves. In the process of adapting to a new world, we see that community organisations, despite their own idiosyncratic histories and circumstances, shaped themselves in ways that brought Chinese Australian communities together. That is, in the face of common difficulties, the need to cooperate overrode the differences between Chinese Australian individuals, communities and organisations. The histories of Perth's Chung Wah Association, Darwin's Chung Wah Society and Melbourne's See Yup Society are good examples: respectively a small metropolitan community in Australia's West; a medium-sized rural community in the North (though proportionally large compared to the surrounding non-Chinese communities); and a large metropolitan community (among other large communities) in the Southeast. Though very different to each other, they encountered similar experiences and responded to them in similar ways.

The Chung Wah Association (Perth)

Perth's Chung Wah Association (CWA) experienced a sustained decline under racially discriminatory government policies before being revitalised in the 1970s. When CWA formed in 1909, it became a surrogate community for the approximately 840 ethnic Chinese living in Perth. Later self-published histories of the organisation described CWA as a vehicle for societal and political action from its outset; the early Chinese Australian community it claimed to represent had a history of protesting the restrictive immigration and residency laws in Western Australia.[30] Accordingly, CWA served as an intermediary

---

29 Yong, *The New Gold Mountain*, 189.

between its community and the state and federal governments, as well as helping individuals with legal representation in criminal or industrial matters. As a representative body, it also engaged with other Chinese community organisations in the eastern states to fight against racially discriminatory policies. In this last regard, they had some success in securing immigration concessions for merchants and their families.[31] As wealthy merchants typically steered these organisations, it shows that solidarity extended along class as well as ethnic lines – and that in White Australia, wealth could open doors that racism had shut.

The origin of Chinese in Perth and Western Australia was as indentured labour, primarily from Singapore. These indentured labourers were sought by the Western Australian authorities to address the colony's labour shortages in the mid to late 19th century. As Jan Ryan shows, the flow of people and products profited both colonial outposts.[32] Though crucial to building the colony, indentured labourers occupied a marginalised position in society, and in the 1890s, Western Australian authorities followed the examples set in the eastern colonies and moved to restrict Chinese numbers. As in other parts of Australia, and indeed other settler colonial societies (the USA the most prominent among them), these restrictions were fuelled by xenophobia, fears of "cheap" Chinese labour replacing White labour, and White notions of Chinese racial inferiority.[33]

Under these unwelcoming conditions, Perth's Chinese migrants created a "Friendly Society" in 1898 to provide welfare services to its members.[34] It was probably this body that petitioned the first

---

30 CWA, *Chung Wah Association Centenary Celebration Souvenir Publication, 1910-2010* (Perth: Chung Wah Association, 2010), 40.
31 Tian Cai, "Astride Two Worlds: The Chinese Response to Changing Citizenship in Western Australia (1901–1973)", *Theses: Doctorates and Masters*, 1 January 1999, 113–20, https://ro.ecu.edu.au/theses/1199.
32 Jan Ryan, *Ancestors: Chinese in Colonial Australia* (South Fremantle: Fremantle Arts Centre, 1995), 18–21.
33 Philip A. Kuhn, *Chinese Among Others: Emigration in Modern Times* (Lanham, US: Rowman & Littlefield Publishers, 2008), 197–238; Peter Charles Gibson, *Made in Chinatown: Chinese Australian Furniture Factories, 1880–1930* (Sydney: Sydney University Press, 2022), xiii–xvii.
34 CWA, *Chung Wah Association Centenary Celebration Souvenir Publication, 1910-2010*, 40.

1 Chinese Australian community organisations

Australian Prime Minister, Edmund Barton, to ameliorate the conditions of the White Australia policy and entreated the Dowager Empress for "protection" – likely meaning a consul-general in Western Australia.[35] When neither eventuated, Perth's Chinese resolved that a more "official" community organisation was needed to respond to their worsening circumstances. Consequently, CWA was formed.[36] Along the way, interactions with Chinese Australians from the eastern colonies (and later states) of Australia inspired the organisation of Perth's Chinese migrants. Yet unlike their counterparts in eastern Australia, whose communities were large enough that they grouped themselves according to their clans or counties of origin, Perth's Chinese were like "scattered sand": without immediate kith and kin, Chinese residents from disparate origins came together to form a local Perth community organisation that avoided much of the rivalry and provincialism seen in Sydney and Melbourne.[37] Their ability to set aside their differences to present a united front to advance their interests is reflected in the CWA's name itself. Rather than referencing a particular county or clan, the translation of its name from Cantonese is simply "the Chinese Association".

Although rich enough to raise some £1,200 in September and October of 1911 for Sun Yat-sen's Revolutionary Army in China, by 1922 CWA found itself struggling to repay the mortgage on its meeting hall. It resolved to lease the building to the Western Australian branch of the Australasian Kuomintang (AKMT), a body representing the Chinese Nationalist Party in Australia and beyond, which continued operating in the hall into the 1940s.[38] Their fundraising and chosen tenants give some indication of CWA's political and ideological sympathies, suggesting Perth's Chinese community was still strongly connected to the politics of its old home.

---

35 Yong, *The New Gold Mountain*, 15–17.
36 CWA, *Chung Wah Association Centenary Celebration Souvenir Publication, 1910–2010*, 40.
37 Ryan, *Ancestors*, 21–5; Cai, "Astride Two Worlds", 80–8, 113–18.
38 CWA, *Chung Wah Association Centenary Celebration Souvenir Publication, 1910–2010*, 40–1.

CWA's charity can also be interpreted as a survival strategy. The logic emerging from the nascent Chinese nationalism of the time was that "a strong, progressive China" could protect and win respect for its peoples abroad and thus funds were directed to the causes of the Chinese Republic.[39] Suggesting local connections, CWA's charity was directed to other causes, too. During its zenith at the start of the century, CWA raised monies for the Royal Perth Hospital, the Red Cross Society, the European War Fighting Fund and the Children's Hospital and Orphanage.[40] As Tseen Khoo and Rodney Noonan suggest, Chinese philanthropy was an opportunity to both "celebrate the Chinese cultural identity, while also asserting their support for Australia as members of local, community-based campaigns".[41] In this way, CWA's charity can be read as both an expression of Chinese and Australian identity as well as a strategy to claim belonging in a society that was disinclined toward a Chinese presence.

Unfortunately, CWA's generosity did not save it from the fate experienced by other community organisations around Australia. In its own historical account, CWA uses census data to calculate that by 1933 there were only 363 Chinese living in Perth. It puts this down to the cumulative effect of the Great Depression, immigration restrictions and aged Chinese returning to their homeland.[42] Tian Cai also uses census data to show that the number of those born in China and residing in Western Australia dropped from 465 in 1954 (383 male, 82 female) to 313 in 1961 (227 male, 86 female) as older individuals passed away.[43]

The use of the census data by CWA and Cai is interesting for the way it constructs Perth's "Chinese community" solely around migrants from the Mainland. Omitted from the 1961 figure, for example, are 189 people born in Hong Kong and 618 people born in Singapore (many

---

39   Kuhn, *Chinese Among Others*, 240–57.
40   CWA, *Chung Wah Association Centenary Celebration Souvenir Publication, 1910–2010*, 40–1.
41   Tseen Khoo and Rodney Noonan, "Wartime Fundraising by Chinese Australian Communities", *Australian Historical Studies* 42, no. 1 (March 2011), 94–5, https://doi.org/10.1080/1031461X.2010.541472.
42   CWA, *Chung Wah Association Centenary Celebration Souvenir Publication, 1910–2010*, 41.
43   Cai, "Astride Two Worlds", 228–32.

of whom must have considered themselves "Chinese").[44] The omission is made more interesting when the Singaporean origin of many of Western Australia's Chinese migrants is considered. As previously explained, place of birth does not always match ethnicity. But to this end, the census also asked respondents to record their "race". From this data, Western Australia had 793 men and 197 women who identified as "full-blood" Chinese, and another 147 individuals who identified as "European and Chinese" in 1961.[45] Combined, that makes 1,137 Chinese Australians in Western Australia. Moreover, according to census responses, there were 566 people who considered themselves "full-blood" Chinese but who were not born in China. Immediately, this tells us that Perth's Chinese Australian community was not predominantly from China at this point – and by a large margin. Instead, they were probably *huayi* or, more crucially, locally born.

The figure of 1,137 Chinese Australians is not large, but evidently enough to keep CWA alive. In its self-recorded history, CWA referred to a "small number of families" that kept the organisation going until the 1970s, hinting that its membership was locally born and suggesting the shifting demographic profile of Perth's Chinese Australian community. Further evidence of the shift is that CWA updated its constitution in 1951 to reflect its changing membership. While the original had stated CWA was to be "a place of resort for Gentlemen of the Chinese nationality residing in Australia" (nationality often being synonymous with race at this time), the new constitution now welcomed persons "substantially of Chinese descent" to their ranks to pursue Chinese cultural activities, literature and education.[46] The amendment reveals the progeny of these first migrants and the existence of inter-ethnic marriages among CWA's membership. Lowering the racial barrier for membership might also signify that members were, by then,

---

44 K.M. Archer, "Birthplaces of the Population of Australia by States and Territories", Census, Census of the Commonwealth (Canberra: Commonwealth Bureau of Census and Statistics, 1961), 7.
45 K.M. Archer, "Race of the Population: Australia, States and Territories", Census, Census of the Commonwealth (Canberra: Commonwealth Bureau of Census and Statistics, 1961), 5–6.
46 CWA, *Chung Wah Association Centenary Celebration Souvenir Publication, 1910–2010*, 40–2.

recognising both their Chinese and Australian identities. A combination of English and Chinese names on a list of past CWA presidents is another clue this might be the case.[47] In fact, a 1923 photo of Perth's AKMT committee members, with which CWA shared a close relationship, depicts an intermingling of peoples. Mei-fen Kuo and Judith Brett suggest that the KMT back in China would have disapproved of any "non-Chinese" joining the ranks of overseas branches.[48] Such a sentiment alludes to the contemporary understandings of the intersections of race and nationalism, as much as beliefs about "Chinese authenticity". However, the photographic and membership records suggest that these community organisations were willing to change their rules and expectations to survive in their changing, local realities.

The Chung Wah Society (Darwin)

The history of the Chinese Australians who comprised Darwin's Chung Wah Society (CWS) is comparable to Perth's CWA. Darwin's Chinatown was formed by the first 186 Chinese migrants who arrived in 1874 – only five years after the settlement of Darwin itself was established.[49] Like that in Perth, the Chinese community in Darwin was enmeshed with the broader community but suffered under racially discriminatory legislation. Yet the economic expedience and moral indifference of early Anglo-Australians toward Chinese settlers is exceptional, perhaps owing to Darwin's unique demographic composition.

Between 1880 and 1900, indentured labour was crucial to the construction of Palmerston (Darwin's original name). Indentured labour built Darwin's first Catholic church, the town hall and many of the first

---

47 CWA, 76.
48 Mei-fen Kuo and Judith Brett, *Unlocking the History of the Australasian Kuo Min Tang, 1911–2013* (Melbourne: Australian Scholarly Publishing, 2013), 24–5.
49 Shane Stone and Roger Steele, "Progress of the Chinese Community of the Northern Territory", *Northern Perspective* 18, no. 1 (n.d.), 28–9, https://doi.org/10.3316/ielapa.960201915; Diana Giese, *Beyond Chinatown: Changing Perspectives on the Top End Chinese Experience* (Canberra: National Library of Australia, 1995), 2.

homes and stores. Beyond this, Chinese migrants occupied the full spectrum of trades and commercial enterprises that could be imagined in a new settlement: carpenters, ironsmiths, miners, agricultural labourers and stockmen, cooks, fishermen, artisans and storekeepers.[50] Dozens of photographs held by the National Archives of Australia, however, show how Anglo-Australian authorities perceived the Chinese presence as vexatious rather than vibrant. The photos of "condemned Chinese hovels near the heart of Darwin" and Pine Creek captured both the impoverished conditions some Chinese migrants endured in the first decades of the 20th century, as well as the disdain the public health board had for the Chinese.[51] The photographer included perfunctory descriptions like "group of decrepit men repatriated to China", "hovels built mostly out of flattened kerosene tins", and "Chinese Urinal. Urinal is never emptied and ground in vacinity [sic] is saturated with decomposing urine".[52] The photographer did not connect the indignity of these living arrangements to the exploitative conditions Chinese migrant-workers typically endured. One is struck by the similitude of the images, but this was likely the photographer's intention. As McAndrew Chua argues, sanitation concerns created a medico-legal pretext for authorities to excise the Chinese Australian presence from the Northern Territory.[53] With the work of building Darwin done, toilworn Chinese were to be repatriated and their dwellings demolished.

The large role Chinese played in Darwin's construction may also be the cause of their victimisation.[54] Oral historian Diana Giese, who interviewed many of the descendants of these early Chinese migrants,

---

50 Giese, *Beyond Chinatown*, 2–3; Eric C. Rolls, *Sojourners: The Epic Story of China's Centuries-Old Relationship with Australia: Flowers and the Wide Sea* (Brisbane: University of Queensland Press, 1993), 276.
51 "Photographs of the Northern Territory, NT1912/1022 – NT1915/1028" (item, Canberra, 1925 1912), A3, ALBUM 1, National Archives of Australia, https://tinyurl.com/yzemunk9; "Photographs of the Northern Territory, NT1915/1028 – NT1917/383" (item, Canberra, 1925 1912), A3, ALBUM 2, National Archives of Australia, https://tinyurl.com/3c88kj5x.
52 "Photographs of the Northern Territory, NT1912/1022 – NT1915/1028" Item No. 7802042, 7649237, 7802038.
53 McAndrew Chua, "The Racial Politics of Public Health in 1910's Darwin Chinatown", *Journal of Northern Territory History*, no. 21 (n.d.), 59–78, https://doi.org/10.3316/informit.032944074798518.

points to the example of the parliamentarian (and briefly the 21st premier of South Australia), V.L. Solomon. Despite employing a number of Chinese in his mining and conveyancing business, Solomon stoked fear and antipathy toward Chinese in the South Australian Assembly and later the Commonwealth Parliament.[55] During debates over Australia's Immigration Restriction Bill, soon to be known as the cornerstone of the White Australia policy, Solomon argued that it was because of "their virtues, their industry, their indomitable perseverance, their frugality" that Chinese specifically should be stopped from immigrating to Australia. Solomon insisted that these qualities would allow Chinese migrants to outcompete the European migrants in the processes of colonisation and settlement. He pointed to Darwin as an example where he claimed 7,000 Chinese settlers outnumbered the 1,000 Europeans.[56]

Solomon's argument was based on economic and cultural reasons – if we take Solomon's observation of Chinese "work ethic" to be a comment on Chinese values and habits. At the time, this was quite unusual. As Allan O'Neil points out, Solomon's avoidance of racial slurs contrasted strongly with other ministers' arguments, such as Prime Minister Edmund Barton's reference to "inferior races" and "higher civilisations" when discussing the Chinese and the virtues of White Australia.[57] Perhaps Solomon's Jewish identity gave him some aversion to using baser forms of racism. Solomon's "socio-economic" argument against Chinese immigration was more insidious and evidently more lasting. While ideas about racial purity became taboo after the Second World War, fears of Chinese or Asians taking jobs for less pay and replacing Anglo/White Australians appear perennially (see chapters

---

54 Northern Territory Museums and Art Galleries Board, *Sweet & Sour: Experiences of Chinese Families in the Northern Territory* (Darwin: Museum and Art Gallery of the Northern Territory, 1997), 39.
55 The Northern Territory was part of South Australia from 1862 until 1911. Giese, *Beyond Chinatown*, 5.
56 "Immigration Restriction Bill" (Melbourne: Commonwealth Hansard, 26 September 1901), 5239–40, https://tinyurl.com/4tz52jcj.
57 Allan O'Neil, "More Cooperation and Less Conflict: Chinese-European Relationships in South Australia's Northern Territory", *Journal of Northern Territory History*, no. 16 (2005): 81.

1 Chinese Australian community organisations

on the Blainey and Hanson debates). Solomon's self-interests are additional and telling characteristics of this type of politically expedient racism. Until 1880, Solomon had been a proponent of Chinese immigration, hiring many Chinese labourers in his mining ventures and even representing Chinese litigants in court. It was only when Chinese businessmen began competing with White businesses for White customers that Solomon transformed into a "vehement opponent" of Chinese immigration.[58]

The accuracy of Solomon's assessment of Darwin's population is uncertain. In 1901, when "Port Darwin" was still part of South Australia and around the time Solomon made his argument to restrict Chinese immigration to the new federal parliament, there were 3,253 China-born residents in South Australia's "total population" of 363,157 (Aboriginal and Torres Strait Islander peoples were not counted in censuses until 1971, following the 1967 referendum).[59] In a speech prepared with the assistance of CWS members Ron Chin and Albert Chan, Northern Territory Chief Minister Shane Stone claimed "on the eve of Federation [...], the Territory's population consisted of 1003 Europeans and 2928 Chinese".[60] In 1911, when the Northern Territory was separated from South Australia, the Northern Territory's population included 1,165 China-born persons and South Australia's population included 242.[61] If counted by "race" (including "full-blood" and "half-caste"), South Australia had 359 Chinese Australians in 1911 and the Northern Territory had 1,339.[62] Whatever the number of Darwin's Chinese population just prior to Federation, it was evidently large enough for

---

58 O'Neil, 80–1.
59 G.H. Knibbs, "Official Year Book of the Commonwealth of Australia 1901–1907", Census, Official Year Book (Melbourne: Commonwealth Bureau of Census and Statistics, 1908), 165, 168.
60 Stone and Steele, "Progress of the Chinese Community of the Northern Territory", 29.
61 G.H. Knibbs, "Part II. – Birthplaces", Census, 1911 Census of the Commonwealth of Australia (Melbourne: Commonwealth Bureau of Census and Statistics, 1917), 116.
62 G.H. Knibbs, "Part VIII. – Non-European Races", Census, 1911 Census of the Commonwealth of Australia (Melbourne: Commonwealth Bureau of Census and Statistics, 1917), 905.

several family clans – the Yuen, the Chin and the Wong – and other organisations to form by the turn of the century.[63]

Darwin's Chinese Australian communities maintained separate clan associations and an active chapter of the AKMT, despite the effects of restrictive immigration and the Great Depression. The Second World War, however, put an end to this organisational diversity.[64] After the bombings of 1942 and the consequent evacuation of the city (with some Chinese Australians enlisting or working for the city's defence), many of Darwin's families returned to find Chinatown completely destroyed. Other families did not return at all.[65] Of all the groups that had once been, just the Wah On Society remained, and with only meagre financial resources at that. Realising that the 600 or so Darwinian Chinese Australians who remained would stand better odds of rebuilding Chinatown and reclaiming property in the aftermath of the war if they stood together, the Wah On Society called a meeting for all local Chinese Australians to pool their efforts into a new, single organisation.[66] Thus in 1946, the Chung Wah Society (CWS) came into existence as an organisation to serve the common interests of all Darwin Chinese irrespective of clan background, language or, as Julia Martínez emphasises, political background.[67] Like the early Chinese in Perth, the war had turned Darwin's Chinese Australians into "scattered sand". With dwindling numbers and resources, a new, united "Chinese Society" was established.

---

63 Stone and Steele, "Progress of the Chinese Community of the Northern Territory", 30–3.
64 Giese, *Beyond Chinatown*, 16; Daryl N. Chin and Diana Giese, *Daryl Chin Interviewed by Diana Giese for the Post-War Chinese Australians Oral History Project*, sound recording, Post-War Chinese Australians Oral History Project (Darwin, 1996), TRC 3540, National Library of Australia; Stone and Steele, "Progress of the Chinese Community of the Northern Territory", 34; Julia Martínez, "Chinese Politics in Darwin: Interconnections between the Wah On Society and the Kuo Min Tang", in *Chinese Australians*, eds Sophie Couchman and Kate Bagnall (Boston: Brill, 2015), 240–66, https://tinyurl.com/ym334v7v.
65 Giese, *Beyond Chinatown*, 42.
66 Chin and Giese, *Daryl Chin Interviewed by Diana Giese*; Giese, *Beyond Chinatown*, 49.
67 Martínez, "Chinese Politics in Darwin", 258–1; Giese, *Beyond Chinatown*, 39.

1 Chinese Australian community organisations

Despite the respect of White locals for the resilience and generosity of their Chinese Australian neighbours during the Great Depression and the Second World War, there was still a campaign against rebuilding Chinatown.[68] Darwin resident Jimmy Ah Toy remembered his community's hurt at being labelled sojourners and the Darwinian authorities' insistence that Chinese Australian residents be repatriated back "home". Again, it was history repeating. In 1905, representatives of Darwin's Chinese Australians had claimed their right to stay in Darwin as legitimate settlers after sustained attacks in the South Australian Parliament. "We have made [Darwin] our home," they then declared.[69] Less than a century later, their descendants were defending the same claim.[70] For the early members of CWS, their determination to rebuild Chinatown after the Second World War was thus also an assertion that they belonged to the city and Australia.[71] However, like Perth's CWA, CWS also asserted its place in Australian society at the same time as its community's population was shrinking. In 1933, 316 Chinese comprised 20 per cent of Darwin's population of 1,566 (again, Aboriginal and Torres Strait Islander peoples were not yet counted in the census).[72] By 1942, this had fallen to 10 per cent. In 1967, only 3 per cent of Darwin's population claimed to be Chinese.[73]

The See Yup Society (Melbourne)

On the other side of the continent, Melbourne's See Yup Society (SYS) also followed a trajectory of social prominence into decline.[74]

---

68 Giese, *Beyond Chinatown*, 16, 39; Stone and Steele, "Progress of the Chinese Community of the Northern Territory", 34.
69 Ben Silverstein, "'Throwing Mud' on Questions of Sovereignty: Race and Northern Arguments over White, Chinese, and Aboriginal Labour, 1905–12", *Australian Historical Studies*, 22 April 2021, 1, https://tinyurl.com/49va7ta7.
70 Giese, *Beyond Chinatown*, 11–12.
71 Stone and Steele, "Progress of the Chinese Community of the Northern Territory", 34–5; Giese, *Beyond Chinatown*, 49.
72 Martínez, "Chinese Politics in Darwin", 242.
73 Giese, *Beyond Chinatown*, 11.
74 Note that though I use the form "See Yup Society", the name of this organisation also appears as "Seeyup Society" or, more historically, as "See Yap Society" (among others).

Established in 1854 in South Melbourne by some of the first Chinese migrants to seek their fortunes on Victoria's goldfields, SYS is one of the oldest continuing Chinese Australian community organisations in Australia. As a native place association, it represented Chinese from the See Yup or "four counties" region of Guangdong province (comprised of Toishan, Sunwui, Hoiping and Yanping).[75] Like CWA, SYS offered assistance in members' legal affairs, provided community representation and petitioned government for better treatment of Chinese in Australia.

In its 150th anniversary memorial publication, SYS fit itself into the "Chinese sojourner-goldminer narrative" widely known in Australian history, recounting the racial oppression of Chinese miners on the goldfields.[76] Prominently featured is the well-known overland trek that Chinese prospectors took from South Australia's port of Robe to Victoria's goldfields – an effort to avoid the racist tax Victoria's colonial authorities imposed on any Chinese landing in its ports.[77] SYS's claim on this history is notable. The Chinese miners' presence is quintessential in retellings of Australia's colonial past, even in the most Anglo-centric examples, although SYS frames the Chinese miner squarely within a history of oppression.

Historical oppression illuminates other sides of SYS's history, too. In *Big White Lie*, John Fitzgerald describes SYS's adoption of Western standards of dress and manners, and the Victorian-style renovations of its Daoist temple in the 1860s – including a bas-relief of two men in top hats and tailcoats encompassing the world in their arms – as symbols of their self-perceived and aspirational cosmopolitanism.[78] Participation in public life, such as in the parade to celebrate the visit of the Duke of York in 1901, further support Fitzgerald's argument that the Chinese of

---

75　SYS, 四邑特刊: *Seeyup Society 1854–2004 (Siyi Tekan "Seeyup Special Issue")* (Melbourne: Seeyup Society, 2004), 4, 23. The standard Mandarin names for these places are Taishan, Xinhui, Kaiping and Enping.
76　"白澳政策時代" for "White Australia policy" (and variations on it) is a term that reappears in SYS's 150 Year Anniversary booklet in multiple articles.
77　SYS, *Seeyup Society 1854–2004*, 23, 93.
78　John Fitzgerald, *Big White Lie: Chinese Australians in White Australia* (Sydney: UNSW Press, 2007), 224.

1 Chinese Australian community organisations

the early SYS wanted to belong in Australian society and demonstrate affection and allegiance to their new home.

The image of an oppressed Chinese miner in traditional garb clashes with that of the cosmopolitan Chinese in top hat and tails. But perhaps depictions of the latter could also be seen as an example of Chinese Australians addressing the expectations and anxieties of the Anglo-Australian society that surrounded them. The self-imposed direction to SYS members to adopt Western dress codes, for example, implies that it was not because Chinese *liked* Western clothes but rather Chinese clothes were "very much disliked by Europeans". Further directions clarify that Western dress was adopted because members must avoid being "laughed at by Europeans". Another direction warned its members that:

> Should anyone get embroiled in a quarrel with Europeans, and receive insults from them, the services of an interpreter must be called into requisition, to make up matters. The offending Chinese shall first be chastised and his case afterwards gone into; and this will serve as a warning for his presumption.[79]

The fact that the Chinese "offender" would be chastised before their case is even gone into suggests a default submission to White authority.

In truth, SYS and its membership display qualities both as targets of assimilative expectations and as historical agents able to adopt and reject aspects of Australian society. SYS's 1854 constitution sets out the traditions and aspirations of these early arrivals. A temple and ancestral shrines for departed companions were to be built "when the Society has ample funds" and it was done so in a combination of Feng Shui principles and Victorian architectural aesthetic. It committed the SYS to "render all possible assistance whenever and wherever there occurs cases of famine and flood, [and] in such charitable activities as the maintenance of hospitals", and this it did toward its members' new

---

79   W.M. Young, "Report of the Condition of the Chinese Population in Victoria", Report (Melbourne: Houses of Parliament, 1868), 17–20.

and old homelands.[80] SYS's history is not one purely of oppression, but also of adaptation.

Despite still being one of Melbourne's largest Chinese Australian community organisations in the 1920s and 1930s, SYS was affected by the restriction of Chinese immigration and its membership dwindled like those of other community organisations around Australia.[81] Long-time president Maurice Leong recalled that when his father encouraged him to join in 1947, SYS's situation was dire. To illustrate its inability to recruit new members, only three regional trustee positions existed when once there were twelve. Though SYS still held multiple properties in Melbourne, the rental income it could draw from these was irregular.[82] As a result, SYS went into a caretaker mode and its temple closed and fell into disrepair – so much so that in 1962 the local council threatened to demolish the building.[83] The attrition of membership and finance that began in the 1900s only worsened into the 1960s. The society recounts the period as a low point in its history.[84] During this time, many of SYS's earliest organisational records were lost to neglect or accidents. According to the former president Maurice Leong, the earliest written record now is a book of minutes dating back to the 1920s.[85]

Yet SYS did not fold. Moreover, it did not combine with other organisations to form a new one. This is interesting because SYS had a particularly close relationship with another community organisation, the Kong Chew Society (KCS). Formed in 1853, one year before SYS, KCS was another native place association taking in migrants from

---

80   Yong, *The New Gold Mountain*, 272.
81   Fitzgerald, *Big White Lie*, 141; Mei-fen Kuo, *Making Chinese Australia: Urban Elites, Newspapers and the Formation of Chinese-Australian Identity, 1892–1912*, Monash Asia Series (Melbourne: Monash University Publishing, 2013), 190.
82   Maurice Leong and Diana Giese, *Maurice Leong Interviewed by Diana Giese for the Chinese Australian Oral History Partnership Collection*, sound recording, Chinese Australian Oral History Partnership, 2000, TRC 4583, National Library of Australia.
83   Leong and Giese; Sophie Couchman, "Melbourne's See Yup Kuan Ti Temple: A Historical Overview", *Chinese Southern Diaspora Studies* 8 (2019), 75–6.
84   SYS, *Seeyup Society 1854–2004*, 32.
85   Leong and Giese, *Maurice Leong Interviewed by Diana Giese*.

1 Chinese Australian community organisations

Guangdong as members.⁸⁶ However, KCS was, in effect, a more exclusive society than SYS, as it drew its membership only from Xin Hui County – one of the four counties comprising the "See Yap" ("Kong Chew" is a Cantonese cognate for 岡州/Guangzhou, an old name for Xin Hui).⁸⁷ The relationship between these two organisations was close. SYS's constitution recorded that SYS was first housed within KCS's premises before it could afford its own.⁸⁸ According to Yong, these organisations maintained different purposes: SYS being devoted to charitable causes in Melbourne (for Chinese and non-Chinese alike) and in China, and KCS working as an arbitrator between different native place and clan associations throughout the colony. SYS also held a monopoly over the passage of Chinese back to China (typically miners), while KCS leadership held sway over Chinese commerce in Melbourne. Nevertheless, SYS and KCS repeatedly cooperated, especially in instances that would benefit Chinese migrants: for example, paying the upkeep for the Chinese consulate-general premises and funding the China-Australia Mail Steamship Line.⁸⁹ When there was cause to work together, SYS and KCS typically did so.

That these organisations remained distinct, despite drawing their memberships from an overlapping pool of See Yap emigrants, demonstrates the size of Melbourne's Chinese Australian population and its capacity to sustain multiple organisations. As C.F. Yong outlines, in 1857 there were 25,424 Chinese in Victoria, and it was only around 1891 that this number dropped below 10,000.⁹⁰ And, as both Yong and Fitzgerald point out, there were still enough Chinese Australians around after Federation for rivalries to exist between organisations – sometimes even "fighting one another in the streets".⁹¹ Mei-fen Kuo also describes rivalry and occasional violence between Chinese Australian community organisations in Melbourne and Sydney during this period.⁹² Of course, rivalries and violence existed in cities with smaller

86 KCS, "About Us", Kong Chew Society, https://tinyurl.com/39szvw9b.
87 Fitzgerald, *Big White Lie*, 141–2.
88 Yong, *The New Gold Mountain*, 272.
89 Yong, 191–3.
90 Yong, 275.
91 Fitzgerald, *Big White Lie*, 66, 82; Yong, *The New Gold Mountain*, 193–4.
92 Kuo, *Making Chinese Australia*, 159–66.

Chinese Australian populations, too. One incident in 1918 involved a CWA member shooting another member over disputed committee election results.[93] CWA survived this crisis (though omitted it from its own telling of history) and continued to be the premier organisation representing the interests of Perth's small Chinese Australian community. In 1911, there were 1,872 "full and half-blood" Chinese in Western Australia (many living in the state's regional oasis of diversity, Broome).[94] In 1921, the number reduced to 1,443 with only 714 living in the state's metropolitan areas.[95] In comparison, Melbourne counted 2,449 Chinese Australians in 1921, and Sydney 3,953.[96]

As the decades continued into the 20th century, the number of Chinese Australians in Melbourne dwindled and many of the city's community organisations ceased to exist. SYS and KCS, however, managed to hold on. If SYS's membership was ageing and shrinking, as past-president Maurice Leong described, then it is likely that KCS's membership was as well. In 1962, KCS had managed to source funds from Melbourne's local Chinese Australian residents to open Victoria's first aged care home for elderly Chinese. Again, this was a cause for the community to come together: as SYS remembered, its support ensured that the aged care home could afford to operate.[97] Despite the hardships apparent in White Australia, these organisations did not amalgamate. For their continued existence, SYS and KCS have the honour of being organisations that both pre-dated and outlasted the White Australia policy. Still, Melbourne's Chinese migrants from the four counties only survived the White Australia policy period by pulling together when needed.

In the histories of CWA, CWS and SYS, there is a common pattern of formation under pressing circumstances and then decline upon the advent of the White Australia policy. This decline continued in the

---

93 "Chews V. Lees: A Chinese Wounded", *Register*, 22 January 1918; "Rival Chinese Factions", *Sydney Morning Herald*, 22 January 1918.
94 Knibbs, "Part VIII. – Non-European Races", 926.
95 Chas. H. Wickens, "Part V. – Race", Census, 1921 Census of the Commonwealth of Australia (Melbourne: Commonwealth Bureau of Census and Statistics, 1924), 312.
96 Wickens, 300, 303.
97 SYS, *Seeyup Society 1854–2004*, 33–4, 87.

1 Chinese Australian community organisations

various communities and organisations around Australia well into the 1960s, and new, local Chinese Australian identities were formed in the process. Pressures of decline and discrimination caused differences to be put aside, and their commonalities brought them, and their community organisations, together. These histories also suggest that the size of a local Chinese Australian population naturally affects the diversity of community organisations of a given locale.

New community organisations

Whereas the older community organisations were founded largely for mutual protection, those formed during Australia's turn to multiculturalism had other imperatives for coming together. The desire to maintain and pass on Chinese culture for future generations – cultural maintenance – was by far the primary driver for them. The creation of Chinese-language schools, and social and cultural activities, were therefore formative objectives. With the growing public regard for multiculturalism and increasing number of ethnic Chinese migrants, the formation of new community organisations led to greater diversity overall. In these more favourable conditions, some of these new organisations nevertheless appealed for unity of the Chinese Australian community by different means and for different ends – such as for the allocation of government resources or to pursue a socio-political ideal. Yet, in the absence of a pressing need to come together, it is clear that the new community organisations maintained their diversity.

There are additional differences between old and new organisations, such as their typically different gender compositions. Those formed in the late 19th and early 20th centuries were overwhelmingly if not entirely made up of men and focused on supporting these men to settle in this new land (as well as to return to the old land when needed). By comparison, community organisations formed during the multicultural turn took the family as the basic unit of its membership and, as a result, their organisational focus widened. Language schools and childcare or excursions and picnics for families with children were common features of these organisations, as were youth or women's committees. Again, the creation of Chinese-language schools co-aligned with the larger presence of young Chinese Australian families and a concomitant desire to pass on cultural knowledge and identity. Whereas older community organisations catered to the immediate needs of Chinese Australian men in a foreign land, newer organisations grew their focus to include the needs of Chinese Australian families. Where older community organisations put a strong focus on ensuring migrant men received their traditional rites upon death, new community organisations looked to building future generations in a land they saw as their home.

While the memberships of these organisations achieved a great gender balance, this did not lead to greater balance on the executive committees of these organisations. They remained overwhelmingly led by men. Though Chinese Australian women have begun to take leadership positions, progress in this regard has been very limited. In one of the better examples of women occupying places of leadership, four women have served as president of the Australian Chinese Community Association (ACCA) over its history. Yet the fact that 15 men have filled this role shows equality is still far off.[98] The further fact that female presidents of other community organisations have often served immediately after their husbands – such as in case of the Chinese Association of Victoria (CAV) and the ACT Chinese Australian Association (ACTCAA) – are further indications that patriarchal structures remain strong. As Angeline Low shows in her study of women in Sydney's Chinese Australian community organisations, men often enlist their wives, female relatives and friends into voluntary work within their chosen organisations. As a result, there are typically more women in community organisations than men, but more men in leadership positions than women. Family time constraints that disproportionally affect women and a propensity for men to "play politics" compound this situation.[99]

---

98 ACCA, "Past and Current Presidents of ACCA", Australian Chinese Community Association 澳華公會, https://tinyurl.com/9bate6mk.
99 Angeline Low, "The Roles and Contributions of Chinese Women Entrepreneurs in Community Organizations in Sydney", in *Voluntary*

1 Chinese Australian community organisations

Another difference between the new and old organisations is the degree to which they fitted with the contemporary social and political moods around them. In this regard, the constitutions of organisations (much like the community organisations themselves) were products of their times. Formed under racially discriminatory policies in a newly federated Australia, CWA, for example, stated it would "do its utmost" to investigate cases where members were bullied or ill-treated.[100] In the context of China's republican movement, AKMT's 1921 constitution encouraged Chinese Australians to "take a greater interest in the political economy of their native country" and "appreciate the advantages" of democratic government, and encouraged "an appreciation … of a friendly relationship between the Great Powers".[101] During the multicultural turn, commitments to promote mutual understanding between Chinese and non-Chinese Australians, foster the integration of new migrants into Australian society, and cooperate with like-minded community organisations were common objectives.[102] These ideals fostered an active Chinese identity as well as an active Australian one.

As one of my interviewees reflected, many migrants who came to Australia during the 1960s and 1970s were enthusiastic and optimistic about partaking in their new homeland's social and political affairs because similar opportunities did not exist in their old homelands.[103] But it was not just new migrants. Again, reflecting the times,

---

Organizations in the Chinese Diaspora, eds Khun Eng Kuah-Pearce and Evelyn Hu-Dehart (Hong Kong: Hong Kong University Press, 2006), 215–20.

100 CWA, ed., *Chung Wah Association, 1910–1995: 85th Anniversary* (Perth: Chung Wah Association, 1995), 11.
101 Yong, *The New Gold Mountain*, 268.
102 ACCA, ed., 澳洲紐修威省澳華公會會刊 *Àozhōu Niǔxiūwēishěng àohuágōnghuì huìkān* (*The Australian-Chinese Community Association of NSW Journal*) (Sydney: ACCA, 1977), 75; CASA, "News Bulletin November 1978" (Chinese Association of South Australia, November 1978), 5, National Library of Australia; CAV, ed., *Chinese Association of Victoria: 1982–1992: The First Ten Years* (Melbourne: Chinese Association of Victoria, 1992), 10; ACTCAA, "Newsletter August 1988" (ACT Chinese Australian Association, August 1988), 1, National Library of Australia.
103 Interviewee 1, Researcher with Anonymous Interviewee 1, interview by Researcher, 20 July 2018.

In the Face of Diversity

Australian-born Chinese Australians also partook in the formation of new community organisations. In doing so, they seized the opportunities for political and social goals which were not or could not be pursued by their forebears. Large community organisations that formed at this time provided ample evidence of this in the materials they created and the local and national significance they went on to achieve. Two examples given here – the Chinese Association of South Australia (CASA) and the Chinese Fellowship of Victoria (CFV) – showed similar ends could be achieved despite different circumstances.

The Chinese Association of South Australia

CASA formed in Adelaide in 1971. It focused on cultural maintenance and community welfare: opening a language school that taught Mandarin and Cantonese for children and adults, celebrating events on the traditional Chinese calendar, providing translation and interpreter services, and assisting new migrants to settle into their new community.[104] It hosted various cultural activities for members, English language classes for restaurant workers, and staged Chinese cultural displays at public events.[105] CASA's diverse membership of students, academics, small business owners and professionals, including many from Hong Kong, Malaysia, Singapore and Indonesia, meant that CASA's membership overall had a higher degree of education, English proficiency and wealth comparative to the community organisations formed decades prior.[106] CASA's membership was typically younger and included university students and young families. Moreover, CASA's

---

104 Australian Department of Social Security, *National Groups in Australia: A Directory. South Australia 1975* (Canberra: Australian Government Publishing Service, 1975), 16.
105 CASA, "News Bulletin December 1979" (Chinese Association of South Australia, December 1979), National Library of Australia; Qinghuang Yan and Hongbo Zhou, 南澳中華會館: 四十周年紀念特刊 *Nan'ao Zhonghua Huiguan: Si Shi Zhou Nian Jinian Tekan (CASA 40th Anniversary Commemorative Magazine): 1971–2011* (Black Forest: The Chinese Association of South Australia Inc., 2016), 120–4.
106 Yan and Zhou, *CASA 40th Anniversary Commemorative Magazine: 1971–2011*, 118.

membership accounted for a greater proportion of Adelaide's small Chinese Australian population. CASA claimed that by 1973 it had a membership of 228 from a total Chinese Australian population it thought did not exceed 400.[107] It is likely Adelaide's Chinese Australian population – and therefore the pool for potential CASA members – was larger than CASA estimated. According to the 1971 census, South Australia counted 631 China-born residents and another 194 from Hong Kong, 318 from Singapore and 1,011 from Malaysia for a total of 2,154.[108] In 1976, residents born in these places (plus eight from Taiwan) totalled 2,868.[109] Many more ethnic Chinese also began arriving in South Australia in this decade as refugees from Indochina (as will become more relevant below). Nevertheless, the organisation could boast an excellent representation of Adelaide's Chinese Australian population, especially in the first years following its foundation.

Its founding member and first president, Edmund Young, was an Australian-born Chinese Australian. Young was a man of strong opinions. In one brash example, he wrote to *The Bulletin* to correct its "erroneous distorted impressions of Chinese".[110] Young's motive for founding CASA was similarly an attempt to right a perceived wrong – this time his personal experience of being denied membership of the Australian-Asian Family Association of South Australia. Because it limited its membership to "mixed-couples", the association rejected Young and his Chinese-born wife for being a "Chinese couple". Young was born and raised in Queensland. Clearly, the Australian-Asian Family Association understood being Australian as being White.

It was this injustice that drove Young to start his own organisation to serve the interests of South Australia's Chinese Australians.[111]

---

107 CASA, *40th Anniversary Commemorative Magazine*, 123.
108 J.P. O'Neill, "Bulletin 1. Summary of Population: Part 4. South Australia", Census, Census of Population and Housing, 30 June 1971 (Canberra: Commonwealth Bureau of Census and Statistics, 1972), 2.
109 R.J. Cameron, "Populations and Dwellings: Summary Tables – South Australia", Census, Census of Population and Housing, 30 June 1976 (Canberra: Commonwealth Bureau of Census and Statistics, 1979), 2.
110 Edmund Young, "Letters: Chinese in Australia", *The Bulletin*, 7 October 1967, 85.
111 Yan and Zhou, *CASA 40th Anniversary Commemorative Magazine: 1971–2011*, 259.

Nonetheless, Young's transformation of his negative experience into positive action exhibited some of the confidence of the 1970s. Along with another founding member, historian Ching-hwang Yen, the two used their networks among Chinese Australian business owners and recently arrived university students to recruit interested people.

After its inaugural meeting in December 1971, CASA was quick to arrange festivities and events. Naturally, these served as platforms for CASA to display and express its cultural identity and familiarise South Australia's public with facets of Chinese culture. These events also afforded opportunities for CASA members to mingle with other sections of Adelaide's society. CASA's inaugural "Dragon Ball" in 1972 was promoted as a chance to rub shoulders with the city's elite and raise the reputation of the organisation.[112] Indeed, most social events afforded multiple opportunities to promote the organisation. "Asian food fairs" and events organised by the South Australian Ethnic Communities Association allowed CASA to do more than promote Chinese cuisine: they were opportunities to build relationships with other communities and government bodies.[113] Through events like these, CASA built a familiarity with local and state governments and other ethnic community bodies, which shored up its reputation as a leading ethnic community organisation.

Before long, CASA was recognised as *the* organisation representing local Chinese Australian interests. Though the ethnic Chinese refugees from Indochina, whom CASA had helped to settle into Adelaide, had formed their own organisation in 1980 (the Indochina Chinese Association of South Australia, ICASA), it was only CASA that was invited to represent Chinese Australian interests on the Police-Ethnic Liaison Committee of South Australia or the Multicultural Education Co-Ordinating Committee of South Australia.[114] The slippage between a community organisation and the wider community it claimed (and was officially recognised) to represent was often self-perpetuated and sometimes inaccurate. If a community organisation proclaimed itself to represent a wider community, a government body could engage with

---

112 Yan and Zhou, 119–20.
113 Yan and Zhou, 121–2.
114 Yan and Zhou, 138–9.

1 Chinese Australian community organisations

it on that basis. This engagement in turn validated the community organisation's original claim, irrespective of the claim's original legitimacy.

Claims of community representation also entailed material benefits. For CASA and ICASA, the claim to community representation became the basis to claim resources from the government, and therefore engendered competition. The competitive nature of government funding meant where one won, the other lost out. After ICASA was able to differentiate its largely refugee community from the more established community that CASA represented, it obtained funding for an in-house social worker ahead of CASA.[115] Understandably, somewhat paradoxical claims could emerge where community organisations might claim to have a larger or more niche community representation according to the conditions of the funding.

The issue of representation notwithstanding, CASA's achievements benefitted local Chinese Australians beyond its own membership. CASA's Edmund Young had been an outspoken supporter of criminalising forms of racism and discrimination, and later was also a supporter of Indochinese refugees.[116] In 1973, CASA successfully lobbied for Mandarin to be taught at the South Australian Institute of Technology (later the University of South Australia).[117] CASA saw this as raising the prestige of Chinese language and culture in South Australia, allowing the children of migrants to learn Mandarin at the tertiary level and build interest in Chinese language and culture among non-Chinese Australians.[118]

At its inception, CASA was a community organisation with good coverage over the relatively small Chinese Australian community in Adelaide, but more community organisations would follow in the years

---

115 Qiuping Pan, "Ethnic Identity and Immigrant Organizations", *Journal of Chinese Overseas* 14, no. 1 (23 April 2018), 41–2, https://tinyurl.com/42438jca.
116 Edmund Young, "Letters: Chinese Suffer", *The Bulletin*, 25 August 1973; Edmund Young, "Letters: Perkins' Views Racist", *The Bulletin*, 6 October 1981.
117 Edmund Young, "Chinese Language Course", *Overseas Trading*, 14 December 1973, 658.
118 Yan and Zhou, *CASA 40th Anniversary Commemorative Magazine: 1971–2011*, 126.

soon after – especially after an influx of Indochinese refugees. The issue of representation intersected with the new multicultural topography of Adelaide and Australia in general. Chinese Australian communities had the confidence to create their own new organisations, but government funding for those organisations would rely on the nature of their community representation; this could be broad or narrow depending on the organisation's aims or the government's funding stipulations.

The Chinese Fellowship of Victoria

Just a little older than CASA, the Chinese Fellowship of Victoria (CFV) was founded in August 1971. CFV is another organisation that held community and cultural maintenance as central tenets. Like CASA, CFV assisted migrant settlement, created a Mandarin-language school and library, screened Chinese movies and hosted social functions.[119] It also ran a Chinese choir, painting classes and a dance troupe. Notable for the time was that it also organised group tours to the PRC and Hong Kong.[120] According to CFV, these activities attracted students, and both blue- and white-collar workers to CFV's membership, as well as older Chinese Melburnians who lacked the English skills needed for mingling with the broader community.[121] CFV's membership therefore differed from CASA's. Unlike Adelaide's relatively young Chinese Australian community, CFV had connections to Melbourne's long-established communities to draw upon. CFV's inaugural

---

119 CFV, "About Us", Chinese Fellowship of Victoria, 2018, https://tinyurl.com/32ryebr9; CFV, "Newsletter August 1974" (Chinese Fellowship of Victoria, August 1974), 1–2, State Library of Victoria.
120 CFV, "Newsletter February 1975" (Chinese Fellowship of Victoria, February 1975), 6–11, State Library of Victoria.
121 CFV, *Aodaliya Weisheng qiao youshe er shi wu zhounian yinxi jinian tekan 澳大利亞維省僑友社二十五週年銀禧紀念特刊 (Chinese Fellowship of Victoria, Australia: 25th Anniversary Commemorative Journal)* (North Melbourne: Chinese Fellowship of Victoria, 1996), 17, 28; CFV, "Newsletter July 1975" (Chinese Fellowship of Victoria, July 1975), 9–10, State Library of Victoria; CFV, "Newsletter November 1975" (Chinese Fellowship of Victoria, November 1975), 13–14, State Library of Victoria.

vice-president, Maurice Leong, was also many times the president of SYS and founder of an early pro-PRC group, Chinese Unity.[122] With broad appeal and potential for growth, CFV openly expressed its goal to unite and represent all Chinese in Melbourne.[123]

Within three years of its formation, the group had outgrown its clubhouse on Franklin Street. CFV's old site is notable for being close to Melbourne's Queen Victoria Market, an important site for Chinese grocers and blue-collar workers. It was only a short distance from the city's Chinatown where the local AKMT still held sway. According to Leong, AKMT had earlier convinced the local Wesley Church not to lease its Nicholas Hall to "communists" when the CFV was first looking for a home (proving the relative openness after the Menzies years, neither Leong nor CFV kept their support for the PRC secret).[124] Procuring larger premises became a rallying cause for CFV's members, and within a few months almost $13,000 was raised and a new premises secured.[125]

CFV was proud of its quick expansion and it endeavoured to keep increasing its local presence and patronage. In 1975, CFV created a public relations and promotion subcommittee to manage the group's image, raise awareness about its services, and ultimately attract more members.[126] Throughout this period, CFV stated that its mission was to unite "all groups" of Melbourne's Chinese Australian community. For its leadership, it seemed imperative that Chinese Australians' similarities outweighed any of their differences. Yet CFV's hope for unity was at times asserted with hostility. "While in the process of uniting, you must be vigilant; if unity is destroyed you will be kicked while you're down", it warned in one newsletter.[127] Who was imagined

---

122 Leong and Giese, *Maurice Leong Interviewed by Diana Giese*; CFV, *Chinese Fellowship of Victoria, Australia: 25th Anniversary Commemorative Journal*, 10.
123 CFV, "Newsletter August 1974", 1.
124 Leong and Giese, *Maurice Leong Interviewed by Diana Giese*.
125 CFV, "Newsletter August 1974", 7–8.
126 CFV, "Newsletter April 1975" (Chinese Fellowship of Victoria, April 1975), 1, State Library of Victoria; CFV, "Newsletter May 1975" (Chinese Fellowship of Victoria, May 1975), 1, State Library of Victoria; CFV, "Newsletter July 1975", 1–3, 6–10.

to be doing this "kicking" was not clarified, but it gives an idea of how strongly CFV believed it could and should represent all local Chinese Australians.

In its early newsletters, it is clear that CFV's call for Chinese Australian unity was predicated on a commitment to the PRC, equating love for the ancestral homeland with adherence to the CCP's political and patriotic line. This stance fitted with one existing story for CFV's origin. According to one early newsletter, it was during the 1971 Senkaku/Diaoyu Islands dispute between Japan and China that a group of Melbourne Chinese endeared to Chinese socialism struck on the idea to form CFV. Despite being "intimidated" by other organisations bitter about the Communist victory in 1949, the group believed Melbourne needed a "truly patriotic community organisation".[128] When Australia switched its recognition from the ROC to the PRC in 1972, CFV felt its support for the CCP was vindicated. "Two years since [Australia's recognition of the PRC], a visible result is that the social standing of Chinese compatriots has greatly increased", CFV declared to its members.[129] (Interestingly, 25 years later, another testimonial claimed CFV's formation "was not politically motivated, although it appeared to be the case at the time").[130] The idea that a strong China would protect the interests of Overseas Chinese harkened back to the rationale for supporting the Chinese republican movement more than half a century earlier. CFV's contemporary messaging was that Chinese Australians should uniformly get behind the PRC if they wanted to maintain or improve their social standing.

In taking this position, CFV placed itself in clear opposition to community organisations that were historically and ideologically aligned with the Kuomintang (KMT) and Republic of China (ROC).

127　CFV, "Newsletter August 1974", 1–2.
128　"侨友社是三年前在保卫钓鱼台运动中诞生的。当时，在墨尔本有一些华侨，他们都热爱社会主义中国，但是由解放治上受到恐吓，真正有组织的华侨爱国社团并没有." CFV, "Newsletter September 1974" (Chinese Fellowship of Victoria, September 1974), 8, State Library of Victoria.
129　CFV, 7.
130　CFV, *Chinese Fellowship of Victoria, Australia: 25th Anniversary Commemorative Journal*, 28.

1 Chinese Australian community organisations

It is very probable that CFV's suggestion of intimidation was pointed at Melbourne's branch of the AKMT. Melbourne's AKMT had a relationship with local Chinese Australians that had been built over many decades.[131] A public example came in 1969, when most of Melbourne's community organisations – including SYS and KCS – joined the local AKMT branch in wishing President Chiang Kai-shek a happy birthday. In concert with other AKMT branches and community organisations around Australia, they took out a joint advertisement in the *Canberra Times* to send their salutations.[132] The advert is an interesting historical footnote. SYS's appearance among the well-wishers clashes with the pro-PRC position that leaders later portrayed in SYS's 150 year chronicle – a reminder that opinions and memories change over time (or according to the intended audience).

In its early years, CFV did not appear set to "unite" the local Chinese Australian community as much as it appeared hopeful of displacing an older organisation – AKMT. The path CFV took to do this was sometimes provocative. When Chiang Kai-shek died, CFV ridiculed Taiwan's dictator as a lackey for Japanese and American interests and castigated him for Taiwan's separation from the Mainland. Again, pushing the point of Chinese (Australian) unity, CFV trumpeted that Taiwan separatism was foolish as it went against the patriotism and love of Overseas Chinese everywhere:

> [And] once China is reunified, our business as Overseas Chinese organisations becomes easier to handle, and even greater unity of the Chinese people can be achieved![133]

Such a statement was not so much an appeal to unity among existing Chinese Australian communities and their organisations as it was a

---

131 Kuo and Brett, *Unlocking the History of the Australasian Kuo Min Tang, 1911–2013*, 148–78.
132 ACT Chinese Club of Canberra et al., "Congratulations on the Occasion of His Excellency President Chiang Kai-Shek's Birthday", *Canberra Times*, 31 October 1969.
133 "中國統一了，我們的僑團的事也好辦了，華人也會更團結起來的！" CFV, "Newsletter May 1975", 1–3.

unilateral declaration of how CFV believed intra-ethnic relations should be.

CFV's early one-eyed support for the PRC and CCP ran contrary to other new Chinese Australian communities, too; namely those coming as refugees from Indochina. CFV's celebration of Vietnam's victory over "the American Imperialists" was little comfort to the ethnic Chinese arriving in Australia as refugees from the ashes of that conflict.[134] In striking contrast to CFV's vision of the CCP as the saviour of oppressed peoples across the world, one community organisation later created by Indochinese refugees, the Indo-China Ethnic Chinese Association of Victoria (ICECAV), saw the CCP as an "accomplice" to their suffering.[135] Moreover, ICECAV derided community organisations that toed the PRC's political line as self-serving opportunists.[136] Although these were new Chinese Australian communities (especially the very recent Indochinese communities), they were nevertheless repeating a historical pattern. As it had been in the past, Chinese politics remained a double-edged sword: it brought some communities and organisations together, but it kept others apart.

From scattered sands to a new beginning

Now encouraged to express their cultural identities openly, Chinese Australian communities generated new organisations to embody their values and cater to their needs. For new organisations like CASA and CFV, whose memberships included families with young children, cultural maintenance was a fundamental objective. Thus, initiatives like language schools were undertaken. At the same time, these organisations offered a selection of cultural activities for the benefit

---

134 CFV, 10.
135 Note that I use the form "Indochina" however the organisation uses the "Indo-China" form in its name. ICECAV, "The Bridge July 1999" (Indo-China Ethnic Chinese Association of Victoria, July 1999), 7, State Library of Victoria.
136 ICECAV, "The Bridge February 2001" (Indo-China Ethnic Chinese Association of Victoria, February 2001), 8, State Library of Victoria.

1 Chinese Australian community organisations

of the next generation and for the enjoyment of the old. Their memberships quickly grew accordingly.

New organisations also exhibited other values through their activities and communications. CASA showed an eagerness to embed itself in Adelaide's social landscape as the city's premier Chinese Australian community organisation. CFV was guided by a socio-political vision for Melbourne's local communities. In each case, these imperatives for unity differed from the old community organisations' more urgent reasons for pursuing Chinese Australian unity and cooperation. For CWS, CWA and SYS, these were primarily the pressures resulting from the White Australia policy, and for CWS the aftermath of the Second World War was another reason. While not unlike earlier uses of overseas patriotism for political causes in China, CFV's appeal to Chinese Australian unity by way of patriotic support for the PRC lacked the urgency of comparable appeals during the Second World War (or the Chinese Civil War, for that matter). CASA's representation of a united Chinese Australian community for government funding or initiatives was markedly different because such programs simply did not exist during the White Australia policy period.

Most important to point out here are the patterns of cooperation and diversity among community organisations. As seen in the histories of CWA, CWS and SYS, as local Chinese Australian populations became smaller and social environments more hostile, the resultant pressures forced individuals to put aside differences and compelled community organisations to amalgamate or cooperate. Likewise, the histories of CASA and CFV after the multicultural turn show how diversity began to flourish as adversities diminished. This established a pattern that continues into contemporary histories.

New or old, Chinese Australian community organisations began to forcefully (re)assert their social ambitions and political beliefs as part of their organisational remit during the multicultural turn. As will be seen in the next chapter, the newfound optimism of community organisations helped them to pursue these ambitions, which in turn coloured the way they "did" multiculturalism. Moreover, it gave them the confidence to assert their belonging in Australia and respond to the nascent challenges to the nation's new multiculturalism.

2
Early optimism and challenges

> I never dreamed of staying back in Australia, really. I just came to study and I'm going back to practise in Malaysia because I was always very socially conscious and I wanted to help Malaysia at that time. But when Gough Whitlam came to power, and he changes this policy, and then I listened to one of his speeches one day, and he said, "we must treat all migrants as equal, otherwise how do you expect them to contribute wholeheartedly to Australia?" And so he abolished this White Australia policy and then established [the] anti-racial discrimination act and all that. And that made me stay in Australia.[1]

As the interviewee above conveys, the 1970s was a period of hope for a new multicultural Australia. For Chinese Australian communities and the organisations that represented them, the turn to multiculturalism engendered new confidence to express publicly their Chinese (Australian) identities. The 1970s was also a period in which Chinese Australians re-examined and reconfigured their personal and collective

---

1 Interviewee 3, Researcher with Anonymous Interviewee 3, interview by Researcher, 18 September 2018.

identities, allowing them to define Chinese Australianness afresh. The confidence to assert Chinese Australian identity meant that community organisations were also more prepared to insist on how non-Chinese Australians should see or define them – ensuring they were participants in Australia's common multicultural process, rather than conforming to what White Australian authorities had envisioned *for* them.

In terms of community organisations and their own approaches to multiculturalism, a hundred flowers bloomed. Alongside the new possibilities of inter-ethnic interactions were new possibilities for intra-ethnic relations. Sharing the prevailing confidence of the era, community organisations were optimistic about brokering unity among Australia's diverse Chinese Australian communities. For some, this would involve familiar attempts to use a transnational political ideology to unite disparate communities; that is, drumming up support for the PRC in spaces where support for the KMT had once predominated. Differentiating themselves from these well-worn plays and demonstrating some fresh ideas, organisations that consciously avoided political overtures were more effective at brokering lasting cooperation between communities.

However, Australia's turn to multiculturalism energised reactionary organisations that longed to restore the previous racialised ideals of White Australia. In search of sensational material, Australia's media often provided a platform for these racist organisations. Moreover, Australian media displayed its own "White Australian hangovers" through insensitive or plainly racist content. True to the diverse ways of enacting multiculturalism, Chinese Australian community organisations responded differently to these issues but, as will be seen, the turn to multiculturalism fundamentally changed the dynamic between the proponents and opponents of racist ideas in Australia.

The confidence to be Chinese Australian in multicultural Australia

James Jupp used the growth of Australia's non-White population to measure the impact of White Australia's end. Alongside his quantitative metric, we could consider a qualitative one: the confidence of ethnic

2 Early optimism and challenges

community organisations to assert their respective identities in Australia's public space or enact their own ideals. It could be the courage to make a political stand or the comfort to rejoice with others. In August 1974, as thanks for the Chinese Fellowship of Victoria's (CFV) open support and political advocacy during a strike for better conditions, Hong Kong sailors feted CFV representatives as guests of honour in celebrations aboard their ship, the *An'da*. Also present at the celebration were representatives of the Victorian branch of the Seamen's Union of Australia (SUA), who had also supported the sailors' strike. CFV was chuffed to have played its part. In its newsletter, CFV extolled the experience as an example of international camaraderie of workers against capitalist oppression.[2]

CFV's actions speak to the confidence of Chinese Australian community organisations during the multicultural turn. Despite the heightened political sensitivity of the Cold War, CFV did not hide its socialist sympathies. Every month it mailed its newsletters to the State Library of Victoria for collection. Almost every one of these early issues made some mention of the folly of American imperialism – especially in Vietnam – and the inevitable triumph of the Maoist cause. As other community organisations and leaders could attest, before the 1970s, such opinions could cause social stigma or put you on the watchlists of the Australian Security Intelligence Organisation (ASIO).[3]

This marked a huge change in the way Australian authorities treated Chinese Australian communities and their representative organisations in a relatively short amount of time. The strong anti-communist sentiments of the preceding Coalition governments, from the push to ban the Communist Party of Australia to the fear of the "Domino Theory", were still fresh in people's minds. Now it was more likely for Australian authorities to support Chinese Australian

---

2 CFV, "Newsletter August 1974", 9–10.
3 Arthur Gar Lock Chang and Ann Turner, *Arthur Lock Chang Interviewed by Ann Turner*, sound recording, 1991, National Library of Australia; Leong and Giese, *Maurice Leong Interviewed by Diana Giese*; "Chinese Youth League of Australia – Volume 1" (Item, Canberra, 1958 1944), A6122, 1914, National Archives of Australia, https://tinyurl.com/43u8p364; "Chinese Youth League of Australia – Volume 2 [227pp]" (item, Canberra, 1962 1958), A6122, 1915, National Archives of Australia, https://tinyurl.com/5n6mfud5.

community organisations than put them under surveillance. It had only been in 1962 that the South Melbourne Council threatened to demolish the See Yup temple. This may well have happened if not for a philanthropist who donated £10,000 at the last moment (she was the wife of a Chinese herbalist who had made a fortune in Ballarat during the Spanish flu epidemic).[4] A decade later, public money saved the temple. In 1973, the See Yup Society (SYS) was able to raise $20,000 from local members for restoration works. This time, however, instead of threatening foreclosure, the state and federal governments chipped in $40,000.[5]

Here was an inversion of the historical relationship between Chinese Australian community organisations and government authorities. Where government had once extracted money from Chinese Australians through discriminatory taxes and levies, state and federal governments were now funding the preservation of Chinese (Australian) culture and communities. As SYS's Maurice Leong reflected, the 1970s seemed to be a period of new acceptance and open-mindedness in Australian society, which made life easier for Chinese Australian communities and in turn made the lives of individuals easier. Of course, this didn't mean that Chinese Australian residents ran into Australia's now open arms. After years of living under the White Australia policy, Leong was taken aback when one day an immigration officer suggested naturalisation rather than renewal of his residency permit. "Oh," was Leong's response, "let me think on it," Leong's previous encounters with ASIO had left him perhaps wary, but eventually (years later) he took on permanent residency. He kept his Chinese citizenship for the rest of his life.[6]

Shifts in government treatment were matched with shifts in community attitudes. Darwin's Chung Wah Society (CWS) sensed the shift and by 1974 described having "re-established" itself within the Darwin community. It opened its first language school in 1972 and began hosting an annual "Dragon Ball" for Chinese and non-Chinese

---

4   Couchman, "Melbourne's See Yup Kuan Ti Temple: A Historical Overview", 76.
5   SYS, *Seeyup Society 1854–2004*, 31–2, 99.
6   Leong and Giese, *Maurice Leong Interviewed by Diana Giese*.

2 Early optimism and challenges

Australians to come together. Although CWS's temple was destroyed by Cyclone Tracy on Christmas Day 1974, local community support and government relief led to the temple's reconstruction and reopening in 1978.[7] Here, too, the local community and government's attitude was far removed from its earlier reluctance to rebuild Chinatown after the Second World War, or determination to demolish "Chinese hovels" in the 1910s.[8] The changing attitude was seen in other ways, as well. In 1975, CWS won best float and its own Joanne Stokes was crowned the Queen of Darwin's first Bougainvillea Festival Parade.[9] While the long-standing emphasis on being Australian still existed – heard in the self-described "very, very Australian attitudes" of some of its members – CWS found its Chineseness was more appreciated in the surrounding community.[10]

For a long time, the latter half of "Chinese Australianness" appeared to be the more salient part of Chinese Australians' identities – especially among those who had grown up under the White Australia policy. Daryl Chin, a leading member of CWS in Darwin, reflected on the "Australian way of thinking" that had seeped into him during his education. In boyhood he had wondered why his ancestors were absent from classes about Australia's historic settlers. Nevertheless, in adulthood the sites he visited in his ancestors' China felt alien. The

---

7 Northern Territory, *Sweet & Sour*, 46–7; William Fong and Diana Giese, *William Fong Interviewed by Diana Giese in the Post-War Chinese Australians Oral History Project*, sound recording, Post-War Chinese Australians Oral History Project, 1993; Darwina Fong and Diana Giese, *Darwina Fong Interviewed by Diana Giese in the Post-War Chinese Australians Oral History Project*, sound recording, Post-War Chinese Australians Oral History Project, 1992.
8 Chua, "The Racial Politics of Public Health in 1910's Darwin Chinatown".
9 Northern Territory, *Sweet & Sour*, 46–7.
10 Ernie Chin and Diana Giese, *Ernie Chin Interviewed by Diana Giese for the Post-War Chinese Australians Oral History Project*, sound recording, Post-War Chinese Australians Oral History Project (Darwin, 1993), TRC 3007, National Library of Australia; Chin and Giese, *Daryl Chin Interviewed by Diana Giese*; Joe Sarib, Diana Giese and Daryl N. Chin, *Joe Sarib Interviewed by Diana Giese with Daryl Chin for the Post-War Chinese Australians Oral History Project*, sound recording, 1997, TRC 3665, National Library of Australia.

overwhelming European-colonial focus of his education about Australia's past, he reflected, had made him associate with one culture far more than the other. It was only later in life that he began to think about his Chinese Australian identity in a more complex way.[11] For Chin's personal shift in perspective to occur, the multicultural shift in Australian society needed to become firmly established and accepted.

If multiculturalism allowed for the re-examination of one's Chinese Australian identity, then it also allowed for individuals to consider which aspects of each culture they wished to adopt for themselves. Slightly older than Chin, Wellington Lee was another Darwin native. He boarded in Queensland as a youth and served with the Royal Australian Air Force during the Second World War. Afterwards he became secretary of the Victorian branch of the Returned and Services League of Australia (RSL), as well as the founding president of the Federation of Chinese Associations (FCA) in Melbourne in 1979. As FCA was an umbrella organisation of 17 Chinese Australian community organisations in Victoria, Lee encountered many leaders of Chinese Australian community leaders. By his own accounts, they often frustrated him. In an interview with Diana Giese, Lee explained he was proud that his mother gave him a strong set of Chinese family values. On the other hand, he derided some supposed Chinese qualities, complaining that the reticence of the "Chinese community" had kept it from being a part of the "mainstream community". He criticised many for clinging to a "Chinese way of thinking", which he thought was parochial, jealous and self-serving. Regarding community service, Lee exclaimed, "Everyone wants to be an emperor," but "they don't know what it's about, they don't want to work for it."[12] He pointed to his own life as an example of being a proper Chinese Australian – seemingly one who overcame a few hard knocks along the way.

While some Chinese Australians were coming to define themselves subjectively, others were also making sure that they would not lose this prerogative to official multicultural initiatives. Put another way,

---

11   Chin and Giese, *Daryl Chin Interviewed by Diana Giese*.
12   Wellington Lee and Diana Giese, *Wellington Lee Interviewed by Diana Giese for the Post-War Chinese Australians Oral History Project*, sound recording, 1998, TRC 3699, National Library of Australia.

2 Early optimism and challenges

Chinese Australian communities wanted to be their own agents in the new multicultural Australia. They did not want to be fitted into the multicultural policies the White majority (namely, Anglo-Australians) were creating for ethnic minorities.

In 1975, the Chinese Fellowship of Victoria (CFV) strongly opposed a $500,000 proposal by local and state governments to revamp Melbourne's Chinatown. Offended by the new "old" orientalist aesthetics, CFV launched a letter campaign among residents and business owners. They argued such a makeover would only exoticise and alienate Chinese Australians from the broader Australian community to which it belonged. To be clear, CFV did not oppose displays of Chinese culture for non-Chinese Australian society. It was happy to perform Chinese dances at Melbourne's Moomba Festival or exhibit Dragon Boat racing on the Yarra River. But CFV felt that anachronistic ornamentation for the city's Chinatown was representative of neither modern China nor modern Chinese Australian communities who, CFV argued, should "look to the future".[13] It became clear in the local press that Chinatown's residents did not much care for the "multicultural colour" proposed by the city and state governments.[14]

The issue might have been more to do with the lack of consultation than with gaudy aesthetics. Ten years later, Chinatown was made over in an "oriental style" much like the original plan. A major difference between the proposal of the mid-1970s and that of the mid-1980s was that local Chinese Australian communities had gained a degree of control over the character of the Chinatown precinct. This came in the form of a Chinese History Museum and the creation of a Chinatown governing committee consisting predominantly of local community leaders – including three chosen by FCA.[15] Had the local and state

---

13   CFV, "Newsletter November 1975", 1–3.
14   Michael Prain, "Chinatown is Planned for the City", *The Sun*, 7 June 1975; Richard Goodwin, "Chinese Don't Want to Become a Sideshow for City Tourists", *The Age*, 19 January 1976.
15   Victorian Parliament, *Chinatown Historic Precinct Act 1984* (1984), http://www.legislation.vic.gov.au/; For further discussion see: Lok Yee Lotte Wong, "Melbourne Chinatown Redevelopment: The Unwritten Perspective

governments sought residents' views for its original proposal, it likely would have faced less opposition.

The New South Wales government's proposal to redevelop Sydney's Chinatown in the early 1980s attracted the attention of the Australian Chinese Community Association (ACCA). Just as the CFV had opposed the redevelopment of Melbourne's Chinatown, the ACCA also raised concerns about the makeover of Sydney's Chinatown. In its submission to the state and city's building authorities, ACCA recommended that, more than touristy decorations, the local Chinese Australian residents needed a space where their community could meaningfully exist and function. Demonstrating what good community representation looked like, ACCA had conducted local surveys and consultations to support its recommendations – and the greatest concern among locals was the transformation of the character and social make-up of Chinatown.[16]

The consultation and control carried out by local Chinese Australian communities thus challenged views of these neighbourhoods as examples of orientalism. While Kay Anderson argues that ACCA's intention was to save its neighbourhood from the "dandification" that Melbourne's non-Chinese architects had planned to impose on their "celestial alleyways", she is accurate only if attention is kept to CFV and ACCA's initial opposition.[17] Charges of orientalism against both Melbourne and Sydney's Chinatowns becomes shaky when we consider the input of local community organisations into their designs. Anderson's claim that Sydney's Chinese Gardens were "the ultimate in imagined ancestral symbols of Chineseness" ignores the fact that local Chinese Australians had fought to develop the gardens in the

---

from the Chinese Community" (Honours Thesis, Melbourne, University of Melbourne, 2018), https://tinyurl.com/6d55e4e5.
16   ACCA, "ACCA News September 1980" (Australian Chinese Community Association, September 1980), 1, State Library of New South Wales; ACCA, "ACCA News October 1981" (Australian Chinese Community Association, October 1981), 3, State Library of New South Wales; ACCA, *Chinatown in the 1980s* (Sydney: Australian Chinese Community Association, 1982), 70–86.
17   Kay Anderson, "'Chinatown Re-oriented': A Critical Analysis of Recent Redevelopment Schemes in a Melbourne and Sydney Enclave", *Australian Geographical Studies*, 28, no. 2 (1 October 1990), 143, 148–50.

2 Early optimism and challenges

face of non-Chinese Australian opposition – as outlined in ACCA's own submission to the NSW Department of Environment and Planning.[18] The "ancestral symbolism" is a predictable result, considering the city of Guangzhou assisted the local community to develop the garden; Guangzhou and the surrounding counties of Guangdong province hold great ancestral significance for many Chinese Australians, especially those in Sydney in the 1980s. In fact, ACCA said it was proud to "offer our excellent heritage to the country and let our culture beam with Australia's development". More importantly, in communications to its membership and to the broader public, ACCA claimed that it was "the outspokenness of people from our community" that led to the project's fruition.[19] Rather than an example of orientalism, the gardens were a site for Chinese Australian communities to assert control of multicultural developments. In both the Melbourne and Sydney cases, it was not necessarily *what* Chineseness looked like but *how* multiculturalism was done that mattered.

Chinese politics and intra-ethnic (dis)unity

While the multicultural turn enabled inter-ethnic relations to become sites for Chinese Australians to assert control of Chineseness, it also enabled intra-ethnic relations to offer similar opportunities for communities to define Chineseness between themselves.

Since the earliest days of Chinese emigration to Australia, connections to China and other source places of Chinese migrants influenced the form of communities and the function of organisations.[20] These connections continued to influence the paths of the many Chinese Australian community organisations during the multicultural turn. Among the other influences of the period, the

---

18 Anderson, "'Chinatown Re-Oriented'", 151; "Letter to Mr R.B. Smyth, Director, NSW Department of Environment and Planning, 29 May 1982" in ACCA, *Chinatown in the 1980s*, Appendix 2.
19 Joseph Glascott, "Garden Site a Battleground", *Sydney Morning Herald*, 21 December 1984; ACCA, "ACCA News July 1985" (Australian Chinese Community Association, July 1985), 4, State Library of New South Wales.
20 Wang, "Among Non-Chinese".

politics of the Cold War and the ideology emanating from the PRC's Cultural Revolution loomed large in the social space shared by Chinese Australians.

The multicultural turn coincided with Australia's recognition of the People's Republic of China, its abandonment of official diplomatic relations with the Republic of China in Taiwan, and, in 1975, the death of Chiang Kai-shek. Following these developments, CFV was optimistic that the Mainland versus Taiwan or communist versus nationalist divides among Chinese Australian communities would be resolved in a manner to its liking. As a pro-PRC organisation, CFV claimed that:

> us Overseas Chinese require Taiwanese liberation and Chinese unification not just because we all have patriotic hearts, but also because of the disuniting and divisive quarrels among Overseas Chinese organisations.[21]

Ignoring the PRC's history of influencing Overseas Chinese communities – and CFV's own partisan position among Melbourne's Chinese Australian community organisations – the organisation repeatedly blamed the divisions of Overseas Chinese on "the overseas activities of the Taiwan regime".[22] But the division between pro-PRC and pro-ROC camps did not quickly dissolve. Decades later, they remained. In an interview in the year 2000, founding member of CFV Maurice Leong was still complaining that unity among Melbourne's Chinese Australians had long been "disrupted" by the infiltration of pro-Taiwanese factions into the city's community organisations. He suggested that without such disruption (or other trouble "traced back to Americans"), there would be no disunity among Chinese Australians.[23]

---

21 "我们海外华人要求台湾的解放，中国的统一，不单是因为所有华人都有爱国心，而且因为华侨中不统一不团结社团间的争吵，很多是根源于台湾政权在海外的活动": CFV, "Newsletter September 1974", 7; CFV, "Newsletter May 1975", 3; CFV, "Newsletter August 1975" (Chinese Fellowship of Victoria, August 1975), 2, State Library of Victoria.
22 CFV, "Newsletter September 1974", 7; CFV, "Newsletter May 1975", 3; CFV, "Newsletter August 1975", 2.
23 Leong and Giese, *Maurice Leong Interviewed by Diana Giese*.

2 Early optimism and challenges

Leong's accusations reveal his own political convictions. His assessment ignores how organisations sympathetic to the PRC (like his own CFV) also stoked division. In the 1970s, CFV's consistent appeals for "patriotic Chinese" to come together in unity were undermined by provocative positions. In one incendiary example, CFV gloated about the PRC's ability to seize Taiwan by force.[24]

Leong is not alone in blaming Taiwanese sympathisers or foreign influences for causing division among Chinese Australian communities; some interviewees for this research expressed the same views.[25] But counter-balancing them are other Chinese Australian community leaders who held that pro-PRC people had a negative influence on their own or other community organisations.[26] The situation illustrates how uniquely intractable the political divisions between Chinese Australian communities can be and why the idea of unifying communities behind a single political ideology is so chimerical.

The Chinese Youth League

The recent history of the Chinese Youth League provides an example of political convictions being used, for better or worse, as a force to unite local Chinese Australians. In 1979, to mark CYL's 40th anniversary, Al Grassby declared that CYL had been "part of a Chinese renaissance in Australia". In an obvious nod to developments in China's political sphere, he mused that CYL had seen "the rise and fall of the fortunes of man in many parts of the world".[27] Indeed it had. By way of their respective transnational connections, the Australasian Kuomintang

---

24 CFV, "Newsletter August 1975", 2.
25 Interviewee 5, Researcher with Anonymous Interviewee 5, interview by Researcher, 24 September 2018; Interviewee 6, Researcher with Anonymous Interviewee 6, interview by Researcher, 25 September 2018, 6.
26 Interviewee 7, Researcher with Anonymous Interviewee 7, interview by Researcher, 16 November 2018; Interviewee 10, Researcher with Anonymous Interviewee 10, interview by Researcher, 13 July 2019.
27 CYL, *40th Anniversary Chinese Youth League of Australia: Commemorative Bulletin* (Sydney: Chinese Youth League, 1979), 3, https://tinyurl.com/yh45dx8u.

(AKMT) was reaching a nadir of community relevance as it approached the multicultural turn while CYL was reaching its zenith.[28] It is clear from CYL's materials that the organisation ascribed its relevance and prominence among Chinese Australians to its connections with the PRC. As a symbol of this connection, CYL's president, Ching Tan, wrote in his organisation's 80th anniversary chronicle that "CYL was proud to be the first organisation in Sydney to raise [its] homemade national flag of China" in a celebration of the PRC's founding on 1 October 1949.[29] As it stood, CYL had backed history's winner. The AKMT had not.

Like AKMT, CYL was the product of patriotic sentiments for China. CYL's forerunner organisation, the Chinese Youth Dramatic Association, was founded in 1938 to raise funds for China after Japan's invasion. The following year, the association reformed as CYL as it broadened its attention to social welfare and political activities, especially for the sake of Chinese sailors in Australia.[30] In fact, during the Second World War, CYL had cooperated with AKMT to raise funds for the war effort in China. In what Shirley Fitzgerald describes as a "confusing" time of cooperation between nationalist and communist aligned organisations, it became difficult to keep track of which organisation did what in their mutual efforts. Everything was geared toward helping China resist Japan's invasion, and political differences were eclipsed by this common concern. As Fitzgerald remarks, the events of the war "unified Sydney's Chinese" and it was not until the end of the war that a "clear-cut division between political left and right" returned.[31]

During the Cold War, CYL's support for the PRC and the international communist movement saw some members become alienated and then withdraw from the organisation in the early 1960s.[32] ASIO sources suggested that the Sino-Soviet split and reports about the

---

28 Kuo and Brett, *Unlocking the History of the Australasian Kuo Min Tang, 1911-2013*, 169-78.
29 CYL, *80 週年紀念冊 Bashi Zhounian Jinian Ce (80th Anniversary Commemorative Edition)* (Sydney: Chinese Youth League, 2019), 3.
30 CYL, *40th Anniversary Chinese Youth League of Australia: Commemorative Bulletin*, 52-3.
31 Shirley Fitzgerald, *Red Tape, Gold Scissors: The Story of Sydney's Chinese* (State Library of New South Wales Press, 1997), 136-8.

2 Early optimism and challenges

Cultural Revolution drove away more of CYL's members. Of course, ASIO was itself a cause of CYL's dwindling membership. As one of CYL's old leaders suggested, the knowledge of ASIO surveillance kept some people away from the organisation.[33] From over 200 members in 1957, the CYL had only around 80 members in 1968.[34]

Using PRC patriotism to unite Chinese Australians

Chinese Youth League's staunch support for the PRC's socialist cause also won it admirers. In 1975, the Chinese Fellowship of Victoria extolled CYL:

> For 36 years, this healthy overseas Chinese organisation has been defending justice, introducing socialism and Chinese culture, promoting friendship and understanding between the peoples of Australia and China, strengthening Chinese unity and welfare services, and more.[35]

Like CYL, CFV wished to re-frame local Chinese Australians' attachment to the old homeland as an attachment to the "New China".[36] This seemed possible to them with their main competitor in the ideological arena, AKMT, out of the picture.

The CFV and CYL's cultural-political connections to the PRC were maintained symbolically and materially through the community organisations' connections with Chinese sailors. CYL's connection to

---

32 "Chinese Youth League Monthly Tea Meetings", 26/08/1962 "NSW Chinese Workers' Association Volume 1" (Item, Canberra, 1970 1953), 22, A6122, 2235, National Archives of Australia, https://tinyurl.com/5yh63w5t.
33 Interviewee 6, Anonymous Interview.
34 "Chinese Youth League of Australia, February 1970", 9 "NSW Chinese Workers' Association Volume 1".
35 健康的僑團三十六年岁在维护正义，介绍社会主义中国文化，促进澳中两国人民的友谊和了解，搞好华人团结福利事业等等: CFV, "Newsletter May 1975".
36 CYL, *40th Anniversary Chinese Youth League of Australia: Commemorative Bulletin*, 40.

Chinese and Hong Kong sailors especially explains how this organisation fared better than many others under the White Australia policy. At the end of the Second World War, CYL attracted many Chinese sailors who were stuck in Australian ports at the war's end. This situation is unsurprising. Like those Chinese men who first came to Australia in the 19th century, here were more who wished to connect with those who shared their language and culture.[37] Shirley Fitzgerald describes the relationship between CYL and the sailors as symbiotic: sailors became involved in the production of Cantonese and Hainanese operas, and CYL helped to raise funds for the Chinese Seamen's Union and other China-related causes by staging operas and grassroots campaigns.[38] Over the years, this arrangement evolved into a steady stream of Chinese sailors bringing news and cultural materials (like films, recordings, books and so forth) from the PRC to CYL. As a result, CYL became a source of the latest news in China and a place to meet "real" Chinese. While some community organisations in Perth or Melbourne struggled to attract new members during the 1950s and 1960s, CYL could boast over a hundred attendees at its film screenings and banquets.[39] In the early 1970s, CFV established similar transnational connections, sources for cultural materials, and strong community credentials following the example of its comrade organisation in Sydney, CYL.[40]

While the cultural and political connection to China was of primary importance here, the sailors and the organisations' support for them also point to another imagined transnational community. Both CFV and CYL assisted the sailors' multiple industrial actions against their international employers for better pay, thereby giving the organisations the cause and opportunity to enact their political beliefs.[41] Providing material aid to striking Chinese sailors throughout the 1950s, 1960s and 1970s, CYL and CFV relished their role in the

---

37 "Chinese Youth League of Australia, February 1970", 2-3 "NSW Chinese Workers' Association Volume 1".
38 Fitzgerald, *Red Tape, Gold Scissors*, 137.
39 "Chinese Youth League of Australia, February 1970", 1-16 "NSW Chinese Workers' Association Volume 1".
40 CFV, "Newsletter August 1974", 9; CFV, "Newsletter February 1975", 4-6; CFV, "Newsletter May 1975", 2.

2 Early optimism and challenges

international struggle of workers against capital. Newsletters from the time and later interviews celebrated their involvement.[42] References to class struggle also appear in CFV's support for socialist and anti-imperialist forces in Vietnam, Cambodia and East Timor.[43] Thus, in addition to transnational linkages to China, CYL and CFV were projecting their organisations' solidarity with an international community of peoples freeing themselves from the nefarious effects of colonialism, imperialism and capitalism.

Nevertheless, the internationalist cause remained secondary to the aim of fostering Chineseness with socialist characteristics. Many of CYL and CFV's activities in the 1970s seemed configured to achieve this aim. Normalised relations between Canberra and Beijing enabled freer travel to China. Consequently, both CFV and CYL quickly organised tours for Chinese Australian adults and youth to visit the land of their ancestors.[44] The tours were about discovering the "new China" as much as uncovering old roots. To be sure, they were self-conscious attempts to prove China's improved material conditions. Members who visited China to celebrate the 25th anniversary of the PRC's foundation relayed that China was progressing further toward its socialist ideals under Mao Zedong, but that it also possessed department stores bustling with shoppers "just like the local Myers".[45] Of course, the effusive positivity also belied some insecurities about China's progress. In its early years, CFV constantly reported on the successes of China's socialist system and often with comparison to the West. Numerous articles about the unprecedented speed of social

---

41 "Chinese Crew Wins in Stand for Human Rights", *Tribune*, 24 February 1971; "Seaman's Official: 'Owners' Extortion'", *Tribune*, 17 September 1974.
42 "Chinese Youth League of Australia, February 1970", 1-16 "NSW Chinese Workers' Association Volume 1"; Chang and Turner, *Arthur Lock Chang Interviewed by Ann Turner*, CFV, "Newsletter August 1974", 9; CFV, "Newsletter May 1975", 4-6.
43 CFV, "Newsletter April 1975", 3-4; CFV, "Newsletter May 1975", 10; CFV, "Newsletter June 1975" (Chinese Fellowship of Victoria, June 1975), 7-8, State Library of Victoria; CFV, "Newsletter October 1975" (Chinese Fellowship of Victoria, October 1975), 3, State Library of Victoria.
44 CYL, *40th Anniversary Chinese Youth League of Australia: Commemorative Bulletin*, 41.
45 CFV, "Newsletter August 1974", 5-7.

and technological modernisation in the new China appeared along with more pointed articles about the superiority of Chinese teaching methods over Western methods or Chinese beauty standards over Western standards.[46] These descriptions clashed with the impressions of the members who had seen the "real China". One of the leaders of CYL's early trips to China was surprised to find it "totally different to how the Chinese magazines report it". He was struck by the poverty and deforestation of inland China. He remembered his cousins appeared under-nourished when they met. Subsequently, he "questioned what was reported by the Chinese media".[47] Despite the glowing reports, for some, travelling to the new China took away the imagined country's sheen.

Despite the growing obviousness that the new China was not as glorious in real life, CYL and CFV continued pushing Chinese propaganda to foster unity among Chinese Australian communities through attachment to the PRC. Picnics in celebration of China's National Day on 1 October became annual events for CYL and CFV along with traditional calendar events. Along with martial arts films or documentaries about life in China, CFV screened military parades on National Day and showed Cultural Revolutionary films and ballets such as *The White-Haired Girl* and *Taking Tiger Mountain by Strategy*.[48] In so doing, CFV and CYL were not simply trying to project a favourable (if fanciful) image of the PRC; they were also blurring the distinction between the Chinese state and the imagined Chinese homeland.

The blurring of cultural and political identities is evident in the text of CFV's newsletters. Throughout the 1970s and beyond, CFV's newsletters played into what Leo Douw terms the "sojourner" or "*huaqiao* discourse" – the mobilisation by China's rulers of Overseas Chinese communities by fostering nostalgia for China and an expectation that Overseas Chinese would one day return.[49] As a term

---

46 CFV, 8; CFV, "Newsletter September 1974", 7–10; CFV, "Newsletter April 1975", 5–6; CFV, "Newsletter May 1975", 9; CFV, "Newsletter September 1975" (Chinese Fellowship of Victoria, September 1975), 4–5, State Library of Victoria.
47 Interviewee 6, Anonymous Interview.
48 CFV, "Newsletter August 1974", 3–4; CFV, "Newsletter April 1975", 2; CFV, "Newsletter May 1975", 11.

2 Early optimism and challenges

for self-description by Overseas Chinese, Douw and others note that *huaqiao* fell into disuse in the 1950s when the transnational, ethno-nationalism connotations of the term conflicted with the burgeoning settler- and anti-colonial nationalisms of the Asia-Pacific.[50] It is curious, then, to see CFV use the term prolifically in its newsletters throughout the 1970s and into the 1980s.[51] As Gungwu Wang describes the term, *huaqiao* "was openly used to bring about ethnic if not nationalist or racist binding of all Chinese at home or abroad", which in turn enacted a "militant commitment to remaining Chinese or restoring one's 'Chineseness'".[52] CFV's use of the term alongside other words like 侨胞 (*qiáobāo*, Overseas Chinese compatriots) and 爱国 (*àiguó*, patriotism) in articles about Overseas Chinese patriotism or reunification with Taiwan fit with Wang's description.[53]

As Ien Ang points out, *huaqiao* and other rhetorical affirmations of a fixed, unitary Chinese diaspora was, like nationalism, another sort of imagined community: "one based on the presumption of internal ethnic sameness and external ethnic distinctiveness".[54] The use of terms

---

49 Leo Douw, "The Chinese Sojourner Discourse", in *Qiaoxiang Ties: Interdisciplinary Approaches to "Cultural Capitalism" in South China*, eds Leo Douw, Michael R. Godley and Cen Huang (Kegan Paul International in association with International Institute for Asian Studies, 1999), 22–44.
50 Douw, 34–6; Pál Nyíri, "Expatriating in Patriotic?: The Discourse of 'New Migrants' in the People's Republic of China and Identity Construction among Recent Migrants from the PRC", in *State/Nation/Transnation: Perspectives on Transnationalism in the Asia Pacific*, eds Katie Willis and Brenda S.A. Yeoh (Florence, US: Taylor & Francis Group, 2004), 121; Ien Ang, "Beyond Transnational Nationalism: Questioning the Borders of the Chinese Diaspora in the Global City", in *State/Nation/Transnation: Perspectives on Transnationalism in the Asia Pacific*, eds Katie Willis and Brenda S.A. Yeoh (Florence, US: Taylor & Francis Group, 2004), 183–4.
51 See for example: CFV, "Newsletter September 1974", 7–9; CFV, "Newsletter April 1975", 5–6; CFV, "Newsletter May 1975", 3; CFV, "Newsletter January 1984", 1.
52 Gungwu Wang, *Community and Nation: Essays on Southeast Asia and the Chinese*, Southeast Asia Publications Series, no. 6 (Sydney: Published for the Asian Studies Association of Australia by Heinemann Educational Books (Asia) Ltd and Allen & Unwin, 1981), 2, 7.
53 CFV, "Newsletter September 1974", 7–8; CFV, "Newsletter May 1975", 3.
54 Ang, "Beyond Transnational Nationalism", 184–5.

like *huaqiao* and other patriotic language conveyed the type of political diaspora of which CFV saw itself a part. CFV and CYL employed strategies similar to AKMT and other (trans)nationalist organisations. The concurrence of political opposites like CFV and AKMT should show the folly of such strategies for unity. Not all Chinese Australians answered the transnational calls, let alone shared the same politics. Political loyalties could make one organisation's membership antipathetic toward the other, throwing up obvious problems for ethnic unity. Moreover, as one CYL member reflected, some people simply liked to socialise and participated in the activities of both AKMT and CYL.[55] They totally ignored the mutual exclusivity implied by each organisations' competing political positions.

Using multiculturalism to unite Chinese Australians

In contrast to the homogeneity demanded by political ideologies, the multicultural turn offered a way for communities to come together while accepting each other's differences. A number of community organisations took the opportunity to enact the multicultural ideal of strength through diversity.

In the states with the largest Chinese Australian communities, New South Wales and Victoria, multiple organisations came together to form federated bodies or "umbrella organisations". In 1977, the Council of Chinese Organisations (CoCO) formed in New South Wales and the Federation of Chinese Associations (FCA) formed in Victoria in 1979. Each reflected fresh will to put aside differences for the sake of addressing the common interests of Chinese Australian communities. These included interests like holding shared Chinese New Year festivals or publishing joint statements against racism. These federated bodies were representative of the good faith required between parties. For example, the pro-PRC CFV was a founding member of FCA, along with the pro-ROC and AKMT-affiliated Chinese Youth Society.[56] The constituent organisations did not surrender their political ideals, said one former FCA leader, which naturally led to impasses on certain

---

55 Interviewee 6, Anonymous Interview.

2 Early optimism and challenges

issues. However, the federated model of FCA encouraged compromise between organisations.[57] To enshrine political non-alignment, FCA only involved itself in traditional Chinese cultural calendar dates and, at least at its outset, avoided endorsing National Day celebrations.[58] Defying the pattern of intra-ethnic rivalry, FCA is now in its fourth decade.

The Australian Chinese Community Association

A shared ethnic identity was the basis for another new community organisation that strove to represent "all" of Sydney's Chinese Australian community without being a federated body. Prior to CoCo, the Australian Chinese Community Association of New South Wales (ACCA) formed in 1974. ACCA's invocation of a shared ethnic identity was distinct from others. Whereas the Chinese Association of South Australia (CASA) had used ethnic identity to unite a small and relatively homogenous group in Adelaide, ACCA's formation was an attempt to bring together several pre-existing and emerging communities, each of which had conceptions and misgivings about the others. Moreover, the proposed new organisation would not dissolve the organisations which comprised it (as was reminiscent of the formation of Darwin's CWS). Among the community leaders driving the proposal were Arthur Locke of CYL, Michael Yap of the Chinese Language Broadcast Association (2AE), and the man who would become the inaugural president of ACCA, Kip Fong.

Creating something united from fractious parts was a formidable task. On 7 July 1974, 350 people gathered at ACCA's inaugural meeting. "High hopes and jubilation for the future" mixed with lingering feelings that "the community was far too divided by suspicion and interests ever to unite into one association". After all, ACCA aimed to unite camps

---

56 FCA, "关于华联会历史 guanyu hualianhui lishi (About FCA's History)", 维省华联会 Federation of Victorian Community Associations, https://www.vicfca.org.au/vicfcahistory?lightbox=dataItem-juumat123.
57 Interviewee 2, Researcher with Anonymous Interviewee 2, interview by Researcher, 24 August 2018.
58 FCA, "关于华联会历史 guanyu hualianhui lishi (About FCA's History)".

of long-established and locally born Chinese Australian Sydneysiders with young and ambitious recent migrants from Hong Kong, and (later more so) ethnic Chinese who had escaped the wars and political upheavals of Southeast Asia.[59] To ameliorate their differences, the leaders of the initiative hammered out a constitution that made ACCA distinctly "non-political, non-religious and non-sectarian".[60] Shared Chinese culture and common migrant experiences would be ACCA's cause. It founded a Chinese-language school and held exhibitions and workshops, as well as a committee dedicated to settlement and integration issues. The executive committee "formed the habit" of scanning the news for issues relevant to Chinese Australian communities and took to responding on their behalf. To ensure its leadership did not ossify, the executive committee and the presidency regularly changed – which was something quite rare for the time.[61] In short, ACCA built itself on a firm foundation of apolitical common interests and eschewed matters that might excite differences.

ACCA's formation was surely guided by the multicultural ideals of the time, but it was also the result of new multicultural policy. In 1973, the Whitlam government held the National Population Inquiry and canvassed public opinion on matters about the country's future composition. To respond to this inquiry, Chinese Australian community leaders formed the committee that became ACCA.[62] In its submission, the preliminary ACCA committee suggested the government accept more Chinese migrants. In making its case, it argued that Chinese had long been migrants to Australia. They already had established communities, making integration into Australian society easy. It also pointedly added that encouraging Chinese migration would right the historic wrong done by the White Australia policy.[63] In so doing, ACCA insisted that present policy be informed by

---

59   ACCA, *The Australian-Chinese Community Association of NSW Journal* (1977), 2, 24–6.
60   ACCA, 75.
61   ACCA, 24–35.
62   ACCA, 24.
63   ACCA, 39–40.

the effects of past policy, and in the years following, ACCA continued to connect multicultural ideals with policy outcomes.

For one, ACCA demanded Chinese Australian community organisations be represented at the Good Neighbour Council of New South Wales. Funded by the Commonwealth, the Good Neighbour Council was a nation-wide network that was, in part, tasked with welcoming and assisting immigrants to settle in Australia. Increasingly in the 1960s (though with varying degrees of success), the councils became an intermediary between ethnic communities and government. However, the Good Neighbour Council's past assimilationist imperative and strong predilection toward British migrants – especially at its executive level – had seen previous approaches by Chinese Australian organisations rebuffed.[64] The Good Neighbour Council, however, admitted an ACCA representative soon after ACCA's formation. ACCA attributed this to two things. One was the government's fresh attitude toward race and nation – signalling ACCA perceived a causal relationship between new multicultural ideals and real-world change. The other was that ACCA represented a broad cross-section of Chinese Australians rather than a single, narrow community.[65] As such, ACCA's attention to multicultural policy extended from a formative purpose to the cause to sustain its existence. ACCA showed that a successful formula for uniting Chinese Australian communities was to move focus away from internal politics and onto multicultural policy.

Of course, multicultural policies did not instantly dispel Australian racism. The repeal of discriminatory immigration policy notwithstanding, ACCA fulminated against the lingering and pervasive racism in government structures:

> We encountered still, albeit camouflaged, racial discrimination and the White Australia policy alive and well, resisting tooth and nail, every inch of the way our demands that Chinese Australians be treated equally like other Australians.[66]

---

64 Jupp, *From White Australia to Woomera*, 13, 22, 86–8.
65 ACCA, 24.
66 ACCA, 2.

The Commonwealth government attempted to reassure Chinese Australian communities of its commitment to multicultural ideals, not least through the personal efforts of its Commissioner for Community Relations, Al Grassby. In late 1974, Grassby spoke to multiple Chinese Australian community organisations, including ACCA, of the government's desire to correct the absence of the Chinese in Australian history and begin a new chapter of multicultural equality. About this, ACCA felt vindicated.[67] When Grassby spoke to CFV, he was applauded and praised for his role in "burying" the White Australia policy. Adapting a characteristically Maoist slogan, CFV assured Grassby that it would help him "sweep (racists) into the rubbish bins".[68]

There was equal enthusiasm for being Australian, albeit in ways that aligned with the principles of the community organisation. At the same function where Grassby spoke, CFV declared it would continue the long tradition of loyalty that Overseas Chinese had shown their adoptive country. Evidently, there was enough room in the hearts of CFV's membership for two patriotisms. "We live here as Australians and we look to Australia as our country", it declared.[69] In comparison, ACCA and CASA grasped at a feeling of belonging in Australia without necessarily framing it as "loyalty" to the state. Encapsulating their sentiments was an essay written by a Chinese Australian primary school student, Alysia Chew, entitled "I am an Australian too". Winning the NSW Ethnic Community Council's essay competition in 1974, the essay's final passage was reprinted by both CASA and ACCA:

> Despite the fact that I occasionally face problems as described above, my life has been very much enriched on the whole because in my unique position I can learn so much from both cultures. I can in a sense, say that I live in the best of both worlds. I am Chinese, but I am an Australian too.[70]

---

67 ACCA, 27.
68 CFV, "Newsletter November 1974" (Chinese Fellowship of Victoria, November 1974), 3, State Library of Victoria.
69 CFV, 2–3.
70 ACCA, "ACCA News November 1979" (Australian Chinese Community Association, November 1979), 3, State Library of New South Wales; CASA, "News Bulletin December 1979", 4.

2 Early optimism and challenges

With the advent of multiculturalism, being able to declare publicly "I am Chinese" was both an act of pride and a demonstration of how much things had changed. Likewise, as the roots of multiculturalism grew deeper into the nation's soil, the refrain "I am an Australian too" gained greater legitimacy. However, the optimism of multiculturalism was soon to meet opposition from those sections of White Australia that were unwilling to accept diversity. As this resentful opposition swelled into later debates about Asian immigration, the Chinese Australian claim "I am an Australian too" also grew from a self-affirmation to a public attestation.

Racism under the multicultural turn

From 1978, the Commission for Community Relations began issuing annual reports of the complaints of racism it received. These reports include cases of racial vilification directed at Chinese Australians as well as "Asian Australians" (it was at times unclear whether "Asian Australian" was a category created and used by the commission when a specific ethnicity was unknown or unstated, or was a term of self-identification used by a complainant, or was to identify the quality of the racist act itself – for example, a pamphlet calling for an end to "Asian immigration"). In 1978, 16 complaints were made by Chinese Australians that included public ridicule, racist newspaper articles and "standover tactics" employed by country police in New South Wales.[71] A year later there were nine complaints, which included workplace discrimination and complaints against heavy-handed immigration officers.[72] By 1980, there were only four cases of discrimination made by Chinese Australians (though 18 were attributed to "Asians").[73] The next year there were only three complaints lodged – compared to 15

---

71 Office of the Commissioner for Community Relations, "Commissioner for Community Relations: Annual Report", Annual Report (Canberra: Australian Human Rights Commission, 1978), 125–47.
72 Office of the Commissioner for Community Relations, "Commissioner for Community Relations: Annual Report", Annual Report (Canberra: Australian Human Rights Commission, 1979), 139–79.

lodged by German Australians, 11 by Vietnamese Australians, 33 by Italian Australians and 38 by "Asians". Far out-stripping these were the 338 complaints by Aboriginal Australians.[74] The figures are a blunt reminder of the disparity between the treatment and acceptance of "multicultural communities" and Indigenous communities in this country.

The declining rate of Chinese Australians reporting incidents of racism is curious. It is unlikely that Chinese Australians simply did not know about the provisions of the Commission for Community Relations. These same reports show that the declining number of complaints made by Chinese Australians coincided with an increasing number of requests to the commission for migration assistance from Chinese Australians – with 22 such requests in 1980. Moreover, organisations like CASA and ACCA held information sessions that covered issues like racial discrimination and citizens' rights to recourse under the law.[75] When questioned about instances of racism at this time, interviewees often made reference to the stoic or non-confrontational disposition of Chinese Australians, or claimed that they did not recall racism being too great an issue.[76] However, attention paid to racism in community organisations' newsletters showed it was an important issue. Much of the focus here was not necessarily on particular incidents of racism, but on racist

---

73 Office of the Commissioner for Community Relations, "Commissioner for Community Relations: Annual Report", Annual Report (Canberra: Australian Human Rights Commission, 1980), 116–17.
74 Office of the Commissioner for Community Relations, "Commissioner for Community Relations: Annual Report", Annual Report (Canberra: Australian Human Rights Commission, 1981), 82–3.
75 Yan and Zhou, *CASA 40th Anniversary Commemorative Magazine: 1971–2011*, 138; ACCA, "ACCA News September 1981" (Australian Chinese Community Association, September 1981), 6, State Library of New South Wales.
76 Interviewee 1, Anonymous Interview; Interviewee 3, Anonymous Interview; Interviewee 4, Researcher with Anonymous Interviewee 4, interview by Researcher, 24 September 2018; Interviewee 6, Anonymous Interview; Interviewee 9, Researcher with Anonymous Interviewee 9, interview by Researcher, 12 July 2019; Interviewee 10, Anonymous Interview.

2 Early optimism and challenges

organisations and the extent of racist sentiment in Australia's new multicultural society.

This, too, seemed to be the focus of the Commission for Community Relations. While the reports singled out more egregious examples of racism, they put most focus on the activity of racist organisations. These included the circulation of pamphlets which warned of "Chinese floods" and the importation of Asian "sex-marriage-murder rites" into the country, and publications of racist articles or advertisements in newspapers. Though many of these articles were picked up by newspaper editors and passed on to authorities, some still made it to publication. In one instance, an advertisement was placed offering cash rewards for information about Australian parents who had adopted Asian babies. When the commission questioned the group responsible about what it intended to do with that information, it threatened that it "was prepared to go to any lengths to keep this country white".[77]

Other organisations would make themselves known by posters or graffiti with variations of "Asians Out!" or "Asians Go Home!", sometimes accompanied with swastikas or other white supremacist iconography.[78] Members of racist organisations aired their views through talkback radio and letters to the editor and likewise abused and threatened White Australians who attempted to defend non-White Australians.[79] Residents in Melbourne, Sydney, Perth and Adelaide received letters pretending to be from the Commission for Community Relations. The sham letters advised recipients that their household had been assigned to host a refugee family for several months. While many saw through the ruse immediately, the use of the commission's real address and a forgery of Commissioner Al Grassby's signature fooled others. The commission consequently received outraged refusals and worried supplications.[80]

---

77 Office of the Commissioner for Community Relations, "Commissioner for Community Relations: Annual Report", 1978, 101–2.
78 Office of the Commissioner for Community Relations, "Commissioner for Community Relations: Annual Report", 1979, 16–17.
79 Lorna Lippmann, "Punch-up Threat on TV Denied", *Canberra Times*, 27 May 1974.

By 1980, there were some 30 racist organisations operating in Australia, the most prominent of these being the Australian League of Rights, the National Alliance, the Immigration Control Association and the National Front.[81] Though these groups counted few official members, their persistent and intimidating methods effectively projected their views throughout the wider community. The ethnic communities they targeted also grew concerned.[82] Attacks on clubhouses, non-English newspaper offices, and resource centres damaged not just property but morale.[83] An accumulative effect began to build. As Grassby reflected:

> On Monday you got in your letterbox a racist pamphlet. Then on Tuesday you happen to be listening to a radio talkback show and you hear a voice saying "we must clean up the nation and all these people must go". On Wednesday you read in your newspaper a letter to the editor saying that Australia should be preserved of [sic] pure Aryans. You begin to wonder what kind of country you are living in.[84]

The media's amplification of these issues was another concern for the commission and community organisations alike. Newspapers regularly printed reports of foreign white supremacist organisations like the United Kingdom's National Front or the USA's Ku Klux Klan reaching into Australia. Stories and interviews with homegrown supremacist organisations like the Australian League of Rights and the National

---

80 Office of the Commissioner for Community Relations, "Commissioner for Community Relations: Annual Report", 1980, 10–11; Lorna Lippmann, "Racist Propaganda and the Immigration Debate", in *Multicultural Australia Papers*, vol. 33 (Melbourne: Ecumenical Migration Centre, 1984), 1–3.
81 Office of the Commissioner for Community Relations, "Commissioner for Community Relations: Annual Report", 1980, 10.
82 Office of the Commissioner for Community Relations, 10.
83 Office of the Commissioner for Community Relations, 11, 100–01; Human Rights and Equal Opportunity Commission, *Racist Violence: Report of the National Inquiry into Racist Violence in Australia* (Canberra: Australian Government Publishing Service, 1991), 139–40.
84 John Jesser, "Upsurge in Race-Hate Campaign", *Canberra Times*, 21 November 1979.

2 Early optimism and challenges

Front of Australia were also frequently printed and thereby became familiar to the public.[85] The *Sydney Morning Herald* interviewed the founding member of the National Front, Robert Cameron, multiple times.[86] Founder of the League of Rights, Eric Butler, also found audiences through the *Sydney Morning Herald* and the ABC.[87] While the outlets mostly took the angle of concerned exposés, they inevitably gave racist organisations a valuable platform from which to communicate their views to the wider public.

The effect of this racism can be measured by its penetration into public life. The League of Rights, for example, claimed tens of thousands of members through multiple front organisations.[88] Though that figure is perhaps fanciful, in October 1975, the league boasted that "actionists" from every state had attended its "National Action Seminar". Demonstrating the international linkages of the organisations, representatives from the New Zealand League of Rights and the British League of Rights also attended.[89] According to multiple journalists, racist organisations like the League of Rights had infiltrated Australia's National and Liberal parties.[90] To Grassby, most disturbing

---

85 Office of the Commissioner for Community Relations, "Commissioner for Community Relations: Annual Report", 1979, 14; "Racial Discrimination Day: Australian UN Association Statement", *Canberra Times*, 21 March 1979; "State Attacked for Racist Attitudes: Members of the Ku Klux Klan", *Canberra Times*, 17 October 1979; "The Grim Politics of Extremism", *Sydney Morning Herald*, 28 February 1972.
86 Malcolm Brown, "Racist Group Expects Nation-Wide Membership", *Sydney Morning Herald*, 8 June 1978; Malcolm Brown, "A Growing Audience for Messages of Hate", *Sydney Morning Herald*, 8 February 1984.
87 "Pushing a 'Cure-All' Gospel: League of Rights Has Strong Support", *Sydney Morning Herald*, 22 March 1976; "Censored History – A Selection of the Thoughts of Eric Butler", *Sydney Morning Herald*, 22 March 1976; Malcolm Brown, "League of Rights to Condemn Leaders' Meeting", *Sydney Morning Herald*, 21 September 1981; "Eric Butler, National Director Australian League of Rights", Television, *Monday Conference* (Australia: Australian Broadcasting Corporation, 26 June 1972).
88 Office of the Commissioner for Community Relations, "Commissioner for Community Relations: Annual Report", 1981, 15–16; "Pushing a 'Cure-All' Gospel: League of Rights Has Strong Support".
89 Eric Butler, "League of Rights Surges Forward", *Intelligence Survey*, October 1975, 25th ed., 1, National Library of Australia.

was the significant number of new police cadets who held racist views. On the eve of their graduation in 1981, he heard cadets claim "Chinese commit the most crime" and "Asians are taking over the country".

Chinese Australian responses to racism

In the contemporary materials made by Chinese Australian community organisations, there was an awareness of racist currents in Australian society and an interest in how different racist voices might attract public support. It was the latter that seemed to be the greater concern. Consequently, the responses coming from Chinese Australian community organisations were not just in defence of their own members but also in defence of multicultural Australia in public forums.

In November 1974, CFV's president wrote to television station Channel 9 to complain about the "Charlie Who" character on the popular *Hey Hey It's Saturday* program.[91] While John Blackman's ham-fisted portrayal of a Chinese man was embarrassing in itself, President Gim Wah Yeo's principal concern was the character's appearance on a children's morning program. He conveyed his concern that it could "foster harmful stereotypes in the minds of child audiences" and that Chinese Australian schoolchildren might "endure the same crude humour from their classmates". Yeo connected his concerns about children to Australia's future as a fair society:

> We are living in an era when all men are equal, and we wish to educate our children to grow up without racial prejudices. Your programme, on the other hand, exploits lingering prejudices against "foreigners".

---

90   Mike Richards, "A Foot in the Coalition Door", *Sydney Morning Herald*, 28 February 1979; "The Lilly-White Principle", *Canberra Times*, 9 December 1978; "We Seek to Influence Politicians", *Sydney Morning Herald*, 22 March 1976; Terence Michael Craig, "The Australian League of Rights and Its Divisions", manuscript (1987).
91   CFV, "Newsletter June 1975", 3.

2 Early optimism and challenges

CFV and Channel 9 exchanged correspondence on the matter, but Yeo's complaint seemed to have little impact. As the decades wore on, Australia's tastes changed but *Hey Hey It's Saturday* stayed the same (in 2010, Blackman considered reviving Charlie Who and other stereotype "characters" for the *Hey Hey It's Saturday* reunion show).[92] The glacial change was frustrating. CFV's newsletter editor wrote:

> ... while the majority of the Australian communities are working very hard to make Australia a truely [sic] multi cultural society, there are, however, still some people who are basically racist.[93]

ACCA also engaged with media racism in a way that defended Chinese Australians' place in Australian society and appealed to multicultural ideals. On 12 September 1977, an article in the *Daily Telegraph* claimed Dixon Street (the heart of Sydney's Chinatown) was suffering a Triad crimewave. Apparently, "the traditional Chinese code of silence" was uniquely allowing lawlessness to go unchecked. ACCA quickly demanded an apology from the paper. The following week, an editorial in the paper read:

> ... there is no more highly respected citizenry than the Chinese who over the years have made an invaluable contribution to the cultural, economic and social development of Australia.

ACCA noted that some in Sydney's Chinese Australian community were worried that the complaint to the *Herald* might goad non-Chinese Australians to respond negatively, but the organisation defended its actions:

> We can flatly say that racial prejudice is by no means dead, and there are still many who hark back to the old White Australian

---

92 This reunion became infamous for a "Black-face" performance in one of its segments. David Knox, "Hey It's Still Blackers", *TV Tonight*, September 2009. https://tvtonight.com.au/2009/09/hey-hey-its-still-blackers.html/.
93 CFV, "Newsletter June 1975", 3.

days. But the ACCA will certainly not stand idle and allow our community to be insulted.[94]

Community organisations' treatment of racist organisations differed from their responses to instances of racism or prejudice in the media. Indeed, the absence of news about racist organisations in the newsletters of Chinese Australian community organisations during the 1970s and early 1980s is surprising given the attention paid to racist organisations by Australia's English-language media. Perth's Chung Wah Association (CWA) made limited direct reference to racial prejudice and only directly acknowledged the presence of National Action in Perth neighbourhoods in 1984 (after the Blainey debate had made Asian immigration a national issue).[95] This was despite Western Australia having a reputation as Australia's "most racist state".[96] Vashti Jane Fox notes that:

> Between 1984 and 1989 over 40,000 lampposts, letter boxes and bus stops in suburbs across Perth in Western Australia were covered with neo Nazi posters declaring amongst other things: "No Asians", "No Coloureds", "White Revolution the only solution" and "Jews Are Ruining your Life".[97]

Owing to the growing presence of racist acts and actors, Perth's John Ang created an anti-racist vigilante group in 1989. His "World Ninja Society" offered a "Dial a Ninja" service for people requiring emotional support or physical protection.[98]

---

94 ACCA, "ACCA Newsletter October 1977" (Australian Chinese Community Association, October 1977), 3, State Library of New South Wales.
95 CWA, "Chung Wah News October 1984" (Chung Wah Association, October 1984), 9.
96 "Racial Discrimination Day: Australian UN Association Statement"; "State Attacked for Racist Attitudes: Members of the Ku Klux Klan"; "Anti-Asian Campaign in Perth", *Sydney Morning Herald*, 3 December 1979; Office of the Commissioner for Community Relations, "Commissioner for Community Relations: Annual Report", 1979, 15.
97 Vashti Jane Fox, "Fascism and Anti-Fascism in Perth in the 1980s", in *Histories of Fascism and Anti-Fascism in Australia* (Routledge, 2022), 158.

2 Early optimism and challenges

What accounts for the different responses to racist organisations and the racism seen in the media? One obvious explanation is that there was a danger (real or perceived) in directly confronting racist organisations. Another possible explanation, however, lies in how community organisations positioned themselves in Australian society at the end of the 1970s and early 1980s.

Interviewees suggested that many migrants from Southeast Asian countries had a powerful desire to participate in Australia's democratic society and political processes. This desire had been prompted not simply by the multicultural turn itself, but by their previous experiences of authoritarian regimes and racial discrimination in the countries of their birth, too.[99] The desire to participate is reflected in the common expressions of faith in Australia's multicultural society and the inclusivity it afforded their communities. ACCA encouraged its members to:

> take an intense interest in the social and political matters and well-being of this country ... Let us enjoy the privileges and fulfill the obligations. Let us all work together to make this country an even better place to live in. COME ON, AUSTRALIANS.[100]

Community organisations that could remember Australia when it was not welcoming of ethnic difference also felt the shift toward inclusivity. An editorial in CWA's *Chung Wah News* reported that:

> Many of us have insulated ourselves from active community services and have built up an apathy in our attitudes. It is time that we come out of this retreat and be more active and constructive in the society we live.[101]

---

98 Fox, 171.
99 Interviewee 1, Anonymous Interview; Interviewee 2, Anonymous Interview; Interviewee 3, Anonymous Interview.
100 ACCA, "ACCA News December 1979" (Australian Chinese Community Association, December 1979), 1, State Library of New South Wales.
101 CWA, "Chung Wah News September 1983" (Chung Wah Association, September 1983), 3.

After long histories of social marginalisation, community organisations now saw themselves as purposefully occupying a more integral position in Australian society.

In contrast, racist organisations were described by media and politicians as being on the fringes of Australian society. This was not just because such a small number of Australians were members of racist organisations, but also because multicultural and anti-racist policy had become central to Australian society – the *Racial Discrimination Act 1975* being both a symbolic and legislative example of this. Of course, Australian society was not free of racism, but such developments indicated the diminishing acceptability of individuals – let alone organisations – publicly espousing racist beliefs.

Yet there remained a fear among Chinese Australian community organisations that racist ideologies could be carried by influential people or organisations back from the fringes of Australian society to be embraced by the mainstream once more. Community organisations thus remained vigilant to this possibility, despite the optimism they still had for Australia's multiculturalism. This vigilance was not unwarranted. In 1978, the United Nations Association of Australia had warned that even small racist groups operating on the periphery of society could quickly grow into more influential movements.[102] Their opinion might well have been informed by the example of Robert Menzies becoming a patron of the National Australian Association (NAA) just two years prior. He resigned after several months, not because he disagreed with their cause to control immigration and keep Australia racially homogenous – "the objects of the National Australian Association, as set out in their constitution, are such as to produce my complete support", said Menzies – but because he disliked the media attention he received for taking up the position.[103] The "resurgence of racialist groups" seen in the media was cause for alarm for ACCA. In March 1976, it wrote that the Menzies example should "surely shake

---

102 "Racial Discrimination Day: Australian UN Association Statement".
103 "Sir Robert a Patron for Last Time", *Canberra Times*, 24 March 1976, http://nla.gov.au/nla.news-article110809630; John Jesser, "Some Tensions, but Bigoted Propaganda Failed, Grassby Says: Upsurge in Race-Hate Campaign", *Canberra Times*, 21 November 1979, https://tinyurl.com/3jnk228s.

2 Early optimism and challenges

the complacency out of members who think that we do not face racial discrimination in the late 70s". ACCA called for a "serious effort" to combat the spread of racism through better contact and information sharing among Chinese Australian communities.[104] However, trying to call out racism while at the same time denying public attention to racist organisations was hard.

CASA confronted this problem when an Australian chapter of the Ku Klux Klan (KKK) emerged in South Australia in 1978. Frank Chiu, president of CASA at this time, recalled the racist organisation created a wave of anxiety from Perth to Adelaide, spreading lies about Indochinese refugees and migrants being poised to "stealthily Asianise Australia".[105] Because the media already appeared to be exacerbating the public perception of refugees as a threat, CASA decided that it was best not to provide more oxygen to the issue. In newsletters circulated to its members, CASA condemned the actions of racist organisations but stated that it would not publicly engage with such groups: "Until such organizations could demonstrate that they had significant support in South Australia then we would not do them the honour of speaking out against them in the press."[106] CASA was consciously attempting to keep racist organisations on the periphery of Australia's attention.

Instead, CASA used its own forums to raise the issue with politicians. In February 1979, the same month that CASA decided to avoid public discussion on racism, Chiu gave a speech at a Chinese New Year banquet. South Australia's Governor, Keith Seaman, and John Bannon, Minister of Community Development and assistant to the Minister of Ethnic Affairs, were guests of honour.[107] In the speech, Chiu expressed CASA's concerns about the rise of racist organisations in

---

104 ACCA, "ACCA Newsletter March 1976" (Australian Chinese Community Association, March 1976), 2, State Library of New South Wales.
105 "State Attacked for Racist Attitudes: Members of the Ku Klux Klan"; Yan and Zhou, *CASA 40th Anniversary Commemorative Magazine: 1971–2011*, 307.
106 Yan and Zhou, *CASA 40th Anniversary Commemorative Magazine: 1971–2011*, 142–3; CASA, "News Bulletin February 1979" (Chinese Association of South Australia, February 1979), 3.a, National Library of Australia.
107 Yan and Zhou, *CASA 40th Anniversary Commemorative Magazine: 1971–2011*, 307.

South Australia, but also stated his "great confidence in the Australian general public and their rejection of any form of racism in the community". Both Seaman and Bannon gave their own condemnations of racism in the speeches that followed, suggesting prior discussions about racism between CASA and these politicians.[108] As mentioned above, CFV and ACCA had similar interactions with Commissioner Al Grassby at their own functions. By going directly to government leaders, community organisations could communicate concerns and recommend action without appearing as victims in the press or giving free publicity to racist organisations.

Participation in government consultative bodies was another avenue for community organisations to use, and CASA again provides an example. The Police-Ethnic Liaison Committee of South Australia, formed in 1980, was designed to build mutual understanding between South Australia's police force and its minority ethnic communities. CASA, the only Asian ethnic community organisation invited to join, saw its participation as a chance for information exchange and to protect local communities against the effects of racism.[109] Two years later, CASA pushed forward with its anti-racist objectives by participating in the Multi-Cultural Education Co-Ordinating Committee. Though the committee was primarily a forum to advocate teaching Mandarin in South Australian schools and universities, CASA took the opportunity to have out-dated and racist materials removed from state school libraries.[110] True to CASA's intention to limit public attention to racist organisations, its involvement in consultative bodies guided government and community attention toward the prevalence of racism in Australian society without directing attention to racist organisations. Moreover, CASA was playing a part in curbing the proliferation of racism in the public-facing areas of policing and education, thereby keeping racism to the fringes of Australian society and protecting multiculturalism.

---

108 Yan and Zhou, 143; CASA, "News Bulletin February 1979", 3.a.
109 Yan and Zhou, *CASA 40th Anniversary Commemorative Magazine: 1971–2011*, 138.
110 Yan and Zhou, 138–9.

2 Early optimism and challenges

ACCA, too, had been monitoring developments related to racism and racial equality since the mid-1970s and was involved in a police community liaison committee in the early 1980s.[111] As part of its welfare remit, ACCA also educated its members about workplace discrimination, its illegality under the *Racial Discrimination Act 1975* and the committees charged to enforce this Act. With each complaint treated confidentially, ACCA encouraged all who believed themselves to be a victim of workplace discrimination to lodge their complaints with the relevant committee within the Commission for Community Relations.[112] While information like this empowered ACCA's community to respond to the individual instances of racism its members experienced, the very act of evoking legal protection under the *Racial Discrimination Act* was to fulfil the rationale behind the Act's creation: to create a safe and equitable society by curbing racism.

One good turn ...

The multicultural turn heralded a new period of optimism for Chinese Australian community organisations. Because Australian government and society now encouraged the expression of ethnic identities, community organisations could now project their Chineseness unselfconsciously. Importantly, community organisations projected their own versions of Chineseness, ranging from CWS and its very "Australian" way of being Chinese, CFV and its concerns about "old-fashioned" Chineseness, to ACCA and its contribution toward establishing a "traditional" Chinese garden in the middle of Sydney. These latter two organisations also highlighted the importance of community agency when it came to expressing Chineseness –

---

111 ACCA, "ACCA Newsletter May 1976" (Australian Chinese Community Association, May 1976), 1–3, State Library of New South Wales; ACCA, "ACCA News April 1984" (Australian Chinese Community Association, April 1984), 6, State Library of New South Wales; ACCA, ed., 澳華公會十週年紀念特刊 *Ao Hua Gonghui Shi Zhou Nian Jinian Tekan (ACCA 10th Anniversary Year Book) 1974–1984* (Sydney: Australian Chinese Community Association of NSW, 1984), 57–60.
112 ACCA, "ACCA News September 1981", 6.

implementation of "multiculturalism from above" would not work without community consultation. The optimism of the multicultural turn allowed community organisations to become confident in their actions and their identities.

This went the other way, too, with some (perhaps overly) confident community organisations becoming optimistic about creating a sense of unity among the historically divided Chinese Australian communities. As the histories of the CYL and CFV showed, what was happening in China could have ramifications for the prominence and relevance of community organisations in Australia. In the case of these organisations, we saw community organisations come together over a shared political ideology, but that same political ideology also alienated other communities and organisations. In particular, the aspiration of CFV or CYL to push ideological harmony with the PRC to unite Chinese Australian communities was unlikely, if not impossible, to achieve – just as it had been for the AKMT with the Republic of China. As the formation of ACCA or the other federated and umbrella organisations showed, cooperation and unity among Chinese Australian communities was far more likely when politics were deliberately kept out of an organisation's purview.

Multicultural Australia also stirred reactions from individuals who wished to restore White Australia. These people formed organisations that committed acts of racist intimidation and violence. Nevertheless, Chinese Australian community organisations, though vigilant, did not appear to be too greatly intimidated by these racist organisations and responded to them in ways that suited their own interests. Because community organisations seemed to be more concerned with racist beliefs (re)gaining currency in Australian society, they were more active in calling out examples of racism in the Australian media. Despite the lingering racism in Australian society, community organisations maintained a belief in the decency of the vast majority of non-Chinese Australians and that the country's new multicultural ideals could withstand backlash. Again, this suggests that the multicultural turn was a time of new optimism and confidence for Chinese Australian community organisations.

Though Chinese Australian community organisations had always mounted their responses to racism from a humanistic and moral high

2 Early optimism and challenges

ground, after the end of White Australia and turn to multiculturalism, they now expected to be supported by the majority of Australians, too. The promises of multiculturalism marked the 1970s as a period of optimism for Chinese Australian community organisations. But the optimism existed alongside challenges. While confident in the country's preparedness to embrace multicultural ideals, community organisations nonetheless tempered their hope with a vigilance against the vestiges of the White Australian mentality.

In such an optimistic atmosphere, and with community organisations so confident in their assertions of Chineseness and Australianness, there was no reason for differences to be set aside for the sake of Chinese Australian unity. ACCA's care for common cultural and settlement welfare interests did not cause the dissolution of the different community organisations whose leaders instigated ACCA's formation. Instead, greater national identification with Australia seemed to surpass a diasporic or transnational identification with China – the stress on "being Australian" rendered the multicultural turn a nationalist turn also – thereby illuminating the success of multicultural policy as an inclusive national vision. Amid the prevailing optimism, the threat posed by racist organisations or examples of racism in the Australia media – though deplorable – was not great enough for community organisations to come together either. Though sensitive to the possibility that racist values could return from the fringes of Australian society and be accepted by the mainstream once more, Chinese Australian community organisations stayed focused on developments in their local environments. This focus changed after the Blainey debate in 1984.

3
The "Blainey debate"

> I had the feeling that [Blainey] was a wolf under sheep's clothing. No doubt some of the things had some reasons behind it, but he soon deteriorated into some language that revealed himself as not speaking from a very reasonable ground. But he revealed his displeasure at the ethnic profile of Asian people, as expressed in his book, *All for Australia*.[1]

> The *huayi* always have the three wise monkeys approach to life. Until they are completely attacked, like by Geoffrey Blainey, then they don't do anything ... So they say, "Okay, we must have a national organisation, we must have a voice." So a few people got together and they had this national conference ... we want to have a voice but we can't decide how we're going to organise to have a voice. "Oh, can't do this, this one wants this, this one wants that." And in the end we say, "Oh, we need to postpone this. We need to have another conference." Eventually nothing happened.[2]

---

1   Interviewee 4, Anonymous Interview.

On 17 March 1984, Professor Geoffrey Blainey delivered a speech in Warrnambool to the city's local Rotary chapter. He used the opportunity to attack the Hawke government for favouring Asian immigration ahead of British or European. The current migration policy was disingenuous, he argued; the product of historical guilt and a desire to impress neighbouring countries. He claimed it was like the "White Australia policy inside-out" and he warned that the present pace of Asian immigration could "explode" the public consensus on multiculturalism and "jeopardise the tolerance built up in the last thirty years".[3] Clarifying his position a few days later in *The Age*, he cautioned that the Hawke government's "Asianisation" of Australia was short sighted because using "taxes [to pay] the dole to Asians flocking into [the] neighbourhood" would inevitably provoke the wrath of "poorer" and "least educated" Australians.[4]

Blainey's high public standing added to the impact of his speech. He was a professor of history at the University of Melbourne and Dean of its Arts Faculty. He had written several influential books, and his own television series *The Blainey View* added to his public reputation.[5] Additionally, he held multiple positions on civic boards and committees. In fact, he had earned special regard from Chinese Australian community organisations as the inaugural chair (1978–84) of the Australia-China Council – a body promoting Sino-Australian relations and cultural exchange.[6]

---

2   Interviewee 8, Researcher with Anonymous Interviewee 8, interview by Researcher, 12 July 2019.
3   "The Warrnambool Speech: 'Too Many Asians', 1984", in Kate Darian-Smith and Michael Cathcart, *Stirring Australian Speeches: The Definitive Collection from Botany to Bali* (Melbourne: Melbourne University Press, 2004), 294–5.
4   "The Dilemma of Asian Immigration", in Geoffrey Blainey, *Blainey, Eye on Australia: Speeches and Essays of Geoffrey Blainey* (Melbourne: Schwartz & Wilkinson, 1991), 26–30.
5   Bongiorno, *The Eighties*, 63; Kelly Boyd, ed., *Encyclopedia of Historians and Historical Writing* (New York: Routledge, 2019), 93–5, https://tinyurl.com/ycyxzaks.
6   Paul J. Farrelly, *The Australia-China Council: The First Forty Years* (Canberra: Australia-China Council, 2018), 4; ACCA, "ACCA News April 1984" (Australian Chinese Community Association, April 1984), 2, State Library of

3 The "Blainey debate"

Scholars, politicians and media pundits rose to attack or defend Blainey's position, thereby also making statements on Asian immigration and the place of multiculturalism in Australia.[7] As years passed, popular and scholarly understanding of the debate was incorporated into longer histories of Australian racism and anxieties about immigration.[8] One name for this historical moment was the "immigration debate", but its other name, the "Blainey debate" helps to differentiate this episode from other debates about immigration (and specifically Asian immigration) in Australian history.

If the arrival of Indochinese refugees in 1976 was the first "test" of the end of White Australia, the Blainey debate can be seen as the first sustained and widespread attack on multicultural Australia.[9] This reason alone makes the Blainey debate a significant moment in Australian history. However, the Blainey debate also had a profound effect on Chinese Australian communities and the organisations which represented them. The debate immediately dampened the multiculturalist optimism that had, until then, abounded. Chinese Australian community organisations interpreted it as a "wake-up call": a call to people of Chinese origins to bestir themselves from political complacency and take action.

As one interviewee put it:

> I think Blainey, the so-called Blainey debate, was very much a turning point. A landmark development which prompted many of us to become more active.[10]

New South Wales; CFV, "Newsletter May 1984" (Chinese Fellowship of Victoria, May 1984), 8, State Library of Victoria.

7 See: Renata Singer and Michael Liffman, *The Immigration Debate in the Press, 1984* (Melbourne: Clearing House on Migration Issues, 1984).

8 See for example: Andrew Markus and M.C. Ricklefs, *Surrender Australia? Essays in the Study and Uses of History: Geoffrey Blainey and Asian Immigration* (George Allen & Unwin, 1985); Laksiri Jayasuriya and Pookong Kee, *The Asianisation of Australia?: Some Facts about the Myths* (Melbourne University Press, 1999); Tavan, *The Long, Slow Death of White Australia*; Jupp, *From White Australia to Woomera*; Bongiorno, *The Eighties*, 59–83, 227–62.

9 Jayasuriya and Kee, *The Asianisation of Australia?*, 14; Higgins, *Asylum by Boat*, 20–1, 56.

10 Interviewee 1, Anonymous Interview.

Another interviewee felt rudely jolted:

> I was just blindly imbibing this wonderful Garden of Eden. And then came 1984. Geoffrey Blainey really woke me up. And it was then that I began to get interested in the history of the Chinese in Australia.[11]

The Blainey debate was thus a moment for action and reflection – a time for Chinese Australian communities to defend their sense of belonging, but also to assess the values and character of Australian society.

Two ideas began to take shape in response to the debate: that Chinese Australian communities should seek to embed themselves more deeply into the social and political fabric of Australia, and that some kind of unity should be brokered across Australia's various Chinese Australian communities. These two ideas were not mutually exclusive, and both were intended to offer protection against racism. But as this chapter shows, it was easier for community organisations to defend their place in Australian society than it was to achieve lasting "Chinese Australian unity": organisations could do the former on their own terms, while the latter naturally meant negotiating the differing, sometimes competing views on unity held by other organisations. In this regard, the 1986 National Conference of the Australian Chinese Community was the pinnacle of Chinese Australian responses to the Blainey debate, while at the same time being an anti-climax for aspirations of Chinese Australian unity.

Alongside these implications, a third significant aspect of the debate was the way community organisations fitted it into Australian histories of racism, prejudice and xenophobia. The historical uniqueness of the Blainey debate aside, Chinese Australian community organisations tend to see the debate in a continuum of Australian anti-Asian and specifically anti-Chinese histories. It is easy to see why. The Chinese Australian community organisations encountered in this book stressed that later phenomena – like the rise of John Howard's social conservatism and Pauline Hanson's politics of social grievances

---

11 Interviewee 8, Anonymous Interview.

3 The "Blainey debate"

– grew from the Blainey debate. By the same token, they stressed that the debate created a platform for those who resented Australia's multiculturalism and longed for a return to White Australia.

Chinese Australian community organisations' initial responses to the debate

For many community organisations, the first response to the Blainey debate was to inform themselves about the arguments. Perth's Chung Wah Association (CWA) circulated extracts of Blainey's articles featured in *The Age* and *The West Australian*, as well as rebuttals from political journalist Laurie Oakes and Michael Liffman of the Ecumenical Immigration Centre in Melbourne.[12] The Chinese Fellowship of Victoria (CFV) went further. It reprinted entire articles that analysed Blainey's attack on the Hawke government for "pro-Asian bias" and the politicking that ensued, tables of immigration data, and "Asian migrant success stories".[13] The Australian Chinese Community Association (ACCA) reprinted Blainey's full Warrnambool speech in its newsletter and asked its readers: "What is your opinion of the 'Blainey view'?"[14]

Blainey's previous position on the Australia-China Council added to the shock and disappointment of community organisations.[15] "I appreciate the good professor's concern for the welfare of the nation," wrote Stanley Hunt, the president of ACCA:

> but a person of significant standing in the community should perhaps exercise greater responsibility in his public utterances. It is somewhat amazing that Professor Blainey, a professed historian,

---

12 CWA, "Chung Wah News April 1984" (Chung Wah Association, April 1984), 4.
13 CFV, "Newsletter March 1984" (Chinese Fellowship of Victoria, March 1984), 16–19, State Library of Victoria.
14 ACCA, "ACCA News April 1984", April 1984, 2.
15 ACCA, 5; CFV, "Newsletter May 1984", 8.

should demonstrate such a high degree of ignorance of Man's migrational habits since time began.[16]

Hunt later warned that the Blainey debate would encourage others to spread their own racist views.[17]

The concern that Blainey's public standing would legitimise more extreme racist views or embolden racist organisations was common. CFV feared Blainey's speech gave racists "a golden opportunity to cash in their campaign against the Asian Community in Australia".[18] As evidence, CWA reprinted a racist pamphlet that National Action had circulated during the debate. "Are you aware that this was circulated in some suburbs?" CWA asked its membership.[19] The question could also have been put to Blainey, drawing a line between his public statements and the types of people his words had subsequently emboldened.

In his admonishment of Blainey, ACCA president Hunt also foreshadowed a common conception among Chinese Australian community organisations that, having legitimised racist opinion in public discourses, Blainey had enabled politicians to appeal to racist sentiments for political gain.[20] To CFV, it was "regrettably clear that the Liberal/National Opposition is seizing this issue in the hope of gaining political inroads and most probably they will try to keep this issue very much alive until after the expected election".[21] To illustrate its meaning, CFV reprinted a cartoon of Opposition Leader Andrew Peacock (known for his refined decorum) dressing up the monstrous embodiment of racism in more tasteful Gucci attire. Gim Wah Yeo, president of the CFV, wrote directly to the Prime Minister to register his community's concerns. He requested that greater support be given

---

16 ACCA, "ACCA News May 1984" (Australian Chinese Community Association, May 1984), 3, State Library of New South Wales.
17 ACCA, "ACCA News July 1984" (Australian Chinese Community Association, July 1984), 2, State Library of New South Wales.
18 CFV, "Newsletter March 1984", 13.
19 CWA, "Chung Wah News October 1984", 9.
20 CWA, "Chung Wah News June 1984" (Chung Wah Association, June 1984), 2; CWA, "Chung Wah News August 1984" (Chung Wah Association, August 1984), 2; CFV, "Newsletter May 1984", 8.
21 CFV, "Newsletter March 1984", 13.

3 The "Blainey debate"

to the Community Relations Commission and to limit the Opposition's attempt to exploit the "Asianisation issue" for political advantage. CFV members were encouraged to write their own letters to the Prime Minister and other parliamentarians as part of a campaign around this issue.[22] In their own campaigns, the Chinese Association of South Australia (CASA) and CWA lobbied politicians to condemn racism in Parliament, as well as the racist organisations operating in Australian society and now benefitting from the public debate on Asian immigration.[23]

These community organisations understood that the ability for racist thinking to spread in Australian society depended on the extent to which multiculturalism and Asian immigration would become politicised issues. In this relationship, they saw the media as a catalyst, and numerous letters from Chinese Australian community organisations to newspapers or to parliamentarians expressed as much. In June 1984, ACCA's Hunt wrote to the *Sydney Morning Herald* to criticise its editorials of Blainey as "biased, provocative and totally irresponsible". He pointed to Australia's history of Sinophobia and the media's propensity to amplify the voices of a disgruntled few. "What are you trying to prove?" Hunt asked.[24] In reply, the editor defended his position: "Division is more likely to be cured by rational discussion rather than by pretending that it does not exist or that democracy is too frail to stand the stress of differing opinions."[25]

Although voices in the media often appealed to the need for "rational discussion" to cure the problem of racism in Australia, there were many instances where journalists and television or radio hosts were unable to maintain civility. Hunt reported his dismay at the televised "debate" in which he and other ACCA representatives had participated on Channel 7's *Terry Willesee Tonight*. A panel consisting of Blainey, Stewart West and Michael Hodgman (respectively the

---

22 CFV, 7, 13–14.
23 CWA, "Chung Wah News June 1984", 13; CWA, "Chung Wah News November 1984" (Chung Wah Association, November 1984), 7–10; Yan and Zhou, *CASA 40th Anniversary Commemorative Magazine: 1971–2011*, 144.
24 ACCA, "ACCA News June 1984" (Australian Chinese Community Association, June 1984), 8, State Library of New South Wales.
25 ACCA, "ACCA News July 1984", 2.

Minister and Shadow Minister for Immigration and Ethnic Affairs) fielded questions from members of political groups, ethnic communities, racist organisations and the RSL. Hunt called the event a "fiasco":

> A few undesirables in the audience disrupted what was to be a debate on immigration intake. In the absence of what is the reality with the immigration programmes, uninformed individuals hurled oral abuse at others in the audience and the panel of speakers.

The *Sydney Morning Herald* reported that some audience members ("a group of Asian immigrants") staged a walk-out until Ross May, leader of the National Socialist Party, was ejected from the audience for his abuse.[26] The producer of the program claimed May's attendance had not been planned. However, media outlets courting lurid characters and publishing sensationalised copy was (and today remains) a common occurrence.

The Blainey debate was obviously a boon for talkback radio, which relied on provocative themes for listener engagement. Higher ratings translated to higher advertising revenue, so the incentive for sensationalism was clear. On radio station 3AW, "human headline" Derryn Hinch asked listeners if "immigration should be banned for two years so Australians could get the jobs available". Of 26,520 callers, 23,580 agreed, and Hinch (who is, ironically, a New Zealand immigrant) proclaimed immigration should be stopped. The Blainey debate was often discussed in simplified and evocative language designed to elicit visceral rather than considered responses. Especially in the talkback format, simply voicing an opinion seemed more important than the substance of that opinion or the consequences of sharing it. "No matter what you think of his views, Hinch stirs action", said one advertisement for Hinch's program.[27] That was entirely the

---

26 Francis Lee, *Out of Bounds: Journey of a Migrant* (Sydney: Universe Books, 2010), 137; ACCA, "ACCA News July 1984", 2; "Immigration Issue Causes TV Audience Row", *Sydney Morning Herald*, 16 June 1984.
27 3AW, "Immigration Should Be Banned", *The Age*, 20 March 1984.

3 The "Blainey debate"

point. Such media content was not meant to spur discussion about the Blainey debate, let alone inform the audience about the issues – it was intended to "stir [re]action".

Newspapers also used the debate to elicit emotional responses from readers by way of think pieces on racist organisations, and a mutually beneficial relationship between newspapers and racist organisations developed: the former being able to use the provocative content to sell papers, the latter gaining a public platform. For their own credibility however, both newspapers and racist organisations distanced themselves from the reality of this arrangement and the fact that the Blainey debate had enabled it. National Action's leader, Jim Saleem, acknowledged to an interviewer for *The Age* that "Professor Geoffrey Blainey may have encouraged some people to think more about the Asian immigration issue", but he denied a "correlation between National Action's propaganda and statements by the professor". But as a "propaganda organisation [...] attempting to convert some people to a particular attitude and a particular world view", Saleem's National Action surely benefitted from the respectability Blainey leant to anti-immigration agendas like its own – not to mention the platform provided by *The Age*.[28] In the view of *The Sun's* Tom Prior, "undoubtedly there is an argument against giving [National Action] publicity" (in what he called "the newspaper with by far the biggest daily circulation in Australia"). But he maintained that National Action and their supporters "will not go away simply because they are ignored". It was, however, Prior's choice to depict Mark Ferguson, National Action's 1984 candidate for the seat of Wills (in a futile run against the incumbent Bob Hawke), as "a misguided idealist rather than a hardline racist or bigot".[29] Because racist organisations benefitted from the articles that normalised them and their messages, Prior should have also understood that positive coverage would not make them go away either.

As the debate around immigration spilled ever more into issues of race, leaders of Chinese Australian community organisations stepped

---

28   Karen Cooke, "Reasonable Tones Carry the Message of Hate", *The Age*, 25 July 1984.
29   Tom Prior, "Wills Man Likes Asians – in Asia", *The Sun*, 8 November 1984.

up their responses. Ching-hwan Yen, president of CASA and a historian at the University of Adelaide, wrote to *The Advertiser* to publicly refute Blainey's claims of pro-Asian bias regarding migration and the conflation of refugee and immigration intakes and issues.[30] Francis Lee, an engineer and head of the Cantonese language department at SBS radio, went further with a full-page rebuttal published in *The Australian*. In opening, Lee hinted at some of the characteristics that set the Blainey debate apart from other instances of anti-Asian racism:

> Like most Asian people in Australia, I kept hoping the present anti-Asian campaign would die away without my having to combat it. But when I saw an article by Professor Geoffrey Blainey, which claimed the Asian people in Australia are on his side in rejecting Asian immigrants, I felt it was time for Asians to at least clarify their position.[31]

What goaded Lee into action, then, was not simply Blainey's claim to know what average (White) Australians thought about Asian immigration, but also his claim to know what Asian Australians thought about it. In the process, Lee turned the democratic rhetoric of "rational discussion" back upon those who invoked it:

> The most objectionable aspect of Professor Blainey's campaign is not whether it would result in fewer Asians in Australia, but the thoughtless way it has been conducted, and the underlying tone which runs against the principles of human dignity that we, Asians and non-Asians alike, hold dear.[32]

In this way, Lee opened the possibility that it was supporters of Australia's multicultural reality who were in fact the true Australians – it was those who were critical of multiculturalism who should

---

30 Yan and Zhou, *CASA 40th Anniversary Commemorative Magazine: 1971–2011*, 143–4, 278.
31 Francis Lee, "From the Asian Side of the Blainey Debate", *The Australian*, 5 October 1984.
32 Lee.

3 The "Blainey debate"

re-evaluate the quality of their Australianness. Garry Leong quipped in ACCA's April 1984 newsletter that it was Blainey who was out of step with public opinion, because "Asians enjoy respect and in turn respect Australia as a country".[33] As such, an important outcome of Blainey's Warrnambool speech was the social and political activation of Chinese Australian communities and organisations. The CWA even thanked Blainey for "waking us up out of our complacency".[34] As CWA's president, Kee-Yong Yee, went on, Chinese Australians:

> ... must participate fully in all activities of the community at large so as to fulfil the duties and responsibilities of a good citizen whether it be in social, education, sports, welfare or politics. This will not only help to erase the ignorance about us but also the common allegation of [our] incompatibility.[35]

A good Chinese Australian citizen, therefore, was a citizen active in society and politics. Likewise, other community organisations like ACCA and CFV urged their members to become socially participatory citizens; variously reminding members that "goodwill begins with me" and encouraging the use of their talents for the benefit of the nation.[36] To these organisations, active citizenship – through societal participation, engagement with media or political action – assured their place in Australia and acted as a bulwark to racism.

The Australian Chinese Forum

While the Blainey debate pushed existing Chinese Australian community organisations to play a greater role in Australian society, it also brought a whole new organisation into being. In late 1984, a series of informal meetings and dinner conversations about Blainey and the debate laid the foundation for a new Chinese Australian organisation. Meeting formally for the first time in March 1985, the Australian

---

33 ACCA, "ACCA News April 1984", April 1984, 5.
34 CWA, "Chung Wah News November 1984", 7–10.
35 CWA, "Chung Wah News June 1984", 2.
36 ACCA, "ACCA News July 1984", 2; CFV, "Newsletter March 1984", 13.

Chinese Forum (ACF)[37] aspired to raise "the profile of the Chinese community in Australia".[38] Its founding members were typically wealthy and well-educated: lawyers, engineers, doctors, academics, businesspeople and (aspiring) politicians. If not born in Australia, they were migrants from Hong Kong, Malaysia and Singapore and educated in Australia. They were middle-aged or older and had strong English-language skills.[39] They were also well-connected to Sydney's Chinese communities. Inaugural vice-chairman, King Fong, for example, was also secretary of the Dixon Street Chinese Committee, sat on the executive committee of ACCA and belonged to numerous other community groups.[40] This elite composition did not worry ACF's members, who saw themselves as the best placed among Chinese Australians to achieve their objectives.

Like other community organisations, ACF believed increased political awareness and societal participation among Chinese Australians would provide the best protection from incendiary racial issues like those coming from the Blainey debate.[41] ACF did not concern itself with social welfare and cultural maintenance roles and rather saw itself as a training ground for future (Chinese) Australian leaders.[42] ACF strongly encouraged its members to join Australia's political parties, though which parties ACF members joined was irrelevant. The organisation's goal to foster political discussion and

---

37 Part of this description of the Australian Chinese Forum appears in Nathan Daniel Gardner, "United We Stood but Divided We Were: Chinese Australian Unity and the 1984 Immigration Debate", *History Australia* 19, no. 2 (3 April 2022): 305–24, https://doi.org/10.1080/14490854.2022.2048038.
38 Lee, *Out of Bounds*, 138–40.
39 Lee, 139–40, 143; ACF, "ACF Newsletter October 1986" (Australian Chinese Forum, October 1986), 15, State Library of New South Wales.
40 ACF, "ACF Newsletter October 1986", 15; ACCA, "ACCA News September 1984" (Australian Chinese Community Association, September 1984), 2, State Library of New South Wales; Fitzgerald, *Red Tape, Gold Scissors*, 173, 175.
41 ACF, "ACF Newsletter March 1986" (Australian Chinese Forum, March 1986), 12–13, State Library of New South Wales; ACF, "ACF Newsletter August 1986", 11.
42 ACF, "ACF Newsletter August 1989" (Australian Chinese Forum, August 1989), 6–7, National Library of Australia.

3 The "Blainey debate"

agreement through reasoned debate overrode the importance of political alignment.[43]

ACF stressed that democratic participation and community engagement were responsibilities for members to uphold. Members strove to do so. Letter writing – to politicians, newspapers, television and radio stations or government departments – was one method by which members could "discharge one's democratic responsibility as an Australian citizen".[44] Additionally, ACF members monitored media for unfair depictions of Chinese Australians and various other ethnic groups, which were then followed up by a dedicated subcommittee.[45] Another subcommittee recorded the activities of racist organisations and reported incidents to authorities. Another, in 1985, made a submission supporting the creation of an Australian Bill of Rights.[46] ACF fostered further political interest through public forums, publishing information about Australia's democratic processes, and excursions to the Parliament Houses in Canberra and Sydney.[47] The educational purpose of ACF's parliamentary visits was two-directional. ACF wanted to demystify political engagement for its members and dispel parliamentarians' misconceptions of Chinese Australians as politically disengaged.[48]

ACF saw political participation as key to ensuring Chinese Australian security in Australian society and the rationale for this participation was frequently connected to the success of Australia as a multicultural society and a modern, cosmopolitan nation.[49] Other organisations agreed that multiculturalism could not be taken for

---

43 ACF, "ACF Newsletter June 1986" (Australian Chinese Forum, June 1986), 6–8, State Library of New South Wales; ACF, "ACF Newsletter December 1986" (Australian Chinese Forum, December 1986), 2–3, State Library of New South Wales.
44 ACF, "ACF Newsletter June 1988" (Australian Chinese Forum, June 1988), 15, State Library of New South Wales.
45 ACF, "ACF Newsletter March 1986", 3–4.
46 ACF, "ACF Newsletter June 1986", 9, 11–13.
47 ACF, "ACF Newsletter November 1987" (Australian Chinese Forum, November 1987), 4, 11, State Library of New South Wales; ACF, "ACF Newsletter August 1989", 6–7; ACF, "ACF Newsletter June 1991" (Australian Chinese Forum, June 1991), 9, National Library of Australia.
48 ACF, "ACF Newsletter June 1988", 2.

granted and the Blainey debate caused them to redouble their support. As CWA put it, multicultural society needed to be maintained and protected through active societal participation as "Australians first, Chinese second".[50] To the same end, the Chinese Association of Victoria (CAV) formed an "anti-discrimination and social action subcommittee" with a duty to strengthen Australia:

> Chinese-Australians, like other Australians ... have an obligation to help build Australia into a strong, peaceful, prosperous and clever country for ourselves and future generations. We shall play our part in assisting the governments of whichever political persuasion to promote mutual respect and peaceful coexistence with all communities in our multicultural society.[51]

The community organisations' interest in all facets of Australian society illustrated their holistic interest in the nation beyond "ethnic issues". At the opening of the Federation of Ethnic Communities' Councils of Australia's (FECCA) new headquarters in Sydney, Bob Hawke pointedly addressed the Blainey debate and the value of Australia's ethnic communities. His words may have missed the mark. Stan Hunt, speaking as the representative of the Council of Chinese Organisations (CoCO) at the function, welcomed Hawke's gesture but said that he would be even more popular among the various ethnic communities in the room (especially ahead of the election) if he instead chose to waive income tax for 12 months.[52] ACF also resisted having its interests pigeonholed as "ethnic issues". It pushed its membership and guest speakers to discuss all matters of modern Australian society.[53] The message was that Chinese Australians were not a minority interest

---

49 ACF, "ACF Newsletter August 1989", 9; ACF, "ACF Newsletter June 1986", 2-3, 11-13; ACF, "ACF Newsletter March 1989" (Australian Chinese Forum, March 1989), 7, National Library of Australia.
50 CWA, *Chung Wah Association Centenary Celebration Souvenir Publication, 1910-2010*, 134-9.
51 CAV, *Chinese Association of Victoria*, 1992, 7.
52 ACCA, "ACCA News May 1984", 2.
53 ACF, "ACF Newsletter June 1986", 9; Lee, *Out of Bounds*, 139-40, 142-3.

3 The "Blainey debate"

group. They were interested in all aspects of society – just like any other Australians.

While the 1970s had been a decade of resurgence of Chinese identity in the Australian public, the 1980s was a decade when Chinese Australian communities sought greater engagement with other parts of Australian society. Overall, the engagement with newspapers, politicians and Blainey himself had led Chinese Australian community organisations to more purposeful public participation and to stronger commitments to Australian multiculturalism. Despite the debate's associated racial tensions, community organisations' assertions of belonging in Australia grew bolder.

Arising conceptualisations of Chinese Australian unity

How different Chinese Australian communities and representative organisations should come together *within* Australian society was another matter.[54] The feeling that Blainey, as CWA put it, woke Chinese Australians "out of complacency" ran widely and deeply across Chinese Australian communities. The idea that Chinese Australian communities should in some way unite to meet the challenge posed by the Blainey debate ran alongside the idea of greater societal participation. In the immediate wake of Blainey's Warrnambool speech, Katie Young, a regular contributor to CFV's newsletter, encapsulated all these feelings and ideas in an article that trumpeted, "It is Time now!":

> As a minority group, we must not only be United, but we must stand up and be counted [...] The Blainey Affair is the indicator, the message. As an ethnic group the Chinese must begin to be vocal, to be aware and to be involved in political, social, economical [sic], educational and all other community issues.[55]

---

54 CFV, "Newsletter March 1984", 15.
55 Parts of this discussion on Chinese Australian unity feature in Gardner, "United We Stood but Divided We Were".

The word "united" was pointedly underlined and forms of community action listed with alliterative effect. CWA and CAV expressed similar sentiments in their own publications.[56] How this feeling would be translated by the various groups into a form of community unity that could effectively respond to the debate was initially unclear, but two and a half years later, CFV, CWA, CAV and other community organisations attempted to do so at the National Conference of the Australian Chinese Community in Sydney.

Convened on 28–29 November 1986, the conference was attended by 159 representatives of 33 community organisations from across the nation.[57] Its primary objective was to create a nationally representative body for Chinese Australians that could advocate collective interests or respond to future xenophobia. Although the conference failed to produce a unified perspective about how to pursue this objective, it nevertheless kindled perennial discussions about establishing nation-wide Chinese Australian unity in one form or another.

The meaning of unity was not consistent across the community organisations during the Blainey debate or indeed at the conference. The singular "Australian Chinese Community" of the conference title, for example, suggested an aspiration for Chinese Australian unity as a single, harmonious whole, and showed the power and attractiveness of ethnicity as collective self-identification.[58] But there were other ideas about unity. As examples, CFV, CASA and ACF displayed three variations on the theme of unity and the reason for pursuing it. Located in different parts of Australia and possessing different membership profiles of age, generation, objectives and political outlook, the groups represented the different possible compositions of Chinese Australian communities and reflected the diversity among the national conference's attending organisations.

For CFV, establishing complete ethnic unity was an end in itself and the Blainey debate more or less served as a rallying cause. For CASA, pursuing unity as an ethnic bloc was proposed as a pragmatic

---

56 CWA, "Chung Wah News June 1984", 2; CAV, *Chinese Association of Victoria*, 1992, 18–21.
57 Young and Yeo, *National Conference of the Australian Chinese Community*, 11.
58 Izenberg, *Identity*, 21–3, 206–12.

3 The "Blainey debate"

means to respond to the debate. ACF believed Chinese Australian unity depended on uniting with the rest of Australia and its shared multicultural ideals.[59] While the three groups' responses to the Blainey debate tended to converge over the period leading up to the national conference, thereby suggesting a more united way of responding, their different conceptualisations of "unity" nonetheless remained evident.

CFV and CASA's invocations of Chinese Australian unity to respond to the Blainey debate grew from their respective histories. CFV's foundational imperative to unite all of Melbourne's Chinese Australian communities and its history of using emotive and didactic rhetoric could be heard in its declaration, "it's TIME". Harkening back to the era of its establishment, CFV echoed Gough Whitlam's 1972 campaign slogan, imbuing a sense of urgency and inevitability into its call for Chinese Australian unity. Likewise, CASA reflected its history of pragmatic community organisation and cooperation in its own call for Chinese Australian unity. After an extraordinary meeting called to discuss responses to the immigration debate, CASA committed itself to renouncing "isolation and silence" and engaged with the debate independently and in cooperation with other groups – Chinese Australian and non-Chinese Australian alike.[60]

In ACF's case, its aspirational character cast a vision of unity with a greater Australian whole rather than one that ended at the borders of the ethnic group. Of the three, ACF seemed to put the greatest weight on its "Australianness". It kept itself distant from foreign nations and, regardless of its members' affections for their places of birth or ancestry, ACF was solely focused on Australia's politics and society.[61] Yet ACF was not uncritical of Australia or its multiculturalism. ACF recognised the importance of maintaining culture and strength in diversity, and it genuinely took multiculturalism as Australia's binding principle. But it also believed multiculturalism must move beyond pageantry and stressed the need for full participation of Australia's minorities in

---

59 From 1996, ACF became known as the "Chinese Australian Forum".
60 CASA, "News Bulletin May 1984" (Chinese Association of South Australia, May 1984), 5, National Library of Australia; Yan and Zhou, *CASA 40th Anniversary Commemorative Magazine: 1971–2011*, 58.
61 ACF, "ACF Newsletter December 1986", 3; Lee, *Out of Bounds*, 139.

politics and society if multiculturalism was to be successful. ACF's regular public forums, policy information evenings and political fundraisers were testament to this ideal.[62] ACF's intention was for Chinese Australians to be united with the nation as an active part of a multicultural whole.

A united response to the Blainey debate

Each organisation demonstrated their participation in the debate to their respective memberships. Both CFV and ACF took materials related to the Blainey debate from newspapers and reprinted them in newsletters alongside copies of their own letters to politicians, the press and other players. The "Voice of the ACF" was reprinted alongside editorials on the "Twisted Eloquence" of Blainey. Marginalia accompanying articles in one CFV newsletter instructed "bigots [to] take note" of the public support for multiculturalism and the positive examples of citizenship provided by Asian Australians.[63] Importantly, these (re)publications suggested a greater community formed by shared experiences and perspectives. The organisations curated materials in a way that outlined the arguments and counter-arguments of the debate and provided specific "Chinese Australian perspectives" on them. By identifying allies and antagonists of Chinese Australians, and Asian Australians more broadly, the organisations presented the idea of a single community respectively befriended and beset by these parties.

The heightened visibility of Chinese Australian groups in the public domain during the Blainey debate shows that the willingness of CFV, CASA and ACF to speak for Chinese Australians collectively became more pronounced over time. There were signs of this from the outset of the Blainey debate. Taking another example from CFV's newsletters:

> We the Asian communities of Australia must work closer together on common issues such as this. We must show our compassion and understanding towards each other whether you are the old

---

62   ACF, "ACF Newsletter March 1986", 15–16; Lee, *Out of Bounds*, 140.
63   CFV, "Newsletter March 1984"; ACF, "ACF Newsletter March 1986".

3 The "Blainey debate"

residents or the new comers ... It is through this solidarity, we shall then be able to make a stronger contribution towards a better multicultural Australia.[64]

Putting this idea into action, community organisations increasingly participated in or engaged with governmental and community bodies. Often the organisations spoke on behalf of Chinese Australians and even "Asian Australians", who were obviously not part of the organisations' respective memberships. Nevertheless, these actions helped community organisations gain greater public recognition and project the impression of a unitary ethnic body.

In this vein, CASA's Rick Yuan at the South Australian Ethnic Affairs Commission conference stated ethnic communities needed to move beyond "tokenism" and put greater political pressure on the prevailing social system to effect change and build a truly multicultural society.[65] This was not unlike ACF's own vision. In CASA's case, it had already involved itself in a Police-Ethnic Liaison Committee and other similarly "ethnic-focused" consultation committees, partly in response to racist activity in Adelaide during the late 1970s and early 1980s.[66] Donning this mantle of community representation, CASA became very visible to the South Australian Human Rights Commission. The commission entrusted CASA to complete a survey of the extent and manner of racism and discrimination in the state with particular attention paid to how the Blainey debate had negatively affected Chinese and, notably, *other* Asian Australian communities.[67] Jen Tsen Kwok has pointed to the establishment of multi-ethnic groups that distributed information and lobbied government and media in the wake of the Blainey debate – such as the Australian-Asian Community Welfare Association, the Asian Australian Resource Centre and the Asian Australian Action Committee – as examples of turning ethnic

---

64 CFV, "Newsletter March 1984", 13.
65 CASA, "Newsletter January 1985" (Chinese Association of South Australia, January 1985), 7, National Library of Australia.
66 Yan and Zhou, *CASA 40th Anniversary Commemorative Magazine: 1971–2011*, 138–9.
67 Yan and Zhou, 144–5; CASA, "Newsletter March 1985" (Chinese Association of South Australia, March 1985), 9, National Library of Australia.

identity into political agency.[68] CASA's participation in civic bodies shows its political agency was likewise couched in its ethnic identity.

A comparable range of activities was undertaken by ACF; participating in government and community roundtables and drafting parliamentary submissions on issues like racism.[69] As previously mentioned, ACF made a submission to the Senate Standing Committee of a proposed Bill of Rights for Australia, recommending that the incitement of racial hatred be outlawed and to allow for class actions against racial offenders. Perhaps they had Blainey in mind. While the Bill of Rights never came to be, the ACF's vision was eventually given credence by the amendments to the *Racial Discrimination Act* a decade later.[70]

In a way, the community organisations' growing will to participate in the political process was matched by a greater will from government and the general community to listen to Asian and Chinese Australian voices. However, the need to listen to a "representative" voice no doubt helped to reify a singular, uniform Chinese Australian community. Similarly, letter-writing, engaging members in political discussions, and participating in community and government initiatives helped community organisations to entertain the possibility of uniting to speak with one voice.

The 1986 national conference

This possibility seemed within sight in 1986 when a national conference of Chinese Australian community organisations was convened. The seeds of the conference were sown in December 1984, when the Federation of Ethnic Communities' Councils of Australia (FECCA), the

---

68 Kwok, "An Etymology of 'Asian Australian' Through Associational Histories Connecting Australia to Asia", 358–62.
69 Kwok, 358–62.
70 ACF, "Submission by the Australian Chinese Forum to Australian Senate" (Parliament Submission, Canberra, 1985), Z567, Box 15, Federation of Ethnic Community Councils of Australia, ANU Archives; Australian Commonwealth Government, *Racial Discrimination Act 1975*, section 18C (1995), https://tinyurl.com/2mks8hu9.

3 The "Blainey debate"

parent body of the Ethnic Communities' Council of Victoria (ECCV), held a conference in Melbourne. CFV, via its president Gim Wah Yeo, was a major player. Yeo was then the ECCV's treasurer and at FECCA's national conference he encountered representatives from analogous state and territory councils who were, like him, members of Chinese Australian community organisations.[71] Together they began discussing the creation of a body that could represent the interests of the Chinese Australian community at the national level.[72]

After lengthy deliberations and the original proposal of Melbourne, they decided on November 1986 in Sydney. Yeo was elected conference secretary. ACF president James Lee was a member of the organising committee, and CASA president Ching-hwang Yen was also an organising member and a keynote speaker for the conference. In March 1986, the committee sent letters to all of the 114 Chinese Australian community organisations listed in the 1984 *Ethnic Communities Directory* (issued by the Department of Immigration and Ethnic Affairs) to gauge their interest and invite them. Extra effort was made to send letters to other newly formed or unlisted groups. Again, demonstrating the intra-ethnic cooperation that the Blainey debate created, responses to the letters indicated strong support for the proposal. Along with fostering the personal connections and exchanges between attendees, the working committee resolved that a core aim of the conference was to consider the establishment of a body that could identify the "common goals and objectives" of Chinese Australians.[73]

The CFV newsletter announced the conference with a sense of occasion and urgency. Wrote Yeo:

---

71 CFV, "Newsletter November 1986" (Chinese Fellowship of Victoria, November 1986), 5, State Library of Victoria; Jasbeer Singh, T. Sandhu and B. Singh, *Australasian Who's Who*, 1st ed. (Adelaide: Oriental Publications, 1987), 139, https://tinyurl.com/2dtfu3eb; Migrant Resource Centres were begun around Australia under the proposals contained within the 1978 Galbally Report: Galbally, *Report of the Review of Post-Arrival Programs and Services for Migrants*.
72 Young and Yeo, *National Conference of the Australian Chinese Community*, 3.
73 Young and Yeo, 2–3.

The success of the conference will rely on all Chinese Australian community organisations and individuals' enthusiastic support and participation. Federal Minister for Ethnic Affairs, Chris Hurford, has sent a letter of praise and encouragement and all state government members also unanimously see this historic and pioneering undertaking as the most important work of Chinese living in Australia.[74]

Yeo's complete confidence in the conference's success was consistent with CFV's established ethos and ideology. He urged, but also presumed, the unanimous support of Chinese Australians, and triumphantly claimed the support of "all state government members". The ethnic unity of Chinese Australians that CFV had long described and desired was apparently within his reach.

Yet by the time the national conference was in train, other community organisations had grown confident in their own methods of dealing with the fallout of the Blainey debate. While interested in partaking in the conference, some had grown ambivalent toward the idea of unity formalised in a national body. Among them, ACF raised concerns about the hidden or self-serving motivations of organisations and self-styled community leaders.[75] ACF president James Lee asked:

> can the national body formed as the result of this conference honestly claim to have the support of all Chinese communities in the whole of Australia and to be a truly representative body of these people?

Beyond the matters of legitimacy and representation, he also queried the practical need for a national body as "it was open to question what [it] could do that a meeting of regional representatives cannot".[76]

---

74 聚會的成功，基於全澳大利亞華人社團及個人的熱烈支持和參與，聯邦政府移民及民族務部部長赫福先生特地來函讚揚和鼓勵，個省市政府官員，也一致認為這歷史性的創舉，是華人在澳居住的切身主要工作. CFV, "Newsletter November 1986", 6.
75 ACF, "ACF Newsletter August 1986", 4.
76 ACF, 2–3.

3 The "Blainey debate"

Concerned by the prospect of a national body misrepresenting its member organisations or becoming a vehicle for personal ambitions, Lee was cautious. To him, Chinese Australian organisations would more effectively serve their distinct communities if they focused on their own interests and came together over issues only as their respective memberships felt necessary.

CASA took an in-between position. Like ACF, CASA supported a national body if it could bring together Chinese communities in Australia and deal with issues commonly affecting them – the Blainey debate being an example. This pragmatic approach to unity aligned well with James Lee's view of community representatives coming together as necessary. But as Yen saw it, a national body would coordinate responses from all communities around Australia and foster understanding between them. This meant more than unity as a means to an end – it could be a pragmatic means to other ends, too. While Yen did not see the creation of a national body as a foregone conclusion, he nevertheless shared Yeo's view that its creation was needed to "increase the strength and influence" of lobbying on issues affecting all Chinese in Australia.[77]

After the national conference began, however, it became clear that the formation of a national body would be stymied not only by the competing understandings of such a body's purpose but also by the different conceptualisations of "Chinese Australian unity" itself.

The first keynote speech of the conference, delivered by Professor Manning Clark, put the position of the "Chinese in Australia" on a very broad plain. As the historian spoke to his desire for fraternal relations between all peoples and a duty to protect our shared "Mother Earth", his millennium-long view of "Chinese and Australian encounters" shrank the significance of national and ethnic groupings.[78] Clark was perhaps the only other Australian historian to loom as large as Blainey at this time and so his presence was noteworthy. Clark's humanist history served as a neat counterpoint to the Anglo-Australian fears that filled the speech Blainey had delivered to Warrnambool's Rotarians in 1984.

---

77 CASA, "Newsletter December 1986" (Chinese Association of South Australia, December 1986), 6, National Library of Australia.
78 Young and Yeo, *National Conference of the Australian Chinese Community*, 6.

Expecting memories of the debate were still fresh, Ching-hwang Yen, as the second keynote speaker, returned the attendees to the purpose of their gathering:

> [Chinese Australians] must unite and organise themselves into a national body which could act as an effective pressure group and they must exercise influence over the policies on immigration, education and ethnic affairs. They must not waste their time and energy engaging in in-fighting over trivial issues and they must devote more of their energy in promoting a good image in the society and help to create a strong, powerful and multicultural Australia.[79]

Yen's additional imperative for Chinese Australian unity was to protect Australia's still fledgling multiculturalism and, throughout his speech, he pointed to Australia's historical mistreatment of Chinese as a cautionary rationale for doing so. Although attendees concurred with protecting multiculturalism, they clearly had doubts regarding how a national representative body would serve this purpose or the individual interests of communities. The conference's first session, "Our Status in Australia", for example, revealed that the unique histories of different communities underpinned their present needs, interests and approaches to community engagement. These differences would likely challenge agreements about the types of policies Yen identified in his keynote. Accordingly, by the second day attendees agreed that *if* a national body were to be formed, it should be focused on matters of social welfare and cultural maintenance and "not concern itself with politics" (this had been ACCA's recipe for success). Furthermore, their consensus was that Australian multiculturalism would best be served by Chinese Australians "mainstreaming" themselves in all aspects of Australian society "rather than becoming ethnic enclaves".[80]

A spectrum of positions was again evident in the wake of the conference, which concluded without agreement to form a national body. Organisations' stated reasons for the conference's failure reflected

---

79 Young and Yeo, 9.
80 Young and Yeo, 10.

3 The "Blainey debate"

some significant differences of language and politics. The otherwise upbeat conference proceedings compiled by Gim Wah Yeo and Katie Young cryptically stated that, in the second general session, titled "Working Together", a "disruption occurred" and an adjournment of ten minutes was made to "restore order". A language barrier was cited as the cause of misunderstandings – the conference was delivered predominantly in Mandarin and English, which was potentially unsuited to those who predominantly spoke Cantonese or other Chinese dialects.[81]

CASA's Ching-hwang Yen explained it differently. To him, the conference was ruined by clashes of pro-Taiwan and pro-China groups.[82] He lay special blame on an Indochinese organisation and its protests that the conference had a pro-China bias.[83] Years later, ACF's Benjamin Chow remembered the incident that had almost deteriorated into a "fist fight", but thought it was more accurately described as a clash between a pro-PRC group and a vehemently anti-communist group (the latter having a membership that came predominately from Vietnam).[84]

Sydney's ACCA, too, pointed to partisanship, but on the part of leaders of community organisations who used "skewed reasoning and strong emotions" to dismiss views divergent from "the interests of political forces outside Australia". While these political forces were left unidentified, ACCA warned that the proposed national body's independence would be compromised if it sought endowments from overseas.[85] While not necessarily a China-versus-Taiwan concern, the issue here was with being beholden to "foreign interests".

---

81 Young and Yeo, 10.
82 Yen Ching-hwang, *Ethnicities, Personalities and Politics in the Ethnic Chinese Worlds* (Singapore: World Scientific, 2016), 354.
83 Yan and Zhou, *CASA 40th Anniversary Commemorative Magazine: 1971–2011*, 142.
84 Benjamin Chow and Diana Giese, *Benjamin Ming Tung Chow Interviewed by Diana Giese for the Post-War Chinese Australians Oral History Project*, Post-War Chinese Australians Oral History Project, 1998, TRC 3707, National Library of Australia; Correspondence with the Author, 17 January 2024.
85 ACCA, "ACCA News December 1986" (Australian Chinese Community Association, December 1986), 3, State Library of New South Wales.

Muted discussion in publications produced after the conference showed further disillusionment. ACF included a report which noted that those in favour of forming a national body "carried the day" but did not mention the conference's disturbances.[86] The brevity of this report nonetheless suggested an underwhelmed response. Interestingly, at a prior point in the newsletter, ACF conspicuously reiterated its political neutrality and non-alignment with affairs of any "motherland". It was a statement that dovetailed with ACCA's concerns about foreign interests.[87]

Newsletters put out by CFV after the conference were strangely silent about it, despite the dominating role played in its organisation by Yeo. It was only in June of the following year that CFV returned to the subject of Chinese Australian unity with a reprinted article written by CASA's Yen. The article explained the diversity of Chinese Australian communities and insisted on the need for cultural maintenance while also participating in Australia's multicultural society wholeheartedly. It thereby gave a conciliatory nod toward some of the issues of the previous year's conference. Yen nonetheless remained insistent on the need for a national representative body – with the Blainey debate given as the exemplary reason.[88]

CWA had a rosier view of the conference, perhaps because one of the only resolutions to emerge from it was the appointment of its president, Eric Tan, as national coordinator of the next conference.[89] Even so, Tan opined that Chinese Australian communities "are neither in the position nor ready to form a national body today".[90]

These reflections on the conference again revealed the presumptions underlying shared identity. Though all participants were certainly "Chinese", they ascribed different languages and dialects, ideologies, values, connections, places of origin, past experiences, and future aspirations to being Chinese. Demonstrably, what was held as

---

86 ACF, "ACF Newsletter December 1986", 15.
87 ACF, 2–3.
88 CFV, "Newsletter June 1987" (Chinese Fellowship of Victoria, June 1987), 9, State Library of Victoria.
89 CWA, *Chung Wah Association Centenary Celebration Souvenir Publication, 1910–2010*, 42.
90 ACF, "ACF Newsletter December 1986", 15.

3 The "Blainey debate"

essentially Chinese by some participants (being pro-PRC, for example) was not equally held by others. Nor did the urgency of past or prospective challenges (like the Blainey debate) see Chinese Australian unity overcome these differences. Instead, the failure of the conference was perhaps a demonstration that Chinese Australian unity existed as a process rather than a fixed state. The conditions that compelled unity could themselves wax and wane. The conflict at the conference and the various explanations for it show that the quality that was held to be uniting – being Chinese – was itself multifaceted, dynamic and contested.

Katie Young, who had called for Chinese Australians to stand as one at the beginning of the Blainey debate, opened the national conference with another call: "As friends, with one voice, we'll have the strength and capability to overcome obstacles in order to gain equity and identity." In the context of the Blainey debate, Young's call had resonances among Chinese Australian community organisations. But the community organisations heeding that call responded in different ways. While the Blainey debate can be considered the impetus for Chinese Australian community organisations across the nation to cooperate, their efforts to come together at the national conference revealed the great diversity of Chinese Australian communities and thus the difficulty of uniting in the form of a national body or otherwise.

The long wake of the Blainey debate

While Chinese Australian community organisations identified the Blainey debate as the first challenge to multiculturalism since the end of the White Australia policy, their contemporary and later reflections also fitted the debate into a continuum of Australian racism and Sinophobia. The long history of prejudice in Australia does give some explanation for the difficulty of countering Blainey's position. During the debate, many of Blainey's opponents attempted to disprove his arguments by pointing to the relatively low rates of immigration from Asia and highlighting the miniscule percentage of Asian Australians relative to other Australians. Though these counter-examples were rational and true, they did not effectively dispel the evocative and emotive appeals Blainey had made in the first place.

For example, Blainey leaned heavily on the perception that Indochinese refugees and Asian migrants did not integrate well into Australian society. Quoting from letters he received from "average Australians" who were on "the front line of the immigration process", Blainey projected images of Asians as people who "spit everywhere and spread germs", who "dry noodles on clothes lines" and fill the air with "greasy smoke and the smell of goat's meat". While Blainey maintained that multiculturalism's gains should be defended, he nonetheless pandered to class antipathies by characterising multiculturalism as a quixotic ideology for highly educated and wealthy urbanites to indulge in from a distance. Such intellectuals and social elites, he claimed, were detached from multiculturalism's reality. In Blainey's reality, Asian migrants were coming to Australia at too great a rate, from uneducated, poor and culturally unassimilable backgrounds, and were in direct competition with working-class Australians for jobs, homes and welfare. At a time of economic downturn, Blainey sent a message that many Australians could feel to be true.

While Blainey mourned the average Australian as the ultimate victim of multiculturalism, he claimed to be sympathetic to both parties in this quandary. "It is not the fault of the Asians or the fault of the average Australians who feel their jobs are under threat," Blainey suggested, as it was just in each group's nature to be mutually competitive and loathing. Blainey blamed the government for letting immigrants in and allowing the inherent natures of Asian migrants and working Australians to come into conflict in the first place.[91] Blainey posed the predicament as two problems: one, the "natural" opposition of cultures and economic competition; the other, the government's favouritism toward Asian immigration. Here, Blainey tapped into two Australian worries that had deep historical roots.

These were worries that had been mounting over the last decade. In April 1976, the first boat carrying Indochinese refugees landed in

---

91   Richard Goodwin, "'Too Many Asians' Immigration Policy Question", *Warrnambool Standard*, 19 March 1984; Blainey, *Blainey, Eye on Australia*, 26–30; Darian-Smith and Cathcart, *Stirring Australian Speeches*, 294–5.

3 The "Blainey debate"

Darwin with much sensation. Combined with those that followed, it left a lasting impression on the Australian psyche of rickety vessels heavily laden with strange and desperate people landing on the country's northern shores.[92] Some members of Darwin's Chung Wah Society themselves had misgivings about the boats' passengers bringing crime or tarnishing the image of other, already established (and thus more accepted?) Asian Australian communities.[93] Despite the evocative image, very few refugees came to Australia by sea.[94] Of the roughly one million refugees who fled Vietnam, Laos and Cambodia between 1975 and 1982, Australia had taken 60,000–70,000. Of this number, perhaps as few as 2,000 had arrived by boat, yet the image of an armada of refugee boats – an image stoked by racist organisations and sensationalist media reporting – resonated with White Australia's historic fears of "Asian hordes" flooding the country.[95] It was an easy vein for the historian Blainey to tap and thereby enrich the credibility of his arguments.

In reality, most refugees from Vietnam, Cambodia and Laos came by air after authorities processed them in Indonesia, Malaysia or Singapore. This form of offshore refugee processing was developed by the Fraser government as a safer and more efficient means of resettling displaced Indochinese peoples in Australia. According to Fraser, Australia's involvement in the Vietnam War and its international human rights commitments obliged the Australian government to resettle Indochinese refugees. For James Jupp, this commitment to resettlement was the crowning achievement of the Fraser government.[96] Other scholars agreed with Jupp's judgement, but also

---

92 Jupp, *From White Australia to Woomera*, 42; Higgins, *Asylum by Boat*, 20–57.
93 Chin and Giese, *Ernie Chin Interviewed by Diana Giese*; Chin and Giese, *Daryl Chin Interviewed by Diana Giese*.
94 Peter Shergold, "Australian Immigration since 1973", in *The Great Immigration Debate*, eds Frances Milne and Peter Shergold (Sydney: Federation of Ethnic Communities Councils of Australia, 1984), 20; Jamie Mackie, "The Politics of Asian Immigration", in *Asians in Australia: Patterns of Migration and Settlement*, eds James E. Coughlan and Deborah J. McNamara (Melbourne: Macmillan Education Australia, 1997), 26.
95 Mackie, "The Politics of Asian Immigration", 22.
96 Jupp, *From White Australia to Woomera*, 42–3.

noted the utility of the Fraser government's resettlement program as a signal to Asian neighbours that Australia had resolutely put the days of White Australia behind it.[97]

Given this history, it is telling that Blainey charged the Hawke and not the Fraser government for showing "favouritism" toward Asian migration. After all, it had also been the Fraser government that in 1982 abolished all assisted passage migration except for refugees – thereby removing the long-running preference for British migrants and enabling greater non-European migration (at the time predominantly from Vietnam and Lebanon).[98] This irony must not have been lost on the many Chinese Australian community organisations. ACCA, CASA and CFV had been posting updates in their newsletters on developments in immigration law on a near monthly basis for decades. They were well aware of Fraser's commitment to multiculturalism and the boons to Asian migration that had flowed from his government.

While the Blainey debate was ostensibly about the rate of immigration and Australia's ability to absorb peoples and cultures different to those that had come before, it was also, from its outset, about framing progressive ideals like multiculturalism against conservative ideals like "traditional Australian values" and the parties that respectively represented them. Blainey's choice to attack one side of politics and not the other for its multicultural principles had the effect (if not the intent) of politicising an idea that had until then enjoyed bipartisan support.[99] The pretence of the debate was not missed by Australian historians.[100] Of course, Chinese Australian community organisations had always given this assessment.

Chinese Australian community organisations also had cause to doubt the class element of Blainey's argument. According to Blainey,

---

97 Shergold, "Australian Immigration since 1973", 19–21; Cox, *Immigration and Welfare*, 82, 185–6; Deborah J. McNamara and James E. Coughlan, "Future Directions: Asian Immigration into the Twenty-First Century", in *Asians in Australia: Patterns of Migration and Settlement*, eds James E. Coughlan and Deborah J. McNamara (Melbourne: Macmillan Education Australia, 1997), 326; Jayasuriya and Kee, *The Asianisation of Australia?*, 29.
98 Jupp, *From White Australia to Woomera*, 16–17, 45.
99 Bongiorno, *The Eighties*, 66–71.
100 Bongiorno, 253–4.

3 The "Blainey debate"

working-class White Australians would necessarily revile migrants as competitors for jobs or burdens on welfare. But the experiences community organisations had just prior to the debate suggested that Asian xenophobia was just as deeply rooted – if not more so – in the neighbourhoods of middle-class Australia. In late 1982, a petition of 79 residents from Adelaide's lower-middle-class-but-aspirational suburb of Black Forest opposed CASA's plan to establish its community centre in the neighbourhood. The names appearing on the petition were all European with the overwhelming majority suggesting British or Irish origins. Along with concerns about the detrimental effects on the traffic, noise and look of the neighbourhood, the residents complained that CASA's community centre was simply not "of beneficial interest to the community surrounding it". Breaking with Blainey's argument that correlated unemployment with antipathy to Asian migrant communities, the Black Forest residents showed their only economic concern was with the potential detriment to "the resale value of [their] houses".[101] Noise (the sound of a non-English language?), property values and neighbourhood façade are hardly the commonly heard concerns of Australia's working classes.

CAV had a similar experience to CASA. Founding member and past-president Franklin Chew recounted that soon after it was established in 1982, CAV sought premises for its community centre. Initially, CAV chose a site in the outer Melbourne suburb of Ringwood as much of its membership lived close by. However, CAV abandoned this idea after "a lot of objections by the neighbourhood". Local residents complained about the impact of the centre on the surrounding community, and Chew also noted the "very racist attitudes" expressed by some in their opposition. It was enough for CAV to reconsider establishing its community in Ringwood. Chew explained:

> Various excuses were given [by residents] and we would not ... we don't feel that we should start something with good intentions

---

101 Yan and Zhou, *CASA 40th Anniversary Commemorative Magazine: 1971–2011*, 272–4.

in such a terrible conflict. So we want to avoid this conflict and looked [sic] for somewhere where there's less residential homes.

Eventually, CAV found five acres in a mixed commercial-residential zoned part of Wantirna.[102] Contrary to Blainey's claims that it was Asian communities who were unable or unwilling to integrate, CASA and CAV's experiences suggest it was the other way around – White, (aspiring) wealthy Australians created and protected their own ethnic ghettoes and resisted integration with others.

This fitted with the fear interviewees had about Blainey's reputation contributing to the proliferation of racist views into mainstream, middle-class Australia.[103] As one former member of the Australian Chinese Forum described:

> When the others came out, you know, they're just racist. And all the people, they don't support [racism] even if they do feel there were too many Asians here. But when Geoffrey Blainey came on, he was a scholar. He was well spoken. He knew how to pick his words. He built up a case that provided a platform. In a way he was more dangerous than the others because he had this air of legitimacy in expanding his views on the subject. And he provided a platform for all the others to jump on to participate.[104]

In another reflection, a former member of CAV also drew a connection from Blainey's concerns with Indochinese refugees to the populist politicians that stepped into the discursive space Blainey provided:

> The sad thing is, you know, Blainey ... Blainey's commentary ... that he, being a highly regarded [and] respected academic making those comments, allowed subsequent, much more ugly views to

---

102 Franklin Chew and Diana Giese, *Franklin Chew Interviewed by Diana Giese in the Chinese Australian Oral History Partnership Collection*, sound recording, Chinese Australian Oral History Partnership, 2000, TRC 4581, National Library of Australia.
103 Interviewee 3, Anonymous Interview; Interviewee 5, Anonymous Interview; Interviewee 8, Anonymous Interview.
104 Interviewee 4, Anonymous Interview.

3 The "Blainey debate"

be expressed. He kind of legitimised, in a sense, more extreme views and that. He might have, as a result, encouraged Pauline Hanson. The other thing that was very much in the minds of Asian Australians and their organisations around that time was also subsequently John Howard. And Howard was making some quite negative comments about the level of Asian immigration.[105]

It is difficult to ignore the lasting effect of the Blainey debate on how race and migration are treated in Australia – especially for political ends. The National Inquiry into Racial Violence in Australia reported that, following the Blainey debate, an Indochinese community centre in Adelaide had its windows smashed three times between 1986 and 1989. Furthermore, nine Chinese restaurants had been firebombed and a Chinese Australian community leader in Perth was threatened to stay out of politics. There were reports of police assaulting Chinese Australians in Sydney and Melbourne, and dozens of cases of verbal abuse and vandalism across the country. In February 1988, Chinese Australian Peter Tan was beaten to death by two youths when his taxi broke down on the outskirts of Perth. As one explained to police: "I don't like Chinese, to start with, so I belted [the] shit out of him." The inquiry's report advised that in many cases this violence was "directly able to be related to contemporary political debate".[106] That same year, Perth was also the site where John Howard launched his "One Australia" campaign. There he declared that it was multiculturalism – not racism – that had "gone off the rails". Hawke called out Howard's cynical opportunism and accused him of "policy by code word", which Frank Bongiorno reminds us is now more commonly known as "dog-whistling".[107]

Howard's and Blainey's "code words", as well as their appeals to the silent majority, hold more than a passing resemblance. On 22 November 1983 (only a couple of months before his Warrnambool speech), Blainey declared at the National Press Club that "[Asian

---

105 Interviewee 1, Anonymous Interview.
106 Human Rights and Equal Opportunity Commission, *Racist Violence*, 140–2, 157–8, 506–13.
107 Bongiorno, *The Eighties*, 253–4.

immigrants] should come on our terms, through our choosing, and in numbers with which our society can cope". It is eerily close to Howard's 2001 election promise that "we will decide who comes to this country and the circumstances in which they come".[108] The connections continue. Howard was (in)famous for attacking what he called the "black armband view" of history during Australia's 2000s culture wars – a phrase (and idea) that had been coined by Blainey.[109] If dog-whistling made it possible to appeal to xenophobic Australians without offending the sensibilities of others, it also normalised the views of the former and desensitised the latter to prejudice. To Chinese Australian community organisations, the careful and eloquent speech from respected voices like Blainey bore this purpose and effect. Racist ideologies returning to the fore of Australian society by these subtle means was the greatest concern for Chinese Australian community organisations. Putting the Blainey debate into its historical context – looking both forward and backward in time – suggests their fears were well founded.

Australia for all

On 24 January 1986, Blainey warned dignitaries gathered for an "Australia Day luncheon" in Melbourne that multiculturalism was "threatening to disperse this nation into many tribes".[110] His claim that ethnic minorities sought rights without taking on responsibilities was inflected with nostalgia for British monoculturalism and a desire that this be Australia's guiding social principle once more. "This country is too good to ruin," he pleaded.[111] Blainey argued for Australia to be unified through a fundamentally British ethno-cultural identity

---

108 Blainey, *Blainey, Eye on Australia*, 24; John Howard, "John Howard: 'But We Will Decide Who Comes to This Country and the Circumstances in Which They Come', Election Campaign Launch – 2001", Speakola, 28 October 2001, https://speakola.com/political/john-howard-election-campaign-launch-2001.
109 Michelle Rayner, "History Under Siege: Battles over the Past, Part 3, Australia", Text, *Radio National*, 2 April 2008, https://tinyurl.com/298udrm8.
110 Blainey, *Blainey, Eye on Australia*, 60.
111 Blainey, 61.

because he believed only a single, shared identity was strong enough to keep a nation together.

But multiculturalism was vibrant and endemic in Australian society and it was only becoming more so – as shown by the actions of Chinese Australian community organisations during the debate. Proposing that all Australians shared a British ethno-national identity or must assimilate into it was not going to unite Australians the way that multiculturalism could and did. Chinese Australian community organisations were adamant about this during the debate. They championed the idea of civic participation in Australia that was actually closer to the democratic principles and values that the likes of Blainey and others claimed to be defending *from* multiculturalism. It was on this basis that Chinese Australian community organisations built their response to the debate and their protection from the resultant racism: by performing the multiculturalism they wanted to see in Australian society, the political participation and the societal engagement, they would realise that multicultural reality for Australia.

But ironically, many Chinese Australian community organisations failed to achieve Chinese Australian unity because many, like Blainey, predicated unity on an ethnic essentialist identity, too. The inherent differences of Chinese Australian communities meant that they each had different ideas about the meaning, shape and need for Chinese Australian unity. Without the urgency of the Blainey debate providing a good reason to put these differences aside for the sake of (temporary) unity, the differences returned to the fore and stymied the possibility of a nationally representative Chinese Australian body. Because of these differences, again, some Chinese Australian community organisations saw that multiculturalism would provide a more stable basis for unity.

There are also ironies in the lingering legacy of the Blainey debate for Chinese Australian communities. As the first great threat to multiculturalism since its establishment, it was a new and unique moment, just as Blainey provided a unique and eloquent challenge quite different from the actions of racist organisations in the 1970s and 1980s. Yet the debate was also seen as a logical continuity of the past racism known during the White Australia period and, as will be seen in coming chapters, a link to future populist xenophobia and Sinophobia.

It was a legacy that became especially obvious to these community organisations during the Hanson debate some ten years later.

4
The Tiananmen Massacre and the "89ers"

> I can always remember this guy who was the [student] leader. He said – and this might not translate very well [or] mean very much in this culture – and he starts off, "有一天" [yǒu yī tiān]. "There will be a day." And I just about wept as soon as I heard. But then it all blew over. And then the next thing we know, you know, Bob Hawke. And then we've got 40,000 of them. And then the world changed.[1]

The 1989 Tiananmen Massacre changed the composition and character of Chinese Australian communities more profoundly than any other single event since the end of the White Australia policy.[2] As the interviewee above conveys, the massacre elicited powerful emotional responses and had enormous political and social consequences for existing communities. Embodying these changes and consequences

---

1 Interviewee 8, Anonymous Interview.
2 The event is also known as the "Tiananmen Square Massacre" but I have dropped the word "Square" in recognition of the fact that much of the violence and the overwhelming majority of deaths associated with this event occurred in the neighbourhoods and streets beyond the square itself.

was a cohort of some 45,000 Chinese students who would eventually become Chinese Australians after gaining the right to settle in Australia permanently in 1993. Because of the significance of the shifts, it is helpful to think of this period in three broadly defined phases.

The first phase was characterised by the immediate reactions from Chinese Australian community organisations to the massacre as a humanitarian, political and moral crisis. Stirring sorrow, horror, incredulity and indignation, the massacre forced many new and old Chinese Australians to take stock of their relations to their ancestral homeland and the regime that ruled it. But the emotional shock of the event was accompanied by localised concerns, too; namely about the fates of tens of thousands of Chinese students residing in Australia and the imminent arrival of many thousands more. In response, many community organisations scrambled to provide aid or advocacy for these students. Others, however, were more subdued in their public statements regarding the massacre or their actions to support the students residing in Australia. Whether outspoken or reticent, the community organisations' reactions give insight into sentiments percolating at the time.

The second phase was characterised by community responses to the students' campaign to permanently reside in Australia. With their own grief and shock subsiding, the students faced the existential problems of their personal futures. Community organisations offered different levels of support to the students according to their own abilities, resources or relationships with the Australian government. With multiple organisations cooperating and coordinating aid and advocacy initiatives, responses to the Tiananmen crisis and the students' campaign for permanent residency presented a renewed motivation for Chinese Australian community organisations to form a nationally representative body. At another national conference in Melbourne in 1990, community organisation delegates discussed these matters and others.[3] Unfortunately, the conference was as fruitless as the last, partly because the massacre (and responses to it) proved to be a source of division.

---

3   CFV, "Newsletter November 1990" (Chinese Fellowship of Victoria, November 1990), 11, State Library of Victoria.

4 The Tiananmen Massacre and the "89ers"

The third phase was characterised by the social affairs of Chinese Australian communities establishing a new equilibrium after the massacre. The decision to grant permanent residency reflected the fact that the student cohort was enmeshed with Australian society, especially its Chinese Australian communities – into which the students brought new vitality. Bringing not just their youth, working as Mandarin teachers, artists, writers, performers and so on, the students brought a wealth of cultural capital that was highly valued by local community organisations. The students also hold the record as the largest single group of asylum seekers ever to have been accepted into Australia. Some have argued that this fact, along with the students' long campaigns themselves, had a profound influence on Australia's immigration policy.[4] Many Chinese Australian community organisations, who had pre-existing interests in amendments to immigration, keenly followed the succession of policy changes in the first half of the 1990s and their attitude toward the changes often bore direct or implicit references to the student cohort. It was also during the early 1990s that Chinese Australian community organisations normalised relations with the PRC, which were hastened by concurrent floods in Eastern China. With the issue of the students' residency largely resolved, most Chinese Australian communities and organisations sought to renew their relations with the ancestral homeland.

This three-phase analytical model helps to track the consequences of the Tiananmen Massacre for Chinese Australians. These consequences are not just the altered form of Chinese Australian communities, but also the communities' outlooks on social and political issues at home and abroad. This community perspective is an important one because existing scholarship has focused almost entirely on the students themselves.[5] The Tiananmen Massacre compelled many

---

4 Jia Gao, "Seeking Residency from the Courts: The Chinese Experience in the Post-White Australia Era", *Journal of Chinese Overseas* 7, no. 2 (2011), 187–210, https://doi.org/10.1163/179325411X595404; Chongyi Feng, "The Changing Political Identity of the 'Overseas Chinese' in Australia", *Cosmopolitan Civil Societies Journal* 3, no. 1 (2011), 121–38.

5 Jia Gao, "Migrant Transnationality and Its Evolving Nature: A Case Study of Mainland Chinese Migrants in Australia", *Journal of Chinese Overseas* 2, no. 2 (2006), 193–219; Feng, "The Changing Political Identity of the 'Overseas Chinese' in Australia"; Edmund S.K. Fung and Jie Chen, *Changing Perceptions:*

Australian citizens to wrestle with their Chineseness and how the social and transnational space they shared with other Chinese (Australians) had changed.

Background

Though appellations of the group can be fraught, I refer to the cohort of Chinese overseas students – those who, through their legal and political campaigns from 1989 to 1993, came to be permanent residents of Australia – as the "89ers". Jia Gao, who has extensively researched (and himself belongs to) this cohort of roughly 45,000 students, categorises it into further sub-groups. One method of categorisation is by level of education. Around 30 per cent of the 89ers were undergraduate or postgraduate students, with a small number of visiting academics included in this figure. The vast majority of 89ers were students who took part in English short-courses as part of the Australian government's "ELICOS" scheme (English Language Intensive Courses for Overseas Students).[6] Gao also adds differences of socio-economic status to these two sub-groups: typically the "degree group" being higher and the "ELICOS group" lower. Additionally, Gao identifies three broad regional groupings of 89ers. One, the Guangdong group, integrated well with many Chinese Australian communities through a shared use of Cantonese. Another shared language, the Wu dialect, formed the basis for the Shanghai group. People belonging to the Guangdong and Shanghai groups were typically ELICOS students. The Beijing group, which incorporated students from the capital and others from across China who used standard Mandarin to

---

The Attitudes of the PRC Chinese towards Australia and China, 1989–1996, Australia-Asian Papers, No. 78 (Centre for the Study of Australia-Asia Relations, Faculty of Asian and International Studies, Griffith University, 1996).

6   This was a scheme developed by the Australian government to attract foreign fee-paying students from overseas. Jia Gao, "Chinese Students in Australia", in James Jupp, ed., *The Australian People: An Encyclopedia of the Nation, Its People and Their Origins* (Cambridge; New York; Melbourne: Cambridge University Press, 2001), 222–5.

4 The Tiananmen Massacre and the "89ers"

communicate, typically undertook higher degrees and had connections to Australian society through their educational institutions.[7]

Additionally, the 89er cohort was sorted by the Australian government into pre- or post-June 20 sub-groups.[8] 20 June 1989 was the government's deadline for Chinese students to apply for permanent residency on humanitarian grounds and thus the "pre-June 20" 89ers were essentially those students who were already in Australia when the massacre occurred. Those students who arrived in Australia after this date – including those who had already paid their tuition fees prior to 20 June and before March 1992 – could only apply for permanent residency by pursuing refugee status.[9] Although the pre-existing Chinese Australian communities and their representative organisations are the focus of this chapter, it is necessary to be aware of these differences among the 89er cohort as they could influence Chinese Australian community groups' actions and attitudes.

Naming the events of June 1989 is also fraught. Along with "massacre", the terms "incident", "riot", "protests", "crackdown" and "6/4" have been used by scholars, journalists and general populations to describe the killings that occurred specifically on 4 June in Beijing, the broader 1989 protest movement around China, or both.[10] In the immediate aftermath of the massacre, the CCP referred to the event as a "counterrevolutionary rebellion" but over the years downgraded

---

7   Jia Gao, *Chinese Activism of a Different Kind: The Chinese Students' Campaign to Stay in Australia*, Social Sciences in Asia: Volume 37 (Leiden: Brill, 2013), 5–8.
8   Gao identified a third sub-group of "later comers", although it was largely left undifferentiated from the post-June 20 sub-group in community organisations' materials. Gao, *Chinese Activism of a Different Kind*.
9   Over-staying a pre-existing visa was another determinant in the government's treatment of pre-June 20 89ers. Gao, 10–14.
10 See for example: Louisa Lim, *The People's Republic of Amnesia: Tiananmen Revisited* (Cary, US: Oxford University Press, 2014); Jean-Philippe Béja, ed., *The Impact of China's 1989 Tiananmen Massacre* (London: Taylor & Francis, 2010); Philip J. Cunningham, *Tiananmen Moon: Inside the Chinese Student Uprising of 1989* (Lanham: Rowman & Littlefield Publishers, 2014); Dingxin Zhao, *The Power of Tiananmen: State-Society Relations and the 1989 Beijing Student Movement* (Chicago: University of Chicago Press, 2001); Joseph Fewsmith, *China Since Tiananmen: The Politics of Transition* (Cambridge, UK: Cambridge University Press, 2001).

it to a "disturbance".[11] The choice of nomenclature for this event remains sensitive and is often interpreted as a signal of political sympathies.[12] My use of the term "massacre" is primarily informed by the materials created by Chinese Australian community organisations immediately following the event. The early references in Chinese-language materials commonly used terms like "(大)屠殺" ((dà) túshā) and "殘殺" (cánshā), which respectively translate as the noun and verb for *massacre*. While some groups and newspapers included the Tiananmen demonstrators in the entirety of the 1989 protest movements, accurately referring to them as part of a broader "群眾運動" (qúnzhòng yùndòng, mass movement) or "民主運動" (mínzhǔ yùndòng, democracy movement), it was specifically the killing of students and workers on 4 June in and around Tiananmen that elicited the most numerous, immediate and passionate responses from Chinese Australian communities.

The first phase: Bitter grief and furious condemnation

Prime Minister Bob Hawke's speech during the "memorial ceremony for those killed in China", held in the Great Hall of Parliament House on 9 June, was symbolic of the deep emotional reaction that the massacre

---

11 Perry Link, "June Fourth: Memory and Ethics", in *The Impact of China's 1989 Tiananmen Massacre*, ed. Jean-Philippe Béja (London: Taylor & Francis, 2010), 18; Link translates *"fengbo"* as "skirmish", but I have translated it as "disturbance", as Michel Bonnin does. See: Michel Bonnin, "The Chinese Communist Party and 4 June 1989", in *The Impact of China's 1989 Tiananmen Massacre*, ed. Jean-Philippe Béja (London: Taylor & Francis, 2010), 39–40.

12 Mike Ingham, "Twenty Years On: Hong Kong Dissident Documentarians and the Tiananmen Factor", *Studies in Documentary Film* 6, no. 1 (21 May 2012), 82, https://doi.org/10.1386/sdf.6.1.81_1; Bin Xu, "Listening to Thunder in the Silence on Tiananmen: Politics and Ethics of the Memory of the June Fourth Movement", *China Information*, 9 September 2020, https://doi.org/10.1177/0920203X20956561; Yasmin Ibrahim, "Tank Man, Media Memory and Yellow Duck Patrol: Remembering Tiananmen on Social Media", *Digital Journalism* 4, no. 5 (3 July 2016), 582–96, https://doi.org/10.1080/21670811.2015.1063076.

stirred in Australia. His tearful delivery is likely remembered by many Australians thinking back to this time.[13] Hawke departed from his script to describe soldiers "bayonetting" demonstrators and bodies "reduced to pulp" under the tracks of tanks.[14] It was perhaps Hawke's own visceral and frank attempt to come to terms with what had happened in Beijing. His shaking hands and voice betrayed the difficulty of putting raw emotions into words.

Hawke's reaction, like those of many Chinese Australian community organisations, conveyed a feeling that a common humanity had been maimed. For a vast number of Chinese Australians, factors of memory, history and family compounded the trauma. In the days, weeks and months that followed, community newsletters carried a seemingly unending stream of responses to the massacre.

Overwhelmingly, the reactions were highly emotional. The Chinese Fellowship of Victoria (CFV), which had since its founding been a stalwart of the People's Republic, expressed on the front page of its newsletter its "bitter grief and furious condemnation" of what the CCP had committed against its own people. Over the image of five wreaths it declared: "We strongly condemn the brutality of the P.L.A. cold bloodedly murdered our defendless patriotic compatriot [sic]".[15] On 27 May, just a week before the massacre, CFV together with 12 other organisations (including Melbourne's KMT-aligned Chinese Youth Association) had published a statement in support of the protests happening in China. It declared the organisations' shared belief that the protests were patriotic movements, urged the Chinese government not to use force against demonstrators, and underscored the right of the Chinese people to protest for greater democracy, freedom and human rights.[16] They forwarded their statement to allies in Hong Kong and

---

13 Mike Seccombe, "From the Archives: Hawke Weeps As He Tells of Massacre", *Sydney Morning Herald*, 17 May 2019, https://tinyurl.com/26efan8j.
14 Hawke's archived speech had a hand-written warning in the margin: "check against delivery". Compare Robert James Lee Hawke, "Speech by the Prime Minister: Memorial Ceremony for Those Killed in China" (Canberra, 1989), 2; "What Hawke's Ultimate Heart-on-Sleeve Moment Says about How He Engaged with the World", 17 May 2019, https://tinyurl.com/mryv5w9x.
15 沈痛哀悼, 慎怒譴責: CFV, "Newsletter June 1989" (Chinese Fellowship of Victoria, June 1989), State Library of Victoria.

authorities in Mainland China as what they held to be the "common view in the overseas Chinese communities".[17] The subsequent massacre, therefore, was a grievous shock. In CFV's June newsletter, president Patrick Yuen shared his "utmost disbelief" that:

> Some units of the People's Liberation Army savagely murdered thousands of Chinese compatriots in Beijing in [sic] 4th June 1989. This most sickening deed only revealed the total madness of those making such a decision, one that is completely incompatible with the standard of our civilisation today. Our hearts almost stopped with grief. We feel shame that such a disgraceful disaster could occur in our respectable motherland of "Middle Kingdom".[18]

The tone marked a dramatic break from CFV's usual veneration of the PRC. Only in the previous newsletter, Yuen had announced that Melbourne's Chinese Consul-General would be attending a CFV dinner. In fact, Yuen had been urging members to quickly book seats to ensure, "a good chat on all aspects of China" with the Consul-General.[19] Whatever may have been discussed at this dinner in April was not, however, revealed. In the following newsletter, the only evidence that the dinner had happened was a small and blurry photograph.[20] CFV's anguish was likely spiked with disenchantment toward socialism and the CCP, too. Six months on, Yuen saw the democratic freedoms coming to Eastern Europe and wondered where the "Gorbachev of China" might be.[21]

Despite earlier declarations not to involve itself in the political affairs of "any previous homeland", the Australian Chinese Forum

---

16 CFV et al., "墨爾本各界團體聲援 (Melbourne Organisations from All Walks of Life Voice Support)", *Australian Chinese Daily*, 27 May 1989.
17 CFV, "Newsletter June 1989", 5.
18 CFV, 5.
19 CFV, "Newsletter March 1989" (Chinese Fellowship of Victoria, March 1989), 3, State Library of Victoria.
20 CFV, "Newsletter June 1989", 9.
21 CFV, "Newsletter February 1990" (Chinese Fellowship of Victoria, February 1990), 2, State Library of Victoria.

4 The Tiananmen Massacre and the "89ers"

(ACF) in Sydney felt compelled to comment on the crisis. Like CFV, ACF had become worried about the potential danger to protesters in China. In a letter to the Chinese Ambassador on 24 May, ACF president James Lee expressed his hope that the restraint the Chinese government had thus far shown would "avoid any possible bloodshed".[22] His hope was dashed and replaced by exasperation. The day after PLA soldiers killed Chinese civilians, Lee and half a dozen Chinese Australian community organisations from Sydney sent a joint letter to the Consul-General that castigated the Chinese government. Among the signatories were the presidents of the Australian Chinese Community Association (ACCA), which was likely Sydney's largest Chinese Australian community organisation at the time, and the president of the Chinese Youth League (CYL), one of Sydney's oldest associations which, like Victoria's CFV, had been a steadfast supporter of the CCP. Lee "ensured that the Chinese government was left in no doubt at all concerning overseas Chinese reactions to the events":

> We deplore the use of the might of the People's Army against her own people. We note that the international prestige of your country is suffering greatly as a result of the wanton application of force and violence. We also note that the continued chaos in China can only be detrimental to the development and financial restructuring of your country. We urge that the Chinese government to bring [sic] an immediate halt to the violence and bloodshed in your country and to refrain from any further action against those participated [sic] in the quest for a more open and accountable government.[23]

ACF's references to Overseas Chinese, China's falling international prestige and the pointed use of "your country" in the letter reveal some of the massacre's transnational dimensions. As ACF and CFV demonstrate, in the eyes of these Chinese Australian community groups, a line was drawn between the Chinese Communist Party and

---

22 ACF, "ACF Newsletter August 1989", 10.
23 ACF, 10.

the Chinese people. Moreover, these organisations declared that they stood by the latter.

On 5 June, the same day the letter to the Consul-General was sent, Lee sent another letter to Chinese students who were organising a public memorial service. Along with lambasting the "absolutely unforgivable" use of force against peaceful demonstrators, Lee conveyed ACF's "salute and our highest esteem to those who have offered the supreme sacrifices for their cause". It shared its grief and pain with the families and friends who had lost loved ones. When the service was held the following day at the Sydney Town Hall, many ACF members attended alongside overseas students and other Chinese Australians from all walks of life in a sign of solidarity.[24]

Likewise, CFV partook in demonstrations in Melbourne to show its "passionate concern", describing its members' participation as "following the tradition of Dr Sun Yat-sen".[25] The description was a nod toward a century of imagining the Chinese diaspora as a community ready to mobilise for political movements on the Mainland. Unlike in the late 19th and the 20th centuries, however, the overseas sympathies mobilised after Tiananmen were not for a particular political party. Like ACF, CFV called for social change and political freedoms:

> Despite the imminent defeat of the movement in the hands of those [CCP] hardliners, it is clear that it will be a hollow victory. Their credibility with the people has been shattered; those courageous martyrs have NOT died in vain.[26]

Chinese (Australians) seemed to be united in grief. A month after the massacre, 89ers and Chinese Australian sympathisers erected a three-metre "Goddess of Democracy" statue in front of the Chinese embassy in Canberra, and town hall meetings in Melbourne and Sydney attracted hundreds of (Chinese) Australians including politicians and community leaders.[27] The consistency of sentiments across Australia and the world, as well as across political lines and social strata, was striking.

---

24   ACF, 11.
25   CFV, "Newsletter June 1989", 5.
26   CFV, 6.

4 The Tiananmen Massacre and the "89ers"

Condemnation of the CCP's actions seemed near universal among Overseas Chinese communities and the view that the party was out of step with the will of Chinese at home and abroad was widespread.[28] CFV remarked that China had lost the support of "many many good friends" around the world.[29] ACF declared that China was "the land of our forebears and no longer our own".[30] If the massacre had put a line between the party and the people of China, it had also completely alienated many Overseas Chinese communities from the CCP.

Nonetheless, the repudiations of the CCP and the massacre from some Chinese Australian community organisations were less forthright. A notable example was the ACT Chinese Australian Association (ACTCAA), which neither mentioned the massacre in its June 1989 newsletter nor discussed the massacre in any issue that followed.[31] It was only in February 1990 that ACTCAA tangentially referenced the matter when requesting funds or assistance in finding employment for some 200 Chinese students in Canberra.[32] It is unclear how ACTCAA's leadership and its general membership saw the massacre or the plight of the 89ers. ACTCAA's annual report in April 1990 mentioned that "an expression of the Association's views [was made] to the Prime Minister concerning the June 4th incident" at some point, but there was no mention of when or how their views were expressed, nor what they were, nor any elaboration on how their views were established or agreed upon. In the absence of any discussion of the massacre in the period immediately following the event, the attention paid instead to the history of Chinese in Canberra, Dragon Boat racing

---

27 STRB, "六・四屠殺」一周月 澳各大城市紀念活動悼英魂", 星島日報 (Sing Tao Daily), 5 July 1989.
28 For a collection of views from around the world, see: *Overseas Chinese Culture*, 海外風, no. 23 (August 1989).
29 CFV, "Newsletter May 1990" (Chinese Fellowship of Victoria, May 1990), 6, State Library of Victoria.
30 ACF, "ACF Newsletter August 1989", 6.
31 See onward from: ACTCAA, "Newsletter June 1989" (ACT Chinese Australian Association, June 1989), National Library of Australia.
32 ACTCAA, "Newsletter February 1990" (ACT Chinese Australian Association, February 1990), 1, National Library of Australia.

and multicultural activities made it look like ACTCAA was trying hard to avoid taking any position on the issue.

Naturally, responses to the massacre were complicated. One former representative to the Federation of Chinese Associations (FCA) believed that Taiwanese communities in Melbourne and other parts of the country were hesitant about wading into the Tiananmen issue. As a minority within a minority, they felt they could become "too big a target" if they became outspoken.[33] Another interviewee from Brisbane's Cathay Community Association (CCA) remembered more tempered responses to the massacre: shock that the army could commit such an atrocity but also a belief that the demonstrators had goaded authorities by not backing down.[34] As CCA was an organisation founded by people who had experienced the Japanese occupation of Papua New Guinea and relocated to Australia after the country gained independence from Australia in 1975, this member's view might have been informed by experiences with realpolitik.

Community organisations' views were also likely affected by the different social landscapes they occupied. Again, using ACTCAA as an example, a non-confrontational stance toward the PRC may have been prudent due to the Chinese embassy looming large over Canberra's small and youthful Chinese Australian community. In the large, vibrant and well-established communities of Melbourne and Sydney, local consul-generals could not hold as much sway over local community discourses. In Canberra, disapproval of the PRC might have been necessarily subtler. ACTCAA had always had close relations with the Chinese embassy, so when functions with visiting PRC delegations or dignitaries suddenly stopped being announced and organised after June 1989, it signalled the sensitivities surrounding such relationships.[35] Considering that the Tiananmen issue was still so raw and Canberra was a small place, ACTCAA's non-confrontational response could have been a prudent decision.

---

33 Interviewee 2, Anonymous Interview.
34 Interviewee 9, Anonymous Interview.
35 See for example: ACTCAA, "Newsletter August 1988", 7; ACTCAA, "Newsletter April 1989" (ACT Chinese Australian Association, April 1989), 1–3, National Library of Australia.

4 The Tiananmen Massacre and the "89ers"

The response of the Chinese Association of South Australia (CASA) is more difficult to gauge. In its July 1989 newsletter it simply wrote: "The tragic event which took place in Tienanmen [sic] Square in Beijing in June shocked the world."[36] CASA had quickly met with Overseas Chinese students in Adelaide to learn of their plight and how it could help, but its gesture was outshone by the generosity of others. Whereas Chinese Australian community groups in Perth already had "a plane load" of supplies ready to send to China, CASA ultimately explained in its newsletter that it would not raise funds or send medical supplies for the victims of the crackdown because "it had not received confirmation" that its aid could enter the country.[37] In contrast, CFV and another 20 or so Chinese Australian community groups and newspapers held a charity concert at Assembly Hall in Melbourne's CBD. Over $6,000 was raised and put into a trust named "Melbourne Chinese Community Foundation for the Support of Chinese Democratic Movement". Donors received a tax-deductible receipt and an acknowledgement in the Chinese-language press.[38]

The measured responses of organisations like ACTCAA and CASA likely had complex explanations, but it must be noted how much their reactions contrasted with those arising from other Chinese Australian communities. ACF, for example, had always kept foreign politics at arm's length and so they'd neither had a precedent to follow nor anything to gain by censuring China. CFV's condemnation of the CCP broke with its long history of support for the party. After years of encouraging Chinese patriotism, CFV's announcement that it would not be observing the 40th anniversary of the founding of the People's Republic on 1 October 1989 was a grand about-face.[39]

It is clear that ACF and CFV's reactions reflected the high emotions in Chinese Australian communities at the time. A past member of ACF recalled a public meeting held to establish a common position

---

36 CASA, "Newsletter July 1989" (Chinese Association of South Australia, July 1989), 11, National Library of Australia.
37 CASA, 11.
38 CFV, "Newsletter June 1989", 5–6.
39 CFV, "Newsletter September 1989" (Chinese Fellowship of Victoria, September 1989), 2, State Library of Victoria.

on the massacre. Scores of Sydney's Chinese Australian community attended – many of whom had been previously unseen at these types of events. As the former ACF member described, the emotions of these newcomers "really took over the floor", so much so that it was difficult for the meeting to reach a productive conclusion. "The predominant feeling at that meeting," he continued, "was one of emotion. 'How can such a thing happen?' 'How can China do this?'"[40] Because many Chinese Australians were openly criticising the PRC and CCP, many more evidently felt safe to join the chorus of condemnation. Yet the vociferousness of large sections of Chinese Australians also made the silence of others more pronounced. Nonetheless, whether silent or outspoken, these reactions show how communities and organisations were ruminating upon their relation to China and the implications that had for "being Chinese".

The second phase: The 89ers as an issue of Chinese Australian unity and division

In his study into the 89ers' campaign for permanent residency in Australia, Jia Gao included some of the 89ers' perspectives on the existing Chinese Australian community organisations. He noted that in the immediate wake of the massacre, the 89ers could see that the local community organisations shared their pain.[41] Gao nevertheless found that the 89ers did not see local Chinese Australian community groups as worthwhile or effective allies in their campaign for permanent residency. While aware of a community delegation meeting with Hawke just 10 days after the massacre, they felt Chinese Australian community organisations had "limited" influence on government decision-making, because "they did not form a united group". Furthermore, there were those students who felt "some Chinese community leaders were not very supportive of their demand to stay in Australia anyway".[42]

---

40 Interviewee 4, Anonymous Interview.
41 Gao, *Chinese Activism of a Different Kind*, 29–34.
42 Gao, 142–3.

4 The Tiananmen Massacre and the "89ers"

Local Chinese Australian communities were indeed diverse. While some community organisations did not offer much assistance to the 89ers, others did. Gao's explanation of Chinese Australian disunity – as a historical hangover of native place groups who bickered about whether or not to align themselves with the Chinese Communist Party – does not fully capture the complex relations that communities had with each other or with various "homelands".[43] There was much more to the story. Though community organisations took the massacre and the 89ers as a cause for intra-ethnic solidarity and cooperation, deciding how to attend to this cause eventually created division. Indeed, the massacre and the presence of the 89ers were factors that complicated pre-existing desires to unite Chinese Australian communities.

After the failure of the 1986 national conference to create a nationally representative body, community organisations had planned another conference for December 1989 in Canberra to again discuss the potential for forming a united voice of Chinese Australian communities. The uncertainty around national air travel during the 1989 "pilots' dispute", however, impeded the organisations' planning and the conference was delayed until April 1990 and then moved again to 7–9 December in Melbourne.[44] In the interim, the Tiananmen Massacre had occurred and the 89ers had begun their campaign for permanent residency in Australia, combining into a rallying cause for the conference.

The massacre's influence on the conference planning was immediate. The day after the massacre, ACCA hosted a meeting of leaders of Sydney's various community organisations to discuss a united response. From the connections available through the conference planning committee, ACCA's meeting quickly transformed into a nation-wide teleconference of community organisations.[45] The groups agreed that the students already in Australia should have their visas extended and their rights to work expanded. To this end, ACF suggested the organisations should lobby the 89ers' case directly to

---

43 Gao, 142.
44 ACTCAA, "Newsletter November 1989" (ACT Chinese Australian Association, November 1989), 1, National Library of Australia.
45 CASA, "Newsletter July 1989", 11; ACF, "ACF Newsletter August 1989", 11.

Prime Minister Hawke. Using the combined clout of the nation's leading community organisations, the conference planning committee secretary, Chung-Tong Wu, requested a meeting with the Prime Minister and one was scheduled for the morning of 16 June 1989.[46] Community representatives from all states and territories attended, including ACF president James Lee. By Lee's account, Hawke welcomed their suggestions – how much so was revealed later that afternoon.

Just one week after his tearful address, Hawke again spoke to the nation about what Australia could do to aid the Chinese students already in the country. He began by acknowledging that his meeting with representatives of Chinese Australian communities had provided an opportunity "to announce a range of important new Government initiatives" to address the needs of the 89ers. He declared extensions to the 89ers' visas, increased access to welfare, increased hours of work allowed per week and permission to work full time should students' courses finish.[47] The extent of the measures came as a surprise to Hawke's colleagues.[48] Lee, however, recognised that what Hawke said was almost a verbatim match to what the community leaders had jointly suggested that morning. To Lee and ACF, the similitude showed that community organisations had helped "set the tone" for the measures and the national conversation around the 89ers.[49] For a moment, they had the ear of the Prime Minister and used the opportunity for the benefit of the 89ers.

CASA was pleased with this example of the "national interim committee in action". It extolled the committee's rapid, cooperative and successful response. By juxtaposing its positive review of its response with a lengthy description of what a future national body could look like, CASA seemed to suggest that the meeting with the Prime Minister demonstrated how a fully-fledged national body would work – as a means to talk directly to the highest decision-makers in the land.[50]

---

46   CASA, "Newsletter July 1989", 11; ACF, "ACF Newsletter August 1989", 11.
47   Robert James Lee Hawke, "Announcement on Chinese Students" (Parliament House, Canberra, 1989).
48   "Cabinet Papers 1988–89: Bob Hawke Acted Alone in Offering Asylum to Chinese Students", *The Guardian*, 31 December 2014, https://tinyurl.com/muxbhv5r.
49   ACF, "ACF Newsletter August 1989", 11.

4 The Tiananmen Massacre and the "89ers"

The successful meeting was thus a self-evident reason for establishing a national body.

But just as before, the 1990 national conference and prospect of a national body accentuated the organisations' different priorities. There were those who wished to form a national peak body to respond to Chinese Australians' common concerns – such as the Tiananmen Massacre or the 89ers' residency campaign. Others saw a national body as a goal in itself and that the formation of such a body *was* (or at least *should be*) the common concern of Chinese Australians. Compared to its position at the 1986 conference, CASA now seemed to align more with the latter position. An early sign of this was when CASA met with student groups on 13 June 1989. Its newsletter stated that "by mutual agreement it was considered inappropriate" for CASA to speak on behalf of the students at the meeting with the Prime Minister on 16 June.[51] CASA's position seems odd when ACF stated the purpose of the conference call, the subsequent appointment with the Prime Minister, as well as Hawke's own stated understanding of that meeting, was to discuss the massacre, the 89ers and what Australia could do to help.[52] Instead, CASA stressed that the meeting with Hawke was to advise him of "the impending formation of a National Chinese body" and did not mention the 89ers in this regard.[53] ACTCAA was another organisation that focused on the conference and the prospect of a united, peak national body for Chinese Australians. ACTCAA repeatedly advertised the second national conference in its newsletters but barely broached the massacre or the plight of the 89ers, let alone propose them as reasons for forming a national body.[54]

---

50 CASA, "Newsletter July 1989", 8–11.
51 CASA, 11.
52 ACF, "ACF Newsletter August 1989", 11; Hawke, "Announcement on Chinese Students".
53 CASA, "Newsletter July 1989", 11.
54 ACTCAA, "Newsletter August 1989" (ACT Chinese Australian Association, August 1989), 5, National Library of Australia; ACTCAA, "Newsletter November 1989", 1; ACTCAA, "Newsletter April 1990" (ACT Chinese Australian Association, April 1990), 2, National Library of Australia; ACTCAA, "Newsletter October 1990" (ACT Chinese Australian Association, October 1990), 4, National Library of Australia; ACTCAA, "Newsletter

In the Face of Diversity

Perhaps unsurprisingly, when the 200 or so attendees of the second conference met, they still could not agree on the formation of a national body. Instead, a "national network" was proposed. In form, it was much like the interim planning committee had been but with double the number of state and territory representatives: four each for NSW and Victoria and two each for the rest. In their assessment, both CASA and ACTCAA thought this was a great success as Chinese Australians were "progressing towards a unified representation of [their] collective interest Australia-wide".[55] Yet causes for coming together were absent from their reports. Neither the 89ers' plight across the country nor the aftermath of the massacre were mentioned by CASA or ACTCAA as issues for Chinese Australian community organisations to consider collectively.

Conversely, some of those not interested in creating a peak body instead rallied together to help the 89ers. For ACCA, expending time and energy setting up a formal national or even a state-wide body was a distraction from its primary objective of providing welfare services to Chinese Australian communities.[56] Indeed, ACCA's assistance in areas of immigration, housing and social work was exactly what was needed by the 89ers to settle successfully. In 1991, ACCA's social and Grant-in-Aid workers received 1,593 contacts for assistance related to day-to-day living and settlement in Australia. Its community refugee settlement scheme had another 545 clients with many 89ers likely among those figures.[57] Forming a national body thus seemed superfluous to ACCA's core work. The maintenance of communication lines across the country, much like what had existed as the second conference's interim planning committee, was demonstrably enough to respond to a national issue like the plight of the 89ers.

November 1990" (ACT Chinese Australian Association, November 1990), 2–5, National Library of Australia.
55 ACTCAA, "Newsletter December 1990" (ACT Chinese Australian Association, December 1990), 5, 7, National Library of Australia; CASA, "Newsletter December 1990" (Chinese Association of South Australia, December 1990), 3, National Library of Australia.
56 ACCA, "1991 Annual Report" (Australian Chinese Community Association, January 1992), 3, State Library of New South Wales.
57 ACCA, 10–12.

4 The Tiananmen Massacre and the "89ers"

In the years after the meeting with Hawke, there were more instances of community organisations coming together to lend their joint political pressure to the 89ers' cause for permanent residency. Peter Wong, a member of ACCA, ACF and other community groups, became instrumental in galvanising community cooperation for the 89ers' benefit. Having established a Welfare Committee for Chinese Students, Wong convened a meeting on 28 September 1992, bringing together his group and representatives of ACF, ACCA, the Chinese Association for Social Services, the Asian Australian Resource Centre, and the NSW Indochina Chinese Association, as well as other welfare and Christian groups. Together they resolved that the government should uphold Hawke's original promise to allow the 89ers to stay in Australia with the possibility of permanent residency. Wong's resolution was subsequently supported by community leaders in South Australia, Western Australia and Victoria before it was presented to the Immigration Minister, Gerry Hand, in Canberra by a community delegation led by Wong on 15 October.[58] The resolution and delegation exemplified the possibility of intra-ethnic cooperation across communities in Sydney and the nation at large without the guidance of a national peak body.

Support for the 89ers therefore became a matter that distinguished those community organisations that sought practical unity to collectively back the 89ers campaign from those that sought institutionalised unity (in the form of a national body) as an end in itself. Why some organisations supported the 89ers and others did not is another issue, one that was more complex than Gao's explanation that community organisations were simply divided along pro-PRC or pro-ROC lines.

Some interviewees said there were organisations that did not have the resources or expertise to deal with the 89ers' needs, but one pointedly described a leader of a native place association in Sydney who had no sympathy for the 89ers because he approved of the CCP's

---

58 ACF, "ACF Newsletter November 1992" (Australian Chinese Forum, November 1992), 6–7, National Library of Australia; ACCA, "ACCA News November 1992" (Australian Chinese Community Association, November 1992), 4, State Library of New South Wales.

crackdown.[59] Gao himself had pointed to Wellington Lee, the former deputy mayor of Melbourne, as an example of a community leader opposed to the 89ers. Gao quotes Lee describing the 89ers as opportunists "duping" the Australian authorities and "living off the blood of the Tiananmen massacre".[60] Lee's insult recalls the Chinese expression "*rén xuè mántou*" ("human blood bun", 人血饅頭), which was a wry description for those perceived to be benefitting from the deaths of others.[61] A term with similar connotations, "*liù sì xuè kǎ*" (六四血卡) or "June 4 blood visa", was heard in Chinese Australian communities then and is still used today to allude to the perceived expedience of the 89ers' quest for residency.[62]

Diana Giese's interview with Lee suggests his opposition to the 89ers was born more from his Australian patriotism and disdain for the self-interests he alleged were rife in Chinese Australian communities. In his view, the decision to grant residency to the 89ers had to be balanced against the needs of other refugee and ethnic communities. "We've got to be balanced. The Chinese community are stupid, they're not balanced in that way. They just want everything done for the Chinese", he said.[63] Rather than simple pro- or anti-PRC bias, Lee's earlier complaints that the 89ers were "living off the blood" of Tiananmen and "all present the same letters saying they are scared to return [to China]" seem to be marked by more local considerations.[64]

---

59 Interviewee 1, Anonymous Interview; Interviewee 2, Anonymous Interview; Interviewee 7, Anonymous Interview, 7; Interviewee 8, Anonymous Interview.
60 Gao, *Chinese Activism of a Different Kind*, 142–3; "Hawke's Move on Chinese Students", *Canberra Times*, 10 June 1990, https://tinyurl.com/2s73673p.
61 The expression "人血饅頭" literally means "human blood steamed bun", which is a reference to an old practice related to executions. Jason Fang, "我们是'吃了"六四"人血馒头'：澳洲学运领袖忆'六四'", 9 June 2020, https://tinyurl.com/5n6dvz2r; Qi Jiazhen, "吃了六四的人血馒头，我们更应该'不忘记、不恐惧、不冷淡、不堕落，不放弃'！," 独立中文笔会 "Independent Chinese Pen Centre", 30 May 2017, accessed 17 March 2021, https://www.chinesepen.org/blog/archives/85931.
62 Interviewee 5, Anonymous Interview; Sun Baoqiang, "孙宝强：澳洲之耻 文明之殇 (特荐)", August 2016, https://tinyurl.com/yb2xnkcy.
63 Lee and Giese, *Wellington Lee Interviewed by Diana Giese*.

4 The Tiananmen Massacre and the "89ers"

Opposition to the 89ers seeking asylum also came from self-described "real refugees" from Indochina, among whom were many ethnic Chinese. Such Chinese Australians staked their "real" status on their personal escapes from decades of war and revolution. These former refugees turned the term *chuánmín* (船民) or boat person into a badge of authenticity, differentiating themselves from the current *jīngjì nànmín* (經濟難民) or "economic refugees" they deemed the 89ers to be.[65] The terms "boat person" and "economic refugee" carried special negative meanings in the Australian context and so their use by Chinese Australians drew the 89ers issue into domestic political dimensions. These dimensions are rather distinct from the transnational ones suggested by Gao. One former refugee's complaint that the government's acceptance of the 89ers had been a waste of resources when there were plenty of "true refugees" still arriving by boat suggests that resource allocation was also an issue.[66]

Likewise, ethnic affinities, such as they were, did not produce instant support for the 89ers. As a past FCA representative reflected, the various community organisations which constituted FCA came from diverse geographic, political, social and linguistic backgrounds, and there was limited consensus on how to treat the 89ers issue.[67] Nevertheless, an underlying concern for the 89ers lingered. At its own dinner function with Gerry Hand in Melbourne on 12 August 1992, FCA expressed frustration at the government's apparent ambivalence toward the 89ers languishing between temporary and permanent residency.[68] Unsatisfied by the immigration minister's response on the night, FCA mailed him further questions, to which he replied with

---

64 "They Said It", *Canberra Times*, 9 June 1990, https://tinyurl.com/5n869hk6.
65 ICECAV, 印支華人相濟會成立十週年紀念特刊 *Yinzhi Huaren Xiang Ji Hui Chengli Shi Zhounian Jinian Tekan Indo-China Ethnic Chinese Association of Victoria Commemorative Magazine, 1981–1991* (Melbourne: Indo-China Ethnic Chinese Association of Victoria, 1992), 32–3.
66 Tac Tam Lam and Diana Giese, *Tac Tam Lam Interviewed by Diana Giese in the Post-War Chinese Australians Oral History Project*, sound recording, 1995, TRC 3214, National Archives of Australia.
67 Interviewee 2, Anonymous Interview.
68 FCA, "Chinese Community Bulletin September 1992" (Federation of Chinese Associations, September 1992), 3, National Library of Australia.

several pages of answers.[69] As another example, ACF (an "elite" organisation consisting of middle-aged-and-above professionals who had nascent political ambitions and were largely from former British colonies) had a membership that was generationally, culturally and socially distinct from the 89ers. Yet ACF was resolute that Australia had a "moral obligation" to support the 89ers in ways beyond temporary visas.[70] On 16 October 1993, ACF held its own function and quizzed the invited politicians on the 89ers' right to reside in Australia.[71] Two weeks after this function – and two weeks before the government's eventual announcement that the 89ers could stay – ACF was still meeting with other government and community leaders to discuss what they could do to help bring a resolution to the 89ers' situation.[72] With the government's interest appearing to wane between 1991 and 1993, these community organisations kept the issue alive until the 89ers achieved permanent residency.

Community organisations' political support for the 89ers was accompanied by material and practical assistance. On 1 November 1993, the government announced that pre-20 June 89ers could now apply for permanent residency and a number of fraudulent "form-filling services" appeared in the Chinatowns of Sydney, Melbourne and Brisbane hoping to cash in on their students' desperation.[73] Consequently, the Chinese Australian Social Services put together a team of volunteers to help 89ers fill in their applications for free. Thousands of 89ers came forward. Recognising the organisation's community service role, the government subsequently made it a disseminator of official information regarding immigration and settlement processes.[74]

---

69 FCA, "Chinese Community Bulletin October 1992" (Federation of Chinese Associations, October 1992), 1, National Library of Australia.
70 ACF, "ACF Newsletter November 1992", 7.
71 ACF, "ACF Newsletter January 1994" (Australian Chinese Forum, January 1994), 6, State Library of New South Wales.
72 ACF, 7.
73 通天曉 "Know It All", "中國留學生「填表熱」/Migration Rush", 澳洲動態 Education & Living in Australia, 11 March 1994, 32–3, National Library of Australia.

4 The Tiananmen Massacre and the "89ers"

At other times, community organisations provided the moral support the 89ers needed to survive. Over the years, organisations around the country saw life becoming increasingly intolerable for these "people-in-limbo".[75] In his interview with Diana Giese, Peter Wong recalled a suicide note written to the Welfare Committee for Chinese Students by a young woman: "[She] said, 'Look, I'm very poor. I've been sleeping in the park for a few nights. And, despite your help, I know there's no future for me and I will disappear from the face of this earth. But before I do that, I would like to thank you.'"[76] Wong's voice had quavered as he spoke. The care and human connection between people ran both ways.

It is difficult to calibrate the value of the political advocacy and social welfare offered to the 89ers by community organisations, but it clearly exceeds any simply material outcome. To refugees lacking any certain future, feeling adrift in an alien world, gestures of support carried profound human meaning. While, as Gao describes, the 89ers were waging a highly strategic political and legal campaign for residency in Australia, Chinese Australian communities were behaving toward them (for better or worse) as if they were already part of their shared multicultural society. From this perspective, any purely materialist or functionalist explanation of the 89ers' campaign to stay in Australia fails to capture the greater human experience of this period.

The third phase: Finding a new status quo

Although it happened beyond Australia's borders, the Tiananmen Massacre had a profound effect on Australian society. Shifts in

---

74 Interviewee 5, Anonymous Interview; CASS, 華人服務社30週年紀念特刊/ *CASS 30th Anniversary Souvenir Book*, eds Nancy Zhiyuan Liu and Rosie Du (Sydney: Chinese Australian Services Society, 2011), 65.
75 ACF, "ACF Newsletter February 1992" (Australian Chinese Forum, February 1992), 7, National Library of Australia; 通天曉, "中國留學生「填表熱」/Migration Rush", 32–3.
76 Peter Wong and Diana Giese, *Peter Wong Interviewed by Diana Giese for the Chinese Australian Oral History Partnership Collection*, sound recording, 2001, TRC 4701, National Library of Australia.

demography, domestic and foreign policy, and Australian inter- and intra-ethnic relations can be traced back to this period, and Chinese Australian community organisations had to find a new equilibrium for the social and political changes (and eventual continuities) that followed. Reflecting the complexity of this period, Chinese Australian community organisations' actions in this final phase often blended their local, national and international interests together.

There was an immediate impact on the size and shape of Chinese Australian communities. As a result of the 1 November 1993 announcement, 45,000 Chinese students gained permanent residency. To this day, the 89ers remain the largest single group of asylum seekers ever to have been accepted into Australia.[77] The absorption of the 89ers into Australia is recognisable in data censuses. "China" (excluding its special administrative regions and Taiwan) did not rank in the "top 10 countries of birth for the overseas-born population" in Australia's 1986 census. However, two years after the massacre and Hawke's pledge to protect the 89ers, the number of Australia's population born in China jumped to ninth position on this list with 77,882 individuals.[78] Thenceforth, China's position on this list has only risen. In 1996, China was the sixth largest contributor to Australia's overseas-born population (111,009 individuals), fifth in 2001 (142,781 individuals) and third in 2006 (206,591 individuals). According to the 2016 census, 8.3% of Australia's overseas-born population came from China (509,558 individuals).[79] In the 2021 census, China (excluding SARs and Taiwan) maintained third position in the top five countries of birth outside Australia with 549,618 people (behind England with 927,490 and India with 673,352).[80] Business, education and lifestyle opportunities for Chinese emigrants have played a role in growing this section of Australia's population in recent years.[81] Nevertheless, the census data shows that this trend of

---

77 Gao, "Seeking Residency from the Courts", 113.
78 Joanne Simon-Davies and Chris McGann, "Top 10 Countries of Birth for the Overseas-Born Population since 1901", Statistical Snapshot, Research Paper Series, 2018–19 (Canberra: Parliamentary Library, Statistics and Mapping Division, 22 November 2018).
79 Simon-Davies and McGann.
80 ABS, "Cultural diversity: Census", Australian Bureau of Statistics, 28 June 2022, https://tinyurl.com/3e7mx5vk.

4 The Tiananmen Massacre and the "89ers"

Mainland Chinese emigration to Australia began with the 45,000 89ers. As the 89ers settled into Australian society, they laid the foundations for future emigrants from the Chinese mainland to follow by establishing new community, business and cultural networks – whether those emigrants were the 89ers' own family members or fresh waves of students following in their paths.[82]

Census data also reveals the changes in languages other than English spoken in Australia. Here, the impact of the 89ers does not appear immediately significant. The 1986 census recorded 130,769 respondents speaking a Chinese language at home.[83] Five years later, the number of people speaking a Chinese language had almost doubled to 251,256.[84] Obviously, the addition of some 45,000 people born in China and educated in standard Mandarin contributed to this growth. However, as Gao identified earlier, Cantonese- and Wu-speaking sub-groups existed within the 89ers cohort, so presumably not all of them spoke Mandarin at home. Indeed, of the 251,256 people speaking a Chinese language at home in 1991, 155,934 of them spoke Cantonese while only 52,861 spoke Mandarin.[85] This Cantonese-speaking majority was in keeping with the historical demographic character of Chinese Australian communities – comprised of people who themselves or whose ancestors had come from Guangdong, Hong Kong or Cantonese-speaking communities in Southeast Asia. By 1996, the number of Cantonese speakers had grown by 21.9 per cent to 190,104 and then by another 18.5 per cent to 225,307 speakers in 2001.[86] Research from Australia and elsewhere attributes the increase in Hong Kong emigrants to anxieties about Hong Kong's

---

81 Jia Gao, "Rediscovering the New Gold Mountain: Chinese Immigration to Australia Since the Mid-1980s", in *Contemporary Chinese Diasporas*, ed. Min Zhou (Singapore: Springer Singapore, 2017), 209–31, https://tinyurl.com/ynubmz5p.
82 Gao, "Migrant Transnationality and Its Evolving Nature", 199–200; Jupp, *The Australian People*, 185.
83 Ian Castles, "Census 86 – Summary Characteristics of Persons and Dwellings, Australia", Census, Census of Population and Housing, 30 June 1986 (Canberra: Australian Bureau of Statistics, 1989), 14.
84 Ian Castles, "Census Characteristics of Australia: 1991 Census of Population and Housing", Census, 1991 Census of Population and Housing (Canberra: Australian Bureau of Statistics, 1993), 16.
85 Castles, 16.

return to Mainland rule in 1997 (with the massacre being a contributing factor).[87]

Notwithstanding the increase in Cantonese-speaking Chinese Australians, the arrival of the 89ers began the shift from Cantonese to Mandarin as the most spoken Chinese language in Australia. Starting with a 65.2 per cent increase in at-home-speakers of Mandarin from 1991 to 1996, there has been a greater than 50 per cent growth in the number of people speaking Mandarin at home every five years. As a result, Mandarin surpassed Cantonese as the most spoken Chinese language at home some time shortly after 2006. In the 2006 census there were 220,597 Mandarin speakers versus 244,557 Cantonese speakers.[88] By 2011, this had changed to 336,410 and 263,675 respectively.[89] Owing to the pre-existing number of Cantonese speakers in Australia, the arrival of the 89ers did not see Mandarin immediately displace Cantonese. But the 89ers began an upward trend which gained greater momentum as family and more Chinese international students followed them in later decades.

---

86 ABS, "1996 Census Community Profiles: Australia, Basic Community Profile", Census, 1996 Census of Population and Housing (Canberra: Australian Bureau of Statistics, 1997), B.08, https://tinyurl.com/yc5r8xa7; ABS, "2001 Census Community Profile Series: Australia, Basic Community Profile", Census, 2001 Census of Population and Housing (Canberra: Australian Bureau of Statistics, 2002), B.08, https://tinyurl.com/57f949fe.

87 Rogelia Pe-Pua, *Astronaut Families and Parachute Children: The Cycle of Migration between Hong Kong and Australia* (Australian Govt. Pub. Service, 1996); Peter S. Li, "The Rise and Fall of Chinese Immigration to Canada: Newcomers from Hong Kong Special Administrative Region of China and Mainland China, 1980–2000", *International Migration* 43, no. 3 (June 2005), 9–32, https://doi.org/10.1111/j.1468-2435.2005.00324.x; Alvin Y. So and Ludmilla Kwitko, "The New Middle Class and the Democratic Movement in Hong Kong", *Journal of Contemporary Asia* 20, no. 3 (August 1990): 384–98.

88 ABS, "2006 Census Community Profile Series: Australia, Basic Community Profile", Census, 2006 Census of Population and Housing (Canberra: Australian Bureau of Statistics, 2007), B12.

89 ABS, "2011 Census of Population and Housing: Australia, Basic Community Profile", Census, 2011 Census of Population and Housing (Canberra: Australian Bureau of Statistics, 2012), B13a.

4 The Tiananmen Massacre and the "89ers"

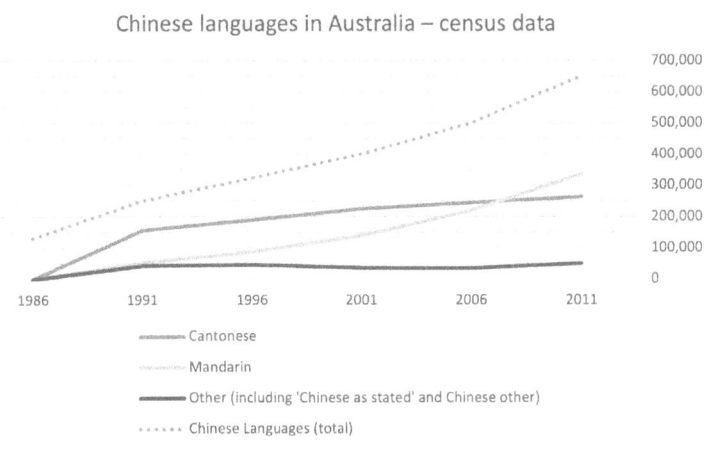

Figure 4.1 Chinese languages spoken at home in Australia. Data compiled from the censuses of the years shown in the graph.

The result of this change is visible in neighbourhoods with large Chinese-speaking populations. Signage in these areas now more commonly uses the Mainland's simplified script rather than the traditional script used by other, typically older, Chinese-speaking communities.[90] This shift is also noticeable in Chinese-language media.[91] The waning of Cantonese in these spaces has caused some concerns among the older communities who fear that Cantonese might disappear completely among younger generations.[92] Beyond the loss of cultural identity, the loss of Cantonese creates problems of equity

90 Xiaofang Yao and Paul Gruba, "A Layered Investigation of Chinese in the Linguistic Landscape: A Case Study of Box Hill, Melbourne", *Australian Review of Applied Linguistics* 43, no. 3 (11 September 2020), 302–36, https://doi.org/10.1075/aral.18049.yao.
91 Wanning Sun et al., "The Chinese-Language Press in Australia: A Preliminary Scoping Study", *Media International Australia* 138, no. 1 (February 2011), 145–6; Wanning Sun, "Chinese Language Media in Australia: Developments, Challenges and Opportunities" (Australia-China Relations Institute, 2016).
92 Lee Lin Chin et al., "Members of Australia's Cantonese Speaking Community Are Concerned about the Declining Number of Second and Third

regarding access to news, information, services and resources that are language-dependent.

Studies suggest that both Cantonese and Mandarin have good language retention rates among second-generation speakers.[93] As the 89ers reached the age and life stability to begin their own families, it is likely many then passed Mandarin on to their children as Cantonese-speaking communities had done before them. However, an additional factor is that many Chinese Australian parents preferred their children learnt Mandarin instead of Cantonese, even if Cantonese was the language spoken by the parents. The reason for this is related to the higher social value many local Chinese Australian communities put on Mandarin – a language all the 89ers were steeped in by virtue of their Mainland origins. CASA's July 1992 newsletter encapsulated the transition to Mandarin exceptionally well: Chinese calligraphy and poetry appeared in simplified, traditional and pinyin (another Mainland-developed transliteration system) scripts; Mandarin classes for children and adults were advertised but not Cantonese; and an "embassy approved" study trip to China was announced. Symbolically, the teacher of CASA's Chinese school contributed an essay in traditional script to this issue, but his student contributed one using the simplified script.[94] Simplified script and Mandarin carried the prestige of being the official language of China and promised a practical benefit for current and future generations who wished to engage with the PRC. It appeared that CASA valued "PRC Chinese" for its potential to imbue a certain "authenticity" into its cultural maintenance practices.

In a similar vein to authenticity, interviewees from various community organisations described the 89er influx as "revitalising". Not only were the 89ers a youthful cohort but, compared to the ethnic

---

Generation Migrants Learning to Speak Cantonese", *SBS News* (SBS TV, 19 May 2018), https://tinyurl.com/3uh37brk.

93 Siew-Mei Wu, "Maintenance of the Chinese Language in Australia", *Australian Review of Applied Linguistics* 18, no. 2 (1 January 1995), 105–36, https://doi.org/10.1075/aral.18.2.06wu; Australian Bureau of Statistics, Population Composition: Languages Spoken in Australia, 24 June 1999), https://tinyurl.com/35pw4np6.

94 CASA, "Newsletter July 1992" (Chinese Association of South Australia, July 1992), National Library of Australia.

4 The Tiananmen Massacre and the "89ers"

Chinese *huayi* (that is, Chinese-descended) "re-migrants" from Malaysia, Singapore and Vietnam, the 89ers also brought with them rich, first-hand knowledge of China.[95] Typically, re-migrants kept to white-collar professions, business or academia. 89ers also went into these fields, leveraging their connections with China and knowledge of its economic systems. But because they were well-versed in the arts and culture of China – its calligraphy, literature, painting, dance, music, philosophy, history and so on – they could also "trade" this cultural capital with the local communities that desired it.[96] In the words of one interviewee from the Chinese Association of Victoria (CAV): "Many of us saw [the 89ers] as a very vibrant, very vital injection into what appeared to be a rather boring Chinese community."[97]

Many Chinese Australian community organisations recruited 89ers to teach the modern, standard Mandarin at their language schools or various Chinese artforms – such as drama, dance, calligraphy, tai chi – at their community centres. Some of these teachers even went on to found their own schools.[98] Community organisations were able to gain additional benefits from the high cultural qualifications of some 89ers. The Chinese Australian Services Society (known later simply as CASS) employed a number of graduates of prestigious acting schools in Beijing and Nanjing to run its dance group and children's drama group and to stage multiple fundraisers for its community projects. These included a variety show held at the Willoughby Town Hall in April 1990 to raise funds for an elderly hostel project, and another the following year to celebrate the Services Society's 10-year anniversary.[99] In this way, the students' cultural capital was being transformed into community prestige and financial benefit.

---

95 Wang, "Among Non-Chinese", 150–3; Jianli Huang, "Conceptualizing Chinese Migration and Chinese Overseas: The Contribution of Wang Gungwu", *Journal of Chinese Overseas* 6, no. 1 (2010), 8–11, https://tinyurl.com/54krjay9; Gao, "Rediscovering the New Gold Mountain", 210.
96 Leo Douw, "Introduction", in *Qiaoxiang Ties: Interdisciplinary Approaches to "Cultural Capitalism" in South China*, eds Leo Douw, Michael R. Godley and Cen Huang (London; New York: Kegan Paul International in association with International Institute for Asian Studies, 1999), 6–10.
97 Interviewee 1, Anonymous Interview.
98 Interviewee 3, Anonymous Interview; Interviewee 5, Anonymous Interview.

As the largest intake of asylum seekers in Australian history, the 89ers also had a profound effect on the immigration policies of Australia. As multiple scholars point out, the Australian government was not enthusiastic about taking on such a large number of Chinese-born individuals in one hit. Chongyi Feng suggests that the 11 amendments to immigration policy between 1989 and 1992 reflected the government's apprehension toward granting permanent residency or refugee status to the 89ers.[100] More pointedly, Gao argues that the 89er episode was the moment when Australians began to "harden their hearts" toward refugees and asylum seekers, henceforth seen in the bipartisan support (and significant public approval) for strict policies toward "irregular immigration" and asylum seekers.[101]

Most Chinese Australian community organisations viewed the government's protracted handling of the 89ers' residency issue with cynicism. In the view of ACCA president Angeline Ouyang, the government's conditional protection of the 89ers had been a gesture to the Australian public that "we are not opening the floodgates to the 'Chinese'".[102] In this respect, there are linkages between the Australian government's responses to the 89ers and the asylum seekers arriving in following decades. The temporary protection visas for refugees that were employed by the Howard government and the governments thereafter have their origin in those temporary protection visas devised by the preceding Hawke and Keating governments.[103]

During this time, Chinese Australian communities followed the changes to immigration policies with keen interest, if not trepidation. The Blainey debate and John Howard's 1988 "One Australia" campaign

---

99 CASS, "Grants Administration and Assessment – Applications – Cultural Exchange Program – Chinese Australian Services Society" (item, Sydney, 20 December 1994), C2943, 64893, National Archives of Australia,; CASS, 華人服務社30週年紀念特刊/CASS 30th Anniversary Souvenir Book, 41; Interviewee 5, Anonymous Interview.
100 Feng, "The Changing Political Identity of the 'Overseas Chinese' in Australia", 125.
101 Gao, "Seeking Residency from the Courts", 113.
102 ACCA, "ACCA News January 1994" (Australian Chinese Community Association, January 1994), 2, State Library of New South Wales.
103 Jupp, *The Australian People*, 190–3.

4 The Tiananmen Massacre and the "89ers"

had already made community organisations sensitive to any changes in immigration policy. As the newsletters of many community organisations showed, this interest seemed to be based on direct relevance to their personal situations – such as changes to the conditions of family reunion or business visas – as much as a concern for broad changes to migrant intakes or attitudes to migrants themselves.[104] After the 89ers' campaign for permanent residency gathered pace in the early 1990s, newsletters show ACTCAA and CASA's interest in immigration laws increased sharply, especially with regard to immigration intake numbers, family reunion visas and business migration programs.[105] In addition to the reservations some community organisations had toward the 89ers' right to stay in Australia, community groups' preoccupation with changes to immigration policy suggest a concern that the 89ers issue might imperil the forms of migration upon which established Chinese Australian communities relied.

During community forums with immigration ministers or their counterparts in opposition, such concern was not dispelled and

---

104 See for example: ACCA, "ACCA News February 1988" (Australian Chinese Community Association, February 1988), 2, State Library of New South Wales; ACCA, "ACCA News March 1988" (Australian Chinese Community Association, March 1988), 5–7, State Library of New South Wales; ACF, "ACF Newsletter June 1988", 3; ACF, "ACF Newsletter March 1989", 4–7, 10–11; CASA, "Newsletter January 1989" (Chinese Association of South Australia, January 1989), 3–7, National Library of Australia; CASA, "Newsletter May 1989" (Chinese Association of South Australia, May 1989), 5–6, National Library of Australia.
105 ACTCAA, "Newsletter April 1990", 2; ACTCAA, "Newsletter August 1991" (ACT Chinese Australian Association, August 1991), 1, National Library of Australia; CASA, "Newsletter September 1990" (Chinese Association of South Australia, September 1990), 11–16, National Library of Australia; CASA, "Newsletter December 1990", 5; CASA, "Newsletter April 1991" (Chinese Association of South Australia, April 1991), 8–9, National Library of Australia; CASA, "Newsletter April 1992" (Chinese Association of South Australia, April 1992), 10, National Library of Australia; CASA, "Newsletter October 1992" (Chinese Association of South Australia, October 1992), 4, National Library of Australia; CASA, "Newsletter September 1993" (Chinese Association of South Australia, September 1993), 12, National Library of Australia.

questions or answers pertaining to the 89ers often overlapped with issues related to broader immigration policy. In one instance, Shadow Immigration Minister Philip Ruddock "fronted critics" at the ACF to explain the Liberal Party's proposed cuts to immigration which, he explained, were due to Australia's economic downturn and consequent lesser ability to absorb new migrants. Although they were asylum seekers, the 89ers were nevertheless drawn into Ruddock's economic explanation for the rate to which Australian society could absorb new members. Ruddock likened the 89ers' temporary protection visas to European "guest worker programs" which allegedly gave one class of people special treatment over other applicants.[106] The Labor Party connected the 89ers to other forms of migration more bluntly. Immigration Minister Gerry Hand explained to FCA that 89ers pursuing marriages of convenience had compelled stricter assessments of partnership visas. "It has proved essential for the Australian Government to be vigilant in ensuring that the goodwill of the Government and the people of Australia is not abused as a result of providing protection to people," he stated.[107]

The politicisation of immigration, asylum seekers and refugees was, of course, not new in Australian history. But it was clear that with the influx of 45,000 Chinese students following in the wake of many more Asian refugees from Indochina – not to mention the recent tumult of the Blainey debate – a popular discomfort about Australia's changing demography was growing. After a period of bipartisan support to make multiculturalism work, many socially conservative politicians took the opportunity to harness populist prejudice for personal gain rather than defuse it for public good.[108] Sensing as much, ACF forecast that the 89ers and immigration would become an election issue in 1993, and by extension Chinese Australian communities would be scrutinised as a migrant or ethnic group seeking special treatment.[109] ACF's prediction was accurate except for being off by a few years. It was in the 1996 election that John Howard won by

---

106 ACF, "ACF Newsletter November 1992", 1.
107 FCA, "Chinese Community Bulletin October 1992", 3.
108 Tavan, *The Long, Slow Death of White Australia*, 220-31.
109 ACF, "ACF Newsletter November 1992", 6-7.

4 The Tiananmen Massacre and the "89ers"

dismissing the "interests of minority groups" and committing to govern "for all of us" in the (White Anglo ethnic) majority. Pauline Hanson then amplified these nationalist imperatives by declaring Australia was being "swamped by Asians".

China's contemporary relationship with Overseas Chinese communities can also be traced to this period. Just as many world leaders mended their relations with Beijing after a short period of sharp condemnation, so too did many Chinese Australian community organisations. In one regard, world leaders and their respective countries had economic imperatives to do so, as did many Chinese Australians. In an increasingly globalised economic system, China's economy was simply too big to be ostracised. But Chinese Australians, like other Overseas Chinese, also had historical and ethno-cultural ties to the land of their forebears. These ties meant that communication with the rulers of that land would eventually need to be reopened if those ties were to be maintained.

For many Chinese Australians, the floods that hit China in 1991 and 1994 were the catalyst for rebuilding connections with the PRC. In 1991, FCA co-ordinated the "China Flood Appeal" and raised $57,000 over a year.[110] In the same year, the Chinese Youth League (CYL) staged a Cantonese opera concert that alone raised $13,881.85.[111] When China experienced deadly floods again in 1994, CYL held another concert to raise more funds.[112] For these floods, ACCA raised over $5,000 and poignantly declared "blood was thicker than water".[113] While ACCA's use of the proverb is obviously a nod to the strength of ethnic ties in the face of natural disaster, it nonetheless appealed to an idea that blood-ties are indelible. This sentiment was more pronounced in CFV's use of the proverb: "That many organisations and individuals gave aid through the Red Cross to the people in disaster-stricken areas

---

110 FCA, "Chinese Community Bulletin August 1992" (Federation of Chinese Associations, August 1992), 1, National Library of Australia.
111 CYL, "CYL News August 1991" (Chinese Youth League, August 1991), 1–4, National Library of Australia.
112 CYL, "CYL News May 1994" (Chinese Youth League, May 1994), 7, National Library of Australia.
113 ACCA, "ACCA News October 1994" (Australian Chinese Community Association, October 1994), 11, State Library of New South Wales.

fully demonstrates the genuine sentiments of patriotism, fraternity and blood being thicker than water for overseas Chinese."[114]

PRC ambassadors and consuls expressed their gratitude to Chinese Australians for their compassion and assistance.[115] In turn, the CCP representatives became conduits for the affection Chinese Australian communities wished to express to their ancestral homeland. In this way, the distinction between China (the place and the people) and the ruling government began to blur once more, undoing the divide created by the massacre and allowing the Communist Party to re-establish authority and esteem. The example of Melbourne's new consul-general Zou Mingrong speaking to the members of CFV at the organisation's 20th anniversary celebration is illustrative in this regard. As it had during meetings with other representatives of the PRC, CFV expressed hopes for the democratisation of China. Consul-General Zou, however, took the stage to make the PRC's position clear:

> Members of the Chinese Fellowship have come forward with your most generous donation, for which, I would like to express, on behalf of the people in disaster areas, our deep appreciation and thanks […] As we are all descendants of the Yellow Emperor, naturally, China's prosperity is our common concern. I am pleased to brief you that at present, China enjoys political and social stability; its economy is developing steadily and continuously, with an annual growth of 6 to 7 per cent; and people are united. They have derived, over the past ten years or so, tangible benefits from China's reform and open-up policy, with their living standard gradually improved.[116]

---

114 支援灾区人民抗灾救灾, 还有不少社团和个人通过红十字会捐助, 充分现了广大侨胞爱国爱民血浓于水的真挚感情: CFV, "Newsletter November 1994" (Chinese Fellowship of Victoria, November 1994), 3, State Library of Victoria.
115 CASA, "Newsletter February 1992" (Chinese Association of South Australia, February 1992), 5–6, National Library of Australia; ACTCAA, "Newsletter August 1991", 2.
116 CFV, "Newsletter October 1991" (Chinese Fellowship of Victoria, October 1991), 2, State Library of Victoria.

4 The Tiananmen Massacre and the "89ers"

Whereas CFV's president Yuen had once believed democracy was "the only road available in this era", Zou here explained that the reunification of the party and the people of China was complete.[117] The PRC would accept aid from the diaspora, but the PRC's chosen path to political stability and economic growth was non-negotiable. For the sake of political and trade relations, Beijing's proviso was accepted by Canberra – as Zou noted, "the Sino-Australian relationship has become normalised since the beginning of the year".[118] Eventually, CFV normalised its relations, too. After shunning the 40th anniversary of the founding of the People's Republic, in October 1994 it celebrated the 45th anniversary with a speech that exalted China's economic growth, common kinship, and Australian–Chinese relations based on commerce, education and cultural exchange.[119] After abruptly turning away from the CCP as a result of the massacre, CFV started coming back around to supporting the PRC once more.

After Tiananmen

Analysing the reactions of Chinese Australian communities and organisations to the Tiananmen Massacre in three phases allows the historically minded to trace the different ramifications that emerged from this event over several years. The initial shock and pain Chinese Australians felt and expressed at news of the massacre on 4 June 1989 is a powerful example of transnational affinities. The reactions of Chinese Australian community organisations at this time showed how the massacre had shaken up imaginings of a global Chinese diaspora – even among those who had strong and long-held connections to the PRC and the CCP, as in the case of CFV. As the initial shock and pain subsided, organisations turned toward responding to the immediate needs of the 89ers, especially their campaign for permanent residency. This saw some community organisations come together to help the 89ers, like ACF and ACCA. Other organisations, as we have seen, were

---

117 CFV, "Newsletter May 1990", 6.
118 CFV, "Newsletter October 1991", 2.
119 CFV, "Newsletter November 1994", 3.

less forthcoming with help for the 89ers. CASA and ACTCAA certainly did not treat the 89ers as a rallying cause for their communities.

Analysing this moment as phases also reveals sites of overlapping issues and consequences. While groups like ACTCAA and CASA seemed apathetic toward the plight of the 89ers or remembering the massacre, they nevertheless enjoyed the apparent cultural authenticity that the 89ers brought into existing Chinese Australian communities. Indeed, all community organisations seemed to benefit in one way or another.

The absorption of these new Chinese Australians also began demographic shifts – of language, migration and generational patterns – that would cascade in decades to come. This was a new stage where the newest Chinese Australians began to leave their mark on existing communities. These shifts went hand in hand with change in the PRC. In contrast to the situation in Eastern Europe and the former Soviet Union, the CCP's power grew through the 1990s. It seemed unaffected by the violence and international outrage toward the massacre. As this reality became more stark, Chinese Australian community organisations, much like the Australian government itself, re-engaged with the PRC. The complexities of that reality continue to be evident in present relations between China, Australia and Chinese Australian communities. Whether due to the trauma of the moment, or the censorship the PRC applies to it, Tiananmen is a topic that remains difficult to discuss.

In the Face of Diversity

Plates

Plates 1–3 These three images depict the rise, fall and rise again of the See Yup Temple in Melbourne. It is one of the oldest Chinese temples in Australia and reflects a mixture of architectual influences from the period of its construction (the present structure, built in 1866, replaced an earlier structure built in 1856). The temple continues to be used as a place of worship and community today.
Plate 1: Lindt, J. W. (ca. 1880-ca. 1890). From the State Library of Victoria.
Plate 2: Collins, J. T. (1963). From the State Library of Victoria.
Plate 3: NAA: A6180, 13/3/75/14. From the collection of the National Archives of Australia.

In the Face of Diversity

Plate 4 On 12 October 1910, Lieutenant Governor Sir Edward Stone laid the foundation stone for the CWA's community hall, where it still stands on James Street in Northbridge, Perth. A mixture of Chinese and Anglo Australian faces can be seen among the offical party, onlookers and labourers. As the decades passed, CWA would change its rules to allow people of mixed heritage to become members. State Library of Western Australia BA1200/168.

Plates

Plate 5 William Fong took this photo in the 1960s, likely part of a Chung Wah Society Chinese new year celebration. Blending the old and new, the procession leaders in traditional garb rode on the back of a truck and marching girls accompanied the lion dancers. Testament to their local presence, Chinese Australian residents had a long tradition of participating in Darwin's parades and festivals. Northern Territory Library.

In the Face of Diversity

Plate 6 With the advent of multiculturalism, parades and festivals became important expressions of community identity and fostered inter-ethnic familiarity. Here, some children are being drawn into the Chinese New Year celebrations. NAA: A6135, K5/3/84/11. From the collection of the National Archives of Australia.

Plates

Plate 7 A member of the Chinese Fellowship of Victoria cooks spring rolls as part of Chinese New Year festivities. Though a traditional food of the Chinese Spring Festival, spring rolls (hence the name) have become a staple for Australian party platters. NAA: A6135, K28/2/86/19. From the collection of the National Archives of Australia.

In the Face of Diversity

Plate 8 As multiculturalism became more accepted as part of Australia's national identity, the country's ethnic diversity was often displayed in its public celebrations, such as in this Australia Day parade in Canberra in 1987. Behind the lion dancers, Kurdish, Ukranian and German (Bavarian) flags and banners can be seen.
NAA: A8746, KN27/2/87/67. From the collection of the National Archives of Australia.

Plates

Plate 9 Professor Geoffrey Blainey had been the inaugural president of the Australia China Council, a body intended to promote understanding and cultural exchanges between the two nations. Here, Blainey and fellow ACC member Tom Keneally flank Mr Liu Gengyin, Vice-President of the Chinese People's Association for Friendship with Foreign Countries, during his visit to Australia in June 1983. Because of Blainey's position on the council, many Chinese Australian community leaders were shocked by his calls to stop Asian immigration during the eponymous 1984 Blainey debate. NAA: A6180, 14/6/83/2. From the collection of the National Archives of Australia.

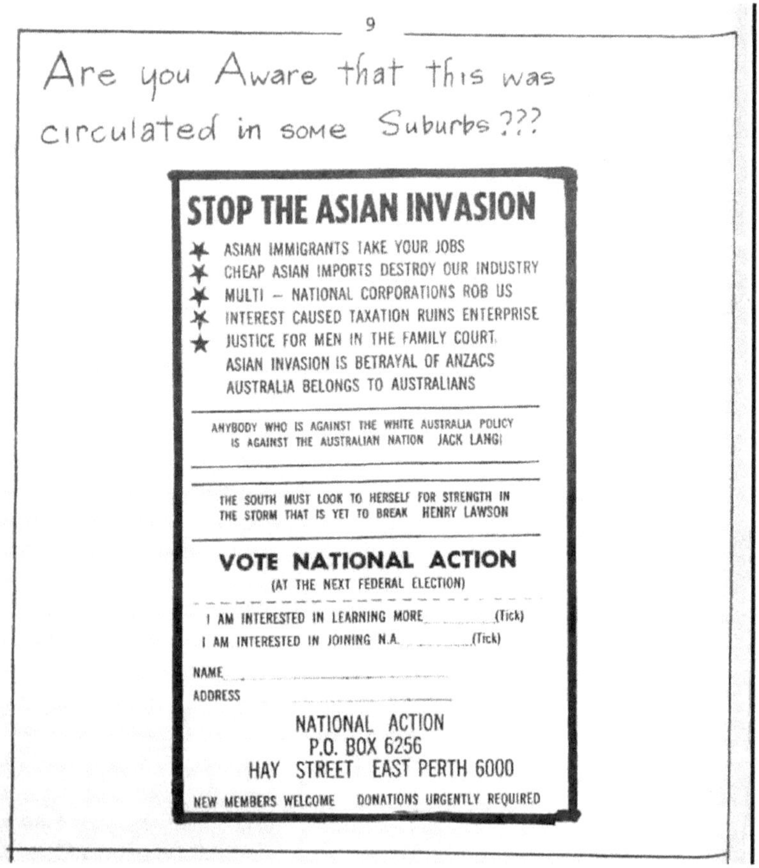

In the Face of Diversity

9

Are you Aware that this was circulated in some Suburbs ???

STOP THE ASIAN INVASION
✱ ASIAN IMMIGRANTS TAKE YOUR JOBS
✱ CHEAP ASIAN IMPORTS DESTROY OUR INDUSTRY
✱ MULTI — NATIONAL CORPORATIONS ROB US
✱ INTEREST CAUSED TAXATION RUINS ENTERPRISE
★ JUSTICE FOR MEN IN THE FAMILY COURT.
ASIAN INVASION IS BETRAYAL OF ANZACS
AUSTRALIA BELONGS TO AUSTRALIANS

ANYBODY WHO IS AGAINST THE WHITE AUSTRALIA POLICY
IS AGAINST THE AUSTRALIAN NATION   JACK LANGI

THE SOUTH MUST LOOK TO HERSELF FOR STRENGTH IN
THE STORM THAT IS YET TO BREAK   HENRY LAWSON

VOTE NATIONAL ACTION
(AT THE NEXT FEDERAL ELECTION)

I AM INTERESTED IN LEARNING MORE _____ (Tick)
I AM INTERESTED IN JOINING N.A. _____ (Tick)
NAME
ADDRESS

NATIONAL ACTION
P.O. BOX 6256
HAY STREET   EAST PERTH 6000
NEW MEMBERS WELCOME   DONATIONS URGENTLY REQUIRED

Plate 10 The Blainey debate stoked anti-Asian sentiments and emboldened racist organisations. National Action was one such racist organisation that increased its activities at the time. Reproduced here is a page from the October 1984 newsletter of the Chung Wah Association, alerting its membership to the circulation of these materials in Perth neighbourhoods. Chung Wah Association, National Library of Australia.

Plates

Plate 11 The Australian Chinese Forum was formed to increase interest and participation in Australian politics among Chinese Australians. One of its methods to do so was to invite politicians and community leaders to speak at its functions. Al Grassby, the commissioner for community relations and "godfather" of Australian multiculturalism, was a recurring guest at such functions. Here he is speaking at ACF's annual dinner in 1986. Australian Chinese Forum, State Library of New South Wales.

In the Face of Diversity

Plate 12 In the wake of the Tiananmen Massacre, Chinese students sought to stay in Australia and eventually became the country's largest single intake of asylum seekers. Here, a student leader adresses a crowd at the Australian National University. The camera crews around him give some indication of the level of public attention given to the students and their plight. ANU Photographic Services; ANU Archives Centre.

Plates

Plate 13 At a rally in front of the PRC Consul General's residence in Toorak, protestors "indignantly condemn" China's government for the "savage massacre" (quoting English and Chinese text shown on the banners). News crews and mounted police add to the gravity of the situation. Anatoly Hue, State Library Victoria.

In the Face of Diversity

Plate 14 Protesters at the rally in Toorak seemed to come from many walks of life, representing both the diversity of Chinese communities and the unanimity in condemning the massacre. Some of the larger banners (translated) read "stop the massacre" and "the world's Chinese people stand united to topple fascist tyranny". Anatoly Hue, State Library Victoria.

Plates

Plates 15-16 Pauline Hanson's politics represented a great threat to multiculturalism in Australia. However, as these two images taken by William Yang in Sydney's Hyde Park show, Hanson's politics also galvanised widespread opposition. The diversity of faces and placards in this crowd shows the capacity of a broad cross-section of Australian communities (not just Chinese or "Asian") to unite for a cause. William Yang, National Library of Australia, PIC/6567/5a; PIC/6567/5b.

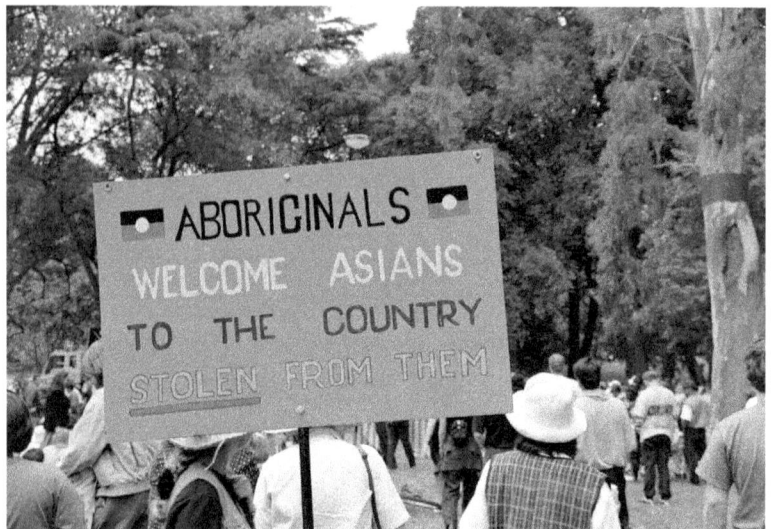

Plate 17 Hanson's divisive politics also had the contrary effect of bringing marginalised communities together. This sign in particular reminds us of the complex relationships between the colonising power, subsequent settler communities and Indigenous sovereignty. Ellis, John B., Anti-racism rally and march through Melbourne, 8th December 1996 (08/12/1996), [UMA-ITE-1999008100276]. University of Melbourne Archives.

Plates

Plate 18 The rise of One Nation prompted many Chinese Australians to take more interest in politics, with some even deciding to run for election. In the 1998 federal election, past president of the Chinese Association of Victoria, Dr Ka-Sing Chua, ran with the Unity Party, a multiculturalist party that formed to oppose Pauline Hanson.

In the Face of Diversity

Plate 19 Around the turn of the century, it was relatively easy to embrace both Chinese and Australian identities. Here, Michael Xu dons a cork hat and raises a glass of beer after becoming an Australian citizen in 1997. Strained political relations between Australia and China would complicate displays of transnational identities in the decades that followed. William Yang, National Library of Australia, PIC/6567/3.

Plates

Plate 20 John Howard had a fraught relationship with Chinese Australian communities during his prime ministership, due largely to the perceptions of his light touch towards Pauline Hanson, his retreat from multiculturalism, and his alignment with Geoffrey Blainey during the 1980s. In November 2001, Howard visited SBS as part of his re-election campaign, where the head of the Cantonese news group, Francis Lee, questioned Howard about his views on multiculturalism. Lee, who was also a co-founder and past president of the Australian Chinese Forum, had previously challenged Howard on his views, even as far back as 1988 when Howard launched his "One Australia" election platform.

In the Face of Diversity

Plate 21 In its early days, the Chinese Youth League was a target of ASIO surveillance for its communist leanings (when the Chinese Communist Party finally won the civil war in 1949, members of CYL paraded through the streets of Sydney with a homemade flag of the People's Republic). Today, CYL is embraced as one of the most vibrant and historically significant community organisations in Sydney. This photo shows CYL members parading through Haymarket as part of Chinese New Year festivities in 2002. [A-01160968]. City of Sydney Archives.

Plates

Plate 22 The "Glory and Dream" concerts planned for the Sydney and Melbourne town halls prompted the formation of the Australian Values Alliance. The concerts were to commemorate the achievements of Chairman Mao Zedong on the 40th anniversary of his death, but AVA opposed them for being pro-PRC propaganda. AVA used this image, which equated Mao with Stalin and Hitler, in its online campaign against the concerts, as well as on posters and placards outside Sydney Town Hall in 2016. Reproduced by permission of Australian Values Alliance.

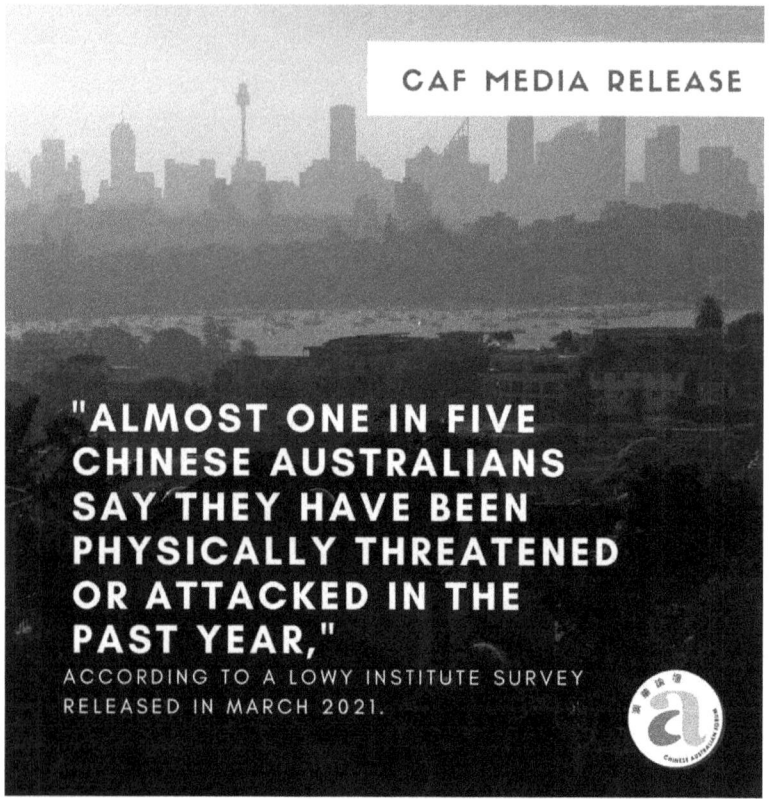

Plate 23 A spike in Sinophobic abuse and assaults followed in the wake of the COVID-19 pandemic; other Australians were also targeted owing to their East Asian appearance. The Chinese Australian Forum stepped forward to spearhead the "Chinese Australian response" to the problem, appealing to the public and politicians for support in multiple ways. Here they are promoting the findings of a 2021 Lowy Institute survey as evidence for the need to oppose Sinophobia. Reproduced by permission of the Chinese Australian Forum.

5
The "Hanson debate"

On 10 September 1996, the representative for Queensland's seat of Oxley, Pauline Hanson, delivered her maiden speech to the Australian Parliament. In it, she described an Australia that was being divided by multiculturalism and "reverse racism". Her once proud country was being exploited by "elites" for their own interests or subject to those of wealthy (Asian) neighbours. She'd had enough, she warned, and so had millions of "ordinary Australians". In line with her claim that Indigenous Australians received too many privileges and welfare benefits due to their race, Hanson claimed that "Asians form ghettoes and do not assimilate". She advocated the abolition of multicultural polices and a return to a racially and culturally homogenous society. She openly called for restrictions on Asian immigration that harkened back to the White Australia policy. Her infamous warning that Australia was "being swamped by Asians" quickly spread into public parlance and became emblematic of her political platform and raw public persona.[1] The speech's effect was immediate and profound. Public debates around national identity, multiculturalism and Asian

---

1 "Appropriation Bill (No. 1) 1996–97 Second Reading" (Canberra: Commonwealth Hansard, 10 September 1996), 3859; Rod Kemp and Marion Stanton, *Speaking for Australia: Parliamentary Speeches That Shaped the Nation* (Melbourne: Allen & Unwin, 2004), 268–72.

immigration began anew, as did increases in anti-Asian rhetoric and instances of racist violence.

On the one hand, the Hanson debate was a singular moment that needs to be analysed on its own terms. In Merle Calvin Ricklefs' view, the Hanson debate was the first time that a racist movement had gained widespread public support *and* established a political base; *and* it was occurring under a government that had its own anti-multicultural and Anglophilic agenda.[2] The attacks on multiculturalism galvanised a great cross-section of Chinese Australian community organisations who responded in their own ways to the debate. The Indo-China Ethnic Chinese Association of Victoria (ICECAV) suddenly became outspoken and compelled members to become politically opinionated and active. The Queensland Chinese Forum (QCF) sought out strategic political and media opportunities to participate in the debate. At a moment when the future of Australia's multiculturalism seemed most imperilled, it was still a moment where multiculturalism was its most vibrant and democratic. At the same time, with the Australian public paying so much attention to multiculturalism, there was an opportunity for certain individuals and organisations to present themselves as figureheads of the "Chinese Australian community".

On the other hand, the Hanson debate is connected to a longer history of xenophobia. Organisations that had responded to Geoffrey Blainey, such as the Chinese Australian Forum (CAF; previously called the Australian Chinese Forum), stepped forth again to respond to Hanson. From one perspective, the Hanson debate was another (White) Australian debate about immigration, race and the "changing face" of the country; one that directly concerned and also engaged Chinese Australians. Different Chinese Australian communities and organisations held diverse views on the Hanson debate and had differing interpretations of it. Chinese Australian opinions from this period offer judgements on how economic, journalistic and political

---

2   M.C. Ricklefs, "The Asian Immigration Controversies of 1984–85, 1988–89 and 1996–97: A Historical Review", in *The Resurgence of Racism: Howard, Hanson and the Race Debate*, eds Christine Winter and Geoffrey G. Gray, Monash Publications in History 24 (Melbourne: Monash University Publishing, 1997), 58–9.

factors culminated in the Hanson debate – as well as on the significance of the Hanson debate for Australia's history and future. They are voices from the frontline of Australian multiculturalism during its greatest crisis that have hitherto not received extensive scholarly attention.

The history of Hanson

Much has been written about the Hanson debate over the years. Journalists and political commentators have analysed and re-analysed Hanson as a populist leader, and scholars of various disciplines have examined "Hansonism" as a collection of socially conservative and economically protectionist policies infused with Anglo-centric, anti-immigration, anti-Indigenous and anti-multicultural ideologies.[3] This same body of work has drawn attention to Prime Minister John Howard's exploitation of the Hanson phenomenon for political advantage, as well as to the momentum contributed by partisan politics and sensationalist media to the spread of the Hanson movement across Australia.

To understand the impact of the Hanson debate on multicultural Australia from 1996 to 1998, it is vital to appreciate the speed with which Hanson jumped from obscurity to founding and leading One Nation, which became the most successful "third party" in the history of Australian politics.[4] Once a member of the Liberal Party, Hanson had been expelled from the party after criticising Aboriginal welfare just prior to the 1996 federal election. To be clear, she had said, among other things, "how can we expect this race to help themselves when governments shower them with money?"[5] Nevertheless, Hanson secured almost a 20 per cent swing in her favour and won the once safe Labor seat of Oxley. Despite being an ex-member of the Liberal Party

---

3   Hage, *White Nation*; Jupp, *From White Australia to Woomera*; Moran, *The Public Life of Australian Multiculturalism*.
4   Jupp, *From White Australia to Woomera*, 138.
5   Kerry-Anne Walsh, *Hoodwinked: How Pauline Hanson Fooled a Nation* (Sydney: Allen & Unwin, 2018), 36–7.

and taking a seat from Labor, neither Labor nor the Liberal–National Party coalition immediately saw her as a serious threat.

After Hanson founded the One Nation Party, it began attracting great support across regional and rural Australia – the National Party's traditional voter base – but this support soon spread to suburban Australia too.[6] One Nation shocked the established parties when it "burst" onto the political scene at the Queensland state election – attracting 22.7 per cent of the total poll and 11 of the 89 seats.[7] Consequently, the major parties, and a large section of the Australian public, grew increasingly nervous about the impact Hanson might have on the 1998 federal election. In hindsight, the Queensland state election was the zenith of One Nation, as its elected parliamentarians proved themselves ineffective and the party highly disorganised. One Nation's success seemed to ride solely on Hanson's personal popularity.[8] Gradually, One Nation's support dwindled with its voter share shrinking again at the 2001 federal election before Hanson was briefly imprisoned for misappropriating party funds in 2003.[9] However, Hanson's meteoric rise (and the real fear that she might not fall) gives some context to the urgency with which Chinese Australian communities and organisations responded to the Hanson debate.

---

6   Iva Ellen Deutchman, "Pauline Hanson and the Rise and Fall of the Radical Right in Australia", *Patterns of Prejudice* 34, no. 1 (January 2000), 51, 60–2; Jupp, *From White Australia to Woomera*, 134–5, 139.
7   Bligh Grant, "Introduction", in *The Rise of Right-Populism: Pauline Hanson's One Nation and Australian Politics*, eds Bligh Grant, Tod Moore and Tony Lynch (Singapore: Springer, 2019), 2; Jupp, *From White Australia to Woomera*, 134.
8   Grant, "Introduction", 2.
9   Jupp, *From White Australia to Woomera*, 137; Walsh, *Hoodwinked*, 118–20; For further discussion on Hanson See: Christine Winter and Geoffrey G. Gray, eds, *The Resurgence of Racism: Howard, Hanson and the Race Debate*, Monash Publications in History 24 (Melbourne: Monash University Publishing, 1997); Tony Abbott et al., eds, *Two Nations: The Causes and Effects of the Rise of the One Nation Party in Australia* (Melbourne: Bookman Press, 1998); Michael Leach, Geoff Stokes and Ian Ward, eds, *The Rise and Fall of One Nation* (Brisbane: University of Queensland Press, 2000); Bligh Grant, Tod Moore and Tony Lynch, eds, *The Rise of Right-Populism: Pauline Hanson's One Nation and Australian Politics* (Singapore: Springer, 2019).

5 The "Hanson debate"

Many writing close to the time of the Hanson debate described it as a moment of degradation in Australian politics. In 1997, Robert Manne wrote that the handling of Hansonism would reveal the "balance" of xenophobic sentiments within Australian conservative politics.[10] Several years later, James Jupp argued that One Nation's lasting political influence was the allure of xenophobia to all parties: it created the myth of one million "Aussie battlers" whose racism could be coddled by the Liberal, Labor and National parties in exchange for votes.[11] Jupp, along with Jon Stratton, interpreted Hansonism's popularity as a sign of the "evolution" of racism in Australian society.[12] In this incarnation, the belief that Eastern and Western cultures were irreconcilably different displaced a more basic belief in White supremacy over other races. The modern argument was that those who grew up in Asian cultures imbibed immutable value systems incompatible with Australia's own. Nevertheless, the logic arrived at the same racist conclusion: large-scale immigration of Asians would degrade Australian society and national identity. Both Jupp and Stratton saw Hanson's claims of unassimability of Asian migrants and the incompatibility of Western and Eastern cultures as extensions of the ideas underpinning Howard's 1988 "One Australia Campaign" and the 1984 "Blainey debate".[13] As will be seen, this line of continuity also ran through the collective memories of Chinese Australian community organisations.

In the years following Hanson's departure from Parliament, other scholars came to see the connections between these moments and others further in the past.[14] Gwenda Tavan argued in *The Long, Slow Death of White Australia* that Hanson's popularity proved White supremacy lived on in the Australian psyche decades after abolishing the last piece of racially discriminatory immigration legislation.[15] In

---

10 Robert Manne, *The Way We Live Now: The Controversies of the Nineties* (Melbourne: Text Publishing, 1998), 100–03.
11 Jupp, *From White Australia to Woomera*, 138–9.
12 Jupp, 129–31; Jon Stratton, *Race Daze: Australia in Identity Crisis* (Pluto Press, 1998), 62–4.
13 Jupp, *From White Australia to Woomera*, 129; Stratton, *Race Daze*, 33–45, 214.
14 Andrew Markus, James Jupp and Peter F. McDonald, *Australia's Immigration Revolution* (Sydney: Allen & Unwin, 2009), 97–9.
15 Tavan, *The Long, Slow Death of White Australia*, 234–9.

Legacies of White Australia, Laksiri Jayasuriya and others further probe the connection between Hanson and Howard's politics and their entanglement with historical racial motifs.[16] This body of scholarship goaded conservative thinkers. In *The White Australia Policy*, Keith Windschuttle on the one hand offered an apologia for Australia's racist past and on the other rejected the connection between Howard and Hanson posited by "by leftist intellectuals". In so doing, he framed rival academics as partisan political actors.[17] In this way, discussion of Hanson and her xenophobic rhetoric entered the "History Wars" of the 2000s. Conservatives charged those who critiqued Australia's racist, colonial history with propagating a "black armband" view, while revisionists countered that those who took a cheerier, apologetic perspective were "White washing" Australia's past.

All this commentary about Hanson demonstrates her ability to capture the popular and political attention of Australia. Indeed, Hanson became something of a celebrity. In 2005, she was a contestant on the popular TV program, *Dancing with the Stars*. After re-election as a senator for Queensland in 2016, she continued to make regular appearances on *Sky News* and Channel 7's *Sunrise*. Despite her prolific public profile and uncritical treatment, Hanson nonetheless complains of being silenced or misrepresented by mainstream media or shadowy political forces.[18] The lamentable irony is that it is actually those people Hanson made a career of vilifying – Aboriginal, Asian, Muslim and African Australians – whose voices are most absent from public discourses.

---

16   Jayasuriya, Walker and Gothard, *Legacies of White Australia*.
17   Keith Windschuttle, *The White Australia Policy* (Sydney: Macleay Press, 2004).
18   Malcolm Farr, "Hanson's 20-Year Conspiracy Theory", *news.com.au*, 14 March 2017, sec. Leaders, https://tinyurl.com/5n977jja; Walsh, *Hoodwinked*, ix–x, 4–6.

5 The "Hanson debate"

The coming of another debate on race and immigration

Like the Blainey debate of the preceding decade, the Hanson debate made a target out of Asian Australians once more. Moreover, Hanson, like Blainey before her, claimed to be the voice for the majority of "ordinary Australians" and railed against the "political correctness" of media, political and intellectual elites who apparently stifled their voices. She based her claims in the everyday experiences she had gleaned as a "mother of four children" and "a businesswoman running a fish and chip shop" and relished in her image as an "unpolished politician" who could relate to the average Australian.[19]

However, the political landscape had changed drastically since the Blainey debate. As Howard himself explained to the Queensland division of the Liberal Party State Council on 22 September 1996:

> One of the great changes that have come over Australia in the last six months is that people do feel free to speak a little more freely and a little more openly about what they feel. In a sense the pall of censorship on certain issues has been lifted.[20]

Race and migration were two of those "certain issues". The new Howard government's mantra of governing for the majority, not "minority interest groups", epitomised how it was ambivalent, even hostile toward multiculturalism and strove to revitalise Australia's "British roots" and "Judeo-Christian values". When Hanson was expelled from the Liberal Party shortly before the 1996 federal election, Howard defended her right to make these and further statements as free speech. He later explained his defence was rooted in his own experience of the politically correct, "McCarthyist smear tactics" used by the previous Keating government.[21] Rather than attempting to quell racist opinions,

---

19 Kemp and Stanton, *Speaking for Australia*, 268–9.
20 John Winston Howard, "Transcript of the Prime Minister the Hon John Howard MP Address to the Queensland Division of the Liberal Party State Council", 1996, 4, https://tinyurl.com/5nfdxb6e.
21 John Howard, *Lazarus Rising: A Personal and Political Autobiography* (Sydney: HarperCollins Publishers, 2013), 302–3.

as the Hawke government had done during the Blainey debate, the Howard government gave them licence – not least due to Howard's own feelings of victimhood.

Conservative politicians' scrutiny of multiculturalism and testing of racial sensibilities reveals the shifting social and political landscape of the day.[22] In the lead-up to the 1996 federal election, the National Party MP for Leichhardt, Bob Burgess, advised the still Opposition Leader John Howard not to court any "ethnic vote" and to trust the "silent majority" of Australians opposing Asian immigration.[23] Bob Katter, then the National Party MP for Kennedy, declared that anyone who opposed critics of Australia's immigration policy were "little slanty-eyed ideologues who persecuted ordinary, average Australians".[24]

Coverage in the *Sing Tao Daily* and responses from the Chinese Australian Forum (CAF) are suggestive of apprehensions building around these matters in Chinese Australian communities ahead of the election. In November 1995, CAF's president, Thiam Ang, wrote to the *Sydney Morning Herald* to say that the "ethnic vote is not unthinking". Many Chinese Australians still remembered Howard's call to limit Asian immigration and were unsure whether his recantation was genuine. Many were familiar with "legalised" racial discrimination in the countries of their birth, he wrote:

> While we can expect anti-Asian remarks by the extremists in our society, similar remarks by political leaders like John Howard in 1988 served only to reopen old wounds.[25]

---

22 Jupp, *From White Australia to Woomera*, 127–9.
23 STRB, "大選關鍵時刻令何華德面紅尷尬 Daxuan Guanjian Shike Ling Hehuade Mianhong Ganga (Critical Election Moment Causes Red Face for Howard)", 星島日報 *(Sing Tao Daily)*, 15 February 1996.
24 STRB, "國家黨侯選人犯眾怒掀巨波 Guojia Dang Hou Xuan Renfan Zhongnu Xian Ju Bo (National Party Candidate Provokes a Huge Wave of Public Anger)", 星島日報 *(Sing Tao Daily)*, 15 February 1996.
25 Thiam Ang, "'Ethnic Vote' Is Not Unthinking", *Sydney Morning Herald*, 16 November 1995, sec. Letters.

5 The "Hanson debate"

This would explain the alarm Ang expressed toward the comments made by Burgess and Katter. Ang wrote to National Party leader Tim Fischer for an explanation of his members' comments and in return received apologies and commitments to multiculturalism.[26] The credibility of such commitments remained to be seen. Ang implored all parties to place unrepentant racist and independent MP Graeme Campbell last in their list of Kalgoorlie electorate preferences for the 1996 election. While Campbell had been expelled from the Labor Party for his racist views, he nonetheless received its preferences along with the Liberals', as each party sought to deny the other the seat. Ang noted the political expediency of Campbell's return to Parliament with disappointment.[27] The moral high ground was surrendered for political advantage, heralding a trend that would become more pronounced over the coming years.

Their racist statements notwithstanding, Burgess, Katter and Campbell each enjoyed large voter swings in their favour at the election. Hanson herself received a 19.3 per cent swing that was described as "astonishing" and, more colourfully, as "kick-arse".[28] Her ability to unseat the incumbent Labor member for Oxley, Les Scott, was attributed partly to the growing public disdain for Keating and partly to the benefit of still appearing on the ballot as the Liberal candidate. However, Hanson's power to tap into latent racism and tensions about political correctness was seen as the critical factor.[29] In the immediate aftermath of the election, Robert Manne noted that media pundits who predicted that these politicians' outspoken racism would damage their election prospects had been proven demonstrably out of touch. In his opinion, the voters of these electorates actually relished in the "politically incorrect brigade".[30] Other politicians might not have had much in common with this "brigade", but they recognised the potential benefits of courting its voter base.

---

26 CAF, "CAF Newsletter May 1996" (Chinese Australian Forum, May 1996), 8, State Library of New South Wales.
27 CAF, 9.
28 John Stone, "Australian for Upset", *National Review* 49, no. 22 (24 November 1997), 32; Walsh, *Hoodwinked*, 39.
29 Stone, "Australian for Upset", 32; Walsh, *Hoodwinked*, 39–40.
30 Manne, *The Way We Live Now*, 67–8.

The expedient handling of Hanson was an issue that defined the debate for Chinese Australian community organisations. CAF cynically observed that a 1996 bipartisan condemnation of racism had come only from fear of losing trade with Asian neighbours and not from any principled standpoint.[31] Rita Wong, the president of the ACT Chinese Australian Association (ACTCAA), wrote to Howard and chastised him for his silence while Chinese Australians were "openly attacked in bigoted and unwarranted statements" by Hanson. While Howard had tried to repair relationships with Asian communities before the election, Wong's words gave warning that such efforts were negated by his failure to rebut Hanson.[32] Indeed, so alike were Howard and Hanson on matters of national identity, multiculturalism and immigration that the Indo-China Ethnic Chinese Association of Victoria (ICECAV) remarked (presumably tongue in cheek) that Hanson's sudden political emergence might have been a political scheme orchestrated by Howard.[33] With Hanson and other openly racist parliamentarians in office, and what appeared to be an apologist for racist behaviour in government, fears of White Australia's return loomed larger than ever. The Chinese Fellowship of Victoria (CFV) and Chinese Association of Victoria (CAV) condemned Hanson and her supporters and urged Chinese Australians to exercise their citizens' rights and responsibilities in protest.[34] "It is time," wrote CAF's Thiam Ang, "that the fair-minded and the rational in our society speak up so that we do not lurch on the road of intolerance."[35]

---

31 Discussed below: CAF, "A Survey of Abuse Suffered by Chinese Australians" (Chinese Australian Forum, 13 November 1996), JV Barry Library, Australian Institute of Criminology.
32 ACTCAA, "Newsletter November 1996" (ACT Chinese Australian Association, November 1996), 3, National Library of Australia.
33 ICECAV, "The Bridge July 1998" (Indo-China Ethnic Chinese Association of Victoria, July 1998), 2–3, State Library of Victoria.
34 CFV, "Newsletter November 1996" (Chinese Fellowship of Victoria, November 1996), 3–5, State Library of Victoria; CAV, ed., *Chinese Association of Victoria: 1982–2007 Silver Jubilee* (Melbourne: Chinese Association of Victoria, 2007), 14–15.
35 Thiam Ang, "The PM and Free Speech", *Sydney Morning Herald*, 27 September 1996, sec. Letters.

5 The "Hanson debate"

The Indo-China Ethnic Chinese Association of Victoria

Alongside its significance in mainstream electoral politics, the Hanson debate marked an important development in Chinese Australian political participation. Specifically, from the mid-1990s, community organisations began to display outspokenness regarding Australian politics and social issues. This is particularly obvious in the case of the Indo-China Ethnic Chinese Association of Victoria. ICECAV's newsletter, *The Bridge*, was filled with long-form articles and brief updates on the Hanson debate that were a mixture of members' own writings, materials from Chinese-language newspapers, and translations of the English-language press. In the brief updates, the editor of *The Bridge* provided commentary that was often sardonic or sarcastic. In the July 1998 issue, one such update related Howard's reluctance to give voting preferences to Labor ahead of One Nation in the upcoming election – for which Hanson described Howard as having "the bearing of a gentleman". The editor was livid:

> From the battering of eyelashes to open teasing and flirtation. This is nothing more than the very meaning of cheap![36]

ICECAV was formed in August 1981 by ethnic Chinese from Vietnam, Cambodia and Laos to provide support and a sense of community to others like themselves who fled these war-torn countries. Though their focus was originally on ethnic Chinese refugees, their scope eventually came to include people of any ethnicity who had been referred to them.[37] These services included access to Cantonese- and Mandarin-speaking social workers, referrals to government services, English classes and other skills workshops like computer classes for women. Recognising its important role in the settlement of refugees, state and federal government agencies provided funding to ICECAV for many of its initiatives.[38] After 15 years it had grown into a sizeable and well-resourced organisation.

---

36 从眉来眼球到公开打情骂俏了。所谓"CHEAP"的意思，莫过于此矣！
   ICECAV, "The Bridge July 1998", 5.
37 ICECAV, *ICECAV Commemorative Magazine*, 11, 19.
38 ICECAV, 19–20, 27.

ICECAV's engagement with the Hanson debate is demonstrative of the way the issue galvanised Chinese Australian communities. In late 1997, the emergence of this "naïve politician" bolstered ICECAV's push to federate Victoria's 30 or so Indochina Chinese organisations.[39] By early 1998, a preliminary committee had been formed, and by February the following year 20 organisations became part of the Federation of Indo-Chinese of Australia (FICA).[40] Through such developments, ICECAV opened the way to greater social and political activism.

In July 1998, nearly two years after Hanson's maiden speech and with the Australian federal election fast approaching, ICECAV canvassed a boycott of any party giving voting preferences to Pauline Hanson's One Nation Party.[41] "All Australia's Chinese should respond to the boycott action. Melbourne should start a petition [for this], too."[42] While its call was directed at Melbourne locals, ICECAV had a readership stretched from Victoria to Queensland.[43] Interestingly, the idea for the boycott had come to ICECAV from Henry Tsang, then Deputy Lord Mayor of Sydney, who warned politicians not to scorn Chinese Australian voters.[44] These signs of co-alignment begin to reveal the degree to which, even in the absence of a formal unification process, different Chinese Australian communities and organisations were coalescing into something resembling a broad-based movement against Hanson and racism.

---

39 ICECAV, "The Bridge November 1997" (Indo-China Ethnic Chinese Association of Victoria, November 1997), 4, State Library of Victoria.
40 ICECAV, "The Bridge January 1998" (Indo-China Ethnic Chinese Association of Victoria, January 1998), 15, State Library of Victoria; ICECAV, "The Bridge February 1999" (Indo-China Ethnic Chinese Association of Victoria, February 1999), 2, State Library of Victoria.
41 Some of the following scholarship on organisations' responses appears in Nathan Daniel Gardner, "All as One to One for All: Comparing Chinese Australian Responses to Racism during the 'Hanson Debate' and COVID-19", *Journal of Chinese Overseas* 18, no. 1 (18 March 2022): 1–30.
42 全澳洲的華人都應該響應杯葛 "一個國家堂" 的行動。墨爾本也應該發起簽名運動: ICECAV, "The Bridge July 1998", 3.
43 ICECAV, "The Bridge May 1998" (Indo-China Ethnic Chinese Association of Victoria, May 1998), 2, State Library of Victoria.
44 ICECAV, "The Bridge July 1998", 3.

5 The "Hanson debate"

Chinese Australian communities and organisations respond to Hanson and the debate

Town hall style meetings or symposia were a common opportunity for cross-community interactions. Melbourne's Museum of Chinese Australian History facilitated an anti-racism symposium on 20 October 1996 that was attended by community representatives from Victoria, New South Wales and South Australia, Chinese Australian politicians, other Asian and non-Asian Australians, and was covered by English- and Chinese-language reporters.[45] The museum had also hosted the "Chinese in Australia and Oceania: International Conference" the month before.[46] The conference gathered representatives of the community, academia and arts over the 21–22 September weekend to discuss the history, culture and social constitution of Chinese in Australia. Among them were five parliamentarians who attended the conference to discuss Chinese Australian political participation: Bill O'Chee, National Party Senator for Queensland; Helen Sham-Ho, Liberal Party, NSW Legislative Council; Hong Lim, Labor Party, Victorian Legislative Council; Bernice Pfitzner, Liberal Party, South Australian Legislative Council; and Richard Lim, National Party, Northern Territory Legislative Council. They took the opportunity to collectively denounce Hanson and racism at the conference once more. A month later, they released another joint statement as "five

---

45 "冷眼" "Lengyan", "婆林·韓琳效應'的省思', 澳洲漢聲雜誌", *Chinese Culture Monthly*, December 1996, 6–8, National Library of Australia.
46 Chinese Museum of Australia, "The Chinese in Australia and Oceania International Conference" (Chinese Museum of Australia, 21 September 1996), Ms Acc17.032, Papers of Diana Giese, File 10, National Library of Australia.

parliamentarians of Chinese descent".[47] Evidently, the importance of responding to the debate eclipsed differences of politics and geography.

Obviously, the cooperation between different communities was mirrored by cooperation between different community organisations. On 14 October 1996, ACCA hosted a meeting with representatives from 17 other Chinese Australian organisations in Sydney to discuss community cooperation in response to Hanson and instances of public racism. One result was a joint letter pushing Howard to show the same kind of strong leadership he had demonstrated during the "gun control debate" months earlier.[48] The Federation of Chinese Associations (FCA) sent a similar letter to the prime minister on 23 September 1996 with signatories representing some 30 community organisations in Victoria.[49] In both cases communities from pro-Taiwan, pro-PRC or anti-communist camps were signatories to the same letter. This degree of cooperation was not insignificant. Groups representing similar Chinese Australian cohorts at the first National Conference of the Australian Chinese Community a decade earlier had clashed.[50]

Showing further solidarity in diversity, Chinese Australian communities and organisations across the country responded to the issue in their own voices, too. Testament to this are the letters sent to the Prime Minister from all over the country. Queensland's Taiwanese community coordinated an open letter with other Taiwanese

---

47 STRB, "独立议员韩珍反移民轮，五华裔议员反应不同 Duli Yiyuan Hanzhen Fan Yimin Lun, Wu Huayi Yiyuan Fanying Butong (Independent MP Hanson Opposes Immigration, Five Chinese-Descendent MPs Respond in the Contrary)", 星岛日报 *(Sing Tao Daily)*, 24 September 1996; STRB, "韩珍反亚言论触发种族紧张，五位华裔议员联合声明谴责 Hanzhen Fan Ya Yanlun Chufa Zhongzu Jinzhang, Wu Wei Huayi Yiyuan Lianhe Shengming Qianze (Hanson's Anti-Asian Remarks Trigger Racial Tension, 5 Chinese-Descendent MPs Announce Joint Statement of Condemnation)", 星岛日报 *(Sing Tao Daily)*, 26 October 1996.

48 Chung to Howard, Letter, "PM 12 November 1996 [Prime Minister's Daily Program; Petitions; Liberal Party Branch Correspondence; Letters of Support; Appointments; Conflicts of Interest; X-Rated Videos; Pauline Hanson; Soldiers Memorial]" (item, Canberra, 1996 1996), M4326, 140, National Archives of Australia.

49 Tchen to Howard, Letter, "PM 12 November 1996".

50 Chow and Giese, *Benjamin Chow Interviewed by Diana Giese*.

5 The "Hanson debate"

organisations around the country urging Howard to tackle Hanson "head-on".[51] Claudia Cream, a lawyer and advisor for three South Australian groups composed primarily of ethnic Chinese refugees, also wrote to Howard about concerns of racial vilification.[52] One dispatch to Howard from the Museum of Chinese Australian History contained "well over one hundred signed letters of concern from the many Chinese Community Organisations all over Australia" – and advised that more were still to come from New South Wales, South Australia and the Australian Capital Territory.[53] Another petition signed by over 500 professionals and graduate students working in a dozen different universities, hospitals, government departments and businesses registered their fears that racism would destroy the multicultural society they had made home. In another, Chinese student associations from each of Victoria's universities collectively expressed regret that the "peaceful and friendly" country in which they had chosen to study had become hostile and dangerous to them and their families. Chinese Australians from all walks of life gave anecdotes of trips where strangers had brought up the racism incited by Hanson, of phone calls from worried relatives overseas inquiring about personal welfare, and of international businesses becoming wary of the Australian market.[54] The rate and variety of responses was impressive. After Hanson's speech in September 1996, Howard received close to 1,000 letters a month for the rest of the year, all condemning Hanson's politics and the racism it stirred.

The great exchange of information and opinions among Chinese Australian communities through newspapers during this period also pointed to broad community engagement with the Hanson debate. Newspapers with circulations in multiple states like the *Sing Tao Daily*, or the local Sydney paper the *United Chinese Times*, provided regular updates on Hanson for readers and a forum through which readers

---

51 Taiwan Institute to Howard, Letter, "PM 12 November 1996".
52 Cream to Howard, Letter, "PM 12 November 1996".
53 Au to Howard, Letter, "PM 12 November 1996".
54 Various to Fischer, Letters, Tim Fischer, "Correspondence – Subject – [Pauline] Hanson", November 1996, M4439, Canberra, National Archives of Australia.

could express their concerns – whether through essays or letters to the editor. Moreover, newspapers advertised anti-Hanson and anti-racism protests and town hall meetings and provided regular updates on community organisations' responses to related issues.[55] This coverage made readers aware of community organisations' actions but also might have encouraged them to become involved themselves. Like the role social media would later play, the Chinese-language press went beyond disseminating community information and toward the function of community building and organising.[56] Protests covered by Chinese-language newspapers and captured on film by William Yang involved crowds of hundreds to thousands of people in Sydney, Melbourne and Brisbane, the participants including young and old, Chinese Australians, Vietnamese Australians, Indigenous Australians, other Asian Australians and White Australians, community leaders, politicians, students, and others coming together under banners reading "Deport Hanson, Not Refugees" and "Asians Welcome, Kick out the Racists".[57]

---

55 STRB, "反種族歧視掀澎湃浪潮，三大城市本周有大集會 Fan Zhongzu Qishi Xian Pengpai Langchao, San Da Chengshi Ben Zhou You Da Jihui (Anti-Racism Actions Surge, Three Big Rallies in Three Big Cities This Week)", 星島日報 (Sing Tao Daily), 18 November 1996; STRB, "紐省18華人社團商對策聯合各族裔抗種族主義 Niu Sheng 18 Huaren Shetuan Shang Duice Lianhe Ge Zu Yi Kang Zhongzu Zhuyi (18 NSW Chinese Community Groups Discuss Countermeasures to Unite All Ethnic Groups in the Fight against Racism)", 星島日報 (Sing Tao Daily), 16 October 1996; UCT, "為反擊種族歧視狂潮各華人群體籌備組堂 Wei Fanji Zhongzuqishi Kuangchao Ge Huaren Qunti Choubei Zu Tang (Chinese Groups Prepare to Organize a Counter-Attack on Racist Frenzy)", 華聯时報 (United Chinese Times), 24 October 1996; UCT, "從種族到文化：反種族歧視大集會 Cong Zhongzu Dao Wenhua: Fan Zhongzu Qishi Da Jihui (From Racism to Culture: Anti-Racial Discrimination Rallies)", 華聯时報 (United Chinese Times), 28 November 1996.
56 Sun et al., "The Chinese-Language Press in Australia", 138–41.
57 UCT, "從種族到文化：反種族歧視大集會 Cong Zhongzu Dao Wenhua: Fan Zhongzu Qishi Da Jihui (From Racism to Culture: Anti-Racial Discrimination Rallies)"; STRB, "反種族歧視掀澎湃浪潮，三大城市本周有大集會 Fan Zhongzu Qishi Xian Pengpai Langchao, San Da Chengshi Ben Zhou You Da Jihui (Anti-Racism Actions Surge, Three Big Rallies in Three

5 The "Hanson debate"

It is important to note the Hanson debate also improved awareness among Chinese Australians about discrimination toward Aboriginal and Torres Strait Islander peoples. In the past, attention to Aboriginal and Torres Strait Islander issues and understanding toward Indigenous cultures had been sporadic but seemingly earnest. In July 1988, Glenn Mar spent $20,000 of his own money to run full-page advertisements that noted the racial violence shown to Chinese and Aboriginal Australians and called for a treaty between non-Indigenous and Indigenous Australians. The ads were significant for appearing in the *Sun-Herald, Sunday Telegraph, Sydney Morning Herald, Australian Financial Review* and *Daily Mirror* as well as for coming in the year of Australia's bicentenary. ACF was deeply impressed:

> ... for many of us, it was the first time that an Australian Chinese publicly dealt with the issue of racism affecting the original inhabitants of this country.[58]

On 10 April 1994, ACF itself claimed to "break virgin territory in multiculturalism" by opening dialogue between Aboriginal and Chinese Australian communities. The event, titled "Indigenous and Ethnic Australians: A Future Together", was televised on SBS with speakers including Irene Moss and Roberta "Bobbi" Sykes recounting the common experiences of racism and violence at the hands of White, mainly Anglo-Australians. It called for Aboriginal and Chinese

---

Big Cities This Week)"; STRB, "華裔韓越裔土著及工會代表慷慨激昂 Huáyì Hányuèyì Tǔzhù Jí Gōnghuì Dàibiǎo Kāngkǎijī'áng (Impassioned Chinese, Korean and Vietnamese Australians, Indigenous and Labor Party Representatives)", 星島日報 *(Sing Tao Daily)*, 25 November 1996; William Yang, *Pauline Hanson Chasing Ethnic Fish and Chips down Oxford St [i.e. Street], Sydney Gay & Lesbian Mardi Gras, 1997*, 1997, Photograph, 1997, 3097590, National Library of Australia; William Yang, *The Era of Hanson, Sydney, 1997*, 1997, Photograph, 1997, 248674, National Library of Australia; William Yang, *The Era of Hanson, Sydney, 1997*, 1997, Photograph, 1997, 1771247, National Library of Australia.

58 ACF, "ACF Newsletter September 1988" (Australian Chinese Forum, September 1988), 9, State Library of New South Wales.

Australians to maintain and share their cultures with each other for the sake of building a stronger Australia.[59]

During the Hanson years, mutual understanding of challenges common to Aboriginal and Chinese Australians spread wider. Amid swirling anti-Aboriginal sentiments of the time, ACCA's newsletter editor, Suling Yap, took umbrage at Peter Sheehan's apologia for British colonisation of Australia: "Anglo-Australia should accept responsibility, fairly and squarely, for its treatment of Indigenous Australians and the disenfranchisement of Indigenous Australians as a result of colonising this country."[60] ACTCAA's Alice Chu framed her bid for the federal seat of Fraser in the 1997 by-election as a direct response to the vilification and abuse of Asian *and* Aboriginal peoples in Hanson's maiden speech. Though she admitted her chances of success were slim, she reconciled that she had to do it for the sake of those people who "have been pushed too far".[61] The sentiments appeared to be reciprocated. A placard held by a contingent of activists at an anti-racism rally through Melbourne on 8 December 1996 read: "Aboriginals welcome Asians to the country that was stolen from them."[62] In addition to the solidarity from other socially marginalised groups, these examples of opposition are indicative of the array of peoples opposing Hanson. The opposition was large and diverse, but still on side. And ultimately this opposition was successful. Australian voters did not return Hanson to Parliament at the following election. In fact, only a single One Nation senator took office.

Sean Scalmer suggests that the movement against Hanson was at its strongest when support for Hanson was also at its peak. As he explains, "only the possibility of [One Nation's] political triumph could stimulate contention on a wide scale".[63] Scalmer does not deal specifically with Chinese Australian responses, but his conclusion seems applicable here.

---

59 ACF, "ACF Newsletter August 1994" (Australian Chinese Forum, August 1994), 264–5, 273, State Library of New South Wales.
60 ACCA, "ACCA News June 1996" (Australian Chinese Community Association, June 1996), 3, State Library of New South Wales.
61 ACTCAA, "Newsletter January 1997" (ACT Chinese Australian Association, January 1997), 3–5, National Library of Australia.
62 John Brant Ellis, "Anti-Racism Rally and March through Melbourne, 8th December 1996" (n.d.), Acquisition: [1999.0081] "Papers of John Brant Ellis", University of Melbourne Archive.

5 The "Hanson debate"

The letters, lobbying, public announcements and protests indicate that the potential for Hanson and One Nation to "triumph" clearly galvanised Chinese Australian communities and organisations.

But Scalmer's point prompts another consideration: with examples of cooperation and sentiments of solidarity abounding, why was there no accompanying suggestion to form a national body as there had been in the context of either the Blainey debate or the 89ers? The urgency of the Hanson debate might have meant there was no time or energy to spare for a project to establish a national body – even though there continued to be national conferences of Chinese Australian communities and organisations.[64] Interim solidarity in the face of adversity might have seemed enough, with each organisation doing its part and adding its voice to the chorus of others. Broad-based opposition to Hanson and One Nation in the wider community could have demonstrated to Chinese Australian community organisations that they did not need a single national body to successfully press their own cause. Perhaps past lessons had convinced community organisations that pursuing a peak body or united voice was superfluous or futile – especially for influential organisations like ACCA and CAF which had historically expressed scepticism toward the idea and were now taking a leading role in coordinating Chinese Australian responses.

The emergence of prominent community leaders and organisations

Solidarity for the sake of immediate action was imperative, but participation in the Hanson debate also augmented the influence and esteem of some individual organisations more than others. These

---

63 Sean Scalmer, "From Contestation to Autonomy: The Staging and Framing of Anti-Hanson Contention", *Australian Journal of Politics and History* 47, no. 2 (1 June 2001), 211.
64 ACTCAA, "Newsletter June 1997" (ACT Chinese Australian Association, June 1997), 5–6, National Library of Australia.

changing fortunes might also inform considerations about the lack of a proposal for a national body.

An important part of the opposition to Hanson was the role played by media-savvy community organisations who became the foremost sources of Chinese Australian commentary and opinions. During the Hanson debate, CAF and the Queensland Chinese Forum (QCF) were two organisations adept at media engagement, allowing them to effectively project their voices and control their narratives in the public sphere.

The Queensland Chinese Forum

QCF is an umbrella organisation for other Chinese Australian community organisations in Queensland. Its first incarnation was as the Council of Chinese Organisations of Queensland, which was formed in response to the Blainey debate in 1984. It was under this name that it took part in the 1986 Australian Chinese national conference.[65] In 1994, the organisation was formally constituted by seven member associations representing the diversity of Queensland's Chinese Australian communities: the Cathay Community Association (made up predominately of ethnic Chinese from Papua New Guinea), the Chinese Business and Professional Association of Queensland, the Chinese Ethnic Broadcasting Association of Queensland, the Chinese Fraternity Association of Queensland, the Hong Kong Business & Professional Association of Queensland, the Queensland Chinese Food and Beverage Hospitality Association, and the Taiwan Friendship Association of Queensland. Like FCA in Victoria, QCF fashioned itself as a "peak" organisation and drew its legitimacy from "the idea that there should be a body representing Chinese Australian interests when important issues affecting the whole community arise".[66] The Hanson debate was taken as one such issue.

Due to its appearance as the representative body for Chinese Australians in Queensland, ABC *Radio National* and SBS sought the

---

65 Young and Yeo, *National Conference of the Australian Chinese Community*, 11.
66 QCF, *Queensland Chinese Forum: Celebrating 20th Anniversary 1994–2014* (Fortitude Valley QLD: Queensland Chinese Forum, 2014), 12–13.

5 The "Hanson debate"

"Chinese Australian perspective" from QCF on matters like immigration policy or critiques of multiculturalism.[67] However, on the Hanson issue, QCF did not always wait to be approached and issued its own media releases. It expressed its outrage when the Liberal Party announced its preference deal with One Nation in the 1998 Queensland state election. Hanson's politics, QCF argued, were inciting racism toward Asian Australians in schoolyards, supermarkets and in the street. QCF explained:

> Since our disgust is total, we have embarked upon a journey to encourage everyone in the Chinese community to withdraw any form of support from the Liberal Party, and to attempt whenever opportune to convince our friends and colleagues in the wider community to do the same.[68]

The *Courier Mail* and *Financial Review* subsequently covered the "influential" Forum's call to shun the Liberals, which in fact preceded those of Tsang and ICECAV coming later in the year.[69] In an indication of their concern, the Liberal parties of other states distanced themselves from the One Nation preference deal that had led to disastrous results for the Liberals in the Queensland election.[70]

CAF also served as a prime source for Chinese Australian opinion during the Hanson debate. Already a veteran of media campaigns since the Blainey debate, CAF was quickly able to turn its experience and expertise to the emergent Hanson issue. On 13 November 1996, CAF called a press conference detailing the rise in racism since Hanson's maiden speech, which featured on the evening news of Channels 9, 10 and SBS, as well as the ABC's *7.30 Report*. Thiam Ang, president

---

67   QCF, "QCF Media Contact Records" (Queensland Chinese Forum, 1998), Member's Personal Papers.
68   QCF, "QCF Press Release: Liberal Party's Shabby Deal on Preferences" (Queensland Chinese Forum, 8 May 1998), Member's Personal Papers.
69   Matthew Franklin, "PM Parries Questions on Hanson", *Courier Mail*, 15 May 1998; Paul Syvret, "Chinese Call for Libs to Be Put Last", *Financial Review*, 13 May 1998.
70   ICECAV, "The Bridge December 1998" (Indo-China Ethnic Chinese Association of Victoria, December 1998), 3–4, State Library of Victoria.

of CAF, also appeared the next day on Channel 9's *Today* to further discuss the rise in racism, including a racially motivated hammer attack on a Chinese Australian woman.[71] Through such appearances, Ang and CAF became the media's first call for Chinese Australian perspectives.

CAF's cardinal position was given some credence by the scale and scope of its initiatives. In late 1996, CAF organised a survey through the *Sing Tao Daily* to gauge pre- and post-Hanson experiences of racism among Chinese Australians. Like its media engagements, this was an action that demonstrated the groups' great organisational capacities and resources. Within a week, the survey had received more than 1,000 responses from the newspaper's readerships in Queensland, New South Wales and Victoria.[72] A total of 345 respondents described experiences of racist abuse before Hanson's maiden speech compared to 710 who did not. After Hanson's speech, these numbers changed to 764 and 291 respectively. Instances of physical and verbal abuse had doubled. Instances of being "spat at" more than tripled.[73] CAF wanted to substantiate what Howard said could not be; that Hanson's maiden speech had encouraged racism in Australian society. The CAF sent the survey results to Prime Minister Howard as proof and requested they be tabled in Parliament. As a highly organised, skilled and well-resourced organisation, CAF reached beyond its membership, gathered the experiences of Chinese Australians and took them to the country's leaders.

The public influence of CAF and QCF can be partly measured by the prime ministers and premiers who, having recognised the organisations as vocal community representatives, attended their functions, gave speeches and fielded their questions over the years.[74]

---

71 CAF, "CAF Newsletter February 1997" (Chinese Australian Forum, February 1997), 6–7, State Library of New South Wales.
72 STRB, "華裔社區勿再緘默, 探行動阻種族主義 Huayi Shequwu Zai Jianmo, Tan Xingdong Zu Zhongzuzhuyi (The Chinese Community Should Not Remain Silent and Explore Ways to Stop Racism)", 星島日報 *(Sing Tao Daily)*, 4 November 1996.
73 CAF, "A Survey of Abuse Suffered by Chinese Australians".
74 Paul Keating, "Tenth Anniversary Dinner of the Australian Chinese Forum", speech, Sydney, 12 October 1995, https://tinyurl.com/2fx8vyru; John Howard, "Address to the Chinese Australian Forum Chinese New Year

5 The "Hanson debate"

While such opportunities allowed for more candid communication of community concerns – and media appearances would benefit the procurement of such opportunities – private lobbying of politicians was not seen by CAF and QCF as particularly effective. As one QCF member put it, the Howard government's support or opposition to Hanson relied on its own calculations of political advantage. The only way to effectively fight Hanson then was to "go public" by way of media engagement.[75] The ability for these organisations to win political redress for Chinese Australian concerns thus depended on the amount of public attention they could muster.

Through initiatives like its survey, media appearances and public forums, CAF made Chinese Australian communities visible and audible. Further, it projected a Chinese Australian voice into sections of Australian society that seldom heard it – just as QCF did. Other organisations were simultaneously taking action. In media engagements and in letters to parliamentarians, the common fear expressed was of racism spreading in Australia and the common demand was for racism (anti-Asian and other forms) to be stopped. An array of individual citizens, community leaders and community organisations were actively airing their concerns. Thus, when CAF or QCF spoke as a "voice" of Chinese Australians in this context, they were not just speaking on behalf of others but as one among many. Nevertheless, these two organisations and their leaders served as a vanguard. From the Hanson debate emerged a trend for certain prominent individuals to become the figureheads of a greater and more diverse movement. After becoming known during the debate, for example, CAF's past-president Ang is still being asked by news services to discuss Hanson decades later.[76]

Dinner", speech, 21 February 1997, Sydney, https://tinyurl.com/3c464tdn; QCF, *Celebrating 20th Anniversary, 1994-2014* (Brisbane: Queensland Chinese Forum, 2014), 12-13.
75 Interviewee 8, Anonymous Interview.
76 Sarah Gerathy, "Pauline Hanson Controversy: Chinese Community Campaigns against 'Racist' Ideas", *ABC News*, 8 July 2016, https://tinyurl.com/3u9azujr; Ian Lloyd Neubauer, "Australia's Pauline Hanson Wins on Anti-Islam Ticket", *Aljazeera*, 11 July 2016, https://tinyurl.com/mv6j832u.

Indeed, the Hanson debate was an opportunity for some Chinese Australian individuals to rise to more significant positions of leadership. Specifically, engagement in the Hanson debate opened a path from community leadership to political leadership. The number of Chinese Australians who retained and took office increased during the Hanson debate.[77] In the cases of Hong Lim, Henry Tsang and Tse-bin Tchen, community leadership led to parliamentary positions. While Lim had been affiliated with Labor since his days at the University of Tasmania, he described his involvement in various Chinese and Indochinese community groups and government liaison roles as what led him to become more directly involved in politics. Lim was already a Victorian legislative councillor before the Hanson debate, but it is clear his star shone brighter because of it:

> This Pauline Hanson business. Suddenly bang! You know, I got faxes, I got phone calls from Chinese leaders: "What are you going to do, Hong?" … they look up to you and you had to do something. So I had to put out a press statement.[78]

Tsang, on the other hand, rose to his position seemingly because of the debate. After years of advocating for Chinese community groups in Sydney, the NSW Labor Party eventually approached him to suggest he "may as well" become a member to better serve those communities.[79] It is more than likely that Tsang's public calls for Chinese Australians to boycott the Liberal Party also appealed to Labor.[80] Tsang became

---

77 Kwok, "Asian Australian Citizenship as a Frame of Enactment in the Parliamentary 'First Speech'"; Jen Tsen Kwok and Juliet Pietsch, "The Political Representation of Asian-Australian Populations since the End of White Australia", *AAPI Nexus: Policy, Practice and Community* 15, no. 1–2 (2017), 109–36.
78 Hong Lim and Diana Giese, *Hong Lim Interviewed by Diana Giese for the Post-War Chinese Australians Oral History Project*, sound recording, 1996, TRC 3502, National Library of Australia.
79 Henry Tsang and Diana Giese, *Henry Tsang Interviewed by Diana Giese for the Post-War Chinese Australians Oral History Project*, sound recording, 1998, TRC 3685, National Library of Australia.
80 Fiona Carruthers, "Leaders Blast Racist Threat", *The Australian*, 28 August 1996; ICECAV, "The Bridge July 1998", 3.

5 The "Hanson debate"

a Labor councillor in the NSW Legislative Assembly in 1999. Tchen's entry into politics deviates somewhat. Over the years, Tchen had organised multiple conferences and seminars to raise political awareness among Chinese Australians. It was at some of FCA's seminars during the Hanson debate that Tchen was asked by attendees why he did not pursue politics himself.[81] As a member of the Liberal Party, Tchen pursued preselection twice before being successfully elected to the Commonwealth Senate in 1998. His efforts in this regard attracted the respect and support of the vocal Hanson critic, Victorian Premier Jeff Kennett.[82]

The Hanson debate even saw the first political party launched by a Chinese Australian. Peter Wong's pro-multiculturalist political group, the Unity Party, encapsulated the mood and political aspirations of many Chinese Australians at the time.[83] It was not an "ethnic unity" party, however, and it was notable for running many Chinese Australian and other ethnic minority candidates. Some of these were long-time community leaders, like Wellington Lee, and others were up and coming, like the young Jason Yat-sen Li. While the party had modest success (and only in urban electorates with high migrant and ethnically diverse populations), it symbolised hope in a time of heightened racism. In Victoria, CFV saw Unity's establishment and opposition to One Nation as the second most important event of 1998 – the re-election of the Coalition government was the first.[84]

Of course, self-interest was also a motivation for community leadership and political pursuits. Though they did not single out any persons, past and present members of community organisations interviewed for this book held strong views that many individuals used the Hanson debate to disguise self-service as community service.[85] Similar sentiments were expressed by Diana Giese's interviewees.

---

81 Interviewee 2, Anonymous Interview.
82 Sandra McKay, "Kennett Promotes Asian Candidate", *The Age*, 7 April 1998; Victoria Gurvich, "Liberal Pick Attacks One Nation", *The Age*, 7 May 1998.
83 Wong and Giese, *Peter Wong Interviewed by Diana Giese*.
84 CFV, "Newsletter February 1999" (Chinese Fellowship of Victoria, February 1999), 4, 7, State Library of Victoria.
85 Interviewee 2, Anonymous Interview; Interviewee 4, Anonymous Interview; Interviewee 8, Anonymous Interview.

Because "everyone wants to be an emperor", Wellington Lee quipped, community interests were sidelined by personal squabbles.[86] One interviewee scoffed at the idea of community altruism and noted community leaders' lust for recognitions like the Order of Australia – apparently for the benefits they were expected to bring to one's personal business. But there was also a degree of acceptance of this; the same interviewee admitted that without any self-interest, no community interests would be served.[87] While it was a crisis for all Chinese Australians, it presented opportunities for some individuals whose personal ambitions could nevertheless benefit others.

In a sense, the Hanson debate produced Chinese Australian community leaders and reified the idea of a "Chinese Australian community". The latter concept seemingly clashes with the image of a gamut of Chinese Australian communities; each responding to the Hanson debate in its own way in a highly participatory and democratic mode. But there is no necessary contradiction. While each organisation might have come to appreciate the value of its own voice, some organisations' voices were more powerful than others. As each organisation – or individual – responded to the Hanson debate according to their own abilities, some were more effective communicators or more successful at reaching wider audiences. These organisations and individuals came to be recognised and treated by the Australian public, its political leaders or its commentariat as speaking for other Chinese Australians.

Organisations projecting themselves as "the voice of the Chinese Australian community" or individuals presenting as "representatives for Chinese Australians" – whether intentionally or not – gave rise to the idea that there indeed was a unitary, distinct and cohesive community. This helps to explain why Howard might have taken his speech at CAF's 1997 Chinese New Year dinner as an opportunity to tell "the Chinese community in Australia, you are an integral part of Australian society. You are welcomed, you are honoured". Howard extended this welcome "on behalf of that modern Australia". Someone should have told him that Chinese Australians did not need to be

---

86   Lee and Giese, *Wellington Lee Interviewed by Diana Giese*.
87   Interviewee 8, Anonymous Interview.

5 The "Hanson debate"

welcomed to a modern country they helped to create (on the unceded lands of Aboriginal and Torres Strait Islanders, no less). Yet this wincing display of pretension should not obscure Howard's address to a unitary "Chinese community in Australia". It is an understandable evocation. Because the Hanson debate was a common concern to all Chinese Australian communities, there undoubtedly was a sense of solidarity that reached across traditional intra-ethnic boundaries. Perhaps something like a national body was not broached at this time because the most prominent voices, those who could have called for something like a lasting community unity, were busy doing their part or saying their piece for a different cause.

Chinese Australian views of the Hanson debate

This view is given credence if we consider that there was no single "Chinese Australian response" to the Hanson debate but rather a variety of responses. These responses were guided by a range of complex understandings of White Australian racism. Giese's interviews with Chinese Australian community leaders commonly contained descriptions of racism, especially anti-Chinese racism, as a perennial problem – though a problem that was shrinking as Australia's peoples embraced multiculturalism and opened up toward their Asian and Pacific neighbours. Even though the Hanson debate heightened anti-Asian sentiments, faith in the decency of the majority of Australians was sustained. Chinese Australian community leaders and organisations cited three common factors for Hanson's rise: social and economic disillusionment, irresponsible media coverage and neglectful or opportunistic politicking.

The majority of Giese's interviewees identified economic insecurity as the leading cause for Hanson's popularity and the accelerated spread of racism during the debate. Chinese Australian politicians seemed especially prone to making this observation. Henry Tsang believed the relative abundance of jobs and more even wealth distribution that had aided the settlement and acceptance of post-war migrants from Southern and Eastern Europe differed from the present economic situation.[88] Along the same lines, Hong Lim, Bernice Pfitzner and

Helen Sham-Ho pointed out that ethnic communities from the Mediterranean and Balkans were hazed by the Anglo ethnic majority before they were socially accepted; they hoped that Asian Australians would eventually be accepted, too. Nevertheless, they noted that their phenotypical differences persistently demarcated them as "Asians" and made them easy targets for disgruntled White Australians.[89] The economic recession of the early nineties had indeed rankled many Australians. Paul Keating's description of it as "the recession we had to have" gave little consolation. These disenfranchised White Australians saw little for themselves in Keating's "Big Picture" social reforms for ethnic minorities. Australia's geopolitical turn toward Asia and away from ethnically familiar Europe made them uneasy.[90] Giese's Chinese Australian interviewees read the March 1996 election as an expression of White Australia's economic and social disillusionment. The observation holds some merit because, at that time, unemployment was at 8.4 per cent nationally (and 9 per cent in Hanson's home state of Queensland).[91]

To Benjamin Chow, president of ACCA from 1997–1999, it was this "mistaken" association of economic downturn with multicultural policy that played into Hanson's popularity. Chow lamented that some Australians remembered a country with full employment as a country without multiculturalism.[92] Federal Human Rights Commissioner and CAF member Irene Moss developed this point further. She did not believe that all who followed Hanson were necessarily racist, though

---

88 Tsang and Giese, *Henry Tsang Interviewed by Diana Giese*.
89 Lim and Giese, *Hong Lim Interviewed by Diana Giese*; Bernice Pfitzner and Diana Giese, *Bernice Pfitzner Interviewed by Diana Giese for the Post-War Chinese Australians Oral History Project*, sound recording, Post-War Chinese Australians Oral History Project, 1996, TRC 3490, National Library of Australia; Helen Sham-Ho and Diana Giese, *Helen Sham-Ho Interviewed by Diana Giese in the Post-War Chinese Australians Oral History Project*, sound recording, Post-War Chinese Australians Oral History Project, 1996, TRC 3514, National Library of Australia.
90 Manne, *The Way We Live Now*, 67–72.
91 ABS, "Labour Force, March Key Estimates", Employment Report, Labour Force (Canberra: Australian Bureau of Statistics, April 1996), https://tinyurl.com/2nk673v4.
92 Chow and Giese, *Benjamin Chow Interviewed by Diana Giese*.

5 The "Hanson debate"

some undoubtedly were. Rather, Moss saw that Hanson's simple socio-economic narrative soothed those who felt the benefits of the modern world had "passed them by".[93]

The argument that economic insecurity was the basis for One Nation support is, however, more nuanced than it seems. Examining data from the 1998 Australian Election Study, Murray Goot and Ian Watson have argued that "where high rates of high unemployment create a political environment conducive to parties of the extreme right, the unemployed themselves were not especially likely to support the One Nation Party". Rather, it was people from various economic backgrounds who were dissatisfied with the major parties and vexed by the cosmopolitan values of the "new class elites", especially values concerning race.[94] The situation is reminiscent of the Blainey debate's fears of racism bubbling out of Australia's poor or working classes, when it was more likely to be the "aspirational" White Australians or "battlers" who vocalised their racial insecurities.

To an organisation like ICECAV, whoever voted for One Nation mattered less than who was being scapegoated "every other time" there was social or economic problems in Australia.[95] Nevertheless, the general impression gained from Giese's interviewees is still in keeping with Goot and Watson's findings. The interviewees who cited economic issues believed that Hanson's supporters might not all be racist per se, but many were misdirecting their fears and frustrations in a racialised way. In the view of James Flowers, member of the Australia China Friendship Society and the Chinese Youth League, multiculturalism was too popularly supported for One Nation to ever dispose of it. Nonetheless, the social and economic changes pushed by Keating (of which multicultural policies were a part) happened too quickly for

---

93 Irene Moss and Diana Giese, *Irene Moss Interviewed by Diana Giese for the Post-War Chinese Australians Oral History Project*, sound recording, Post-War Chinese Australians Oral History Project, 1997, TRC 3612, National Library of Australia.
94 Murray Goot and Ian Watson, "One Nation's Electoral Support: Where Does It Come From, What Makes It Different and How Does It Fit?", *Australian Journal of Politics & History* 47, no. 2 (2001): 191–3, https://tinyurl.com/4ms5zmsf.
95 ICECAV, "The Bridge November 1997", 4.

some (namely Anglo) Australians and led to a disillusionment that was easily tapped by the likes of Hanson and later Howard.[96]

Hanson's ability to use the disillusionment of White voters was augmented by the media's appetite for sensationalism, which was immediately whetted by Hanson's maiden speech. Alan Ramsey, a senior journalist in the press gallery, stated that no parliamentary first speech by a backbench politician had ever "created more continuing controversy – or struck a more responsive public chord".[97] Of course, Hanson's supporters and detractors interpellated her maiden speech for their own political ends. For Scalmer, it is not the content of the speech that was itself "newsworthy", but the fact that the speech (and Hanson's other media appearances) was rich with different possible interpellations – be that as proof of the return of Australia's historic racism, or proof that people who speak uncomfortable truths are vilified by the "woke".[98] Hanson's status as human spectacle gifted her overrepresentation in the media, which in turn allowed Hanson's message to continue resonating. Irrespective of it being positive or negative, the coverage inflated perceptions of Hanson's influence and fed into her followers' belief that they were in Australia's "silent majority".[99]

Letters in support of Hanson sent to Howard and Deputy Prime Minister Tim Fischer demonstrate the belief in this silent majority. Both positive and negative media portrayals of Hanson were cited by the letter-writers as proof of its existence. Multiple letters referenced a poll held by radio shock-jock Alan Jones, where 98 per cent of

---

96 James Flowers and Diana Giese, *James Flowers Interviewed by Diana Giese in the Chinese Australian Oral History Partnership Collection*, sound recording, 2000, TRC 4550, National Library of Australia.
97 Alan Ramsey, "Hanson and a Question of Blame", *Sydney Morning Herald*, 16 November 1996.
98 Sean Scalmer, "The Production of a Founding Event: The Case of Pauline Hanson's Maiden Parliamentary Speech", *Theory & Event* 3, no. 2 (1999), https://muse.jhu.edu/article/32548.
99 Jupp, *From White Australia to Woomera*, 129, 137–8; Andrew Jakubowicz, "White Noise: Australia's Struggle with Multiculturalism," in *Working Through Whiteness: International Perspectives*, ed. Cynthia Levine-Rasky (Albany, US: State University of New York Press, 2002), 114–15.

5 The "Hanson debate"

(variously 36, 37 or) 38,000 callers "supported Hanson's views". These views were not specified, but accordance with them was proof enough that she "voiced what most Australians feel".[100] Others, like the secretary of the Yerong Creek RSL, claimed that the media's negative portrayal of Hanson was unfair as she "called it the way 96% of Australians are thinking".[101] An analysis of mail received by Howard, however, points to the contrary. In the two months following Hanson's maiden speech, Howard had received only 629 letters extolling Hanson and imploring him to support her. In the same time, Howard received 2,742 letters that condemned Hanson and implored him to more stridently oppose her.[102]

This evidence fits Pftizner's belief that the "silent majority" of Australia actually opposed Hanson. In her view, the reality was that the media was amplifying a small number of "angry voices".[103] Though *The Age* claimed it was a "myth that the media made One Nation", the fact remains that it and other media organisations provided Hanson and her party with a means for public dissemination that was crucial for political success.[104] Both CAF's Sham-Ho in her interview with Giese and Opposition Leader Kim Beazley in Federal Parliament cited a letter to the *Daily Telegraph* relating a mother's shame that her son told an Asian classmate to leave Australia because "that's what the lady on TV said".[105] While the media broadcast Hanson because of her potential

---

100 See for example: Correspondence from Janet Baker to Pauline Hanson, 24 September 1996, "Correspondence – Subject – [Pauline] Hanson PART 2" (item, Canberra, September 1996), M4439, 1 PART 2, National Archives of Australia; Correspondence from P.W. Kent to Stephen Mutch to John Howard, 16 September 1996 "PM 12 November 1996"; Correspondence from W. Allen to Tim Fischer, 6 November 1996, "Correspondence – Subject – [Pauline] Hanson PART 3" (item, Canberra, September 1996), M4439, 1 PART 3, National Archives of Australia.
101 Correspondence from S.E. Galvin to John Howard, 28 September 1996, "PM 12 November 1996".
102 Analysis of Mail Registered by MCU 18 November to 29 November 1996, "PM 16 December 1996" (Papers, Canberra, 1996), M4326, 164, National Archives of Australia.
103 Pfitzner and Giese, *Bernice Pfitzner Interviewed by Diana Giese*.
104 Gerard Henderson, "It's a Myth That the Media Made One Nation", *The Age*, 14 July 1998; Scalmer, "The Production of a Founding Event".

to create debate (which made her "newsworthy"), the potential for real harm to result from broadcasting Hanson did not appear to be equally considered. In the view of CAV's Chow and FCA's Lee, a news-making model based on scintillation and outrage only carried Hanson's message forward.[106] The base emotions such coverage stirred complemented the simplistic narrative Hanson's followers viscerally felt to be true and reaffirmed their belief of belonging to a majority.

Journalists often cited society's need to discuss Hanson and evaluate her politics as justification for their coverage. This rested on the idea that debate was a virtue of democracy and that, following this, a democratic society would naturally adopt good ideas and discard the bad if its members could freely discuss them. The era's greatest champion of this principle was, however, Howard. Scholars have often cited Howard's veneration of "free speech" and his denigration of its alleged antonym, "political correctness", as a connection between the two politicians, especially within the context of Hanson's maiden speech.[107] It is an apt connection. Howard's proforma responses to letters about Hanson – irrespective of them being for or against her – reiterated his support for open political debate "in a vigorous fashion" instead of "excessive political correctness". Never condemning Hanson, Howard only counselled letter-writers to undertake political debate "in a tolerant and moderate fashion".[108] As all letters received the same proforma replies (including those from Chinese Australian community organisations), it seemed Howard encouraged Hanson's supporters to create their own standards of debate. Judging by some of the racist

---

105 Sham-Ho and Giese, *Helen Sham-Ho Interviewed by Diana Giese*; "Questions without Notice: Immigration" (Canberra: Commonwealth Hansard, 8 October 1996).
106 Lee and Giese, *Wellington Lee Interviewed by Diana Giese*; Chow and Giese, *Benjamin Chow Interviewed by Diana Giese*.
107 Stuart Macintyre and Anna Clark, *The History Wars* (Melbourne: Melbourne University Publishing, 2004), 133–41; Timothy Kendall, "Using the Past to Serve the Present", in *East by South: China in the Australasian Imagination*, eds Charles Ferrall, Paul Millar and Keren Smith (Wellington, NZ: Victoria University Press, 2005), 128–9; Jakubowicz, "White Noise: Australia's Struggle with Multiculturalism", 111–13; Jupp, *From White Australia to Woomera*, 138.
108 For examples, see correspondence in M4326, "PM 12 November 1996".

5 The "Hanson debate"

language and materials sent to Howard and Fischer, these standards could be quite low. Moreover, Howard's message, like that of the media commentators, was that having a debate was more important than a debate's possible outcomes.

Alarm among community organisations lingered through to the 1998 election and was exacerbated by Howard's equivocation on Hanson. Howard's address to Perth's Chinese Chamber of Commerce at its Golden Jubilee came just before the 1998 election and was filled with familiar praise of Chinese Australian contributions to Australia – especially regarding the conservative aspirational virtues of small business and the strong "family unit". A Chinese Australian mother concerned by the increased racism since Hanson's maiden speech – she said her own children had been called "ch***s" – asked Howard "to tell us how we are going to address this issue and explain to our traumatised children why they are being victimised?" Howard said he sympathised and exhorted all Australians to "fight racism and stamp it out" wherever it occurred. He told the woman and the other attendees to use "facts and effective argument" to persuade others not to "go down that racist path" and then reiterated that not all of Hanson's followers were racist.[109] From his fumbled response to the mother, it is unclear whether Howard was suggesting that his refusal to directly condemn Hanson was an example of effective argument or whether his assertion that not all of the people who just voted for One Nation in Queensland were racist was a persuasive fact (was it unthinkable for a racist to vote for the Liberal or Labor parties?). What was clear though was his side-stepping of the second part of the woman's question. Howard's petty consolation for children being victimised and traumatised was that racist people had a right to free speech and no one had convinced these people (through "facts and effective argument") to be otherwise.

The Queensland election result, in which One Nation received more votes than the Liberal or National parties separately, evidently shook the Coalition. ICECAV interpreted the results as just desserts. Through negligence and intransigence, Howard had "raised a tiger" that now challenged his own political strength.[110] But it was also clear

---

109 John Howard, "Address to the Chinese Chamber of Commerce Golden Jubilee" (Speech, Perth, WA, 24 July 1998), https://tinyurl.com/yp3keatk.

that Howard's demurral on Hanson eroded much Chinese Australian support. In particular, the Liberals' preferencing of One Nation in the Queensland state election and Howard's long refusal to rule out preferencing One Nation ahead of Labor in the federal election caused much consternation among Chinese Australian community leaders and groups who called for a national Liberal boycott.[111] Australia's first Chinese-born parliamentarian, Helen Sham-Ho – who had once loyally defended her party leader and his handling of Hanson – ultimately became disillusioned and left the Liberal Party to sit as an independent in the lead-up to the federal election.[112] In the wake of the federal election some months later, the state Liberal parties of Victoria and New South Wales tried to distance themselves from their federal counterpart – the latter even creating a Chinese Community Advisory Committee to help demarcate themselves from Howard.[113]

To ICECAV's relief, Hanson's political posturing did not equate to prowess, but they recognised Howard's own abilities to exploit social divisions through artifice and innuendo.[114] Peter Wong, a member of CAF (and another former member of the Liberal Party), lamented that Howard's methods for pursuing a uniform society closer to its British roots would lead Australia into a "wilderness" from which a united multicultural society might not return.[115] Five months after his interview, Wong's words became prophetic. As part of the "Tampa Affair", Howard refused 433 Afghan refugees from entering Australia amidst the rhetoric of "strong Australian borders". Two months after this, his government made false claims about refugees throwing their "children overboard" to keep their sinking vessel afloat. In fact, this

---

110 ICECAV, "The Bridge July 1998", 2.
111 QCF, "QCF Press Release: Liberal Party's Shabby Deal on Preferences"; ICECAV, "The Bridge July 1998", 2-3.
112 Helen Sham-Ho, Jackie Huggins and Peter Read, *Helen Sham-Ho Interviewed by Jackie Huggins and Peter Read in the Council for Aboriginal Reconciliation Collection*, sound recording, Council for Aboriginal Reconciliation Collection, 2008, TRC 5961, National Library of Australia; Flowers and Giese, *James Flowers Interviewed by Diana Giese*.
113 ICECAV, "The Bridge December 1998", 4.
114 ICECAV, 4.
115 Wong and Giese, *Peter Wong Interviewed by Diana Giese*.

5 The "Hanson debate"

lie was only keeping afloat Howard's election chances. With pomp and applause, he launched his re-election campaign with the declaration "we will decide who comes to this country and the circumstances in which they come" and pledged to work for the Australian mainstream ahead of "minority interest groups".[116] In sentiment and pitch, he was not too dissimilar from Hanson. Arguably, it was Hanson's support that Howard had siphoned off for a hitherto unexpected election victory.[117] In the view of many Chinese Australian community leaders and organisations, Howard's government made racial scapegoating and political opportunism a staple in contemporary Australian politics.

One Nation and many peoples

The Hanson debate stands out as the greatest threat to Australia's multiculturalism since the end of the White Australia policy. During the debate, Hanson and several other politicians were elected despite (or even because of) their apparent racist attitudes. The Howard government was reluctant to defend multiculturalism and more willing to defend the free speech of multiculturalism's attackers. This was despite, as CAF documented, incidents of racism toward Chinese Australians (let alone other groups) consequently increasing in number and intensity.

The intensity of political action that came as a response to the Hanson debate was in line with the enormity of the challenge. As Scalmer pointed out, it was when the "triumph" of Hanson and One Nation seemed most apparent that democratic counteractions against them were most prolific. The responses of Chinese Australian community organisations fit this pattern. Organisations from across Australia, across various intra-ethnic divides, and across different languages and mediums raised their voices individually and collectively in opposition to Hanson and the debate on race and immigration she

---

116 Howard, "John Howard".
117 Jupp, *From White Australia to Woomera*, 196; Stephen FitzGerald, *Comrade Ambassador: Whitlam's Beijing Envoy* (Melbourne: Melbourne University Press, 2015), 245.

had engendered. The solidarity between many different communities and organisations was unity in the sense that their actions against Hanson amalgamated into a common, united response, but that this is not the same as being a unitary Chinese Australian community.

The creation of a united Chinese Australian body – as had been suggested following the Blainey debate and the Tiananmen Massacre – was not pursued despite the many instances of interstate meetings, inter-organisational joint letters, or other means of cooperation. Practical rather than symbolic solidarity prevailed. Nevertheless, Chinese Australian community leaders largely agreed about the significance and causes of the Hanson debate and expressed a type of de facto Chinese Australian community, even if not one of their own making. According to the Chinese Australian politicians interviewed by Giese and ICECAV, Asian or Chinese Australians were collectively scapegoated by White Australians during times of economic downturn in Australia. In effect, Hanson's supporters imagined a monolithic Chinese or Asian Australian other.

Awareness of this othering by the White (Anglo) Australian majority also informed interviewees' understanding of how the media covered Hanson, and how politicians like Howard could use Hanson for their own advantage. Wong's prediction of Howard leading Australia into a multicultural wilderness had some truth. However, the interviewees also expressed hope for the resilience of multiculturalism. As Flowers said, even if some Australians did not agree with how quickly the change had occurred, multiculturalism was too deeply rooted to be extracted. These observations enrich understandings of Australia's multiculturalism through the lived experiences of those who have fought to defend it at a time of great peril, as do the many examples of small and large acts of opposition to Hanson.

In the process of responding to the Hanson debate, some individuals and organisations became recognisable representatives of the "Chinese Australian" community. Articulate and media savvy, organisations like CAF and QCF became the foremost sources of the "Chinese Australian point of view". Likewise, Chinese Australian politicians like Tsang, Tchen and Lim rose to greater prominence from their community service backgrounds. The prominence of these individuals (indeed, it was because of their social prominence that

5 The "Hanson debate"

Giese interviewed many of them) and the common concerns raised by the debate, allowed them to speak on behalf of other Chinese Australians and become the voices for the "Chinese Australian community". As we will see in following chapters, this arrangement whereby prominent individuals and organisations speak on behalf of others continues with differing degrees of legitimacy. After all, in the absence of a common, unifying issue, the legitimacy of these figureheads as leaders or voices of an imagined Chinese Australian community might begin to weaken.

6
Community organisations in the "Chinese century"

> We believe a very important thing that we can help [the] Australian government [with] is to provide linkage or to promote a very good and stable relationship between Australia and China, which will lead to peace and development and all that for both countries. And we still believe that at this stage. No matter what, who says what. I think this is still the right things and I'm sure ... the Australian government wanted that as well. It's just how to balance some of the pros and cons which the two countries have ... We like to see China is growing and growing well and moving in the right direction, in peace and development. So, if we can help, we can also try and convince them to do better than what they are doing, whatever they're doing. So I think that generally, most Chinese Australians will feel that. Especially of those who settled down here. A lot, you'd be surprised, a lot of members are very critical of China.[1]

---

1   Interviewee 3, Anonymous Interview.

Since the turn of the millennium, many scholars of history, international relations, politics and economics have been analysing what they have dubbed the "Chinese century" or "China's rise": a period in which the PRC's burgeoning economic and political power seems set to challenge the global superiority of the United States. The analysis typically frames China as a "threat" or "opportunity", which is a perception that stretches back to the West's 19th-century encounters with the Middle Kingdom.[2] Many recent works have also considered the places of different ethnic Chinese communities around the world in this "threat" and "opportunity" dynamic. In particular, they are interested in re-imaginings of (trans)nationalism and Beijing's soft-power initiatives, the latter aimed at fostering identification with the PRC and support for the CCP's domestic and international interests.[3]

Notwithstanding the international importance of China and its ability to project its interests beyond its borders, Chinese Australian communities and organisations need to be analysed on their own terms. China was not the only actor exerting a nationalist pull on these communities and organisations. At the turn of the century, Australia,

---

2 C. Fred Bergsten et al., eds, *China's Rise: Challenges and Opportunities* (Washington, DC: Peterson Institute for International Economics and Center for Strategic and International Studies, 2008); David Scott, *"The Chinese Century?": The Challenge to Global Order*, Global Issues (London: Palgrave Macmillan, 2008); Herbert S. Yee, *China's Rise – Threat or Opportunity?* (London: Taylor & Francis Group, 2011); Chengxin Pan, *Knowledge, Desire and Power in Global Politics: Western Representations of China's Rise* (Cheltenham, UK: Edward Elgar Publishing, 2012); Vinod K. Aggarwal and Sara A. Newland, eds, *Responding to China's Rise: US and EU Strategies*, The Political Economy of the Asia Pacific: 15 (Cham: Springer, 2014).

3 There is a lot of literature on this topic. Two collected works that connect this topic to that of Chinese diaspora communities are: Julia Kuehn, Kam Louie and David M. Pomfret, *Diasporic Chineseness after the Rise of China: Communities and Cultural Production* (Vancouver: UBC Press, 2014), http://ebookcentral.proquest.com/lib/unimelb/detail.action?docID=3412881; Bernard P. Wong and Chee-Beng Tan, eds, *China's Rise and the Chinese Overseas*, Routledge Contemporary China Series 170 (London; New York: Routledge, 2018); Hong Liu and Els van Dongen, "China's Diaspora Policies as a New Mode of Transnational Governance", *Journal of Contemporary China* 25, no. 102 (November 2016), 805–21, https://tinyurl.com/5fvdtfhj.

6 Community organisations in the "Chinese century"

too, was appealing to patriotic sentiments and making clear gestures to Chinese Australian communities about national loyalties. Understandably, Ien Ang suggests Chinese Australians "find themselves being pulled in opposite directions, under pressure to display their allegiance to competing national regimes".[4] Nevertheless, Chinese Australian community organisations maintained their own agency in the face of competing PRC and Australian nationalisms. In yet another demonstration of their inherent diversity, they displayed their pride in both China and Australia in ways according to their own predilections. The language of their newsletters, the various events they held or attended, and the relationships they managed with ministers and consuls make it clear that community organisations were cognisant of the two competing "national patriotisms" vying for their patronage. Indeed, as the opening quote in this chapter suggests, organisations made up their own minds on how to engage with or even question the nationalisms presented by the different regimes. This chapter shows that, despite the demands coming from the increasingly muscular forms of Chinese and Australian patriotism at the turn of the century, community organisations were able, for the time being, to position themselves between the two, expressing affinities for either or both nation-states as they chose.

China and Australia at the end of the 20th century

The "Hong Kong handover" can be seen as a harbinger of the Chinese century and a powerful symbol of the end of British imperialism in East Asia. For many Chinese Australians, as for others of Chinese descent around the world, it was a moment to reflect on the past, the present and the possible future. Other developments, international and domestic, also continued to lend significance to China's rise. Whereas the socialist governments of Eastern Europe, Central Asia and Africa had fallen to

---

4   Ien Ang, "No Longer Chinese? Residual Chineseness after the Rise of China", in *Diasporic Chineseness after the Rise of China: Communities and Cultural Production*, eds Julia Kuehn, Kam Louie and David M. Pomfret (Vancouver: UBC Press, 2014), 24.

popular movements, in China the CCP had strengthened its hold. After crushing the protests of 1989, it launched a patriotic campaign to pull the population behind the party-state. The Taiwan Strait Crisis of 1996 and the Hainan spy plane incident in 2001 raised geopolitical tensions between the PRC and the United States, but the 9/11 attacks and the subsequent War on Terror allowed the two powers to de-escalate military posturing and even unite (at least ideologically) against fears of domestic and international Islamist terrorism. Economically, as it escaped the fate of its neighbours during the 1997 Asian financial crisis, the PRC won esteem for its fiscal acumen and experimentation with international commerce infused with "Chinese characteristics". Its entry into the World Trade Organization (WTO) cemented the PRC's important position in global trade and, on this basis, its importance in the process of globalisation itself. It had much to be proud of, and China let this show at the 2008 Beijing Olympics. Marking its renewed stature on the international stage, the Olympics can be taken as "the end of the beginning" of China's rise, which, between this moment and the return of Hong Kong, bookends a decade that encapsulates the dawning of the Chinese century.

Many scholars have pointed out that Beijing adroitly used its international standing to (re)engage with ethnic Chinese communities around the world.[5] The consensus among them is that Beijing's global "charm offensive" toward ethnic Chinese projected a claim over these peoples based on the emotional, cultural and kinship attachments the state presumed Overseas Chinese felt toward China. There are two

---

5   Elena Barabantseva, "Trans-Nationalising Chineseness: Overseas Chinese Policies of the PRC's Central Government", *Asien* 96 (July 2005), 7–28; Ang, "No Longer Chinese?"; Julia Kuehn, Kam Louie and David M. Pomfret, "China Rising: A View and Review of China's Diasporas since the 1980s", in *Diasporic Chineseness after the Rise of China: Communities and Cultural Production*, eds Julia Kuehn, Kam Louie and David M. Pomfret (Vancouver: UBC Press, 2014), 1–16; James Jiann Hua To, *Qiaowu: Extra-Territorial Policies for the Overseas Chinese* (Leiden: Brill, 2014); Wanning Sun, John Fitzgerald and Jia Gao, "From Multicultural Ethnic Migrants to the New Players of China's Public Diplomacy", in *China's Rise and the Chinese Overseas*, eds Bernard P. Wong and Chee-Beng Tan, Routledge Contemporary China Series 170 (London: Routledge, 2018), 55–74.

ostensible motives for the PRC's outreach: to absorb the expertise and resources of Overseas Chinese in the interests of further strengthening the PRC through modernisation and development; and to exercise soft power in the countries where the overseas communities are resident.[6] As Wanning Sun, John Fitzgerald and Jia Gao observed, "China's rise has led to a recentering of China in the diasporic public sphere": it has injected "confidence and pride in its people" and there is a "higher level of willingness on the part of Chinese migrants to answer the PRC's call and 'do their bit' for the motherland".[7] If so, then this suggests Beijing's soft power is meeting and potentially exceeding what Li Mingjiang described as the "defensive purposes [of soft power] for the domestic context".[8]

In this same period, 1997–2008, Australia was itself nation-building and marking momentous occasions. In the space of a few years, Australia ran a referendum on becoming a republic, hosted the 2000 Olympics Games in Sydney (previously beating China's own Olympic bid) and held celebrations marking a centenary of Federation. During the Howard years, Australian militarism, especially the legend of Anzac, became sacrosanct. Those who critically investigated the country's martial history and myths stirred public anger and consternation.[9] Each of these moments offered Australians a chance to reflect on the hopes and the history of their country. But it was also a time of trepidation. The "threat and opportunity" presented by the Chinese century was one source of continual national excitement.

Multiculturalism was another. Though Australia never consigned multiculturalism to failure (as the old colonial powers were

---

6 Elena Barabantseva, *Overseas Chinese, Ethnic Minorities and Nationalism: De-Centering China* (London: Taylor & Francis Group, 2010), 108–37; Kuehn, Louie and Pomfret, "China Rising", 1–9; Ang, "No Longer Chinese?", 17–31; Sun, Fitzgerald and Gao, "From Multicultural Ethnic Migrants to the New Players of China's Public Diplomacy", 63–5.
7 Sun, Fitzgerald and Gao, "From Multicultural Ethnic Migrants to the New Players of China's Public Diplomacy", 63, 69.
8 Li Mingjiang, "China Debates Soft Power: Implications for Chinese Foreign Policy", in *Chinese Scholars and Foreign Policy* (London: Routledge, 2019), 58.
9 Marilyn Lake et al., *What's Wrong with ANZAC?: The Militarisation of Australian History*, 1st ed. (Sydney: UNSW Press, 2010), 1–15.

contemporaneously doing in Europe), belief in the concept was nonetheless rocked by the politics of Pauline Hanson and One Nation, and the Islamophobia that followed the 9/11 terrorist attack and the 2002 Bali bombings. Ultimately, Anthony Moran has argued, support for multiculturalism continued because even cultural conservatives like John Howard acquiesced to it as a nation-building tool more than a national liability – though political expediency still compelled him to lunge enthusiastically toward the latter.[10] Chinese Australian community organisations also expressed some ambivalence toward their place in Australia. Their observations on current and past racism in Australian society reflected poorly on Australia's history and values. It is hardly surprising that they felt "pushed further toward identifying with China".[11] Indeed, Sun, Fitzgerald and Gao have suggested that Australia had to address its own "soft power deficit" through greater outreach to its ethnic minority communities – Chinese Australian among them.[12] Though perhaps sometimes unwieldy, multiculturalism was the only viable model for nation-building Australia had.

Pride in China

Many scholars have taken the arrival of the "Chinese century" as an opportunity to reconceptualise the Chinese diaspora and its relationship to the PRC. New cohorts of Chinese emigrants exuded the confidence of having grown up in an ascendant China and shook up the social and cultural composition of pre-existing communities of Overseas Chinese. At the same time, people also flowed in the other direction with many Overseas Chinese "returning" to China to take advantage of its improved economic opportunities, or otherwise reconnect through personal or professional links.[13] Kuehn, Louie and Pomfret paid particular attention to how diaspora communities have

---

10 Moran, *The Public Life of Australian Multiculturalism*, 11, 110–12.
11 Sun, Fitzgerald and Gao, "From Multicultural Ethnic Migrants to the New Players of China's Public Diplomacy", 66.
12 Sun, Fitzgerald and Gao, 65.
13 Kuehn, Louie and Pomfret, "China Rising", 1.

"engaged with changed, and changing, notions of 'nation' and 'homeland' and the effects these have had on (trans)national consciousness and identity".[14] As Ang has argued, this can be to the detriment of Overseas Chinese as they remain subjected to a meaning of "Chinese" that is "irrevocably tied to the interests of the Chinese nation-state, at the expense of the identification of diasporic Chinese with the countries where they actually live".[15] In such countries (particularly in Western countries), authorities are inclined to suspect that the PRC uses these connections to advance its own national interests (which are implicitly detrimental to their own). Regardless of the foundations for such suspicions, Tan and Wong point out that Overseas Chinese communities are often associated with the PRC, a fact that typically carries negative social and political connotations.[16] The variety of Chinese Australian community organisations is broad enough, and relations with the PRC complex enough, for all these views to be seen.

In the years 1997–2008, pro-PRC community organisations essentialised Chineseness into an ethno-national concept. This concept became especially salient at moments of national pride, such as the return of Hong Kong. As the president of the Chinese Fellowship of Victoria (CFV), C.S. Lo, explained:

> Being an overseas Chinese and a patriot, the witnessing of the return of H.K. back to the Motherland certainly brought to me the immense pride and great sense of achievement [sic]. This event did not only signify a most important turning point in the course of our history – a very significant milestone in our national destiny – it also demonstrated to the world the almost total obliteration of colonialism since the Second World War, and

---

14 Kuehn, Louie and Pomfret, 8.
15 Ang, "No Longer Chinese?", 23–4.
16 Chee-Beng Tan and Bernard P. Wong, "Introduction: Contemporary China's Rise and the Chinese Overseas", in *China's Rise and the Chinese Overseas*, eds Bernard P. Wong and Chee-Beng Tan, Routledge Contemporary China Series 170 (London: Routledge, 2018), 10.

the attainment of our nation as a modern, united and proud country.[17]

Lo's "immense pride" sprang from himself being an Overseas Chinese "patriot", but also the shared sense that it was "a most important turning point in *our* history". Connecting the past to the present, Lo's message hints it was not just Chinese "patriots", members of CFV, or even Chinese Australians to whom he conferred "our national identity", but the entire Chinese ethnos. So, too, does Lo's excitement about plans for the 48th Chinese National Day:

> After more than 30 years arduous and sometimes perilous struggle ... our beloved and proud nation is fast becoming a prosperous, well respected and powerful country on the world stage. So on the eve of the 48th anniversary, we should fill our hearts with pride and joy and to [sic] mark this solemn occasion with proper and fitting action.[18]

Lo's collective, ethnically specific and patriotic language fits in with what Elena Barabantseva identifies around this time as the Chinese nation-state becoming "trans-nationalised" or no longer "territorially bound"; a Beijing-made framework that fixed Overseas Chinese as an extension of China through primordial, cultural and racial ties.[19] Through its Overseas Chinese Affairs Departments, Ambassadors and Consuls, Beijing strengthened these ties to bolster its own soft-power initiatives, such as projecting positive images of the PRC, or galvanising Overseas Chinese support for the country's own domestic programs.

James Jiann Hua To explained that relationship-building programs and policies targeted at overseas Chinese communities, known collectively as *qiáowù* (侨务) or "overseas Chinese affairs work", are

---

17 CFV, "Newsletter August 1997" (Chinese Fellowship of Victoria, August 1997), 5, State Library of Victoria.
18 CFV, 5.
19 Barabantseva, "Trans-Nationalising Chineseness", 8; Elena Barabantseva, "Who Are 'Overseas Chinese Ethnic Minorities'? China's Search for Transnational Ethnic Unity", *Modern China* 38, no. 1 (January 2012): 81–2, https://doi.org/10.1177/0097700411424565.

6 Community organisations in the "Chinese century"

implemented by governmental, diplomatic and non-governmental agencies using formal and informal channels.[20] *Qiaowu* initiatives include dinner invitations to the PRC embassy, all-expenses-paid trips to China, or participation in international conferences. Leaders of community organisations are common targets of these initiatives. Because these favours increased the prestige of leaders and organisations (in addition to the obvious material benefits), community leaders reciprocated the goodwill through public praise (like Lo's article), invitations for PRC representatives to attend community events and the like. A shared pride in China lubricated these exchanges.

In many instances, this pride was sincerely felt and long-standing. CFV's support for the PRC had been a founding principle of the organisation back in 1971 and had endured the crisis of the Tiananmen Massacre.[21] In keeping with this history, CFV hosted a dinner on 30 June at Melbourne's Crown Casino and a cultural gala at the Melbourne Town Hall the following day to mark the return of Hong Kong to Beijing's control. Each event attracted thousands of attendees as well as the audience of the Chinese Consul-General. Demonstrating the reciprocal nature of the relationship, members of CFV's leadership were invited to attend the handover ceremony in Hong Kong as guests of the Chinese government.[22] Among them was Maurice Leong, nine times president of one of Melbourne's oldest continuing native place associations, the See Yup Society (SYS).[23] Over its now 170-year-long existence, See Yup itself had raised small fortunes to develop the "See Yup" counties of Guangdong (Sunwui, Toishan, Yanping, and Leong's native Hoiping), giving some indication of the depth and duration of relations between Chinese Australian communities and the ancestral homeland.[24] Along with Leong's own long history of PRC sympathies and creation of pro-PRC associations, including CFV, Leong showed how historical patriotism continued into more recent contexts.[25]

---

20 To, *Qiaowu*, 1–4, 72–89, https://tinyurl.com/bccmewkw.
21 CFV, "Newsletter September 1974", 8.
22 CFV, "Newsletter August 1997", 3, 5.
23 Leong and Giese, *Maurice Leong Interviewed by Diana Giese*.
24 SYS, *Seeyup Society 1854–2004*, 19–22.
25 Leong and Giese, *Maurice Leong Interviewed by Diana Giese*.

The ACT Chinese Australian Association

Another organisation with pro-Beijing sympathies, the ACT Chinese Australian Association (ACTCAA) organised its own dinner to celebrate the Hong Kong handover. The guest of honour was director of the Hong Kong Economic and Trade Office, Philip Chok. He gave a keynote speech describing the principles of one-country, two-systems, the mutual economic benefit for the PRC and Hong Kong SAR, and the handover itself being a step toward the total reunification of China.[26] As one committee member described it, "Mr. Chok painted a rosy picture for the future of Hong Kong following its handover to China" but also connected the future to the past by linking the "British colonial rule of 156 years" to China's "one hundred years of shame".[27] This historical reminder was clearly aimed at ACTCAA's membership. Yet, with local politicians in the audience, including the ACT's Chief Minister and Opposition Leader, and members of the Department of Foreign Affairs and Trade and the Department of Immigration, Chok's speech overall was as much to assure representatives of the Australian government of a smooth transition of power, economic independence and relative autonomy in Hong Kong as it was to inform local Chinese Australians about this process.[28] ACTCAA here exemplified the role To described for Overseas Chinese community organisations as conduits of PRC soft power; communicating Beijing's policies through informal engagements.[29]

Like CFV, ACTCAA demonstrated the system of reward and prestige for community organisations participating in *qiaowu* efforts.[30] Later that year, the PRC invited ACTCAA's secretary, Alice Chu, along with other overseas Chinese delegates from Australia, USA, Canada, UK and New Zealand, on an all-expenses-paid visit to Beijing, Nanjing, Shanghai, Chongqing and Chengdu. As Chu reported, the 18-day junket was to "enhance mutual understanding and to explore future

---

26 ACTCAA, "Newsletter August 1997" (ACT Chinese Australian Association, August 1997), 6–7, National Library of Australia.
27 ACTCAA, 6.
28 ACTCAA, 2.
29 To, *Qiaowu*, 37–9, 51.
30 To, 50–3.

potentials of establishing and development [sic] economic, trade and cultural cooperation between Australia and China".[31]

How exactly Chu or ACTCAA would facilitate this was not clarified, but a good example of the enhanced cooperation between the PRC and ACTCAA appeared for the 50th anniversary of the founding of the People's Republic. When ACTCAA asked the State Council of Overseas Chinese Affairs to help organise a gala in celebration of the anniversary, the state council sent the Shanghai Performing Arts Troupe.[32] Seven hundred people attended the gala dinner and Chu, now the president of ACTCAA, described the celebration for the PRC's 50th anniversary as a huge success. "It was a great joy for me to see so many ethnic Chinese people in Canberra joining together for this special event," she said.[33] Chu's elision of nationalist and ethnic celebration is telling. Like Lo's fanfare for the Hong Kong handover, national celebrations for a foreign nation became ethno-centric celebrations and re-affirmed an essentialist and patriotic basis for being Chinese.[34]

When ACTCAA was formed on 26 June 1988, its formative goals – to forge unity and speak for Canberra's Chinese Australian community – were not unlike those of the many community organisations that had come before or after.[35] It certainly saw itself as an outlet for Chinese Australians to express pride in their cultural heritage. However, it is likely that attaining personal or organisational prestige were important motivations for ACTCAA's leadership to build relations with the PRC's representatives. As Barabantseva argued, since China's rise, connections with the PRC have come to be a key qualification for overseas community leaders, especially in younger organisations whose leaders lack the business clout or direct community service experience of traditional community leaders. Through these connections with

---

31 ACTCAA, "Newsletter December 1997" (ACT Chinese Australian Association, December 1997), 3, National Library of Australia.
32 ACTCAA, "Newsletter September 1999" (ACT Chinese Australian Association, September 1999), 2, National Library of Australia.
33 ACTCAA, "Newsletter November 1999" (ACT Chinese Australian Association, November 1999), 1–2, National Library of Australia.
34 Kuehn, Louie and Pomfret, *Diasporic Chineseness after the Rise of China*, 5.
35 ACTCAA, "Newsletter August 1988", 1–2.

community leaders, "the Chinese party-state makes an effort to instil commitment to the PRC and its policies of modernisation".[36] In the case of ACTCAA and leaders like Alice Chu, Barabantseva's view seems to have some merit. In October 2004, ACTCAA hosted a roundtable discussion with an official delegation from the Guangdong Overseas Chinese Office. They discussed "the recent overseas Chinese support program development in China and exchanged valuable information regarding Overseas Chinese communities living in Canberra".[37] If ACTCAA was getting something out of the relationship, so was the Overseas Chinese Office.

Longer-established community leaders and organisations seemed to value connections to the PRC, too. Maurice Leong built his reputation on service to Melbourne's Chinese Australian community but seems to have cultivated stronger connections to the PRC due to ideological sympathies. The same is true of the CFV, in which Leong played a formative role. Sydney's Chinese Youth League (CYL), an even older organisation and role model for the early CFV, offered similar examples: providing welcoming committees for new consul-generals and holding friendly table-tennis competitions between its members and consular staff.[38] It also displayed enthusiastic rhetoric. "Indeed the lion has awoken!!" CYL remarked of the PRC's social and economic development after its 2005 tour to China – the "awakened lion" being prominent in the Sinosphere as a nationalist symbol of China's rise.[39] As such, these organisations were not just the "targets" for the PRC's *qiaowu* activities, but were themselves "actors on behalf of China's

---

36   Barabantseva, *Overseas Chinese, Ethnic Minorities and Nationalism*, 126–7.
37   ACTCAA, "Newsletter October 2004" (ACT Chinese Australian Association, October 2004), 4, National Library of Australia.
38   CYL, "Consulate General's Visit", Wayback Machine, Chinese Youth League of Australia, 2005, https://tinyurl.com/4hywhxuz.
39   CYL, "China Tour 2005", Wayback Machine, Chinese Youth League of Australia, 2005, https://tinyurl.com/2am6fkju; Peter Hays Gries, *China's New Nationalism*, 1st ed. (University of California Press, 2004), 43–5; Teddy Ng and Andrea Chen, "Xi Jinping Says World Has Nothing to Fear from Awakening of 'Peaceful Lion'", *South China Morning Post*, 28 March 2014, https://tinyurl.com/4uh95zfd.

public diplomacy".[40] Though receptive to advances of the PRC, these organisations' affinity with the PRC came from within themselves.

Other well-established, community-service-oriented community organisations desired and fostered stronger connections with the PRC without sharing an immediate ideological affinity. In these instances, the pursuit of community prestige or material benefits provides a better explanation for an organisation's amenability to the views of local PRC representatives. PRC patriotism or nationalism per se seems less at issue. As To described it, these organisations were more receptive to PRC representatives who took the time to build trust and offered guidance rather than "overt leadership".[41] From the view of the community organisation, however, a relationship with a PRC representative – like a consul-general – could pay dividends, so long as the organisation expressed agreeable views about China. This arrangement allowed for relations between the PRC and community organisations who were not necessarily ideological allies.

The Chinese Association of Victoria

The Chinese Association of Victoria (CAV) expressed pride in China in ways that gradually became more openly supportive of the PRC. CAV was formed in 1982 mainly by professionals and academics who had emigrated from Malaysia and Singapore.[42] By the 2000s, CAV had grown into one of the largest and most influential Chinese Australian community organisations in Victoria and included people of Chinese background from Southeast Asia, Hong Kong and the PRC who had settled in the more affluent or fast-developing eastern suburbs of Melbourne.[43] CAV's large facilities and membership and impressive cultural programs gave it prominence among Victoria's Chinese Australian communities.[44] Likewise, it would have brought CAV to the attention of the PRC's qiaowu initiatives. Yet in its early days, the

---

40 Sun, Fitzgerald and Gao, "From Multicultural Ethnic Migrants to the New Players of China's Public Diplomacy", 64.
41 To, *Qiaowu*, 49–52.
42 Interviewee 1, Anonymous Interview; Interviewee 3, Anonymous Interview.
43 Chew and Giese, *Franklin Chew Interviewed by Diana Giese*; Interviewee 3, Anonymous Interview.

founders avoided politicised issues due to the experiences they had had in their countries of birth (especially Malaysia).[45] CAV thus avoided wading into the PRC–ROC politics. As past-president Franklin Chew once explained, it was a matter that had divided Melbourne's Chinese Australian communities for so long that CAV, like other organisations, simply deferred to the Australian government's position on matters like the One China Policy.[46]

Of course, this did not inhibit CAV from developing a cordial relationship with the PRC's representatives.[47] CAV held table-tennis tournaments with the staff of the consulate and received books for its school and library from the Consul-General on multiple occasions.[48] Moreover, Chinese consular and embassy representatives were regular guests of honour at CAV functions (as were Australian state and federal politicians).[49] As familiarity grew, it became easier for each party to express admiration for the achievements of the other; CAV for being a premier community organisation and the PRC for its modernisation and economic development.

In 2004, the Chinese consulate invited CAV's president, Vincent Chow, to attend a seminar and study tour in China. He attended another a year or two after, and a third in 2009. The first two trips do not appear to have been covered by CAV's website or newsletters, but a

---

44 Sun, Fitzgerald and Gao, "From Multicultural Ethnic Migrants to the New Players of China's Public Diplomacy", 64.
45 Interviewee 1, Anonymous Interview.
46 Chew and Giese, *Franklin Chew Interviewed by Diana Giese*; Correspondence with the author, 2 February 2024.
47 CAV, "CAV Newsletter November 2008" (Chinese Association of Victoria, November 2008), 4, https://tinyurl.com/yeyvcye4.
48 CAV and Vincent Chow, "President's Report", Wayback Machine, Chinese Association of Victoria, 22 September 2002, https://tinyurl.com/4743j62j; CAV, "News August 2003", Wayback Machine, Chinese Association of Victoria, 2 August 2003, https://tinyurl.com/mvjsxdr8; CAV, "CAV Newsletter February 2008" (Chinese Association of Victoria, February 2008), 10, https://tinyurl.com/3s5p8brn.
49 Chew and Giese, *Franklin Chew Interviewed by Diana Giese*; CAV, "CAV Newsletter May 2007" (Chinese Association of Victoria, May 2007), 27, https://tinyurl.com/42twymc4; CAV, "CAV Newsletter July 2007" (Chinese Association of Victoria, July 2007), 7, 20, https://tinyurl.com/49hcvt37.

report by Chow about his third trip did appear in a newsletter in 2009. This time, Chow provided some insight into what was covered by the study tours. Delegates from around the world were treated to five days packed with dinners and luncheons with officials from the Overseas Chinese Affairs Office and the United Front Work Department. The seminars covered themes intended to foster pride in China's development under the CCP. As Chow reflected:

> They were all interesting topics and some of the papers had given me an in depth knowledge of the old and new China, as well as some controversial issues that's facing China today. For example, not many of us would know that China was a dominant economic powerhouse in the 1600's with 30% of the world GDP. It decreased to 6% in 1900 and down to a miserable 2.2% in 1978 before picking up and increasing to 6.8% in year 2008.[50]

Such lines about the PRC's progress and development would become increasingly familiar to Chinese Australian communities as time went on.

The Australian Chinese Community Association (ACCA) grew more friendly toward the PRC in a similar way. Between 1997 and 2008, ACCA was one of the largest organisations providing settlement assistance, childcare and aged care services for Sydney's Chinese Australian community. In June 2001, the organisation was pleased to have its record of services to the Chinese Australian community recognised by Consul-General Liao Zhi Hong, who gifted ACCA a Chinese translation of the complete *Encyclopaedia Britannica*. Helpfully, he added that if ACCA ever needed funds or other assistance, "the consulate will surely help to the best of its abilities to satisfy any request". His suggestion for ACCA's executive committee to exchange aged care and social welfare knowledge with PRC counterparts in a bilateral program was well-received by the organisation.[51] To this end,

---

50 CAV, "CAV Newsletter January 2010" (Chinese Association of Victoria, January 2010), 20–1, https://tinyurl.com/5c84svpw.
51 ACCA, "ACCA News July 2001" (Australian Chinese Community Association, July 2001), 4, National Library of Australia.

two community groups from Shenzhen and Shanghai visited ACCA in October and November the following year to study its exemplary services.[52] Around the same time as these visits, ACCA held a photo exhibition to demonstrate the "close cooperation and relationship that exists between ACCA and the People's Republic of China". Timed to coincide with Chinese National Day celebrations, the exhibition included Consul-General Hong as guest of honour. Photos from joint student exchange programs or the construction of the Darling Harbour Friendship Garden were displayed to show how a relationship had existed between ACCA and the PRC since 1976.[53]

The gifts and prestige, however, had the potential to overshadow ACCA's own *huayi* identity. In a meeting regarding the donation of new textbooks for ACCA's school, the books' simplified script – and to some degree their contents – became an issue. The benefactor, Sydney's new Consul-General Chen Haoqi, pointed to the trend of simplified text and Mandarin language surpassing Cantonese and the traditional script among Overseas Chinese and further stressed the importance of "canonizing Chinese culture". To some degree ACCA agreed, but it also vouched for the diversity of Chinese cultures and its own "Overseas Chinese culture". Moreover, it explained, Australia was a multicultural country where people were free to practise their own culture as they wished. Nonetheless, ACCA ultimately accepted the consul's offer for the replacement textbooks that taught the PRC's view of Chinese history, geography and culture. ACCA noted that a survey of parents with children enrolled in its language school showed 68 per cent wanted their children to learn simplified script.[54]

In these cases, closer relations with the PRC or its representatives accompanied certain points of view that complemented the PRC's own. Of the community leaders interviewed for this research, there were those who, if not siding with the PRC's views on domestic and international politics exactly, at least believed that Western nations and

---

52 ACCA, "ACCA News March 2003" (Australian Chinese Community Association, March 2003), 24, National Library of Australia.
53 ACCA, "ACCA News December 2002" (Australian Chinese Community Association, December 2002), 18, National Library of Australia.
54 ACCA, "ACCA News July 2001", 4.

6 Community organisations in the "Chinese century"

media routinely portrayed China in a negative light.[55] One interviewee from Sydney said:

> China has become strong. Something that you cannot deny. And it works for China. And China never says that it will export its own ideas to other countries. Not like the West. [Western countries] always say unless you adopt the Western value, your country, your way of running the country is just not up to standard. China has never said that but it has shown to the world that there's certainly another way of running a country.[56]

While stressing he was *not* pro-China, the interviewee was pleased that China was not taking direction from the West. Naturally, community leaders do not need to participate in PRC soft-power initiatives to sympathise with China (a historical understanding of Western prejudice toward China and Chinese will do this). Nevertheless, such sympathies aligned with the objectives of PRC soft power during this period.

Obviously, there were community leaders who were critical of China.[57] One interviewee from a Queensland community organisation that had established closer ties with representatives of the PRC had come by 2019 to feel reservations:

> When it started maybe a decade ago and China started getting strong economically, we all felt proud, which is good. But today, I feel differently now. China is becoming strong and starting to show off herself. Starting to be a little bossy, which can only lead in the long term to real conflict. So, I'm certainly not very happy with the way China's going at the moment.[58]

---

55 Interviewee 3, Anonymous Interview; Interviewee 4, Anonymous Interview; Interviewee 5, Anonymous Interview; Interviewee 6, Anonymous Interview.
56 Interviewee 5, Anonymous Interview.
57 Interviewee 2, Anonymous Interview; Interviewee 7, Anonymous Interview; Interviewee 10, Anonymous Interview.
58 Interviewee 9, Anonymous Interview.

The interviewees' reflections suggest that community organisations are not uncritical of their relationship with China, or rather the PRC. They also implied an awareness of *qiaowu* initiatives and the negative connotations coming from being too closely associated with China. Statements such as "I'm *not* pro-China" or "we all felt proud" but "I feel differently now" signal a desire to distinguish their pride in China and Chineseness from *qiaowu* initiatives, conscious that the latter are complicating their connections with their ancestral land.

It is important to highlight the nuanced perspectives of these community leaders and organisations because it demonstrates their free thinking – something rarely featured in scholarship on the PRC's systematic cultivation of Chinese nationalism among diaspora communities.[59] Between 1997 and 2008, there were Chinese Australian community organisations that were cognisant and critical of the PRC's *qiaowu* initiatives and of the community leaders who sought to benefit from them as "overnight Chinese patriots". The Indochina Chinese Association of Victoria (ICECAV) stands out in this regard. It took a supremely cynical view of Chinese Australian leaders who took up the PRC's "preferable business opportunities" and "free sight-seeing trips to Beijing".[60] To ICECAV, the purpose of cultivating nationalistic pride through *qiaowu* work was clearly linked to the PRC's foreign interests.[61]

The Chinese Australian Forum (CAF) similarly noted with disdain the obsequiousness not of Chinese Australians, but of the Australian government for prohibiting Falun Gong from demonstrating in front of the Chinese embassy:

> ... we can dispute many aspects of the Falun Gong movement, but when the Australian right of peaceful demonstration is threatened by our government's concern of embarrassing a foreign power, then we have a serious problem.[62]

---

59 Kuehn, Louie and Pomfret, "China Rising", 4–5.
60 ICECAV, "The Bridge February 2001", 8.
61 ICECAV, 8.
62 CAF and Jon-Claire Lee, "Press Release: President's Address for Harmony Day Dinner (20/3/02)", Wayback Machine, Chinese Australian Forum, 20 March 2002, https://tinyurl.com/d2yv6hht.

6 Community organisations in the "Chinese century"

CAF's comment also shows that organisations could similarly both take pride in and criticise Australia and its institutions. Evidently, uncritical pride in China was not a common sentiment among community organisations.

Relocation and rediscovery of Chineseness in Australia

After interviewing the former prime minister and researching the history of Sino-Australian relations since 1949, Yi Wang judged that "Howard not only learned to handle the intricacies of diplomacy, but his instinct for pragmatism and compromise helped achieve what had been thought impossible at the start of his prime ministership".[63] What Wang alluded to here was what he and others have termed the "Howard paradox": despite his deep belief in the importance of the US alliance, an Anglo-Australian national identity and the essential differences between Western and Eastern cultures, Howard nevertheless maintained a fruitful and pragmatic relationship with Australia's Asian neighbours, not least of all, the PRC.[64] Wang, however, also paid attention to both directions of Sino-Australian bilateral relations and surmised that each nation was willing and able to compartmentalise issues for their mutual benefit. In practice, this meant avoiding contentious issues (such as each other's human rights record, US relations or the Dalai Lama's international activism) for the sake of focusing on shared interests which were principally related to trade.

Just as China and Australia were able to compartmentalise aspects of their relationship, Chinese Australian community organisations could compartmentalise their relationships with the PRC when interacting with Australian governments and their representatives and vice versa. This compartmentalisation would be prudent considering that *both* PRC and Australian governments attempted to involve Chinese Australian community organisations in their respective diplomatic efforts.

---

63 Wang, *Australia-China Relations Post 1949*, 145–66.
64 Michael Wesley, *The Howard Paradox: Australian Diplomacy in Asia, 1996–2006*. (Sydney: ABC Books, 2007).

In the Face of Diversity

From examples given above, it might appear that ACTAA had been completely absorbed by the PRC's *qiaowu* initiatives. However, viewing ACTCAA from another angle, it could conversely appear as if it was advancing Australian diplomatic efforts. In 2000, the ACT government awarded funds for ACTCAA to buy new traditional Chinese costumes and to print and circulate its newsletters. At the same time, it thanked the organisation for helping it to broker sister-city relationships between Canberra and Beijing, and invited ACTCAA members with business connections to accompany the Chief Minister, Gary Humphries, on a trade mission to China the following year.[65] Moreover, the ACTCAA set aside its good relations with the PRC when dealing with representatives of the Republic of China (ROC). In 1997, its members attended the funeral for the chief of the Taipei Economic and Cultural Office, and in 1999 donated $1,500 through the office for earthquake victims in Taiwan.[66] Compartmentalisation meant good relations with the old country did not preclude good relations with others.

This brief overview of how ACTCAA has acted in relation to China, Australia and other entities raises questions about the tendency of some scholars to describe Chinese Australian community organisations as being co-opted wholesale into the PRC's *qiaowu* objectives. With their focus squarely on China's influence, these scholars overlook the possibility of "host countries" using Chinese diaspora communities to serve their own diplomatic objectives. As such, analyses of overseas Chinese community organisations compartmentalising aspects of their relationships with the governments of both the PRC and their country of residence can be restricted by narrow instrumentalist interpretations.[67] Examples like

---

65 ACTCAA, "Newsletter August 2000" (ACT Chinese Australian Association, August 2000), 3, National Library of Australia; ACTCAA, "Newsletter December 2000" (ACT Chinese Australian Association, December 2000), 1, National Library of Australia; ACTCAA, "Newsletter November 2001" (ACT Chinese Australian Association, November 2001), 2, National Library of Australia.

66 ACTCAA, "Newsletter June 1997", 2; ACTCAA, "Newsletter November 1999" (ACT Chinese Australian Association, November 1999), 1, National Library of Australia.

6 Community organisations in the "Chinese century"

ACTCAA's make it prudent to consider different interests and players within these multifaceted relationships, as well as the necessity to return attention to the communities and their representative organisations themselves.

A study of Chinese Australian community organisations' expressions of pride also challenges the PRC's "reassertion of the mainland as the sole, original and legitimate source of authentic Chineseness" since the beginning of the "Chinese century".[68] This is because, for Chinese Australian communities during this time, expressions of pride about China went hand in hand with the relocation and rediscovery of Chineseness in the Australian setting. Relocation of Chineseness to Australia can be quite literal. Between August and November 2002, ICECAV's exhibition of refugees' journeys and immigration experiences from Indochina to Australia was held at Melbourne's Immigration Museum, attracting local and international patrons. ICECAV boasted that no other Chinese Australian community organisation had ever put on such a display, so it is perhaps unsurprising that their exhibition focused heavily on Indochinese with Chinese ethnic backgrounds like themselves.[69] However, ICECAV emphasised the importance of its new home and pressed all modern ethnic Chinese migrants to commit themselves to it. To ICECAV, a new history should be written to supersede that of the "old" generation of Chinese migrants who remained bound to China and lived in Australia as "guests" wishing to "return home in glory". Challenging the old migrant or sojourner identities bound to China, it proclaimed that "actively integrating into Australian mainstream society is the proper understanding by which we should re-position ourselves as 'new' migrants".[70] In ICECAV's opinion, pride came from being an ethnically Chinese migrant and finding literal and figurative space in Australian

---

67 Ang, "No Longer Chinese?", 27–8.
68 Ang, 28–9.
69 ICECAV, "The Bridge August 2002" (Indo-China Ethnic Chinese Association of Victoria, August 2002), 2–5, State Library of Victoria.
70 積極融入澳洲的主流社會，是我們這一倍"新"移民應該建立的重新自我定位的正確認識: ICECAV, 2.

society. It carried an implicit directive for other Chinese migrants to do likewise.

ICECAV's clear message to Chinese migrants to re-imagine themselves as Chinese Australians can be interpreted as being pointed specifically at "new migrants". As many have noted, *xīnyímín* (新移民) or "new migrant(s)" is a term Chinese government officials and intellectuals have applied to those migrants from Greater China and Southeast Asia since the 1970s. These Chinese opinion-makers believe that a "stable and strong" ethnic identity attached to the Chinese homeland unites these outwardly heterogenous migrant groups, and it is upon this identity that relationships with the PRC are built.[71] Yet ICECAV's criticism of the PRC puts it outside the use of this proposed grouping. Since ICECAV showed familiarity with other PRC soft-power terms like *qiaowu* and showed disdain for opportunistic Chinese Australians who suddenly became "patriotic overseas leaders", it is likely that its use of *xinyimin* carried a deliberate double meaning that refuted the PRC's claim over them and the nature of their connection to China.[72]

Indeed, ICECAV was passionate about relocating Chineseness to the new Australian home. In the context of the current tensions over the Taiwan Strait and the longer animosity between the PRC and ROC camps in the Chinese diaspora, ICECAV implored other Chinese Australian community leaders to join them in doing so:

> Only they who can view the new home as the homeland, the place of residence as the ancestral home, and the mother land as the niangjia, will be able to settle themselves down physically and mentally, blend into the mainstream society, and share in the tragedies and triumphs of Australia. Community leaders, it is time to end our entanglement in the struggles of cross-straits politics.[73]

---

71 Barabantseva, "Trans-Nationalising Chineseness", 15–19; Sun, Fitzgerald and Gao, "From Multicultural Ethnic Migrants to the New Players of China's Public Diplomacy", 69; Feng, "The Changing Political Identity of the 'Overseas Chinese' in Australia", 132–3.
72 ICECAV, "The Bridge February 2001", 8; ICECAV, "The Bridge March 2002" (Indo-China Ethnic Chinese Association of Victoria, March 2002), 10–11, State Library of Victoria.

6 Community organisations in the "Chinese century"

Despite ICECAV's suggestion, the relocation of Chineseness to Australia did not require the severance of ties to the PRC or ROC – it just required being Chinese *Australian*. Throughout this 1997–2008 period, for example, ACCA held "Australian Chinese Day" festivities which included colourful displays of Chinese culture and cuisine.[74] As celebrations dedicated to "friendship and sharing in our multicultural and multi-racial nation", they provided opportunities for Sydney's Chinese Australians to take pride in themselves and their cultural offerings for their non-Chinese Australian compatriots. The theme for 1998, "Let our culture beam with Australia's development", further expressed a desire to weave Chinese culture into the fabric of Australian society.[75] As the sentiment of mutual development implied, the exchange between this Chinese Australian community and wider Australian society went in both directions. Information stalls for community, not-for-profit and government bodies (including WorkCover, the Australian Red Cross, the Australian Taxation Office and World Vision Australia) advertised support programs and volunteer initiatives to festival-goers.[76] Australian Chinese Day celebrations also provided a backdrop for citizenship ceremonies and thereby served a symbolic civic function as well.[77] In 2002, a crowd of

---

73 唯有視新鄉為吾鄉, 將居留地看成祖國, 而母國是娘家, 我們才能身心安頓, 融入主流社會, 以澳洲的榮辱與共, 社團的領導們, 是時候拋卻海峽兩岸糾纏鬥爭了: ICECAV, "The Bridge March 2002", 7. Niángjia (娘家) literally refers to a married woman's old family home, as traditionally a wife was expected to move into the family home of her husband. It also has a figurative meaning, used here, that denotes a place or foreign land where one was educated or resided for a significant time.
74 See for example: ACCA, "Australian Chinese Community Association of New South Wales Inc.: 25th Annual Report 1999" (Australian Chinese Community Association, 1999), 4, National Library of Australia; ACCA, "ACCA News December 2000" (Australian Chinese Community Association, December 2000), 6, National Library of Australia; ACCA, "ACCA News December 2001" (Australian Chinese Community Association, December 2001), 6–8, National Library of Australia; ACCA, "ACCA News December 2002", 6.
75 ACCA, "25th Annual Report", 4.
76 ACCA, 4; ACCA, "ACCA News December 2001", 7.
77 ACCA, "ACCA News December 2001", 7.

15,000 at Darling Harbour's Tumbalong Park witnessed the Minister for Citizenship and Immigration swear in 40 people of Chinese backgrounds as new Australian citizens.[78] Australian Chinese Day celebrations were as much about embedding Chineseness in Australian culture as they were about embedding Chinese Australians in Australian civil society.

Though the Australian Chinese Day celebrations would have been a golden opportunity for public *qiaowu* efforts, such initiatives were not visible, if they were there at all. While Chinese consul-generals sometimes came along, ACCA's written and photographic coverage of the events showed Australian state and federal politicians as the more regular and feted guests of honour. Major sponsorship came from private enterprise and Australian government sources, not from the Chinese government. The event was run by one of Sydney's largest and most influential community organisations, drawing large crowds of Chinese Australians, community leaders and politicians, and thus was an occasion to influence the festivities through sponsorship. Under these circumstances, we might expect to see *qiaowu* attempts to co-opt local communities' participation or at least promote a positive image of the PRC. The fact that, year after year, this opportunity was not taken by representatives of the PRC suggests that the involvement of PRC representatives was not sought by ACCA. Evidently, *qiaowu* efforts were not all-pervasive or persuasive among Chinese Australian communities. Australian Chinese Day seemed to be an unambiguous celebration of being Chinese, being in Australia, and being Chinese Australian.

Of course, there was already a long history of Chinese and Chinese culture in Australia. Alongside the recent relocations of Chineseness to an Australian context, community organisations sought to establish belonging in Australia also through missions to "rediscover" the early roots of Chinese in Australia. Community organisations' newsletters routinely advertised local projects and history workshops, appealing for participants.[79] In one example, interviews with members of Sydney's

---

78   ACCA, "ACCA News December 2002", 6.
79   ACTCAA, "Newsletter November 1999", 4; CAF and Jon-Claire Lee, "Newsletter: The President's Message", Wayback Machine, Chinese Australian

local community were displayed at the Sydney Museum in 2001 in an exhibit fittingly titled *Reclaiming the Past*.[80] In another, Darwin's Chung Wah Society (CWS) opened its own Chinese Museum in the closing months of 1996. The organisation's members co-launched a history book in which many of them featured, *Astronauts, Lost Souls & Dragons*, the following year.[81] Robyn On, a member of CWS's historical subcommittee, explained to those gathered for the launch at Darwin's Parliament House that the "astronauts" were those early Chinese pioneers and later migrants who discovered "a new world" and life in Australia, the "lost souls" were those now "re-discovering their roots" and "learning what it is to be a Chinese Australian", and the "dragons" were those who were now determined to succeed despite hardship. To On, a historiographical shift and community re-evaluation was underway, and from it a new sense of pride was growing:

> Across Australia, Chinese Australians are re-presenting their past from an insider's point of view. Families are rediscovering their past, talking about their present and looking towards their future ... all proud Australians, all contributing in some way to the country they call home, and at the same time proud of their Chinese heritage.[82]

Elsewhere, community organisations were uncovering the wartime contributions of Chinese Australians as a rich source of (Chinese)

Forum, Winter 2000, https://tinyurl.com/d2yv6hht; CAF and Grace Wong, "Newsletter: Reclaiming the Past", Wayback Machine, Chinese Australian Forum, Autumn 2001, https://tinyurl.com/2uk4kdjn; ACCA, "ACCA News March 2001" (Australian Chinese Community Association, March 2001), 12, National Library of Australia; ACCA, "ACCA News December 2002", 23.

80 CAF and Wong, "Newsletter: Reclaiming the Past".
81 Diana Giese, *Astronauts, Lost Souls & Dragons: Voices of Today's Chinese Australians* (Brisbane: University of Queensland Press, 1997); Diana Giese, "Papers of Diana Giese", manuscript (1990), Box 3, folder 18, Ray Yeo, Speech for Book Launch; *Astronauts, Lost Souls, and Dragons* on 18 December, 1996 at Parliament House, Darwin, 18 December 1996.
82 Giese, "Papers of Diana Giese", Box 3, folder 18, Robyn On, Speech for Book Launch; *Astronauts, Lost Souls, and Dragons* on 18 December, 1996 at Parliament House, Darwin, 18 December 1996.

Australian pride. As part of his mission to bring greater attention to the role Chinese migrants played in the creation of Australia, CAF's Jon-Claire Lee was very proud CAF was the major sponsor for a new memorial dedicated to Chinese Australian ex-servicemen in Sydney's Chinatown. Speaking about this at CAF's annual dinner, Lee stoically reflected that "when war came to Australia with the bombing of Darwin in 1942, they [Chinese Australians] were there".[83] Of course, CAF's membership was largely comprised of Hong Kong emigres, so direct connection to the Chinese Australian veterans of the Second World War was unlikely. But this does not matter. As for all Australians, national membership enables claims of pride and ownership over Australia's war legacy regardless of one's own personal links to that history. What is more important here is the presence of an ethnic element. If, as Lee pointed out, Chinese Australians were there then, then Chinese Australians belong here now.

Because Australians seem to uphold military service as the supreme act of patriotism, appealing to Chinese Australian military history was a potent and oft repeated method for demonstrating Chinese Australian belonging.[84] At this time Billy Sing, with a Chinese father and a record as Gallipoli's most lethal sniper, began appearing with more regularity in community histories and memorials as a symbol of (Chinese) Australian patriotism and thus a "model Chinese Australian".[85] The veneration of Sing was not just patriotic, but timely. As Marilyn Lake, Henry Reynolds and others have pointed out, Australia's reverence for its military history only deepened during the Howard years by way of state programs and a revamped school

---

83   CAF and Jon-Claire Lee, "Newsletter: 2000 CAF Annual Dinner Report", Wayback Machine, Chinese Australian Forum, Spring 2000, http://web.archive.org/web/20030925234959/http://www.caf.org.au/.
84   Interviewee 9, Anonymous Interview; Diana Giese, *Courage and Service: Chinese Australians and World War II* (Marrickville, NSW: Courage and Service Project, 1999).
85   Chek Ling, "Move On, Move On! What It Is to Be Chinese in Australia Today", *Cosmopolitan Civil Societies: An Interdisciplinary Journal* 3, no. 1 (24 March 2011): 14–15, https://doi.org/10.5130/ccs.v3i1.1809; John Hamilton, *Gallipoli Sniper: The Life of Billy Sing* (Sydney: Pan Macmillan Australia, 2008); Interviewee 9, Anonymous Interview.

6 Community organisations in the "Chinese century"

curriculum. A sentimentality and sensitivity to all things Anzac swept the land.[86] The fact that Sing had been an unassuming man who later died in relative obscurity and poverty matched the emotional and anti-authoritarian legend of Anzacs who did their duty for their country but were neglected by "the system".[87] As Australia's reverence for military history transformed into sacred mythos during this period, venerating (Chinese) Australian veterans was perhaps the "most Australian thing" one could do at the time.

Pride in Australia

The relocation and rediscovery of Chineseness in Australia gave Chinese Australian community organisations the ability to wade into other current affairs pertaining to the identity of the nation and its past and future direction. Naturally, expressions of pride or shame about Australia on such matters indicated approval or disapproval respectively. At the close of 1998, CAF's Thiam Ang spoke to the political vanquishment of Pauline Hanson with equal measures of triumph and trepidation:

> Nine out of 10 Australians did not fall for the divisive policies of racist parties. So today, as a proud Australian who is also proud of his Chinese heritage, I can proclaim to the world, Australia is a fair and tolerant country ... The Chinese Australian Forum believes that there is now an opportunity to bind the wounds of racial divide of the last 2½ years. To achieve this, we must however confront the ugliness that beset us. Let us not pretend it has gone away, it has not. It will probably be with us for some time to come.[88]

---

86 Lake et al., *What's Wrong with ANZAC?*
87 Joy Damousi et al., "Why Do We Get So Emotional about Anzac?", in *What's Wrong With Anzac?* (Sydney: UNSW Press, 2010), 94–109, https://tinyurl.com/36nhbdzs.
88 CAF and Thiam Ang, "Newsletter: 1998 Annual Dinner President Speech", Wayback Machine, Chinese Australian Forum, 1998, https://tinyurl.com/yc7rcdsh.

Ang's tempered pride in Australia nonetheless demonstrated his commitment to Australia's multiculturalism. He took the victory over Hanson as a sign of the strength of the country's multicultural identity after all. Along these lines, Chinese Australian community organisations treated Australia's republic referendum and its Centenary of Federation as further tests for the nation; sites where hopes for Australia's multicultural future would clash with vestiges of the British colonial past.

CAF's long-held commitment to cultivating greater political awareness and participation among Chinese Australians was prominently on display in its commentary on the referendum. However, it is also clear that CAF was trying to cultivate a position on the referendum that matched its position on Australia's multicultural identity. Consistent with its non-partisan approach to politics, CAF officially took a non-aligned position on the referendum and encouraged its members to become involved with the referendum process and express their views irrespective of what they were.[89] Nevertheless, CAF had a definite republican leaning. In its newsletters, CAF made it clear that most of its executive supported a republic and its events calendar showed its representatives attending multiple functions in support of the republic campaign.[90] CAF's executive explained this position by pointing to Britain's diminishing relevance to Australia and the need for the country to develop its own distinctive democracy. The executive pointedly remarked that "we do not want a foreigner" to be head of state. In a republic "all Australians of any colour" would have the opportunity to be the state's executive.[91] CAF's position points to the referendum as a question about the future of multiculturalism in Australia as much as it was about who its head of state should be. If multiculturalism was truly to be the basis of Australia's identity, then the traces of British supremacy in its government should be removed.

---

89 CAF, "Press Release: The Republic Debate", Wayback Machine, Chinese Australian Forum, 2000, https://tinyurl.com/2uk4kdjn.
90 CAF, "Newsletter: 1999 Diary", Wayback Machine, Chinese Australian Forum, 1999, https://tinyurl.com/2uk4kdjn.
91 CAF, "Press Release: The Republic Debate".

CAF was heartened by the diverse mix of Australians participating in the referendum process. The involvement of those from non-English-speaking backgrounds was interpreted as a "tremendous change" in the character of the country and a validation of CAF's work to increase political participation over the years. CAF was especially proud of its young member Jason Yat-sen Li for his "significant role" in shaping the republican model for the referendum.[92] CAF's disappointment was commensurately deep when the referendum failed, due to what CAF labelled a monarchist "scare campaign". Still, CAF was unmoved in its conviction: "It is about our pride, our dignity, our maturity to have an Australian, one of us, as our Head of State." But more than a matter of pride, the CAF held that a republic could "further strengthen the contemporary multicultural Australia". CAF's point was that Australia would be stronger and its people proud if all its inhabitants felt they equally belonged.[93]

The desire to belong equally to Australia was concomitant with a desire for human equality. This premise made Australia's celebration of its Centenary of Federation a source of consternation for Chinese Australian community organisations. One reason for Australia's Federation had been to curb Chinese immigration, and one of the newly federated government's first Acts of Parliament did just that. In their own newsletters, CAF and ACCA noted this aspect of their country's past with shame.[94] CAF's Autumn newsletter quoted an article written by CAF member Jason Yat-sen Li and published in *The Bulletin*. In it, Li imagined himself as a Chinese person a century ago watching the Federation parades in Melbourne:

---

92 CAF and Thiam Ang, "Newsletter: 1999 Annual Dinner", Autumn 2000, https://tinyurl.com/2uk4kdjn.
93 CAF and Daniel Lim, "Newsletter: Republic Australia – The Way Forward", Wayback Machine, Chinese Australian Forum, Spring 2000, https://tinyurl.com/2uk4kdjn.
94 CAF and Jenny Lim, "Newsletter: A Tale of Two Books", Wayback Machine, Chinese Australian Forum, Autumn 2000, https://tinyurl.com/2uk4kdjn; ACCA, "ACCA News March 2001", 2–3.

I am vaguely aware that it was people like me who inspired all this ... They want nationhood and racial purity. They're worried about the threat of non-white belligerent states and fear Asia.[95]

While CAF and ACCA expressed pride in Australia's achievements and hope for its future, they called upon their fellow Australians to "consider and debate" the problematic parts of its past and present.[96] To celebrate the good in its past, the nation should not forget the bad.

Yet with the so-called History Wars underway, the conservative sections of Australia saw any critical revision of Australia's past, even its White Australia policy, as unnecessary self-flagellation and navel-gazing.[97] Indeed, CAF's Autumn newsletter quoted one reader of Li's *The Bulletin* article who criticised Li's "sour, gloomy, negative, backward-looking" reflection on these grounds.[98] CAF believed such reproachments could only alienate Chinese Australians and lamented that opportunities for national self-criticism were not taken as opportunities for national self-improvement:

> We, too, have as strong a passion and as deep an attachment to this country as those who sit back and pat themselves on the back. The difference is that we say "Yes, this is a great country ... but we can make it better".[99]

The experiences of the referendum and the Centenary showed how pride and shame in Australia were two sides of a coin. Both sentiments were expressed with the intention of directing Australia further down the path of multiculturalism. At the same time, expressing pride or shame was to express belonging to Australia – as was the relocation and rediscovery of Chineseness in Australia. The claim to belong to Australia carried with it a reciprocal claim of ownership over Australia:

---

95 CAF and Jenny Lim, "Newsletter: Celebrating the Centenary", Wayback Machine, Chinese Australian Forum, Autumn 2001, https://tinyurl.com/2uk4kdjn.
96 ACCA, "ACCA News March 2001", 4.
97 Moran, *The Public Life of Australian Multiculturalism*, 101.
98 CAF and Lim, "Newsletter: Celebrating the Centenary".
99 CAF and Lim.

we belong to Australia and Australia belongs to us. As expressed by Chinese Australian community organisations, the legitimacy of this dual claim rested upon the basis of a multicultural Australia – a basis big enough to include all of Australia's peoples. This ownership of Australia – its past, present and future – encompassed all of which there was to be proud of Australia. But if there is pride to be shared in, there is also shame. The idiom used by ACTCAA to describe Chinese Australian communities' situation in Australia, *róngrǔyǔgòng* (榮辱與共, (of friends) to share honour and disgrace), describes not just this pride/shame duality, but also the reality that all members of a group share their weal and woe. If it is true that Chinese Australians do and always did belong to Australia, then what was their place in its history of colonisation or its contemporary treatment of refugees?

Often, Chinese Australian opinions on these issues were as divided as any other Australian opinion. CAF's 2002 Autumn newsletter was largely dedicated to Australia's treatment of refugees arriving by boat in Australia. As many Chinese Australians had been refugees themselves, there was compassion for the largely Afghan and Muslim refugees now arriving by boat a decade or two after them. CAF's Grace Wong criticised the Australian government for offloading its refugee responsibilities to much smaller, poorer nations via the "Pacific solution" and described popular descriptions of refugees as "queue-jumpers" or "illegals" as callous.[100] ICECAV, on the other hand, seemed more understanding of the government's pragmatism when faced with a difficult issue. Despite the organisation heavily representing ethnic Chinese refugees from Indochina – including some who themselves arrived by boat – it described contemporary arrivals as an "endless stream". In an affirmation of commitment to its new homeland, ICECAV warned that from "temporary kindness comes endless troubles".[101] This is rather surprising considering ICECAV's membership of former refugees – not to mention its exhibition at the Immigration Museum based on the experiences of those refugees.

---

100 CAF and Grace Wong, "Newsletter: Recollections", Wayback Machine, Chinese Australian Forum, Autumn 2002, https://tinyurl.com/2uk4kdjn.
101 一時仁慈來無窮後患 —— 源源不絕湧來的中南印尼東南亞成千上萬的船民, 如何解決?: ICECAV, "The Bridge March 2002", 3.

Ironically, ICECAV's views that many refugees were sources of crime were not inconsistent with earlier examples of some Chinese Australian community leaders' concerns about boat arrivals in northern Australia.[102] As Karen Agutter and Rachel Ankeny have shown in their oral history study of South Australia's migrant hostels, divisive and often problematic views exist among many migrant communities – as they do within the study of migrant communities, too. Consequently, they contend that historians and other scholars have a responsibility to discard established assumptions and reconsider "the attitudes of migrants toward their peers, their successors, and the host society into which they had to settle".[103] Being a former refugee does not necessarily mean one will champion future refugees.

More complex were the responses of community organisations to the plights of Indigenous Australia. Again, there was well-placed sympathy. ICECAV, for example, was perplexed by Howard's inability to apologise to survivors of the "Stolen Generation", believing it bespoke his "stubborn" and "arrogant" style of politics.[104] However, deeper understandings of the often-uncomfortable relationship between multicultural and Indigenous Australia were seldom seen. As an exception, CAF held its own seminar on "Building the Reconciliation Bridge" focused on working toward a "strategy for the inclusion of non-indigenous ethnic communities in reconciliation".[105] CAF saw a need to educate migrants and ethnic minorities about the plight of Aboriginal and Torres Straits Islander peoples and recognised language and prevailing prejudices as barriers. It also believed that, due to their "marginalisation from the mainstream society", Indigenous Australians

---

102 Chin and Giese, *Ernie Chin Interviewed by Diana Giese*; Chin and Giese, *Daryl Chin Interviewed by Diana Giese*; Lee and Giese, *Wellington Lee Interviewed by Diana Giese*.
103 Karen Agutter and Rachel A. Ankeny, "Unsettling Narratives: Overcoming Prejudices in the Hostel Stories Project", *Journal of Australian Studies* 40, no. 4 (October 2016): 474–6, https://doi.org/10.1080/14443058.2016.1223151.
104 ICECAV, "The Bridge August 2000" (Indo-China Ethnic Chinese Association of Victoria, August 2000), 4, State Library of Victoria.
105 CAF, "Press Release: Building the Reconciliation Bridge Seminar", Wayback Machine, Chinese Australian Forum, 2000, https://tinyurl.com/2uk4kdjn.

6 Community organisations in the "Chinese century"

might also be ignorant of the plights of migrant and ethnic communities. As CAF's president Jon-Claire Lee explained:

> People from ethnic communities are often in a unique position to understand the experiences of dispossession, marginalisation, racism and minority status, which can form the basis of dialogue about shared experiences with indigenous Australians. As well, both groups have often experienced the consequences of political persecution and loss of identity and homeland.[106]

While the sentiment was well-intentioned and pointed to shared traumas under White hegemony, there was no reflection on the extent to which other non-White migrant groups were themselves settling Aboriginal lands and in so doing were contributing to the "loss of identity and homeland". Later in his address, Lee noted that English was enshrined as the "common language" in the Multiculturalism Bill 2000 recently passed by the New South Wales government. He celebrated this because:

> English unites us, but does not place itself above others. It is also important for all migrants to accept the unifying power and position of English in Australian life.

While the message might be practical for migrant communities, for Australia's original inhabitants, colonialists used the "power and position" of English as a tool of subjugation.

Here, a space between migrant-centric-multicultural Australia and Indigenous Australia appears. Professor Laksiri Jayasuriya, another speaker at the CAF seminar, put it like this:

> The Aboriginal people have, rightly, been lukewarm and indifferent to the current ideology of Australian multiculturalism, which has been framed specifically to cater for the needs and aspirations of immigrant settlers. At the same time, immigrant ethnic groups, until very recently, have failed to recognise and

---

106 CAF.

acknowledge the special status of Aboriginal people and to promote their concerns. Australia could be described as two societies – one multicultural, the other racist. As a result, the agenda of the reconciliation process has had little or no impact on the non-indigenous ethnic minorities. Furthermore, present multiculturalism masks the exclusion and oppression of Aboriginal Australians.[107]

The multicultural framework championed by Chinese Australian community organisations since the end of White Australia upheld the coexistence between the country's majority Anglo-Australian group and the many minority groups. Yet there seemed little recognition of the tension between multiculturalism's emphasis on pluralism, the ongoing settlement of Australia by many (non-White) peoples, and Indigenous Australia's priority for recognition of sovereignty and rights.[108] The pride in Australia that Chinese Australian community organisations espoused was not neutral. In pursuit of belonging in Australia, these Chinese Australian community organisations used the multicultural paradigm to establish social and cultural proximity to the White majority. Chinese Australian pride in Australia could therefore look like part of a collective settler pride that excluded Aboriginal and Torres Strait Islander peoples. It was a problematic truth that Chinese Australian community organisations might also compartmentalise for the sake of better relations with the Anglo-Australian ethnic majority.

---

107 CAF.
108 See for example: Barry Morris and Gillian K. Cowlishaw, eds, *Race Matters: Indigenous Australians and "Our" Society* (Canberra: Aboriginal Studies Press, 1997); Elizabeth A. Povinelli, *The Cunning of Recognition: Indigenous Alterities and the Making of Australian Multiculturalism*, Politics, History, and Culture (Durham, NC: Duke University Press, 2002); Russell McGregor, *Indifferent Inclusion: Aboriginal People and the Australian Nation* (Canberra: Aboriginal Studies Press, 2011).

6 Community organisations in the "Chinese century"

Looking for pride without prejudice

Many scholars have shown the grasp the PRC has tried to exert over the affairs of Overseas Chinese. Tan and Wong argued that the "destiny of Chinese overseas as an ethnic group" is now largely determined by an "emerging strong China":

> With the rise of China as an economic power and her increasing, concerted effort to bring in the Chinese overseas for her soft power diplomacy, the Chinese overseas, willingly or unwillingly, for good or for worse, are once again closely embraced by a strong China.[109]

It is true that some community organisations did "embrace this embrace". But those who did most willingly were already, more or less, within the PRC's purview due to pre-existing sympathies. Organisations like CFV or CYL had championed the CCP and PRC long before the soft-power push at the beginning of the "Chinese century", as had influential individuals like Maurice Leong and Arthur Locke.

Other community organisations seemed more interested in the potential dividends a relationship with China's representatives could pay and expressed pride in the PRC to procure them. Obviously this increased the visibility of pride about China in Australia. Even so, this was not a simple exchange of PRC praise for PRC presents. At this early stage of the Chinese century, community organisations still engaged with the PRC and its representatives in Australia by degrees of their own choosing or comfort. CAV and ACCA are examples of this, as they still placed importance on their own *huayi* identities and even ACTCAA showed some connection to Taiwan. Furthermore, each of these organisations still showed strong emotional and civil connections to Australia. The continuation of community organisations that were critical of *qiaowu* initiatives (ICECAV being the exemplar) and community leaders who came to question these initiatives show that

---

109 Tan and Wong, "Introduction: Contemporary China's Rise and the Chinese Overseas", 11.

the narrative of the PRC simply rolling over community organisations and co-opting them wholesale is an over-simplification. These community organisations and leaders were exercising their own agency, even if they did choose to align themselves with the PRC.

Moreover, we see that through 1997–2008, Chinese Australians also tied their destinies to their present Australian home. ACCA's "Chinese Australian Day", CAF's unending push for greater political participation, and ICECAV's appeal for Chinese Australians to cast off emotional attachments to an imagined old home for the sake of connecting with the new one are examples of enmeshment in Australia. Because of this enmeshment, Chinese Australian community organisations also felt comfortable, even obliged, to point out some of Australia's faults. Australia's Centenary of Federation provided CAF and ACCA's memberships a moment to reflect on how past injustices should be remembered in the present, and the republic referendum was an opportunity to contemplate a future built on Australian multiculturalism rather than British monarchism.

Having pride in China or Australia was not mutually exclusive. In the years between 1997 and 2008, each community organisation found their own balance of pride in (or criticism of) China or Australia according to their own values. The diversity of these expressions, again, shows the diversity of Chinese Australian communities and the organisations that represent them. However, the colour and vitality of these expressions also indicate there was still social and political space for these organisations to display their pride in or criticism of China or Australia. In this early stage of the Chinese century, Chinese Australian community organisations of different types could strike the balance they chose. This balancing act became more difficult as China began to harden the expectations it attached to its soft power, and Australia grew more concerned about the PRC's influence in its domestic affairs.

7
The "China influence" debate

On 14 May 2020, Victorian Labor Senator Kimberley Kitching called for a Senate Inquiry into Issues Facing Diaspora Communities in Australia. Kitching's motivation likely sprang from her long-standing concern about the PRC's influence in Australia.[1] As part of its inquiry, the committee convened six public hearings, held between September and November 2020. It received 90 submissions from various government bodies, ethnic community organisations and individuals. Among these submissions were 11 from Chinese Australian community organisations and individuals. A further five came from organisations that aired interests or concerns related to the Chinese Australian community or China. These included the Asian Australian Alliance, the Uyghur Association of Victoria and the Australian Tibetan Council. In February 2021, the Senate Committee released its report.

The committee was particularly interested in the extent to which the PRC was co-opting and coercing ethnic communities and organisations for its own interests. Some of the examples heard by the

---

1   Latika Bourke, "Four Australian MPs Urge Britain to Ban Huawei", *The Age*, https://tinyurl.com/yc76yw93; Fergus Bagshaw and Eryk Hunter, "'Go for the Whole Hog': MPs Push for Parliamentary Probe into CCP Influence at Universities", News, *Sydney Morning Herald*, https://tinyurl.com/55ckd2zz.

committee included the surveillance and intimidation of individuals, the creation of organisations to stoke division among communities, and the "hijacking and distorting" of local Chinese-language publications.[2] The committee was also concerned about the anti-Chinese racism that grew following the COVID-19 pandemic and in part due to a growing public perception of China's "united front" activities among Chinese Australian communities.[3] The cultural studies scholar, Wanning Sun, in her own submission to the inquiry, attributed this situation to a "Chinese influence narrative" developing in Australian politics and media over recent years.[4] Sun's concerns were proven valid when the Liberal Senator for Tasmania, Eric Abetz, asked three Chinese Australian witnesses to publicly condemn the CCP. The three, Wesa Chau, Yun Jiang and Osmond Chiu, all balked at the request. No one else at the inquiry had been asked to do the same, they pointed out. They stated they had no affections for the CCP, but neither did they see any reason to fulfil demands due to their shared ethnicity with the Han Chinese majority of the PRC. Abetz called their refusal to condemn the CCP "heinous" and labelled them "apologists".[5] Chau described the experience as "race-baiting McCarthyism".[6] The Senate Inquiry thus caught two sides of an ongoing debate about China's interference in Australian society. On one side were those advocating more strident action against an increasingly bullish China and its interference in Australian society. On the other were those concerned about the impact that hawkish commentary on China was having on Chinese Australian communities.

The development of concerns about China's influence in Australian politics and society in little over a decade has seen community

---

2   Kimberley Kitching, ed., *Issues Facing Diaspora Communities in Australia* (Canberra: Senate Printing Unit, 2021), 33–6, 44–5.
3   Kitching, 51–5.
4   Wanning Sun, "Submission to the Senate Inquiry into Issues Facing Diaspora Communities in Australia", 2020, https://tinyurl.com/22mb2dxx.
5   Fitzgerald, "Eric Abetz's War on Chinese Australians Has Beijing Rubbing Its Hands".
6   Naveen Razik, "'Race-Baiting McCarthyism': Eric Abetz Slammed for Asking Chinese Australians to Denounce Communist Party during Diaspora Inquiry", *SBS News*, 15 October 2020. https://tinyurl.com/v973dry6.

7 The "China influence" debate

organisations responding to two competing imaginings of unity among Chinese Australian communities. One is the transnational vision of a "Greater China" pushed by the PRC into Australia. It applies a shared culture to an ethno-nationalist end.[7] A report by the Australian Chinese Workers Association (ACWA) puts it thus:

> Australian Chinese are the same as other overseas Chinese groups in that they possess a strong sense of belonging and cultural identification towards China. The hearts of Australian Chinese community organisations, no matter whether past or current, are tied to the destiny and development of China, paying special attention to China's progress, power and prosperity.[8]

The other competing vision is of civil unity with the Australian mainstream. The pressure to align with one viewpoint or the other has intensified following the first decade of the so-called "Chinese century". It has seen rivalries and disputes arise between organisations holding different views and alienated other organisations that do not wish to become partisan. Indeed, the reactions of various Chinese Australian community organisations have in themselves been grist for the arguments of Chinese and non-Chinese Australian voices in a debate about the form, extent and objectives of China's influence in Australian society. As with the Blainey and Hanson debates on Asian immigration and multiculturalism, the current debate on China's influence is playing

---

7 Harry Harding, "The Concept of 'Greater China': Themes, Variations and Reservations", in *Greater China: The Next Superpower?*, ed. David Shambaugh, Studies on Contemporary China (New York: Oxford University Press, 1995), 8–34; Gungwu Wang, "Greater China and the Chinese Overseas", in *Greater China: The Next Superpower?*, ed. David Shambaugh, Studies on Contemporary China (New York: Oxford University Press, 1995), 274–96.

8 "澳大利亚华人跟其他海外华人华侨一样，对中国具有强烈的归属感和文化认同感。澳大利亚华人社团不管在过去还是现在，都心系中国的命运和发展，关注着中国的进步与强盛"Australian Chinese Workers Association, ed., *Aodaliya Huaren Shequ Fazhan Baogao 2018* 澳大利亚华人社区发展报告 2018 (*Australian Chinese Community Development Report 2018*) (Harbin: Heilongjiang People's Publishing House, 2018), 239.

out in political and media arenas and Chinese Australian communities are caught in the fallout.

In the roughly two decades that this debate has developed, there have also been great changes among Chinese Australian communities – to the point that the degree to which some self-described organisations are representative of a Chinese Australian community at all becomes tenuous. Since the 2000s, Chinese Australian community organisations have changed in form and function as the different migrant cohorts that established them have aged and new waves of PRC emigrants to Australia have arrived. Moreover, entirely new organisations have appeared and come to be major players in the socio-cultural space shared by Chinese Australians. The issue is whether these new organisations – and indeed some of the old ones – still represent *the* or *a* Chinese Australian community in the same way as community organisations did in the past.

Generally speaking, the most outspoken organisations from the 2010s onward have been concerned more with advancing their particular political agendas than with fostering a sense of community among Chinese Australians. Despite the continued growth of Chinese Australian communities, these organisations do not focus primarily on cultural maintenance, welfare services, or increasing societal and political participation for Chinese Australians. Many new groups are better described as political interest organisations: organisations shaped by and dedicated to progressing an often singular ideal or objective and responding to events through the prism of that ideal or objective. This development is not necessarily a negative one and can be seen as reflecting the ever-increasing diversity among Chinese Australian communities. As seen in previous chapters, greater societal and political participation has contributed to the vitality and robustness of Australian multiculturalism. Likewise, these new political organisations have become prominent in debates about China's interests in Australia. Nevertheless, to describe these bodies as community organisations would be misleading when their function lies in pursuing political interests rather than supporting community.

Though some of these organisations' claims to community representativeness are tenuous, it does not stop them from declaring that they represent and are supported by the "Chinese Australian

7 The "China influence" debate

community". Making these declarations, whether true or not, is important for the legitimisation of these organisations' political actions and messages. Since the hardening of China's soft-power initiatives over the last decade, these claims for community support and representation have become more urgent but also shriller. This is because the claims bundle together assertions about the "true" nature and form of the "Chinese Australian community". Competing claims about the nature of the true Chinese Australian community came to a head around the 2016 *Glory and Dream* concerts. A few years later, the COVID-19 pandemic provided another space in which community representation came into question.

Implicating Chinese Australians in the debate

Although academic, political and media attention toward China is primarily focused on the power politics between China and Australia, Chinese Australian communities are nonetheless caught in the crossfire. One reason for this is a tendency in some quarters to elide differences between China and Chinese Australians, not to mention differences between Chinese Australians themselves. In *Silent Invasion*, Clive Hamilton's concern about China's influence in Australia extends to the presence of Chinese Australians in Australian society. Because China expects fealty from Chinese Australians on the basis of race, Hamilton suggests, non-Chinese Australians have cause to suspect the loyalty of any Chinese Australians until proven otherwise.[9] "Espionage on behalf of the PRC is carried out predominantly by those of Chinese heritage", he warns, and Australia must be careful to trust only "those Mandarin speakers whose loyalty to Australia can be assured".[10] Hamilton's intention is to alert Australia to China's infiltration. In the process, he identifies Chinese ethnicity as grounds for suspicions that extend indiscriminately over Chinese Australian communities.

Attempts to distinguish between different types of Chinese Australian communities can also lead to generalisations that put some

---

9 Hamilton, *Silent Invasion*, 39–40, 140; Brophy, *China Panic*, 148.
10 Hamilton, *Silent Invasion*, 151, 181.

communities under greater suspicion than others. In *Red Zone*, Peter Hartcher suggests that a "review of the immigration mix is timely". "Prima facie," he argues, "ethnic Chinese immigrants from Taiwan and Hong Kong are more likely to value Australian liberties." Mainland migrants, on the other hand, should be screened for their ability to "value Australian liberties".[11] Hartcher's reasoning presumably entails a belief that Chinese Australians who grew up under one-party rule somehow retain allegiance to that party. Although Hartcher acknowledges the heterogeneity of Chinese Australian communities, his generalisations about different Chinese backgrounds creates a clear hierarchy of "Australianness" on the basis of one's origin. As Sun points out, where one is born does not dictate one's politics – indeed, many Mainlanders emigrated to escape one-party rule.[12] Moreover, the first president of the Australian Council for the Promotion of the Peaceful Reunification of China (ACPPRC), an overtly pro-PRC organisation, was the Malaysian-born and Australian-educated William Chiu.[13] Prima facie, Chiu does not fit Hartcher's logic.

Sun used the phrase "Chinese influence narrative" to describe the assumptions underpinning the suspicions of Chinese Australian communities. Going one step further, David Brophy has described Australia's angst about China's influence as a "China Panic". Brophy identifies latent Australian racism and historical fears of Asian immigration and invasion as the true root cause for concerns about Chinese Australian communities being part of China's infiltration of Australia.[14] Focusing on the discourses around China's influence and the implications for Chinese Australian communities, Sun and Brophy seemingly bypass much discussion of *qiaowu* initiatives – which remain important because these initiatives have entangled Chinese Australian communities, often unfairly, in the debate about China's influence.

---

11 Hartcher, *Red Zone*, 176–8.
12 Wanning Sun, "Response to 'Red Flag: Waking Up to China's Challenge' by Peter Hartcher", *Pearls and Irritations*, 24 March 2020, https://tinyurl.com/5abw5mnz.
13 ACPPRC, "Chairman", Wayback Machine, ACPPRC, 29 August 2007, https://tinyurl.com/ycx34sy2; Hamilton, *Silent Invasion*, 30–1.
14 Brophy, *China Panic*, 142–4.

7 The "China influence" debate

Hamilton does reflect on the repercussions the current debate has had on Chinese Australian communities. When he asked about the risk that his book *Silent Invasion* might stir up xenophobia, his Chinese Australian friends typically responded along the lines of: "'Well what's the alternative? Should you just say nothing?'"[15] According to Hamilton, his friends were willing to "take some collateral damage to win the larger battle" against China in respect of its influence operations. There are obvious problems with this position. If some are willing to accept "collateral damage", as Hamilton rather brutally puts it, others are clearly concerned about generalisations about Chinese Australians and the ramifications for their communities.

Shifts in Chinese Australian communities

One factor that likely plays into fears about the PRC's influence in Australian society is that China has become the third biggest source for Australia's overseas-born population. Large numbers of young PRC migrants have altered, even displaced many of the previously established Chinese Australian neighbourhoods and communities in Australia's capital cities. Their predominance is noticeable through the prevalence of simplified script and Mandarin language in Chinese-language environments in Australia. According to interviewees, the visibility of Mainland migrants is also enhanced by their displays of wealth and confidence in business and society that is greater than their counterparts from other places.[16]

---

15   Clive Hamilton, "Why Do We Keep Turning a Blind Eye to Chinese Political Interference?", *The Conversation*, 4 April 2018, https://tinyurl.com/9a8tcnrv.
16   Simon-Davies and McGann, "Top 10 Countries of Birth for the Overseas-Born Population since 1901"; ABS, "Cultural Diversity in Australia", Census, Reflecting a Nation: Stories from the 2011 Census (Canberra: Australian Bureau of Statistics, 21 June 2012), https://tinyurl.com/75j4y53f; Samantha Zhan Xu and Wei Wang, "Change and Continuity in Hurstville's Chinese Restaurants: An Ethnographic Linguistic Landscape Study in Sydney", *Linguistic Landscape. An International Journal* 7, no. 2 (16 June 2021): 175–203, https://doi.org/10.1075/ll.20007.xu; Interviewee 1, Anonymous

The demographic shift is obvious in the states with the largest Chinese Australian populations, New South Wales and Victoria, and is reflected in their respective registries of community organisations.

Table 7.1 shows that the number of Chinese Australian community organisations increased over the decades – in step with the growing number of ethnic Chinese immigrants to Australia in the same decades. Two further details should be noted. The first is that many of the community organisations that were established in earlier decades have today ceased to operate. This decline reflects changes in different Chinese Australian communities. From the 1970s to the 2020s, the vast majority of community organisations were created by first-generation migrants. Only those organisations that achieved inter-generational relevance – and therefore inter-generational membership – achieved longevity. For example, many ethnic Chinese refugees from Indochina registered community organisations in Victoria and New South Wales during the 1980s and 1990s to fulfil their communities' specific settlement and welfare needs. As demand to meet these needs decreased, so too did the relevance of some of these organisations. For example, the once large and highly active Indo-China Ethnic Chinese Association of Victoria (ICECAV) has diminished and its primary function now seems to be around social activities and meals for its elderly membership.[17] Likewise, organisations that reflected a highly specific need have disappeared as those needs and circumstances have changed. The Chinese Student's [sic] Association for Safeguarding Human Rights and the Special Committee for Chinese Students, for example, were formed by Chinese students to respond to the Tiananmen Massacre and later campaigned for permanent residency

---

Interview; Interviewee 8, Anonymous Interview; Interviewee 10, Anonymous Interview.

17 ACNC, "Indo China Ethnic Chinese Association of Victoria Inc", Text, Australian Charities and Not-for-profits Commission (Australian Charities and Not-for-profits Commission, 1 April 2021), https://tinyurl.com/mrdujya8; City of Melbourne Council, "Successful Applicants 2023" (Melbourne: Community Meals Subsidy Program, 2023), https://tinyurl.com/4y7crdpp; City of Melbourne Council, "Successful Applicants 2024" (Melbourne: Community Meals Subsidy Program, 2024), https://tinyurl.com/4y7crdpp.

7 The "China influence" debate

Table 7.1 "Chinese" organisations registered and deregistered in New South Wales and Victoria.

Data taken from fairtrading.nsw.gov.au and consumer.vic.gov.au. Community organisations listed had the word "China" or "Chinese" in their title.

Number of new community organisations registered per decade

State	1980s	1990s	2000s	2010s	2020–21	Total
NSW	21	176	281	326	33	837
Victoria	59	132	188	412	31	822

Number of deregistered community organisations by decade of registration

State	1980s	1990s	2000s	2010s	2020–1	Total
NSW	9	118	214	123	0	464
Victoria	30	83	84	61	0	258

Number of community organisations still registered by decade of registration

State	1980s	1990s	2000s	2010s	2020–1	Total
NSW	12	58	67	203	33	373
Victoria	29	49	104	351	31	564

in Australia. These organisations were wound up when the objectives necessitating their existence were met (that is, the students were granted permanent residency).

Other community organisations that are still functioning have changed with the times, too. CFV, one of the most dynamic community organisations throughout the 1970s to 1990s, is now organised almost entirely around its language school program. Accordingly, it has moved from its North Melbourne premises to sites in the outer eastern suburbs of Melbourne where many new generations of Chinese Australian families have settled.[18] In another example, the Cathay Community Association (CCA) once had a focus on social activities for ethnic

Chinese resettling in Brisbane from Papua New Guinea, and even helped settle ethnic Chinese refugees in the 1980s. Interviewees from Brisbane had all noted CCA's history as one of the premier community organisations in the city. The organisation still has a large hall and substantial resources, but as its membership aged, CCA shifted its focus to services and activities more suited to the elderly.[19] Naturally, these community organisations pivoted as the needs of their members changed. But in the process, other issues to which these organisations had once devoted themselves – like responding to racism or settling new migrants – were deprioritised. This fact, combined with the diminished time and energy of ageing memberships, means that some community organisations have lost the capability to respond to the Sinophobia arising from fears of China's soft power.

Table 7.1 also shows the high number of community organisations registered – and deregistered – in New South Wales and Victoria between 2000 and 2020–21. Many of these organisations were highly specific in form and function: language schools, sporting clubs, professional and religious associations. More specialised again were groups catering to niche interests like fishing, bodybuilding or cars. The increase in number and variety of organisations is in line with the increase not only in ethnic Chinese migrants but especially in migrants from the Chinese mainland. The same factor explains the many "neo-native place associations" registered in this period, including the Australian Chinese Jiangxi Association and the Australian Dongbei Chinese Association. Over 100 of these organisations now comprise the membership of the Federation of Chinese Associations in Victoria.[20] Like the native place associations of the 19th century, the neo-native place associations are formed according to members' province or region of origin. However, the past native place associations held parochial attachments to their home counties or clans. Neo-native place associations, on the other hand,

---

18   CFV, "About Us", 澳大利亚墨尔本侨友社中文学校 *Chinese Fellowship Chinese School in Melbourne, Australia*, 2021, https://tinyurl.com/ywkvvanh.
19   Interviewee 9, Anonymous Interview.
20   FCA, "注册会员团体 zhuce huiyuan tuanti (Registered Member Organisations)".

7 The "China influence" debate

accentuate their attachment to China as a whole. Unlike the organisations established by Chinese Australian communities in previous decades, they do not overtly promote welfare or cultural maintenance. Instead, these organisations are most visible when participating in political actions, often at the behest of ACPPRC. At the same time, organisations that are explicitly anti-PRC have formed, many coming out of or associated with the Falun Dafa (otherwise known as the Falun Gong, a spiritual movement persecuted by Chinese authorities). While these organisations also presumably serve a social function (and a quasi-religious one in the case of Falun Dafa), these organisations are politically oriented.

By far the greatest number of organisations registered – and then deregistered – were those geared toward business, tourism, arts and "culture exchange". A common perception among interviewees of these organisations was that they were established only to facilitate business connections with China.[21] While a pecuniary interest was the likely primary motivation for such organisations, they could also become embroiled in more politically charged issues. These (pseudo-)business organisations, along with the pro- and anti-PRC organisations, have very narrow foci and memberships. While they are mostly formed by first-generation migrants from the PRC, the newest and largest Chinese Australian cohort, broader community representation cannot be extrapolated from their memberships as they do not function as community organisations.

Overall, these shifts in the focus and form of Chinese Australian (community) organisations affect the way they might respond to issues surrounding China's influence in Australia or resurgent Sinophobia. Older community organisations, if they still exist, might not be able to respond to such issues as effectively as they did during the Blainey and Hanson debates. The newer organisations that have proliferated in the Chinese Australian socio-cultural space, however, do not seem to espouse the same combination of cultural maintenance, community welfare, and societal and political participation purposes. Where the

---

21 Interviewee 1, Anonymous Interview; Interviewee 4, Anonymous Interview; Interviewee 5, Anonymous Interview; Interviewee 8, Anonymous Interview; Interviewee 9, Anonymous Interview; Interviewee 10, Anonymous Interview.

previous generation of community organisations professed political neutrality and objectivity as a virtue (even if it was not always maintained), the new organisations were formed around clear political or pecuniary interests. These are important considerations for staking out the parameters of the China influence debate, identifying the effect of the debate on Chinese Australian communities, and understanding the responses these communities might enact.

Qiaowu initiatives and transnational Chinese Australian unity

As Hamilton and Hartcher demonstrate, there are major concerns in Australia regarding the PRC's ability to mobilise ethnic Chinese (including Australian citizens) to support its own interests. Hamilton expands on this in his chapter, "Qiaowu and the Chinese Diaspora":

> First-generation migrants living abroad and their children, even if they do not speak Mandarin and know little about China, are targeted for recruitment. Even Chinese babies adopted and raised by Western families become natural targets for enlistment to the cause of the China Dream. On weekends some ethnic Chinese children in Australia attend Chinese schools that teach a CCP view of the world. Free summer camps take teenagers back to China for two weeks of subtle reinforcement of their Chineseness and indoctrination in party views.[22]

Hamilton's description of babies, children and teenagers being recruited and indoctrinated might be alarming (or alarmist?) to parents and community organisations alike. The Chinese Association of Victoria (CAV) sent 10 students to one such youth summer camp in 2010. It reported that 6,000 students from around the world were in attendance and that the camp was opened by Xi Jinping (then First Vice President of China) with an address in the Great Hall of the People. It was clear to CAV that "the Chinese government considered this an important event".[23] Was this youth indoctrination? It seems unlikely.

---

22 Hamilton, *Silent Invasion*, 37–8.

7 The "China influence" debate

The scholarship from which Hamilton draws for his chapter on *qiaowu* comes overwhelmingly from James To's *Qiaowu: Extra-territorial Policies for the Overseas Chinese*. The tenor of To's analysis, however, is slightly different to Hamilton's. To finds that *qiaowu* initiatives trying to build political support for the PRC among second-generation Chinese migrants are "often a failed ritual" due to their connections to the countries of their birth.[24] Rather than being indoctrinated into state programs, To warns that the youth going on these camps are more likely to partake in the kinds of mischief teenagers enjoy when free of their parents' supervision.

To believes *qiaowu* initiatives are more effective among recent Chinese migrant communities than with older ones: what he terms *xīnqiáo* (新侨) and *lǎoqiáo* (老侨) communities, respectively. This is mainly because the connections newer migrants have with the PRC are still fresh, while older migrant communities uprooted themselves from their homelands decades or generations ago, and have since grown roots in their new home country.[25] Hong Liu and Els van Dongen similarly recognise that the PRC's *qiaowu* activities attempt to "attract talent and lure knowledge" from among the Overseas Chinese. But like To, they qualify their findings. The outright co-optation of Overseas Chinese is too simplistic:

> The Chinese overseas are not just passive recipients of state policy, but actors in their own right who benefit from this cooperation with the Chinese state.[26]

As discussed in the previous chapter, the transnational embrace that the PRC extended to Chinese Australian community organisations was welcomed or rebuffed in ways consistent with the organisations' historical views of the PRC (good or bad), as well as with their own

---

23 CAV, "CAV Newsletter August 2010" (Chinese Association of Victoria, August 2010), 15–17, https://tinyurl.com/2mtj5fxz.
24 To, *Qiaowu*, 169–71.
25 To, 158–90.
26 Liu and van Dongen, "China's Diaspora Policies as a New Mode of Transnational Governance".

present interests (such as the dividends a relationship with the PRC could pay). Those that had been historically "neutral" (like CAV) welcomed the benefits that a closer relationship with the PRC could offer, without necessarily advocating or critiquing the PRC's international or domestic positions. This continued to be the case after 2008, despite the intensification of *qiaowu* initiatives. Organisations that have a bad history with the PRC, like Falun Dafa, have railed against the PRC's *qiaowu* program – especially because the program targets organisations like Falun Dafa as dissidents.[27] Conversely, ACWA has been pushing the *qiaowu* agenda forward. In recent years, ACWA has petitioned local Chinese Australians to take up and support the *huayi ka* scheme (a program granting limited residence and work rights to people of Chinese ethnicity in Shanghai and Guangdong) and published an extensive report on how Chinese Australian communities can be better incorporated into "China's soft power" program.[28] Both Falun Dafa and ACWA are organisations largely comprised of recent PRC emigrants. We might then consider the degree to which organisations like Falun Dafa or ACWA (or even older community organisations, for that matter) represent Chinese Australian communities in recent history and what implications this has on understanding support for (or opposition to) the PRC.

From the turn of the century, when the PRC was building its network of overseas influence, there is evidence of community organisations of different descriptions coming together for a common cause, namely to respond to Sinophobia. In 2014, Senator Clive Palmer made racist remarks about China and the Chinese wanting to "take over this country" on ABC's *Q&A* program.[29] Though Palmer tried to clarify that his

---

27 FDA, "Submission to the Senate Inquiry into Issues Facing Diaspora Communities in Australia" (Falun Dafa Association of Australia, 2020).
28 ACWA, "华裔卡 huayi ka (Chinese Descendant ID Card)", WordPress, 澳洲华人总工会, *Australian Chinese Workers Association*, n.d., http://www.acwacoop.org/%e6%b4%bb%e5%8a%a8/%e5%8d%8e%e8%a3%94%e5%8d%a Australian Chinese Workers Association, *Aodaliya Huaren Shequ Fazhan Baogao 2018 澳大利亚华人社区发展报告 2018 (Australian Chinese Community Development Report 2018)*, 240–2.
29 ABC, "Palmer Brands Chinese Government 'Mongrels' Who 'Shoot Own People'", Text, *ABC News*, 19 August 2014, https://tinyurl.com/4ueez4h6.

7 The "China influence" debate

comments were not intended to refer to Chinese people, Chinese Australian "concerns and anger" quickly materialised in the shape of a demonstration representing some 40 community organisations on the lawns of Parliament House in Canberra.[30] Among them were new organisations like ACWA and long-established organisations like the Australian Chinese Community Association (ACCA), CASS Ltd (formerly known as the Chinese Australian Services Society), along with the Korean Society of Sydney, in a show of solidarity.[31] Palmer issued an apology soon afterwards. It was accepted by China's ambassador to Australia, Zhaoxu Ma, but he remarked that "Chinese people are never to be insulted".[32] Because anti-Chinese racism affects all Chinese Australians, it is easy to see how and why different community organisations would come together. At the same time, the involvement of the Chinese ambassador showed how narratives of hurt and insult could blur the line between China and Chinese Australian communities and between organisations new and old.[33]

The convergence of old and new community organisations weakens when the issues at hand are less to do with the general experience of Chinese Australians and more to do with party political interests, including Communist Party interests. This fact notwithstanding, organisations still present their political actions as if they represented the views of the wider Chinese Australian community. When the Australian government cancelled the residency status of ACPPRC's ex-president Huang Xiangmo in February 2019 (due to his suspected role as an agent of foreign influence), ACPPRC quickly

---

30 Felix Lam, "Peak Organisations ACCA, CASS & KSS Visit to Canberra over Senator Palmer's Offensive Insult", *Australian Chinese Community Association*, 29 August 2014, https://tinyurl.com/4cecer5k.
31 ACWA, "Achievements," WordPress, 澳洲华人总工会, *Australian Chinese Workers Association*, https://tinyurl.com/2p9wmjew; Lam, "Peak Organisations ACCA, CASS & KSS Visit to Canberra".
32 Latika Bourke, "Clive Palmer Apologises for China Comments in Which He Referred to Chinese 'Mongrels'", *Sydney Morning Herald*, 26 August 2014, https://tinyurl.com/39ny26hh.
33 Louise Edwards, "Victims, Apologies, and the Chinese in Australia", *Journal of Chinese Overseas* 15, no. 1 (10 April 2019): 71–4, 81–2, https://tinyurl.com/mwvuh2nv.

rallied together 128 Chinese Australian organisations "from across Australia" to protest the decision and protect Chinese Australians' "political participation". Their open letter was published in three Chinese-language newspapers and gained attention in the *Sydney Morning Herald*, too.[34]

ACWA's *Report on the Development of Chinese Community in Australia 2018* included other examples of ACPPRC-led actions, including a joint letter of community organisations opposing the Dalai Lama's visit in 2008, and a rally in Melbourne to protest The Hague's ruling against the PRC's territorial claim over the South China Sea in 2016. ACWA described the latter as the biggest protest from the Chinese Australian community in years. As ACWA's report explained, the strength and use of these protests rested upon the fact that they were legitimate representations of the will of Chinese Australians:

> Chinese community organisations boldly and vocally introduce China's national situation and policies to all parts of Australia, resolving the one-sided views of the Australian masses and energetically advancing the Australian public's knowledge of China, thereby advancing China's national image as well as strengthening China's soft power.[35]

---

34 *Sydney Today*, "力挺黄向墨！全澳128家华人社团联合发声：强烈抗议无良媒体及政客攻讦！Li Ting Huang Xiangmo! Quan Ao 128 Jia Huaren Shetuan Lianhe Fasheng: Qianglie Kangyi Wu Liang Meiti Ji Zhengke Gongjie! (Support Huang Xiangmo! Across Australia, 128 Chinese Community Groups Issue Joint Statement Strongly Protesting against Unscrupulous Media and Politicians!)", *Sydney Today*, 16 February 2019, https://tinyurl.com/6jrn5yx9; Nick Bonyhady, "Chinese Newspapers Dedicate Front Pages to Exiled Billionaire Huang Xiangmo," *Sydney Morning Herald*, 16 February 2019, https://tinyurl.com/6bf26jbx.

35 华人社团勇敢发声，向澳大利亚全方位地介绍中国国情和政策方针，化解澳大利亚民众的片面看法，积极提升澳大利亚公众对中国的认识，从而提升中国的国家形象以及增强中国软实力: Australian Chinese Workers Association, *Aodaliya Huaren Shequ Fazhan Baogao 2018 澳大利亚华人社区发展报告 2018 (Australian Chinese Community Development Report 2018)*, 240.

There was also an implication that Chinese Australian organisations were of one view – which happened to align with China's. The 128 organisations' collective defence of Xiangmo Huang was likewise intended to be seen as a show of unity across Chinese Australian communities.

The degree to which these actions and organisations reflected the views of a large and diverse collective of communities is questionable. In the case of The Hague demonstrations, ACWA's report claimed there were 3,000 attendees representing some 100 community organisations.[36] Video footage of the event suggests a more accurate estimation of attendees would be around 1,000. Moreover, which organisations took part is left unclear as ACWA does not clarify this and there is no signage denoting the participation of any particular community organisation in video footage.[37] If ACWA's claim is taken at face value, however, it would still appear that the 100 organisations participating in the rally had small memberships. The websites of many of the neo-native place associations that were rallied by ACPPRC to support Huang also give the impression of having small memberships (many organisations' websites mirror each other, some have not been updated for years or are incomplete and others have ceased to function).[38] Whether these organisations represent the opinions of Chinese Australians en masse is questioned by Chinese Australians themselves. In response to one article covering the community groups rallying around Huang, a reader scoffed: "What's ridiculous is that ordinary people have something to do with this. I've never heard of any of these 128 groups, let alone ever heard them say

---

36 Australian Chinese Workers Association, 240.
37 *Ruptly*, "Australia: Chinese Protesters Rally against South China Sea Ruling in Melbourne", YouTube, *Ruptly News Watch*, 23 July 2016, https://www.youtube.com/watch?v=jSeaPFxRyxA.
38 See for example: Australian Hokkien HuayKuan Association, "Homepage", *Australian Hokkien HuayKuan Association,澳洲福建会馆*, n.d., http://www.fjhk.org.au/; Australian Hunan Association, "Homepage", *Australian Hunan Association,澳大利亚湖南会*, n.d., https://www.hunan.com.au/; Australian Fujian Association, "Homepage", *Australian Fujian Association,澳大利亚福建乡情联谊会*, n.d., https://www.australianfujianassociation.org/; Australian Jiangxi Association, "Homepage", *Australian Jiangxi,澳大利亚江西同乡会*, http://www.jiangxi.net.au/ (no longer functioning).

anything publicly. They have all just sprung up now, lol."³⁹ Though the claims to community representativeness can be questioned, it is clear that ACWA and ACPPRC placed a lot of importance on appearing to be representative or supported by the community. Legitimacy for their political opinions and actions rested on this representation and support.

The *Glory and Dream* concerts

Both pro- and anti-PRC groups have claimed to represent the "Chinese Australian community" to legitimise their political views. Inherent to these claims are concurrent and competing claims about the true shape, character and opinions of that community. These competing ideas played out during the 2016 *Glory and Dream* concerts which then ignited broader public interest about China's reach into Australia.

The concerts were organised by the International Cultural Exchange Association (Australia) Incorporated (henceforth, ICEAA) for 6 September and 9 September at the Sydney Town Hall and Melbourne Town Hall respectively. ICEAA was another new organisation (registered in 2015) that staged Chinese cultural and artistic performances.⁴⁰ These performances were sometimes overt displays of Chinese patriotism, like ICEAA's gala *Ode to Peace*, which celebrated the 70th anniversary of China's victory in the Anti-Japanese War.⁴¹ *Glory and Dream* was to be a gala of Cultural Revolutionary songs and dances to commemorate the 40th anniversary of Mao Zedong's passing. In advertisements for the events, ICEAA uncritically portrayed Mao as a leader who ushered in a period of peace, stability

---

39 可笑的是，平时老百姓有事情，从来没听过这128家哪个发声，甚至听都没听说过，这回一下全冒出来了，呵呵呵: *Sydney Today*, "Li Ting Huang Xiangmo!"
40 NSW Fair Trading, "Association Summary (ICEAA)", NSW Incorporated Associations Register, 2021, https://tinyurl.com/bd453rb6.
41 ICEAA, "LB 集团《和平颂》音乐晚会再创澳洲海外华人演艺高峰 LB Jituan "Heping Song" Yinyue Wanhui Zai Chuang Aozhou Haiwai Huaren Yanyi Gaofeng (LB Group's "Ode to Peace" Concert Hits a New Peak of Overseas Chinese Performing Arts)", Wayback Machine, *pc181.com*, 28 June 2015, https://tinyurl.com/3cemwcjm.

and development for China – achievements for which he was recognised as a hero "in the eyes of the whole world".[42] As a show of authenticity, ICEAA also displayed certificates from the Mao Clan Exchange Association and the Mao Clan Cultural Corporation – Chinese mainland organisations dedicated to the proliferation of Chairman Mao's legacy – that approved of the forthcoming concerts.[43]

Despite ICEAA's name implying the exchange of culture across borders, the flow of culture through ICEAA seemed directed solely toward a Mandarin-speaking audience. The promotion of *Glory and Dream* appeared only in Chinese-language media. Video footage of *Ode to Peace* shows that ICEAA's performances follow a similar language format: the concert was comprised entirely of performances in Mandarin and moderated by hosts speaking Mandarin only. Examples of (Chinese) Australian culture were absent from the program. With a complete lack of advertisements or accessibility of content for non-Mandarin speakers, it is difficult to see how culture was to be exchanged between China and Australia or Chinese and (Chinese) Australians at these events. Rather than a conduit of cultural exchange, ICEAA appeared to function as a disseminator of PRC-centric Chinese culture.

ICEAA's function here dovetailed with the CCP's *qiaowu* initiatives to project its preferred image into Australia and compel Overseas Chinese to identify with the PRC. Chongyi Feng has publicly linked the organisers of the *Glory and Dream* concerts to the PRC through funding and ideology.[44] Yet the ideological alignment with the PRC is obvious in ICEAA's rhetoric. Promotional materials described the concerts' objective as "entrusting Chinese people at home and abroad" with the mission to carry the glorious past of the Chinese nation toward

---

42 ICEAA, "《光榮夢想》ICEAAI爱西亚艺术团 'Guangrong Mengxiang' ICEAAI Ai Xiya Yishu Tuan ('Glory and Dream' ICEAAI Western and Asian Arts Appreciation Group)", Wayback Machine, *A China Media*, 15 August 2016, https://tinyurl.com/yswes5uh.
43 ICEAA.
44 Chongyi Feng, "Academic Chongyi Feng: Profits, Freedom and China's 'Soft Power' in Australia", *The Conversation*, 6 June 2017, https://tinyurl.com/4x92bx29; Chongyi Feng, "Culture, Free Speech and Celebrating Mao Downunder", *The Conversation*, 24 August 2016, https://tinyurl.com/3n4mdjmv.

its future dreams.⁴⁵ The same message was inherent in the title and content of *Glory and Dream*, which involved a symbolic coupling of the glory of Mao's leadership in the past with the "Chinese dream" currently promoted by Xi Jinping.⁴⁶ ICEAA's collective statements about the form and character of Chinese "at home and abroad" in these materials were premised on the principles of ethnic homogeneity and duty of all Chinese toward the motherland.

These principles were equally apparent in ICEAA's assumptions about the intended audience. In one early promotion of the event on Chinese social media platform *Weibo* (now deleted), ICEAA addressed readers inclusively as "Overseas Chinese" and "travellers abroad", which implied the reader's temporariness in Australia and rootedness in China.⁴⁷ The interchangeability of these terms of address makes us consider whether ICEAA saw a fundamental difference between Chinese expats and Chinese Australians. To arrive at an answer requires making judgements about where ICEAA placed greater importance: on the transnational connections of Chinese (Australians) as the PRC would prefer, or the local rootedness of Chinese Australian identities.

The Australian Values Alliance

One direct outcome of the advance publicity, limited as it was to people literate in Chinese, was the formation of the Australian Values Alliance (AVA). The AVA came together over two petitions started on *change.org*

---

45 ICEAA, "Guangrong Mengxiang".
46 Tianda Yanjiuyuan, Ed., *Zhongguo Meng, Fu Xing Meng: Xi Jinping Dang Xuan Zhong Gong Zhong Yang Zong Shu Ji Quan Qiu Ping Lun Yu Bao Dao Xuan Ji*, 中国梦, 复兴梦: 习近平当选中共中央总书记全球评论与报道选辑 (*Chinese Dream, Revival Dream: Global Comments and Reports on Xi Jinping's Election as General Secretary of the CPC Central Committee*) (Hong Kong: Tianda Yanjiuyuan Chuban, 2013), https://tinyurl.com/55usz3um.
47 Ye Yuan, "《光荣 梦想》海外华人纪念毛泽东逝世四十周年大型文艺晚会即将举行 'Guangrong Mengxiang' Haiwai Huaren Jinian Mao Zedong Shishi Sishi Zhounian Daxing Wenyi Wanhui Jijian Juxing ('Glory and Dream': Overseas Chinese Will Hold a Concert to Commemorate the 40th Anniversary of the Death of Mao Zedong)", Social Media, *weibo.com*, 12 April 2016, https://tinyurl.com/mza5af55.

7 The "China influence" debate

on 16 August to oppose the staging of the *Glory and Dream* concerts in Sydney and Melbourne. The petitions respectively called on Lord Mayor Clover Moore and Lord Mayor Robert Doyle to "immediately terminate the agreement" for the events in each of these cities' town halls and furthermore to ensure that no other council venues would host concerts "glorifying Mao".[48] The petitions denounced Mao's regime and compared Mao to Adolf Hitler and Josef Stalin, holding the chairman responsible for the deaths of over 70 million Chinese people.

AVA opposed the concerts for two main reasons. First, "Maoist thought" was to them a violent and anti-democratic ideology and therefore antithetical to the values upon which Australian society was built.[49] Secondly, the celebration of Mao and his legacy was painful and offensive to survivors of his regime. The concerts would therefore create divisions in Australian communities. Another complaint, that the concerts could incite extremism, terrorism and violence, seemed alarmist but was in keeping with the kind of rhetoric that would later typify AVA.[50]

One member of AVA estimated its membership to be a loose collective of 200 individuals, mostly male and middle-aged or older. He described AVA as having a non-hierarchical structure to prevent the co-optation of leadership by agents of the CCP.[51] He also described an overlap of membership between AVA and other anti-PRC organisations like the Chinese Alliance for Democracy and Falun Dafa. Further demonstrating these connections, some of AVA's earlier content appeared on the webpages of Chinese democratic organisations.[52] Thus, while AVA

---

48 AVA, "Stop Maoist Concert in Sydney", Online Petition, *change.org*, 2016, https://tinyurl.com/2h8rjvyd.
49 AVA, "澳大利亚的公民价值观 Aodaliya de Gongmin Jiazhiguan (Australian Citizen Values)", Blog, *ava.org.au*, September 2016, http://evebch.ava.org.au/2016/09/blog-post_9.html.
50 AVA, "Stop Maoist Concert in Sydney"; AVA, "Stop Maoist Concert in Melbourne", Social Media, *change.org*, 2016, https://tinyurl.com/bdedch22.
51 Interviewee 7, Anonymous Interview.
52 FDC, "Joint Statement of the Chinese Community in Australia on Protest against Maoist Concert", Federation for a Democratic China, 24 August 2016, https://tinyurl.com/mspxrf3u; Xiaogang Zheng, "澳洲應該協助一個類如 ISIS 的'藝術'在墨爾本上演嗎? Aozhou Yinggai Xiezhu Yige Lei Ru ISIS de 'Yishu'

was formed just weeks before the *Glory and Dream* concerts were to be staged, it drew in many people with existing anti-PRC sentiments.

AVA's stated purpose was to alert mainstream Australia of the "red tide" of CCP influence threatening to wash over Australia – here symbolised by *Glory and Dream* but later including other aspects of the PRC's infiltration of Australian society. AVA claimed it could recognise the Chinese threat because its members had lived under the CCP. By the same token, they believed non-Chinese Australians were not alert to this threat because they typically have neither the familiarity with China, nor cultural and language skills to know the true intentions of the PRC.[53] In fact, one post on AVA's website likened Australia to a "frog

---

Zai Moerben Shangyan Ma? (Should Australia Support Staging ISIS-like 'Art' in Melbourne?)", 民主中國陣線（民陣）Federation for a Democratic China (FDC), 6 February 2017, https://tinyurl.com/2a97envh; Xiaogang Zheng, "澳洲价值守护联盟: 澳洲应该协助 – 个类如 ISIS 的'艺术'在墨尔本上演吗? Aozhou Yinggai Xiezhu Yige Lei Ru ISIS de 'Yishu' Zai Moerben Shangyan Ma? (Should Australia Support Staging ISIS-like 'Art' in Melbourne?)", *Australian Values Alliance*, Blog, ava.org.au, 1 February 2017, http://evebch.ava.org.au/2017/02/isis.html.

53   Wensen, "联盟，我以你为荣！Lianmeng, Wo Yi Ni Wei Rong! (Alliance, I Am Proud of You!)", *Australian Values Alliance*, 28 September 2016, http://wensenw.blogspot.com.au/2016/09/blog-post_28.html; AVA, "约定你了，当晚见！（转帖）Yueding Ni Le, Dangwan Jian! (Zhuan Tie) (Promise to See You Tonight! (Reposted))", *Australian Values Alliance*, August 2016, http://evebch.ava.org.au/2016/08/blog-post_75.html; AVA, "'红粉滚回中国！' – 本联盟专稿 'Hongfen Gun Hui Zhongguo!' – Ben Linameng Zhuan Gao (Red Fans Go Back to China! Alliance Special Feature)", *Australian Values Alliance*, August 2016, http://evebch.ava.org.au/2016/08/blog-post_58.html; Wensen, " – 个红色幽灵在澳洲徘徊，华人社区暗流汹涌（特稿）Yige Hongse Youling Zai Aozhou Paihuai, Huaren Shequ Anliu Xiongyong (Te Gao) (A Red Ghost Haunts Australia and Is an Undercurrent of the Chinese Community (Special Feature))", *Australian Values Alliance*, 22 August 2016, http://wensenw.blogspot.com.au/2016/08/blog-post_98.html; AVA, "抵制红潮免祸害华人 – 致澳洲华人同胞的公开信 Dizhi Hongchao Mian Huohai Huaren – Zhi Aozhou Huaren Tongbao de Gongkaixin (Resist the Red Tide and Avoid Harmful Chinese – An Open Letter to Chinese Australian Compatriots)", *Australian Values Alliance*, August 2016, http://evebch.ava.org.au/2016/08/blog-post_78.html.

being slowly boiled", unaware of the extent to which the CCP's influence had already crept into Australia.[54]

Setting AVA apart from other anti-PRC organisations is its overemphasised Australian patriotism. Its self-characterisation as an Australian patriotic organisation appears in part to be calculated. Initially, founding members had considered the name "Universal Values Alliance" as they recognised that the so-called "Australian values" that AVA espoused – democracy, human rights and the rule of law – were not uniquely Australian. Nevertheless, they chose "Australian" values as they thought it would resonate better with mainstream Australians.[55] AVA's other actions reflected its desire to make inroads into the mainstream. These included its use of English on its website, its online petitions, and its early engagements with English-language press and television.[56] AVA's first website post – bilingual lyrics for the Australian national anthem – and its subsequent descriptions of members as "concerned Australian citizens" and "tax-payers" evoked Australia's colloquial patriotism.[57] However, AVA showed aptitude for Australia's colloquial xenophobia, too. "Go back to China!" was a common refrain directed at perceived CCP sympathisers (whom AVA termed "red fans").[58] AVA member John Hugh bluntly explained in an interview with *The Australian* that "if you don't like this

---

54 Baoqiang Sun, "STOP '温水煮青蛙'！ STOP 'Wenshui Zhu Qingwa'! (STOP 'Boiling the Frog'!)", *Australian Values Alliance*, 2017, https://tinyurl.com/2kvshkyr.
55 AVA, "Australian Citizen Values"; Interviewee 7, Anonymous Interview.
56 AVA, "Stop Maoist Concert in Sydney"; AVA, "Melbourne Lord Mayor Robert Doyle: Stop Maoist Concert in Melbourne", Online Petition, *change.org*, 2016, https://tinyurl.com/bdedch22; Callick, "Rebel Chinese Movement Promotes 'Australian Values'"; Philip Wen, "Divisive Mao Zedong Concerts in Sydncy, Melbourne Cancelled", *Sydney Morning Herald*, 1 September 2016, https://tinyurl.com/2nynzncr; Beverley O'Connor, *Concerns over Beijing's Monitoring of Australian Chinese: An Interview with John Hugh*, Interview (Australian Broadcasting Corporation, 2017), 4 April 2017, https://tinyurl.com/p6ntf963.
57 AVA, "Stop Maoist Concert in Sydney"; AVA, "Stop Maoist Concert in Melbourne"; AVA, "让我们高唱澳洲国歌！ Rang Women Gao Chang Aozhou Guoge! (Let's Sing the Australian National Anthem!)", Blog, *ava.org.au*, August 2016, https://tinyurl.com/489d7az5.

country's values, and think constantly of another place as your country, then go back there".⁵⁹

AVA's jingoism demarcated its members as "good Chinese Australians" from the "bad" CCP-sympathising red fans. However, AVA's posturing also seemed like an over-compensation that belied a fear of White Australian racism. AVA believed the increasingly brash Chinese patriotism displayed by some Chinese (Australians) – like that seen at the 2008 Olympic torch relay in Canberra – would inevitably provoke a backlash from mainstream (or, rather, White) Australians. The need to stop these displays (*Glory and Dream* concerts being one) was summed up by one AVA member in an emotive but strategic appeal:

> If we just turn away in silence, it will only make [Australians] believe that all ethnic Chinese are red fans. If this is what they think, then the red tide may be thought of as a yellow-peril and the discriminations we suffered one hundred years ago will again fall on our heads!⁶⁰

Therefore, AVA's desire to identify and castigate the red fans also contained a self-interest for protection from latent Australian racism. If no demarcation was made, AVA feared the consequence would be that non-discerning Australian compatriots would lump all Chinese Australians together as potential CCP sympathisers (as Eric Abetz did

---

58 AVA, "Promise to See You Tonight!"; AVA, "Red Fans Go Back to China!"; AVA, "《请勿作茧自缚！ - 致'颂毛会'支持者的公开信》 Qing Wu Zuojianzifu! – Zhi 'Song Mao Hui' Zhichi Zhe de Gongkaixin (Don't Get Caught in Your Own Web! – An Open Letter to the Supporters of the Mao Gala)", Blog, *ava.org.au*, August 2016, https://tinyurl.com/bddywze7; Wensen, "神圣的使命 – 守护澳洲价值！ Shensheng de shiming – shouhu Aozhou jiazhi! (The Sacred Mission – Protect Australian Values!)", Blog, *ava.org.au*, April 2017, https://tinyurl.com/2nb94ef6; AVA, "联盟快讯 (11) – 抵制'红剧'的小花絮 Lianmeng Kuaixun (11) – Dizhi 'Hong Ju' de Xiao Huaxu (Alliance News (11) – 'Red Ballet' Boycott Update)", Blog, *ava.org.au*, 17 February 2017, https://tinyurl.com/y9cynu7x.
59 Callick, "Rebel Chinese Movement Promotes 'Australian Values'".
60 AVA, "Red Fans Go Back to China!".

at the 2020–1 Senate Inquiry). To AVA, true Chinese *Australians* should demarcate themselves from the CCP crowd by railing against them.

Ostensibly, the conflict between ICEAA and AVA was about the depiction of Mao Zedong. On one side, ICEAA wished to valorise Mao as a hero of the Chinese people in the town halls of two multicultural cities, bringing together overseas Chinese and "[showing] this history to Western society".[61] The concerts would not only tell the "good story" of China, but in themselves be an example of successful multiculturalism. On the other side, AVA demonised Mao as a mass murderer and saw the concerts as both an affront to the Chinese Australians who had escaped Mao's regime and an assault on Australia's democratic values. In the view of AVA and its anti-PRC sympathisers, "multiculturalism in Australia should not be abused to praise criminals against humanity and promote political extremism".[62] In truth, the public conflict between ICEAA and AVA seemed more to do with competing claims about the Chinese Australian community: essentialist claims about Chinese Australian identity and the bonds of that identity to either the Chinese or Australian nation.

On 25 August 2016, a press conference for local Chinese-language media was held in the Sydney suburb of Chatswood to publicise the *Glory and Dream* concerts. Included on the conference panel was ICEAA's president, Yuan Ye, and other representatives from supporting organisations. The representatives took turns extolling the concerts' cultural significance to Chinese Australians, as well as their own personal admiration for Mao and his role in making China a proud and powerful nation.[63] From their comments, it became clear that the

---

61 Yuan, "Haiwai Huaren Jinian Mao Zedong".
62 FDC, "Joint Statement of the Chinese Community".
63 *wxzun.com*, "澳洲华人社区需要正能量！《光荣梦想》音乐会邀请悉尼华人力压反对声音！ Aozhou Huaren Shequ Xuyao Zheng Nengliang! 'Guangrong Mengxiang' Yinyue Hui Yaoqing Xini Huaren Li Ya Fandui Shengyin! (The Australian Chinese Community Needs Positive Energy! 'Glory and Dream' Concert Requests Sydney Chinese to Suppress Dissenting Voices!)", Defunct News Site, *wzxun.com*, 26 August 2016, http://www.wzxun.com/detail/5363880.html (Note the domain and business name difference).

concerts were not simply to rouse Chinese Australians into identifying with the PRC but to unite Chinese Australians though pride in China.

Part of the way through Ye's praise of China, three members of the AVA appeared. A reporter from SBS captured the moment on audio: Ye stopped speaking and an organiser could be heard telling the trio they were not welcome. He directed security to eject them. As they were cleared from the room, a member of the three shouted in Mandarin, "You can't eat Australia's rice and then smash its bowl!"[64] The expression implied that the *Glory and Dream* organisers were jeopardising the society that had allowed them to prosper. A deeper meaning seemed to be that those speaking at the press conference were parasitic and ungrateful.

These different positions on Chinese Australian identity and unity were further reflected in the different responses each organisation had to the press conference incident. The Chinese-language media supporting the concert had little to say about the interruption. One article briefly mentioned a handful of people in opposition to the concerts, but otherwise focused on the panel's admiration for Mao, China's global prestige and the cultural significance of *Glory and Dream* for Chinese Australians. The article also called for Chinese Australians to unite within the Chinese dream and to "lend positive energy to the concert in order to suppress discordant voices".[65] Meanwhile, on the ICEAA's YouTube channel, a video uploaded the day after the conference showed glimpses of the interruption, though bookended it with vox pops about the concerts, Mao Zedong and the right to freedom of speech in Australia.[66]

AVA, on the other hand, employed the burgeoning "China influence narrative" to its advantage. When Mayor Clover Moore refused to meet with AVA about cancelling the concerts, a handful of AVA members

---

64 不要吃澳洲的饭，砸澳洲的锅！"; "纪念毛泽东音乐会发布会屡遭抗议者打断 SBS Your Language, "Mao Concert Press Conference", News, 26 August 2016, https://tinyurl.com/sapyppcx.
65 *wxzun.com*, "The Australian Chinese Community Needs Positive Energy!".
66 Aozhou Da Shiye, "纪念毛主席逝世四十周年《光荣梦想》音乐晚会新闻发布会 Jinian Mao Zhuxi Shishi Sishi Zhounian 'Guangrong Mengxiang' Yinyue Wanhui Xinwen Fabu Hui (Press Conference for the 'Glory and Dream' Music Gala Commemorating the 40th Anniversary of Chairman Mao's Passing)", 27 August 2016, https://tinyurl.com/2u9eaevn.

7 The "China influence" debate

began holding daily protests outside the Sydney Town Hall. Their placards in Chinese and English proclaimed Mao a tyrant and they brandished images of the chairman with a toothbrush-moustache pencilled under his nose. While AVA's public displays attracted attention, its lobbying behind the scenes was of more consequence. According to one member, AVA had connections at Australia's Department of Foreign Affairs and Trade (DFAT) who enjoined the Sydney City Council to reconsider its agreement to stage *Glory and Dream* in its town hall.[67] Fortuitously for the AVA, a scandal involving Federal Labor Senator Sam Dastyari taking money from businessman Huang Xiangmo in return for advocating PRC interests was concurrently unfolding. The case brought widespread attention to Beijing's soft-power initiatives in Australia.[68] Perhaps not wanting to be drawn into similar troubles, Sydney City Council heeded DFAT's advice.

The council announced on 1 September that the concerts would not go ahead. As reasons, it cited concerns for public and patron safety due to protests planned for the night of the event and ICEAA's inability to control admission. Having received the news, ICEAA subsequently cancelled their plans for the Melbourne concert later that same day.[69] In the aftermath of *Glory and Dream*'s cancellation, both ICEAA's and AVA's positions on Chinese Australian unity became clearer. ICEAA released a short statement that, due to a small group of opposition and the inability of local authorities to ensure public safety, *Glory and Dream* was not going ahead. It clarified:

> The organisers have suffered an enormous loss, however there is nothing more important than the solidarity of Chinese Australians. ... The self-improvement of our people requires importance to be attached to unity.[70]

---

67 Interviewee 7, Anonymous Interview.
68 James Massola, "Labor Senator Sam Dastyari Quits over Chinese Donations Scandal", *Sydney Morning Herald*, 7 September 2016, https://tinyurl.com/57j86ka.
69 Wen, "Divisive Mao Zedong Concerts in Sydney, Melbourne Cancelled".
70 ICEAA, "纪念毛泽东逝世四十周年音乐会《光荣梦想》声明 Jinian Mao Zedong Shishi Sishi Zhounian Yinyue Hui 'Guangrong Mengxiang' Shengming (Concert Commemorating the 40th Anniversary of Mao

"We don't want there to be a split in the Chinese community. If this does cause a divide we are willing to abandon the performances", said ICEAA spokesperson Cristina Wang.[71] For ICEAA, unity was paramount.

It was at this moment that AVA declaimed "you should go back to where you came from if you don't adopt Australian values".[72] The problem, as Brophy points out, is that AVA's "'love it or leave it' style of Aussie patriotism" reveals that AVA's vision of Chinese Australian unity with the Australian whole demands blind loyalty and overweening patriotism.[73]

Beyond their own immediate orbits, neither organisation seemed truly representative of Chinese Australian communities. Both were small but highly vocal and visible organisations; one with access to great financial capital, the other to great social capital. But neither could be said to be rich in community support. On the one hand, AVA pointed to two polls run by ImmiAU on WeChat and SBS that revealed that 67 and 79 per cent of respondents respectively were against or indifferent to the *Glory and Dream* concerts.[74] But on the other hand, AVA's low numbers at its Sydney protests showed a similar lack of support or interest. This was reaffirmed by the small turnout and ineffectiveness of AVA's protests against the Cultural Revolutionary ballet *Red Detachment of Women* at Melbourne's Asia TOPA festival the following year.[75] Most interviewees for this research similarly held AVA and organisations like ICEAA in low regard, describing them as groups motivated by their own self-interests rather than by issues that were widely and deeply felt across Chinese Australian communities.

Zedong's Death 'Glory and Dream' Announcement)", News, *yeeyi.com*, 6 September 2016, https://tinyurl.com/yjj7ftu8.
71   Wen, "Divisive Mao Zedong Concerts in Sydney, Melbourne Cancelled".
72   Callick, "Rebel Chinese Movement Promotes 'Australian Values'".
73   Brophy, *China Panic*, 149–51.
74   AVA, "Press Update – Embrace Australian Values Alliance (31 August 2016)", Online Petition, *change.org*, 31 August 2016, https://tinyurl.com/2h8rjvyd.
75   AVA, "Premier Daniel Andrews: Please Stop the Show of the Red Detachment of Women", Online Petition, *change.org*, 4 October 2016, https://tinyurl.com/mwzxvfxc; Naaman Zhou, "Chinese Ballet Show Draws Protests for 'Glorifying Red Army'", *The Guardian* (Australia), 17 February 2017), https://tinyurl.com/bdfpvrp7.

7 The "China influence" debate

COVID-19 and anti-China sentiment[76]

The COVID-19 pandemic has led to a surge in racism toward Chinese Australians. At the 2020 Senate Inquiry, Wanning Sun and community organisations like the Chinese Australian Forum (CAF) and the Asian Australian Alliance (AAA) explained that many Chinese Australians were hesitant to speak out against COVID-charged racism for fear of appearing "anti-Australian" or "pro-PRC".[77] The responses from Chinese Australian community organisations to racism in the context of COVID-19 have indeed been remarkably muted in comparison to their responses during the Hanson and Blainey debates. This would seem to support the claim by Sun and others that a "Chinese influence narrative" was silencing Chinese Australian voices. However, the "influence narrative" was only one factor at work. Others were the changing Chinese Australian demographics and the changing form and function of community organisations.

To illustrate this point, it's worth reflecting on a racially charged incident that occurred almost 30 years before the COVID-19 pandemic hit Australian shores, and how the Chinese Australian communities' reaction then compare to their responses to racist incidents during the height of the pandemic. On 18 October 1991, four Chinese Australian high school boys in the wealthy Sydney suburb of Turramurra were set upon by dozens of White Australian boys of a similar age. The police arrived after the White students had verbally abused and physically assaulted the Chinese Australian students, yet it was the latter who the police arrested. Outraged by the event, ACCA campaigned to have charges against the boys dropped with members willing to fund any legal costs incurred. "In time of need, ACCA has asked for help and the Chinese Australian community responded magnificently," ACCA reported.[78]

---

76 Some of the following analysis of contemporary responses to COVID-19 racism appears in: Gardner, "All as One to One for All".
77 Sun, "Submission to the Senate"; CAF, "Submission to the Senate Inquiry into Issues Facing Diaspora Communities in Australia" (Chinese Australian Forum, 2020), https://tinyurl.com/yceeewyy; AAA, "Submission to the Senate Inquiry into Issues Facing Diaspora Communities in Australia" (Asian Australian Alliance, 2020), https://tinyurl.com/mfcrsmnd.

Nearly 30 years later, in March 2020, two Vietnamese Australian sisters were racially abused in the inner-western (and gentrifying) Sydney suburb of Marrickville. The incident received media coverage as racism connected to COVID-19.[79] Though the young women were not Chinese Australian, the abuse they received, including the instruction to "eat a bat", fitted with the racially prejudiced associations of COVID-19 with China and its hygiene standards that existed at the time. A week later, ACCA issued a condemnation of the racist attack, "regardless of ethnicity", against the two "Asian Australians".[80] Though posted on its website, it is unclear if ACCA's condemnation went further than its own membership. Nevertheless, the difference in the scale of response between then and now is clear.

Differences can also be seen in the responses to broader community experiences of racism. In the context of the Blainey debate, CAV formed an "anti-discrimination and social action subcommittee"; and in the context of Hansonism, the CAV president had openly reproached John Howard at a dinner function for his complicity in platforming Hanson in Parliament.[81] In the face of rising racism following COVID-19, CAV sent a letter of concern to Prime Minister Scott Morrison and other politicians. In reply, CAV received a letter from Gladys Liu MP which it duly published in its newsletter.[82] Though a positive action, it is nevertheless a more modest one when compared to the personal dressing down of a prime minister.

---

78 ACCA, "ACCA News December 1991" (Australian Chinese Community Association, December 1991), 4, State Library of New South Wales.
79 Frank Chung, "'Asian Dog, You Brought Corona Here': Young Women Racially Abused, Spat on in Sydney Street", *news.com.au*, 31 March 2020, https://tinyurl.com/yc42kkcv; Melanie Dinjaski, "Coronavirus: Two Asian Women Target of Spitting Racial Attack in Marrickville, NSW Police Commissioner Mick Fuller", *9news.com.au*, 31 March 2020, https://tinyurl.com/6urm94ds.
80 Tim Feng, "Response to Racial Abuse of Two Sisters in Marrickville", *acca.org.au*, 6 April 2020, http://www.acca.org.au/drupal/en/news/response-racial-abuse-two-sisters-marrickville-1478.
81 CAV, *Chinese Association of Victoria*, 1992, 7; Chew and Giese, *Franklin Chew Interviewed by Diana Giese*.
82 CAV, "The Bulletin Newsletter June 2020" (The Chinese Association of Victoria, June 2020), https://tinyurl.com/ycy2t42b.

7 The "China influence" debate

While the difference between such responses might be due to the "China influence narrative", as Sun and others contend, it should be noted that there are also two to three decades of difference between the community organisations' responses. As such, the age and changing memberships of many of these once outspoken community organisations adds another, complementary explanation. Organisations that had been active during the Blainey and Hanson debates – ICECAV, the Chinese Fellowship of Victoria (CFV), the Queensland Chinese Forum (QCF) – hardly responded to COVID-19 racism at all. The websites or Facebook pages of older community organisations like CAV, CFV and QCF shows that they are still highly active but their organisational focus has shifted as their memberships have changed or aged. Naturally, this has affected their propensity to respond to present social issues like racism.

Related to the changing priorities of older Chinese Australian community organisations is the fact that representation of the "Chinese Australian community" on issues like racism has progressively been concentrated into a smaller number of organisations. In effect, responding to racism had become the domain of "peak organisations". Some of these organisations claimed peak status because they sat atop a federation of other community organisations, like QCF or the Federation of Chinese Associations (FCA) in Victoria. Others, like CAF, claimed to be the foremost advocates of Chinese Australian interests due to their superior expertise and resources.

In the mid-2010s, leaders of peak ethnic community organisations repeatedly came together to oppose the weakening of Australia's racial vilification laws. In 2013, nine such bodies issued a joint press statement supporting stronger anti-racism laws. They included the National Congress of Australia's First Peoples, the Arab Council Australia, the Australian Hellenic Council and the Executive Council of Australian Jewry. The organisation representing the Chinese Australian community was CAF.[83] While not a national peak body like the others, CAF described itself as "the most highly regarded Chinese community group in Sydney" with a purview of "issues of public policy affecting

---

83   Mariana Freri, "Groups Oppose Racial Discrimination Act Change", *NITV*, 22 November 2013, https://tinyurl.com/mracxd7c.

Chinese Australians, including racial discrimination and racial vilification".[84] For good reason, CAF thought itself best placed to represent the Chinese Australian perspective on this issue. Since then, CAF has regularly stepped into this representative role. When Pauline Hanson returned to Australian politics as a senator in 2016, CAF initiated an online campaign encouraging people to upload and share photos of themselves with signs reading "#SayNoToPauline" to social media.[85] Unfortunately, as documented by the Australia Institute, the initial media interest and community support for this campaign dissipated "after little more than a month".[86]

In response to COVID-19 racism, CAF again stepped into the role of community spokes group, releasing an "Open Letter on National Unity During the Coronavirus Pandemic" along with an online petition of over 100,000 signatures calling for a halt to racism and the unity of all Australians.[87] However, this time around the signatories of CAF's open letter seemed to downplay their community credentials. Jason Yat-sen Li's position as CAF president or Benjamin Chow's as CAF's immediate past-president was not noted in the letter. Instead they were listed as company directors. The letter included four other company directors as signatories as well as journalists, authors, TV presenters, artists and an Australian of the Year.[88]

In this case, it is the signatories' exceptional status in business or public spheres, rather than their community roles, that legitimises them speaking for other Chinese Australians. These prominent Chinese

---

84 CAF, "2013 Submission from Chinese Australian Forum Re. Inquiry into Racial Vilification Law in NSW" (Chinese Australian Forum, 8 March 2013), NSW Parliament.
85 Sarah Gerathy, "Pauline Hanson Controversy: Chinese Community Campaigns against 'Racist' Ideas", ABC News, 8 July 2016, https://tinyurl.com/3u9azujr.
86 Philip Dorling, "Still Anti-Asian? Anti-Chinese? One Nation Policies on Asian Immigration and Multiculturalism" (The Australia Institute, May 2017), 4–5, https://tinyurl.com/2xu6ma3x.
87 CAF, "Open Letter on National Unity During the Coronavirus Pandemic", 8 April 2020, https://tinyurl.com/yry7cmtb; CAF, "Denounce Racist Attacks on Asian-Australians: #UnityOverFear During Covid-19", change.org, April 2020, https://tinyurl.com/rhwfw9pr.
88 CAF, "Open Letter on National Unity During the Coronavirus Pandemic".

7 The "China influence" debate

Australians have not been silenced by debates about China's influence and their opposition to COVID-19 racism has been widely published and televised.[89]

In light of the demographic shifts underway at the same time as the China influence debate has been unfolding, it is therefore worth noting that each of these signatories was locally born or came from a former Commonwealth territory (except for Macau-born Tony Ayres) and each was predominantly educated in Australia or in English. Despite its declared aim to speak for all Chinese Australians, the open letter had a narrow community base. None of the signatories came from the recent PRC migrant communities, despite the size and continued growth of that sector, nor were any from the large and now multi-generational Chinese communities that came to Australia as refugees from Indochina. Indeed, the absence of a signatory from one of the new Mainlander communities is especially surprising as many of them are highly educated, wealthy professionals and businesspeople leading in their respective fields (and making similar contributions to Australia as the signatories themselves).[90] Beyond the signatories' wealthy and professional status, then, their defining feature seems to be their suggested status as "model migrants", literate in Australianness and mainstream multiculturalism.

According to Jieh-Yung Lo, director of the ANU Centre for Asian-Australian Leadership and signatory to the open letter, the problem facing "community advocates" is the need to disassociate their campaigns from China's soft-power initiatives: "I feel very saddened by [the situation] because [racism] is a legitimate issue here in Australia, and there are advocates out there working day and night to try and find

---

89 *The Drum Wednesday April 8* (*ABC News*, 2020), https://tinyurl.com/42ek54a9; *Benjamin Law, Author and Journalist Taking a Stand against Racism during COVID-19*, n.d., https://tinyurl.com/247pv6f2.
90 Jock Collins, "Chinese Entrepreneurs: The Chinese Diaspora in Australia", *International Journal of Entrepreneurial Behavior & Research* 8, no. 1/2 (February 2002), 113–33, https://tinyurl.com/85nnfeuf; Ying Lu, R. Samaratunge and C.E. Hartel, "Acculturation Strategies among Professional Chinese Immigrants in the Australian Workplace", *Asia Pacific Journal of Human Resources* 49, no. 1 (1 March 2011), 71–87, https://tinyurl.com/bdf5je66.

solutions to create a more cohesive society."[91] Yet the advocates are not alone in their efforts. As Haiqing Yu points out, there are many Chinese Australian individuals, especially recent migrants from the PRC, who are eager to bring nuance to public and online discussions around racism and "China influence" for audiences in Australia, as well as in China.[92] Thus evidence from within communities shows that many Mainlander Chinese Australians have been active in responding to the racism brought on by COVID-19 and to other challenges posed by the pandemic. For example, new migrants have formed WeChat "neighbourhood watch" groups to respond to instances of racial violence, while others used WeChat groups to procure groceries for neighbours during Australia's civil lockdowns.[93] It was also primarily through WeChat that hundreds of both Chinese and non-Chinese Australians were brought together in Adelaide's Rundle Mall to protest the increase in anti-Asian racism, in an example of inter- and intra-ethnic solidarity.[94] The predominantly new Mainland migrant organisers requested national flags not be brought to the demonstration lest the message of the protest be co-opted.[95] Here a community of people were responding to racism, and furthermore enacting multiculturalism, without community organisations, leaders or advocates acting as mediators.

---

91 Iris Zhao, Erin Handley and Michael Walsh, "China Is Attacking Australia over Racism – but Ordinary People Are Getting Stuck in the Middle", 17 July 2020, https://tinyurl.com/5ar3ufdk.
92 Haiqing Yu, "Chinese Australians' Take on Anti-Chinese Racism in Australia. Part 3 of a Series on Racism", *John Menadue: Pearls and Irritations*, 23 June 2020, https://tinyurl.com/4rbuabtu.
93 Joshua Boscaini, "Chinese Community Helps Families Stuck in Self-Isolation after Coronavirus Outbreak", *ABC News*, 13 February 2020, https://tinyurl.com/y5unrtsf; Anna Hartley, "Chinese Neighbourhood Watch Groups Deny They Are Vigilantes", *ABC News*, 21 October 2019, https://tinyurl.com/3xcnt7z5; Su-Lin Tan, "Chinese-Australians Hunt White Men Who Hit Asian Delivery Rider", *South China Morning Post*, 7 July 2020, https://tinyurl.com/58swvhar.
94 Around Australia, "The Protests at Rundle Mall Adelaide Australia 18 Jul 2020 #shorts", YouTube, 22 January 2021, https://tinyurl.com/yubcufut; "Hundreds Gather in Rundle Mall to Protest against Racial Violence against Asian Community", *Facebook*, 11 July 2020, https://tinyurl.com/38cbt72d.
95 Zhao, Handley and Walsh, "China Is Attacking Australia over Racism".

7 The "China influence" debate

Yu points out that some Chinese Australian voices receive less attention than others.[96] Though she referred specifically to the experiences of the newest Chinese Australians from Mainland China, her point holds for other communities who are not reflected in CAF's open letter, ICEAA's veneration of Mao, AVA's protest against *Glory and Dream*, neo-native place associations marching for the PRC's claim over the South China Sea, or the ACPPRC-led defence of Huang Xiangmo. What Lo's lamentation about advocates "working day and night" to build a better society does not acknowledge, yet at the same time evinces, is that the form of organisations has shifted to be less community-based and that the role of "community advocacy" has been taken up by individuals who are not necessarily tied to community-based organisations.

The changing nature of community representation

With the hardening of China's soft-power initiatives prompting rising alarm in Australia, debates about the PRC's penetration of Australian society have come to colour the political actions and social participation of Chinese Australian community organisations. Unlike in the early years of the 21st century, when community organisations could walk a line between Chinese and Australian nationalisms, today these organisations are increasingly compelled to take one side or the other. As revealed at the 2020–1 Senate Inquiry, many community organisations wished to do neither and consequently stayed quiet in the public domain, lest they incurred the scrutiny of zealous Australian politicians (Abetz), scholars (Hamilton) or journalists (Hartcher). The threat posed by the international reach of an authoritarian China effectively silenced other Chinese Australian community organisations.

As noted, other factors have been at work. Many community organisations that were formed in the 1970s, '80s and '90s now have aged memberships. In the case of ICECAV, this has meant an almost complete loss of vitality. Other organisations have shifted their focus to survive or remain relevant. CFV focused most of its energies on

---

96 Yu, "Chinese Australians' Take on Anti-Chinese Racism in Australia".

its language school, while CCA put a greater focus on social activities suited to its elderly membership. Other community organisations that had formed around the needs of specific cohorts – Indochinese refugees being the exemplar – ceased to exist as their specific needs abated. Consequently, the community organisations that had once pursued such issues have lost much of their capacity to engage with the China influence debate and COVID-19 racism.

Demographic change in the Chinese Australian population coincided with the rise of organisations that are politically focused rather than community focused, even if these political organisations seek public legitimacy through claims of representativeness. These organisations broadly belong in pro-PRC and anti-PRC camps. ACPPRC, ACWA, ICEAA and the many neo-native place organisations belong to the former, and AVA and groups like Falun Dafa to the latter. AVA stands apart by being ardently pro-Australian, if not jingoistic. AVA's dispute with ICEAA over the *Glory and Dream* concerts showed that political divisions in Chinese Australian communities are deep. That dispute also demonstrated competing ideas of what it means to be Chinese Australian – each organisation putting emphasis on one or the other side of that coupled identity.

The newest Chinese Australians, the vast majority being migrants from the PRC, are not prima facie pro-CCP or undemocratic. There are rational counter-arguments to some of Hamilton and Hartcher's essentialist characterisations. A closer look at this cohort reveals an array of interests in niche hobbies, sports, and religious and business organisations. Many eschew organisations altogether, preferring the loose affiliations provided by social media platforms. As seen in response to COVID-19 racism, this manner of loose organisation proved capable of staging a successful anti-racism protest in Adelaide.

These new migrants are producing a different Australia and a larger, highly diversified body of Chinese Australians. If in recent years it appears that the social participation of Chinese Australian communities and organisations has been stifled by competing nationalisms, the last two decades have also been a period of transformation of communities and a time of change in the form and function of the organisations "representing" them.

The Chimera: Chasing unity in the face of diversity

The idea of a unitary, unified or united Chinese Australian community has been advanced at several moments in recent Australian history by multiple actors, in various ways and for different reasons. In the 1980s, after facing down the Blainey debate, Katie Young hoped the Chinese in Australia would "unite and advance", speak "with one voice" and exist as "one big family". Some 40 years later, Peter Hartcher, amid the debate around PRC influence, claimed Australia had built its "Chinese community of 1.3 million without really understanding it or its consequences".[1] Yet the idea or presumption of a Chinese Australian (comm)unity has been hard to define, to grasp or to test, despite the apparent obviousness of its existence. As such, scepticism about the existence of a singular "Chinese Australian community" has sprung from multiple places. Such scepticism should not be a surprise, nor negatively construed, because Chinese Australian communities have themselves sprung from multiple places.

By following the histories of the organisations that, in turn, sprang from these different communities, it is possible to examine how a Chinese Australian community might be, as Ien Ang put it, "imaginatively produced and reproduced" and how concepts of

---

1   Young and Yeo, *National Conference of the Australian Chinese Community*, 5; Hartcher, *Red Zone*, 174.

"Chinese Australian unity" could arise as a reaction to a moment of possibility or crisis.[2] Sometimes appearing as an ethno-nationalist ideal pursued as an end in itself, the idea at other times emerged as a pragmatic goal, expressed momentarily through the solidarity and cooperative actions of separate organisations. But complicating these observations further is the fact that organisations (and the communities that create them) are dynamic bodies that change over time. Thus, when we try to talk about "unity" and "community" historically, our focus must shift nimbly according to the who, what, where and, importantly, *when*. Doing so allows two valuable observations to come into view.

The first concerns the concept of unity that is supposed to underpin this community. In recent history, Chinese Australian unity presented both as a chimera inhabiting the social space shared by Chinese Australians and, relatedly, as a goal sought by Chinese Australian community organisations. The history of community organisations shows that this goal was never realised in a lasting way. Chinese Australian unity remained a chimera, only ever momentarily or partially glimpsed by community organisations. In another sense, Chinese Australian unity is like a chimera because when viewed through the lens of a particular issue at the right time, disparate communities and organisations do appear as a single, composite body – the illusion of unity revealing itself when the same communities and organisations are viewed through the lens of another issue or from a different point in time.

The second observation concerns the ramifications of conceptualising the "Chinese Australian community". While unity might be a quixotic idea and the "Chinese Australian community" more of a discursive term than a fact, "imaginatively producing" Chineseness, Australianness and Chinese Australianness did have real-world implications. Community organisations' actions have been guided by their values and beliefs – including what it means to be Chinese, Australian or both – in tandem with their material needs and capabilities. In the processes of conceptualising, enacting and questioning Chinese Australian unity and the delimitations of a

---

2   Ang, "Beyond Chinese Groupism", 1188.

The Chimera: Chasing unity in the face of diversity

"Chinese Australian community", community organisations show a range of possible connections to their ancestral homeland and their new Australian home. Historically, they have demonstrated a highly participatory mode of multiculturalism, and staked their twin claim of belonging to Australia and Australia belonging to them *as* Chinese Australians – whatever they imagined that to be. These two observations are wrought from recent history.

In the 1970s, Australia's turn from the White Australia policy toward multiculturalism heralded a renaissance for Chinese Australian communities and organisations. The rescission of assimilationist initiatives allowed Chinese Australian communities to express their "Chineseness" publicly. Changed rules for migration slowly led to more Chinese migrants. The role community organisations could play in the settlement process was recognised by state and commonwealth governments and incorporated into their new multicultural policies. Old community organisations that had endured decades of atrophy – of membership, resources and social presence – were revitalised. New community organisations took shape and reflected the optimism and verve of the moment. In terms of organisations, a hundred flowers bloomed – each combining different histories, social backgrounds, languages, resources, objectives (and so on) into a unique blend.

The history of White Australia remains central to understanding the rejuvenation and formation of community organisations because some factors that shape Chinese Australian communities are continuous from Australia's White past into its multicultural present. During the White Australia period, pernicious government policies and societal pressures caused community organisations to decline, but the adversities faced by early Chinese Australians negated differences and promoted cooperation. With its smaller resident population, Perth saw Chinese Australian migrants of disparate backgrounds come together to form the Chung Wah Association (CWA). The evacuation and destruction of Darwin during the Second World War ultimately ended the vibrant communities there, leaving those who remained to amalgamate into the Chung Wah Society (CWS) and rebuild. Melbourne, with its larger population of Chinese Australians, could still sustain multiple community organisations. At the same time, the See Yup Society's (SYS) future was not always certain, and cooperation

309

with the Kong Chew Society (KCS) was sometimes necessary for it to serve the interests of its members and the wider Chinese Australian community in Melbourne. From here begins a pattern whereby pressures – of small communities or hostile social conditions – force communities and organisations to come together and put differences aside.

Likewise, diversity flourished as adversity diminished. From the 1970s onward, community organisations multiplied. They reflected the different Chinese Australian communities establishing themselves in Australia – international or "Colombo Plan" students and young professionals from Southeast Asia, refugees from Indochina, "astronaut" families from Hong Kong and Taiwan, and 89ers and *xinyimin* ("new migrants") from the Chinese mainland – as well as locally born Chinese Australians who came together to preserve and celebrate their Chinese identities and embed their belonging in Australia. Community organisations have confidently re-defined their Chinese, Australian, and Chinese Australian identities on their own terms, as seen, for example, during the redevelopments of Sydney and Melbourne's Chinatowns.

Among the communities' historical differences were political ones. Community organisations that openly supported the PRC, like the reinvigorated Chinese Youth League (CYL) in Sydney or the newly created Chinese Fellowship of Victoria (CFV), found their prominence and relevance rise in accordance with Australia's recognition of the PRC in 1972. Accordingly, the influence of the Australasian Kuomintang – with its connections to Taiwan – gradually receded. Nevertheless, community organisations that attempted to use political ideology and (trans)nationalist sentiments to unite Chinese Australian communities, like CYL and CFV, found limited success. Instead, organisations like the Australian Chinese Community Association of New South Wales (ACCA) had far greater success bringing together Chinese Australians of different backgrounds by being overtly apolitical toward the PRC–ROC divide, and committed to the common interests of cultural maintenance, social welfare and settlement assistance.

Successful multicultural policy and practice required a shift in ideology – that is, new language and new ideas with which Australians could collectively describe and think about themselves. But the shift from White Australia was not trouble-free. Sections of Australia's White population pushed back against the turn to multiculturalism. In the beginning, racist organisations like National Action or the Australian League of Rights mounted campaigns of intimidation, abuse and violence against those representing Australia's multicultural change, Chinese Australian communities among them. Although these racist attacks were typically mounted by small groups through self-publications, graffiti and talkback radio, Chinese Australian community organisations feared that racist ideas might proliferate in mainstream Australia. Accordingly, organisations such as ACCA, CFV and the Chinese Association of South Australia (CASA) engaged directly with racist representations in Australia's media. For this same reason, community organisations opposed Geoffrey Blainey and the debate he ignited in 1984 around Asian immigration. Because Blainey attacked the "Asianisation" of Australia from his position as a well-respected academic, community organisations feared he would lend respectability to more extreme voices and thereby spread racist sentiment through Australian society. Giving credence to these fears, the 1991 *Report of the National Inquiry into Racist Violence in Australia* found that many complaints of racism and racist violence were directly related to the Blainey debate.[3]

The threat posed by the Blainey debate to multiculturalism and Chinese Australian communities prompted calls for greater cooperation among community organisations and ideas of uniting the community were mooted. This was exemplified by the 1986 national conference with its goal to form a peak body and a united voice for the Chinese Australian community. The failure of the conference to produce such a body can be attributed to the inherent differences of the participant organisations. With the urgency of the Blainey debate gone, there was less reason to cooperate. Moreover, the organisations brought different conceptualisations of what Chinese Australian unity was supposed to be: a pragmatic means to respond to issues commonly affecting Chinese Australians, an end in itself to be realised on the basis of common ethno-cultural ties, or a union with the greater

---

3   Human Rights and Equal Opportunity Commission, *Racist Violence*, 140–1.

multicultural Australian whole, as shown by CASA, CFV and the Australian Chinese Forum (ACF), respectively.

These differences would frustrate another attempt to create a peak body at the second national conference in 1990, amid the pain of the Tiananmen Massacre and the uncertainty of the 89ers' future in Australia. At this time, many community organisations recognised that formalised unity in the shape of a national body was unnecessary for addressing Chinese Australian concerns. Organisations that wanted to aid the 89ers in their campaign for permanent residency, like CAF and ACCA, cooperated to do so. Curiously, the organisations most eager to form a national body at this time, CASA and the ACT Chinese Australian Association (ACTCAA), were also reticent about the massacre and not forthcoming with support for the 89ers.

The massacre had immediately provoked "bitter grief and furious condemnation" from the vast majority of community organisations.[4] It compelled a stalwart of the Chinese Communist Party, CFV, to question its support for China's leadership and the socialist project and the connection between the party and the people of China. The massacre compelled CAF, an organisation that had hitherto avoided engaging with any "foreign politics", to publicly censure the CCP. Nevertheless, the shock and outrage gradually subsided and relationships between many community organisations and the PRC normalised and grew stronger in later decades – not least because of the PRC's outreach to Chinese Australian communities through its consuls and departments for Overseas Chinese affairs.

The eventual settlement of 45,000 89ers had a profound demographic impact on Chinese Australian communities, injecting fresh vitality and cultural capital into them. Even before permanent residency was granted to the 89ers, Chinese Australian communities and organisations were already treating them as part of (Chinese) Australian society, incorporating 89ers into their language schools to teach "standard Chinese" or otherwise enjoying "authentic Chinese culture" through the 89ers' familiarity with Chinese art forms. The settlement of the 89ers began the transition from Cantonese to Mandarin as the most widely spoken Chinese language in Australia,

---

4   CFV, "Newsletter June 1989", 1.

aided by a common penchant among Chinese Australians for Mandarin to be taught to second- and third-generation children. It was also the 89ers that set Mainland China on a course to become the primary source of Chinese Australians. These trends strengthened in the 1990s until Mandarin and Mainland Chinese assumed leading positions in Chinese Australian demographic statistics in the 2000s.

However, the resettlement of the 89ers (Australia's largest single intake of asylum seekers), as well as of many Indochinese refugees, apparently incensed Pauline Hanson leading to her 1996 claim that Australia was being "swamped by Asians".[5] As Hanson's anti-Asian immigration and anti-multicultural rhetoric gained traction, it became clear that multiculturalism was facing its greatest challenge since inception. Yet the Hanson debate was also a moment of great multicultural and democratic vibrancy, as was visible in Chinese Australian responses. Chinese Australian opposition to Hanson was another moment of intra-ethnic solidarity between Chinese Australian communities and organisations. Despite the heightened cooperation, a united voice for Chinese Australia in the shape of a nationally representative body was not sought by community organisations at this time. Instead, it appears that community organisations raised a chorus of voices for a widespread movement opposing Hanson. This movement, in conjunction with other popular opposition to Hanson across Australian society, was ultimately validated: Hanson was not returned by Australian voters at the 1998 federal election.

Chinese Australian community organisations and leaders attributed Hanson's popularity among Australians to economic malaise, irresponsible media coverage and Howard's expedient handling of her. Nevertheless, they maintained faith that Australia's commitment to multiculturalism would withstand the Hanson debate. Here community leaders and organisations showed an ability to constructively critique aspects of Australian society and history in order to build a stronger multicultural future. Australia's Centenary of Federation and the republic referendum offered more opportunities for CAF and ACCA to reflect on the legacy of the White Australia policy (a formative reason for Federation) and envision a future without a

---

5   Kemp and Stanton, *Speaking for Australia*, 268–72.

"foreigner" as Australia's head of state.⁶ These reflections on what constituted the essence of Australia are evidence of Chinese Australians growing increasingly comfortable with claims of belonging in Australia since the multicultural turn. The defence of Australia's multicultural ideals was also a claim that Australia belonged to them, too. Indeed, throughout the Blainey and Hanson debates, community leaders and organisations questioned the congruity of racism in modern Australia and the belonging of those who held racist views. As Francis Lee implied in his rebuttal to Blainey's *All for Australia*, it was the multiculturalists, not the racists, who now belonged in Australia.⁷

Over the years, communities and organisations underwent processes of relocating Chineseness to Australia as part of developing this sense of belonging. In collaboration with historians, CAF did so by uncovering Chinese Australian contributions to Australia's war efforts. ACCA's "Chinese Australia Day" offered both symbolic and practical entwining of Chinese and Australian identities, especially through the naturalisation of Chinese emigrants at these festivities. The Indo-China Ethnic Chinese Association of Victoria (ICECAV) implored Chinese Australians of all backgrounds to uproot connections to ancestral lands so as to form deep and lasting attachments to the new land.

ICECAV's desire to sever ties to old homes was in part due to its concern with Beijing's (and Taipei's) influence over Chinese Australian communities – a concern informed by the rise of Beijing's *qiaowu* efforts since the turn of the century. In the late 1990s and early 2000s, community organisations were able to walk a line between Australia and China by freely expressing pride in both – though expressions of pride in the PRC brought exceptional dividends. PRC consuls and ambassadors lavished long-friendly community organisations (like CFV, CYL, ACTCAA) with expenses-paid trips to China and troves of cultural resources. PRC dignitaries visited organisations and honoured them as brokers of China–Australia relations. Such relations became a measure of a community organisation's esteem. Over time, organisations that had once been more neutral, like ACCA or the

---

6   CAF, "Press Release: The Republic Debate".
7   Lee, "From the Asian Side of the Blainey Debate".

Chinese Association of Victoria (CAV), built closer relations with the PRC and procured similar benefits.

With China hardening its soft power in the 2010s, and Australia growing increasingly alarmed about China's reach into its society, organisations became either more politically polarised or reticent. The Australian Values Alliance (AVA) has been the most vocal in raising the alarm about China's political influence in Australia or the "red fans" in Chinese Australian communities. On the other side stands the Australian Council for the Promotion of the Peaceful Reunification of China (ACPPRC) and its associated neo-native place associations, which are most active when pushing Beijing's foreign and diplomatic interests. Other community organisations and leaders have grown concerned that the prevalence of a "China influence narrative" in Australia has marginalised Chinese Australian communities and silenced efforts to call out racism.

Since a renaissance in the 1970s, Chinese Australian community organisations grew in variety and verve, reaching a peak of political and social participation in the late 1990s during the Hanson debate. After that point, the membership base of many community organisations aged or changed their focus to remain relevant. In this vacuum, CAF has risen in prominence to become, demonstrably, Australia's premier political voice for Chinese Australians. On the whole, community organisations now have less capacity to enter into political and social debates, but are also less willing to do so, arguably owing to the effect of the "China influence narrative" and the dominance of vociferous and partisan political organisations in this space. New migrants, predominantly from the Mainland, are young, reasonably wealthy and well-educated. Compared to the Indochinese refugees or the young families arriving from Hong Kong and Southeast Asia, this cohort has less reliance on the settlement and welfare services historically provided by community organisations. Moreover, this new cohort is tech-savvy and socially networked online. The traditional means of building community, maintaining culture and coordinating political action through formal organisations are less relevant. Today, in the 2020s, community organisations might be reaching a nadir of community relevance.

As technology and modes of social networking advance, traditional "bricks and mortar" organisational structures appear increasingly obsolete. If community organisations are becoming less active in today's Chinese Australian communities, one might even wonder if they remain relevant at all. However, while their forms might change, I would venture that community organisations will remain relevant as long as there are people who share ideas, identities and values. Perhaps it is more prudent to consider when or if it is even useful to try fitting Chinese Australians into communities based on ethnic background, as there is now so much diversity among Chinese Australians and their communities are so porous. From this, we might consider if discrete Chinese Australian communities even exist beyond the memberships of Chinese Australian community organisations.

While many of the community organisations studied in this book have appeared separately in other studies (and many are coming to scholarly attention for the first time), a comparative analysis of them over different periods and issues of Australian history has wrought fresh insights into the similarities and differences, the continuities and contingencies, and the societal and demographic changes that make up the rich diversity of Chinese Australian communities. Moreover, these community organisations are shown to have been important local and national actors, bringing fresh perspectives to familiar historical moments like the end of the White Australia policy, the Blainey debate and the Hanson debate. They are thereby framed as creators of history, rather than communities or groups that were merely subject to historical developments. The use of oral history interviews and materials created by community organisations has served to make Chinese Australian voices central in these episodes of Australian history.

Simultaneously, Chinese-language sources can pose a challenge to the "suffocating monolingualism" of Australian history.[8] As Samia Khatun argues, different languages offer different narratological architectures with which scholars can renovate and refurbish well-worn historical understandings and take new passageways into the past. Following the example set by her study of South Asians in Australia,

---

8   Khatun, *Australianama*, 4.

this book carries a hope that more Australian histories will be written from materials in languages other than English. Australia is, after all, a land of many languages.

Highlighting the diversity of Chinese Australian communities and organisations serves to counteract the homogenisation of these groups. This is necessary work. Essentialisation is one of the abuses that is perpetuated by lingering racism in Australian society. Today, understanding this diversity is urgent due to the essentialisation of Chinese Australians taking place in the China influence debate, as well as within the framework of the PRC's transnational *qiáowù* initiatives.

On a more positive note, highlighting the diversity of Chinese Australian communities has also offered a view of Australian multiculturalism that is more participatory than previously described. As one interviewee explained:

> Well, for a lot of people, multiculturalism seems to be implied as an end product, right, "we will finish with a multicultural Australia". But to me it has never been, actually, the right approach to it. Even though, at the beginning, there's a lot of people that did believe that. Even today, a lot of people still assume that when we talk about multicultural Australia it just means that big mixing bowl. [...] [But in] the Australian multiculturalism, we emphasise the process of respecting the contribution that each component of the population, from different backgrounds ... different cultural backgrounds, different heritages ... who can make a contribution to the development of an Australian culture. And that's a process, not an end product.[9]

The history of Chinese Australian community organisations demonstrates that Australia's multiculturalism has been a process; a democratic practice rather than an "end product", or perhaps a verb rather than a noun. The histories of these organisations show that multiculturalism (and its protection) has been a force for inter- and intra-ethnic civil unity and is, therefore, a rebuttal to critics on the right who see multiculturalism as a culture of social division and historical

---

9   Interviewee 2, Anonymous Interview.

erasure.[10] They also pose a response to critics on the left who cast multiculturalism as a perpetuation of White nationalism and ethnic or racial difference.[11] As shown in the materials they created, the community organisations practised their own multicultural ideals. They showed multiculturalism is a journey without a final destination.

On 12 February 2022, Jason Yat-sen Li retained the electorate of Strathfield for Labor in a New South Wales state by-election, despite his opposition attempting to paint him as a CCP sympathiser. Peter Hartcher described the victory as an important demonstration that Australians could "pick the fearmongering from the reality and support a Chinese Australian candidate". The ability for Australians to "sensibly differentiate" was imperative for national unity, Hartcher explained, because "we have 1.3 million Chinese Australian citizens whom we have to value, embrace and protect from the Chinese Communist Party".[12] This is the same community of 1.3 million that Hartcher contends Australia had "built" without understanding it or knowing the consequences.[13] Perhaps the election of Li shows Australia is starting to understand its own Chinese Australian identity. But we will never know the "consequences" of having a single Chinese Australian community because Australia has never "built" a single, cohesive and unitary Chinese Australian community. And for that matter, neither have Chinese Australians. Rather, many diverse Chinese Australian communities – among myriad other communities – helped to instate a practice of multiculturalism in Australia. It is this reality and its consequences that we should turn our attention toward.

---

10 Blainey, *Blainey, Eye on Australia*, 58–61.
11 Ang, *On Not Speaking Chinese*, 14–16; Ghassan Hage, *White Nation [electronic resource]: Fantasies of White Supremacy in a Multicultural Society* (Hoboken: Taylor & Francis, 2012), 22–4.
12 *Insiders* (Melbourne: Australian Broadcasting Corporation, 13 February 2022), https://tinyurl.com/239hxand.
13 Hartcher, *Red Zone*, 174.

Bibliography

3AW (1984). "Immigration Should Be Banned". *The Age*, 20 March.
AAA (2020). "Submission to the Senate Inquiry into Issues Facing Diaspora Communities in Australia". Asian Australian Alliance. https://tinyurl.com/mfcrsmnd.
Abbott, Tony, Robert Manne, Judith Brett, Malcolm Fraser and Ron Brunton, eds (1998). *Two Nations: The Causes and Effects of the Rise of the One Nation Party in Australia*. Melbourne: Bookman Press.
ABC (2014). "Palmer Brands Chinese Government 'Mongrels' Who 'Shoot Own People'". Text. *ABC News*, 19 August. Accessed 7 October 2021. https://tinyurl.com/4ueez4h6.
ABS (1997). "1996 Census Community Profiles: Australia, Basic Community Profile". Census. 1996 Census of Population and Housing. Canberra: Australian Bureau of Statistics. https://tinyurl.com/yc5r8xa7.
——— (2002). "2001 Census Community Profile Series: Australia, Basic Community Profile". Census. 2001 Census of Population and Housing. Canberra: Australian Bureau of Statistics. https://tinyurl.com/57f949fe.
——— (2007). "2006 Census Community Profile Series: Australia, Basic Community Profile". Census. 2006 Census of Population and Housing. Canberra: Australian Bureau of Statistics.
——— (2012). "2011 Census of Population and Housing: Australia, Basic Community Profile". Census. 2011 Census of Population and Housing. Canberra: Australian Bureau of Statistics.

——— (2012). "Cultural Diversity in Australia". Census. Reflecting a Nation: Stories from the 2011 Census. Canberra: Australian Bureau of Statistics, 21 June. https://tinyurl.com/75j4y53f.
——— (1996). "Labour Force, March Key Estimates". Employment Report. Labour Force. Canberra: Australian Bureau of Statistics, April. https://tinyurl.com/2nk673v4.
——— (2022). "Cultural diversity: Census". Australian Bureau of Statistics, 28 June. https://tinyurl.com/3e7mx5vk.
ACCA (1992). "1991 Annual Report". Australian Chinese Community Association, January. State Library of New South Wales.
——— (1984). "ACCA News April 1984". Australian Chinese Community Association, April. State Library of New South Wales.
——— (1979). "ACCA News December 1979". Australian Chinese Community Association, December. State Library of New South Wales.
——— (1986). "ACCA News December 1986". Australian Chinese Community Association, December. State Library of New South Wales.
——— (1991). "ACCA News December 1991". Australian Chinese Community Association, December. State Library of New South Wales.
——— (2000). "ACCA News December 2000". Australian Chinese Community Association, December. National Library of Australia.
——— (2001). "ACCA News December 2001". Australian Chinese Community Association, December. National Library of Australia.
——— (2002). "ACCA News December 2002". Australian Chinese Community Association, December. National Library of Australia.
——— (1988). "ACCA News February 1988". Australian Chinese Community Association, February. State Library of New South Wales.
——— (1994). "ACCA News January 1994". Australian Chinese Community Association, January. State Library of New South Wales.
——— (1984). "ACCA News July 1984". Australian Chinese Community Association, July. State Library of New South Wales.
——— (1985). "ACCA News July 1985". Australian Chinese Community Association, July. State Library of New South Wales.
——— (2001). "ACCA News July 2001". Australian Chinese Community Association, July. National Library of Australia.
——— (1984). "ACCA News June 1984". Australian Chinese Community Association, June. State Library of New South Wales.
——— (1996). "ACCA News June 1996". Australian Chinese Community Association, June. State Library of New South Wales.
——— (1988). "ACCA News March 1988". Australian Chinese Community Association, March. State Library of New South Wales.

Bibliography

——— (2001). "ACCA News March 2001". Australian Chinese Community Association, March. National Library of Australia.
——— (2003). "ACCA News March 2003". Australian Chinese Community Association, March. National Library of Australia.
——— (1984). "ACCA News May 1984". Australian Chinese Community Association, May. State Library of New South Wales.
——— (1979). "ACCA News November 1979". Australian Chinese Community Association, November. State Library of New South Wales.
——— (1992). "ACCA News November 1992". Australian Chinese Community Association, November. State Library of New South Wales.
——— (1981). "ACCA News October 1981". Australian Chinese Community Association, October. State Library of New South Wales.
——— (1994). "ACCA News October 1994". Australian Chinese Community Association, October. State Library of New South Wales.
——— (1980). "ACCA News September 1980". Australian Chinese Community Association, September. State Library of New South Wales.
——— (1981). "ACCA News September 1981". Australian Chinese Community Association, September. State Library of New South Wales.
——— (1984). "ACCA News September 1984". Australian Chinese Community Association, September. State Library of New South Wales.
——— (1976). "ACCA Newsletter March 1976". Australian Chinese Community Association, March. State Library of New South Wales.
——— (1976). "ACCA Newsletter May 1976". Australian Chinese Community Association, May. State Library of New South Wales.
——— (1977). "ACCA Newsletter October 1977". Australian Chinese Community Association, October. State Library of New South Wales.
——— (1999). "Australian Chinese Community Association of New South Wales Inc.: 25th Annual Report 1999". Australian Chinese Community Association. National Library of Australia.
——— (1982). *Chinatown in the 1980s*. Sydney: Australian Chinese Community Association.
——— (2021). "Past and Current Presidents of ACCA". Australian Chinese Community Association 澳華公會. 10 December. https://tinyurl.com/9bate6mk.
———, ed. (1977). *澳洲紐修威省澳華公會會刊 Àozhōu Niǔxiūwēishěng àohuágōnghuì huìkān (The Australian-Chinese Community Association of NSW Journal)*. Sydney: ACCA.
———, ed. (1984). *澳華公會十週年紀念特刊 Ao Hua Gonghui Shi Zhou Nian Jinian Tekan (ACCA 10th Anniversary Year Book) 1974–1984*. Sydney: Australian Chinese Community Association of NSW.

ACF (1986). "ACF Newsletter August 1986". Australian Chinese Forum, August. State Library of New South Wales.

——— (1989). "ACF Newsletter August 1989". Australian Chinese Forum, August. National Library of Australia.

——— (1994). "ACF Newsletter August 1994". Australian Chinese Forum, August. State Library of New South Wales.

——— (1986). "ACF Newsletter December 1986". Australian Chinese Forum, December. State Library of New South Wales.

——— (1992). "ACF Newsletter February 1992". Australian Chinese Forum, February. National Library of Australia.

——— (1994). "ACF Newsletter January 1994". Australian Chinese Forum, January. State Library of New South Wales.

——— (1986). "ACF Newsletter June 1986". Australian Chinese Forum, June. State Library of New South Wales.

——— (1988). "ACF Newsletter June 1988". Australian Chinese Forum, June. State Library of New South Wales.

——— (1991). "ACF Newsletter June 1991". Australian Chinese Forum, June. National Library of Australia.

——— (1986). "ACF Newsletter March 1986". Australian Chinese Forum, March. State Library of New South Wales.

——— (1989). "ACF Newsletter March 1989". Australian Chinese Forum, March. National Library of Australia.

——— (1987). "ACF Newsletter November 1987". Australian Chinese Forum, November. State Library of New South Wales.

——— (1992). "ACF Newsletter November 1992". Australian Chinese Forum, November. National Library of Australia.

——— (1986). "ACF Newsletter October 1986". Australian Chinese Forum, October. State Library of New South Wales.

——— (1988). "ACF Newsletter September 1988". Australian Chinese Forum, September. State Library of New South Wales.

——— (1985). "Submission by the Australian Chinese Forum to Australian Senate". Parliament Submission. Canberra. Z567, Box 15, Federation of Ethnic Communities' Councils of Australia. ANU Archives.

ACNC (2021). "Indo China Ethnic Chinese Association of Victoria Inc". Text. Australian Charities and Not-for-profits Commission. Australian Charities and Not-for-profits Commission, 1 April. https://tinyurl.com/mrdujya8.3.

ACPPRC (2007). "Chairman". Wayback Machine. ACPPRC, 29 August. Accessed 27 February 2022. https://tinyurl.com/ycx34sy2.

Bibliography

ACT Chinese Club of Canberra et al. (1969). "Congratulations on the Occasion of His Excellency President Chiang Kai-Shek's Birthday". *Canberra Times*, 31 October.

ACTCAA (1989). "Newsletter April 1989". ACT Chinese Australian Association, April. National Library of Australia.

——— (1990). "Newsletter April 1990". ACT Chinese Australian Association, April. National Library of Australia.

——— (1988). "Newsletter August 1988". ACT Chinese Australian Association, August. National Library of Australia.

——— (1989). "Newsletter August 1989". ACT Chinese Australian Association, August. National Library of Australia.

——— (1991). "Newsletter August 1991". ACT Chinese Australian Association, August. National Library of Australia.

——— (1997). "Newsletter August 1997". ACT Chinese Australian Association, August. National Library of Australia.

——— (2000). "Newsletter August 2000". ACT Chinese Australian Association, August. National Library of Australia.

——— (1990). "Newsletter December 1990". ACT Chinese Australian Association, December. National Library of Australia.

——— (1997). "Newsletter December 1997". ACT Chinese Australian Association, December. National Library of Australia.

——— (2000). "Newsletter December 2000". ACT Chinese Australian Association, December. National Library of Australia.

——— (1990). "Newsletter February 1990". ACT Chinese Australian Association, February. National Library of Australia.

——— (1997). "Newsletter January 1997". ACT Chinese Australian Association, January. National Library of Australia.

——— (1989). "Newsletter June 1989". ACT Chinese Australian Association, June. National Library of Australia.

——— (1997). "Newsletter June 1997". ACT Chinese Australian Association, June. National Library of Australia.

——— (1989). "Newsletter November 1989". ACT Chinese Australian Association, November. National Library of Australia.

——— (1990). "Newsletter November 1990". ACT Chinese Australian Association, November. National Library of Australia.

——— (1996). "Newsletter November 1996". ACT Chinese Australian Association, November. National Library of Australia.

——— (1999). "Newsletter November 1999". ACT Chinese Australian Association, November. National Library of Australia.

——— (2001). "Newsletter November 2001". ACT Chinese Australian Association, November. National Library of Australia.
——— (1990). "Newsletter October 1990". ACT Chinese Australian Association, October. National Library of Australia.
——— (2004). "Newsletter October 2004". ACT Chinese Australian Association, October. National Library of Australia.
——— (1999). "Newsletter September 1999". ACT Chinese Australian Association, September. National Library of Australia.
ACWA (n.d.). "Achievements". Wordpress. 澳洲华人总工会, Australian Chinese Workers Association. Accessed 7 October 2021. https://tinyurl.com/2p9wmjew.
——— (n.d.). "华裔卡 huayi ka (Chinese Descendant ID Card)". Wordpress. 澳洲华人总工会, Australian Chinese Workers Association. Accessed 7 October 2021. https://tinyurl.com/jt8prhz6.
Aggarwal, Vinod K. and Sara A. Newland, eds (2014). *Responding to China's Rise: US and EU Strategies*. The Political Economy of the Asia Pacific: 15. Cham: Springer.
Agutter, Karen and Rachel A. Ankeny (2016). "Unsettling Narratives: Overcoming Prejudices in the Hostel Stories Project". *Journal of Australian Studies* 40, no. 4 (October): 464–77. https://doi.org/10.1080/14443058.2016.1223151.
Anderson, Kay (1990). "'Chinatown Re-Oriented': A Critical Analysis of Recent Redevelopment Schemes in a Melbourne and Sydney Enclave". *Australian Geographical Studies* 28, no. 2 (1 October): 137–54.
Ang, Ien (2014). "Beyond Chinese Groupism: Chinese Australians between Assimilation, Multiculturalism and Diaspora". *Ethnic and Racial Studies* 37, no. 7 (7 June): 1184–96. https://doi.org/10.1080/01419870.2014.859287.
——— (2004). "Beyond Transnational Nationalism: Questioning the Borders of the Chinese Diaspora in the Global City". In *State/Nation/Transnation: Perspectives on Transnationalism in the Asia Pacific*, edited by Katie Willis and Brenda S.A. Yeoh, 179–96. Florence, US: Taylor & Francis Group.
——— (2014). "No Longer Chinese? Residual Chineseness after the Rise of China". In *Diasporic Chineseness after the Rise of China: Communities and Cultural Production*, edited by Julia Kuehn, Kam Louie and David M. Pomfret, 17–31. Vancouver: UBC Press.
——— (2001). *On Not Speaking Chinese: Living Between Asia and the West*. London, UK: Taylor & Francis Group.
Ang, Thiam (1995). "'Ethnic Vote' Is Not Unthinking". *Sydney Morning Herald*, 16 November, sec. Letters.
——— (1996). "The PM and Free Speech". *Sydney Morning Herald*, 27 September, sec. Letters.

Bibliography

Aozhou Da Shiye (2016). "纪念毛主席逝世四十周年《光荣梦想》音乐晚会新闻发布会 Jinian Mao Zhuxi Shishi Sishi Zhounian 'Guangrong Mengxiang' Yinyue Wanhui Xinwen Fabu Hui (Press Conference for the 'Glory and Dream' Music Gala Commemorating the 40th Anniversary of Chairman Mao's Passing)", 27 August. Accessed 19 January 2022. https://www.youtube.com/watch?v=NvvEQ_vng1A.

"Appropriation Bill (No. 1) 1996–97 Second Reading" (1996). Canberra: Commonwealth Hansard, 10 September.

Archer, K.M. (1961). "Birthplaces of the Population of Australia by States and Territories". Census. Census of the Commonwealth. Canberra: Commonwealth Bureau of Census and Statistics.

——— (1961). "Race of the Population: Australia, States and Territories". Census. Census of the Commonwealth. Canberra: Commonwealth Bureau of Census and Statistics.

Around Australia (2021). "The Protests at Rundle Mall Adelaide Australia 18 Jul 2020 #shorts". YouTube, 22 January. https://tinyurl.com/yubcufut.

Australian Bureau of Statistics (1999). Population Composition: Languages spoken in Australia, 24 June. https://tinyurl.com/35pw4np6.

Australian Chinese Workers Association, ed. (2018). *Aodaliya Huaren Shequ Fazhan Baogao 2018* 澳大利亚华人社区发展报告 2018 *(Australian Chinese Community Development Report 2018)*. Harbin: Heilongjiang People's Publishing House.

Australian Commonwealth Government (1995). *Racial Discrimination Act 1975*, section 18C. https://tinyurl.com/2mks8hu9.

Australian Department of Social Security (1975). *National Groups in Australia: A Directory. South Australia 1975*. Canberra: Australian Government Publishing Service.

Australian Fujian Association (n.d.). "Homepage". Australian Fujian Association, 澳大利亚福建乡情联谊会. Accessed 15 December 2021. https://www.australianfujianassociation.org/.

Australian Hokkien HuayKuan Association (n.d.). "Homepage". Australian Hokkien HuayKuan Association, 澳洲福建会馆. Accessed 15 December 2021. http://www.fjhk.org.au/.

Australian Hunan Association (n.d.). "Homepage". Australian Hunan Association, 澳大利亚湖南会. Accessed 15 December 2021. https://www.hunan.com.au/.

Australian Institute of Aboriginal and Torres Strait Islander Studies (2020). "Indigenous Australians: Aboriginal and Torres Strait Islander People", 7 December. https://tinyurl.com/3pm7dypm.

Australian Institute of Multicultural Affairs (1982). *Evaluation of Post-Arrival Programs and Services*. Melbourne: Australian Institute of Multicultural Affairs.

Australian Jiangxi Association (2021). "Homepage". Australian Jiangxi, 澳大利亚江西同乡会. Accessed 15 December 2021. http://www.jiangxi.net.au/.

Australian Parliament (1973). *Australian Citizenship Act 1973*.

AVA (2016). "Melbourne Lord Mayor Robert Doyle: Stop Maoist Concert in Melbourne". Online Petition. *change.org*. https://tinyurl.com/bdedch22.

——— (2016). "Premier Daniel Andrews: Please Stop the Show of the Red Detachment of Women." Online Petition. *change.org*, 4 October. https://tinyurl.com/mwzxvfxc.

——— (2016). "Press Update – Embrace Australian Values Alliance (31 August 2016)". Online Petition. *change.org*. https://tinyurl.com/2h8rjvyd.

——— (2016). "Stop Maoist Concert in Sydney". Online Petition. *change.org*. https://www.change.org/p/sydney-lord-mayor-clover-moore-embrace-australian-values-stop-maoist-concert-in-sydne

——— (2016). "抵制红潮免祸害华人 – 致澳洲华人同胞的公开信 Dizhi Hongchao Mian Huohai Huaren – Zhi Aozhou Huaren Tongbao de Gongkaixin (Resist the Red Tide and Avoid Harmful Chinese – An Open Letter to Chinese Australian Compatriots)". *Australian Values Alliance*. Blog. August. http://evebch.ava.org.au/2016/08/blog-post_78.html.

——— (2016). "澳大利亚的公民价值观 Aodaliya de Gongmin Jiazhiguan (Australian Citizen Values)". Blog. *ava.org.au*, September. http://evebch.ava.org.au/2016/09/blog-post_9.html.

——— (2016). "'红粉滚回中国！' – 本联盟专稿 'Hongfen Gun Hui Zhongguo!' – Ben Linameng Zhuan Gao (Red Fans Go Back to China! Alliance Special Feature)". *Australian Values Alliance*. Blog. August. http://evebch.ava.org.au/2016/08/blog-post_58.html.

——— (2016). "约定你了，当晚见！（转帖）Yueding Ni Le, Dangwan Jian! (Zhuan Tie) (Promise to See You Tonight! (Reposted))". *Australian Values Alliance*. Blog. August. http://evebch.ava.org.au/2016/08/blog-post_75.html.

——— (2017). "联盟快讯（11）– 抵制'红剧'的小花絮 Lianmeng Kuaixun (11) – Dizhi 'Hong Ju' de Xiao Huaxu (Alliance News (11) – 'Red Ballet' Boycott Update)". Blog. *ava.org.au*, 17 February. http://evebch.ava.org.au/2017/02/11.html.

——— (2016). "让我们高唱澳洲国歌！Rang Women Gao Chang Aozhou Guoge! (Let's Sing the Australian National Anthem!)". Blog. *ava.org.au*, August. http://evebch.ava.org.au/2016/08/blog-post_74.html.

Bibliography

——— (2016). "《请勿作茧自缚！- 致 '颂毛会' 支持者的公开信》Qing Wu Zuojianzifu! – Zhi "Song Mao Hui" Zhichi Zhe de Gongkaixin (Don't Get Caught in Your Own Web! – An Open Letter to the Supporters of the Mao Gala)". Blog. *ava.org.au*, August. http://evebch.ava.org.au/2016/08/blog-post_62.html.
Bagnall, Kate and Julia Martínez (2021). *Locating Chinese Women: Historical Mobility Between China and Australia*. Hong Kong: Hong Kong University Press.
Bagshaw, Fergus and Eryk Hunter (2020). "'Go for the Whole Hog': MPs Push for Parliamentary Probe into CCP Influence at Universities". News. *Sydney Morning Herald*, 7 August. https://tinyurl.com/55ckd2zz.
Barabantseva, Elena (2010). *Overseas Chinese, Ethnic Minorities and Nationalism: De-Centering China*. London: Taylor & Francis Group.
——— (2005). "Trans-Nationalising Chineseness: Overseas Chinese Policies of the PRC's Central Government". *Asien* 96 (July): 7–28.
——— (2012). "Who Are 'Overseas Chinese Ethnic Minorities'? China's Search for Transnational Ethnic Unity". *Modern China* 38, no. 1 (January): 78–109. https://doi.org/10.1177/0097700411424565.
Béja, Jean-Philippe, ed. (2010). *The Impact of China's 1989 Tiananmen Massacre*. London: Taylor & Francis.
Benjamin Law, Author and Journalist Taking a Stand against Racism during COVID-19 (n.d.). Accessed 18 January 2022. https://tinyurl.com/247pv6f2.
Bergsten, C. Fred, Charles Freeman, Nicholas R. Lardy and Derek J. Mitchell, eds (2008). *China's Rise: Challenges and Opportunities*. Washington, DC: Peterson Institute for International Economics and Center for Strategic and International Studies.
Blainey, Geoffrey (1991). *Blainey, Eye on Australia: Speeches and Essays of Geoffrey Blainey*. Melbourne: Schwartz & Wilkinson.
Bongiorno, Frank (2015). *The Eighties: The Decade That Transformed Australia*. Melbourne: Black Inc. Books.
Bonnin, Michel (2010). "The Chinese Communist Party and 4 June 1989". In *The Impact of China's 1989 Tiananmen Massacre*, edited by Jean-Philippe Béja, 33–48. London: Taylor & Francis.
Bonyhady, Nick (2019). "Chinese Newspapers Dedicate Front Pages to Exiled Billionaire Huang Xiangmo". *Sydney Morning Herald*, 16 February. https://tinyurl.com/6bf26jbx.
Boscaini, Joshua (2020). "Chinese Community Helps Families Stuck in Self-Isolation after Coronavirus Outbreak". *ABC News*, 13 February. https://tinyurl.com/y5unrtsf.

Bourke, Latika (2014). "Clive Palmer Apologises for China Comments in Which He Referred to Chinese 'Mongrels'". *Sydney Morning Herald*, 26 August. https://tinyurl.com/39ny26hh.
——— (2020). "Four Australian MPs Urge Britain to Ban Huawei". *The Age*, 23 January. https://tinyurl.com/yc76yw93.
Boyd, Kelly, ed. (2019). *Encyclopedia of Historians and Historical Writing*. New York: Routledge. https://doi.org/10.4324/9780203825556.
Bradley, Kevin and Anisa Puri (2017). "Creating an Oral History Archive: Digital Opportunities and Ethical Issues". In *Oral History and Australian Generations*, edited by Katie Holmes and Alistair Thomson, 75–91. Oxon, UK: Routledge.
Brophy, David (2021). *China Panic: Australia's Alternative to Paranoia and Pandering*. Melbourne: Black Inc.
Brown, Malcolm (1984). "A Growing Audience for Messages of Hate". *Sydney Morning Herald*, 8 February.
——— (1981). "League of Rights to Condemn Leaders' Meeting". *Sydney Morning Herald*, 21 September.
——— (1978). "Racist Group Expects Nation-Wide Membership". *Sydney Morning Herald*, 8 June.
Butler, Eric (1975). "League of Rights Surges Forward". *Intelligence Survey*, October, 25th ed. National Library of Australia.
CAF (2013). "2013 Submission from Chinese Australian Forum Re. Inquiry into Racial Villification Law in NSW". Chinese Australian Forum, 8 March. NSW Parliament.
——— (1996). "A Survey of Abuse Suffered by Chinese Australians". Chinese Australian Forum, 13 November. JV Barry Library. Australian Institute of Criminology.
——— (1997). "CAF Newsletter February 1997". Chinese Australian Forum, February. State Library of New South Wales.
——— (1996). "CAF Newsletter May 1996". Chinese Australian Forum, May. State Library of New South Wales.
——— (2020). "Denounce Racist Attacks on Asian-Australians: #UnityOverFear During Covid-19". change.org, April. https://tinyurl.com/rhwfw9pr.
——— (1999). "Newsletter: 1999 Diary". Wayback Machine. Chinese Australian Forum. https://tinyurl.com/2uk4kdjn.
——— (2020). "Open Letter on National Unity During the Coronavirus Pandemic", 8 April. https://tinyurl.com/yry7cmtb.
——— (2000). "Press Release: Building the Reconciliation Bridge Seminar". Wayback Machine. Chinese Australian Forum. https://tinyurl.com/2uk4kdjn.
——— (2000). "Press Release: The Republic Debate". Wayback Machine. Chinese Australian Forum. https://tinyurl.com/2uk4kdjn.

Bibliography

——— (2020). "Submission to the Senate Inquiry into Issues Facing Diaspora Communities in Australia". Chinese Australian Forum. https://tinyurl.com/yceeewyy.

CAF, and Thiam Ang (1998). "Newsletter: 1998 Annual Dinner President Speech". Wayback Machine. Chinese Australian Forum. https://tinyurl.com/yc7rcdsh.

——— (2000). "Newsletter: 1999 Annual Dinner", Autumn. https://tinyurl.com/2uk4kdjn.

CAF, and Jon-Claire Lee (2000). "Newsletter: 2000 CAF Annual Dinner Report". Wayback Machine. Chinese Australian Forum, Spring. https://tinyurl.com/2uk4kdjn.

——— (2000). "Newsletter: The President's Message". Wayback Machine. Chinese Australian Forum, Winter. https://tinyurl.com/d2yv6hht.

——— (2002). "Press Release: President's Address for Harmony Day Dinner (20/3/02)". Wayback Machine. Chinese Australian Forum, 20 March. http://web.archive.org/web/20021123013154/http://www.caf.org.au/.

CAF, and Daniel Lim (2000). "Newsletter: Republic Australia – The Way Forward". Wayback Machine. Chinese Australian Forum, Spring. https://tinyurl.com/2uk4kdjn.

CAF, and Jenny Lim (2000). "Newsletter: A Tale of Two Books". Wayback Machine. Chinese Australian Forum, Autumn. https://tinyurl.com/2uk4kdjn.

——— (2001). "Newsletter: Celebrating the Centenary". Wayback Machine. Chinese Australian Forum, Autumn. https://tinyurl.com/2uk4kdjn.

CAF, and Grace Wong (2001). "Newsletter: Reclaiming the Past". Wayback Machine. Chinese Australian Forum, Autumn. https://tinyurl.com/2uk4kdjn.

——— (2002). "Newsletter: Recollections". Wayback Machine. Chinese Australian Forum, Autumn. https://tinyurl.com/2uk4kdjn.

Cai, Tian (1999). "Astride Two Worlds: The Chinese Response to Changing Citizenship in Western Australia (1901–1973)". *Theses: Doctorates and Masters*, 1 January. https://ro.ecu.edu.au/theses/1199.

Callick, Rowan (2016). "Rebel Chinese Movement Promotes 'Australian Values'". 4 September. https://tinyurl.com/46wk49zb.

Cameron, R.J. (1979). "Populations and Dwellings: Summary Tables – South Australia". Census. Census of Population and Housing, 30 June 1976. Canberra: Commonwealth Bureau of Census and Statistics.

Canberra Times (1990). "Hawke's Move on Chinese Students". 10 June. http://nla.gov.au/nla.news-article120891437.

——— (1979). "Racial Discrimination Day: Australian UN Association Statement". 21 March.

——— (1976). "Sir Robert a Patron for Last Time". 24 March. http://nla.gov.au/nla.news-article110809630.

——— (1979). "State Attacked for Racist Attitudes: Members of the Ku Klux Klan". 17 October.
——— (1978). "The Lilly-White Principle". 9 December.
——— (1990). "They Said It". 9 June. https://tinyurl.com/5n869hk6.
Carruthers, Fiona. "Leaders Blast Racist Threat". *The Australian*, 28 August 1996.
CASA (1979). "News Bulletin December 1979". Chinese Association of South Australia, December. National Library of Australia.
——— (1979). "News Bulletin February 1979". Chinese Association of South Australia, February. National Library of Australia.
——— (1984). "News Bulletin May 1984". Chinese Association of South Australia, May. National Library of Australia.
——— (1978). "News Bulletin November 1978". Chinese Association of South Australia, November. National Library of Australia.
——— (1991). "Newsletter April 1991". Chinese Association of South Australia, April. National Library of Australia.
——— (1992). "Newsletter April 1992". Chinese Association of South Australia, April. National Library of Australia.
——— (1986). "Newsletter December 1986". Chinese Association of South Australia, December. National Library of Australia.
——— (1990). "Newsletter December 1990". Chinese Association of South Australia, December. National Library of Australia.
——— (1992). "Newsletter February 1992". Chinese Association of South Australia, February. National Library of Australia.
——— (1985). "Newsletter January 1985". Chinese Association of South Australia, January. National Library of Australia.
——— (1989). "Newsletter January 1989". Chinese Association of South Australia, January. National Library of Australia.
——— (1989). "Newsletter July 1989". Chinese Association of South Australia, July. National Library of Australia.
——— (1992). "Newsletter July 1992". Chinese Association of South Australia, July. National Library of Australia.
——— (1985). "Newsletter March 1985". Chinese Association of South Australia, March. National Library of Australia.
——— (1989). "Newsletter May 1989". Chinese Association of South Australia, May. National Library of Australia.
——— (1992). "Newsletter October 1992". Chinese Association of South Australia, October. National Library of Australia.
——— (1990). "Newsletter September 1990". Chinese Association of South Australia, September. National Library of Australia.

Bibliography

——— (1993). "Newsletter September 1993". Chinese Association of South Australia, September. National Library of Australia.

CASS (1994). "Grants Administration and Assessment – Applications – Cultural Exchange Program – Chinese Australian Services Society". Item. Sydney, 20 December. C2943, 64893. National Archives of Australia. https://recordsearch.naa.gov.au/scripts/AutoSearch.asp?O=I&Number=31791499.

——— (2011). 華人服務社30週年紀念特刊/CASS 30th Anniversary Souvenir Book. Edited by Nancy Zhiyuan Liu and Rosie Du. Sydney: Chinese Australian Services Society.

Castles, Ian (1989). "Census 86 – Summary Characteristics of Persons and Dwellings, Australia". Census. Census of Population and Housing, 30 June 1986. Canberra: Australian Bureau of Statistics.

——— (1993). "Census Characteristics of Australia: 1991 Census of Population and Housing". Census. 1991 Census of Population and Housing. Canberra: Australian Bureau of Statistics.

CAV (2010). "CAV Newsletter August 2010". Chinese Association of Victoria, August. https://tinyurl.com/2mtj5fxz.

——— (2008). "CAV Newsletter February 2008". Chinese Association of Victoria, February. https://tinyurl.com/3s5p8brn.

——— (2010). "CAV Newsletter January 2010". Chinese Association of Victoria, January. https://tinyurl.com/5c84svpw.

——— (2007). "CAV Newsletter July 2007". Chinese Association of Victoria, July. https://tinyurl.com/49hcvt37.

——— (2007). "CAV Newsletter May 2007". Chinese Association of Victoria, May. https://tinyurl.com/42twymc4.

——— (2008). "CAV Newsletter November 2008". Chinese Association of Victoria, November. https://tinyurl.com/yeyvcye4.

———, ed. (1992). *Chinese Association of Victoria: 1982–1992: The First Ten Years*. Melbourne: Chinese Association of Victoria.

———, ed. (2007). *Chinese Association of Victoria: 1982–2007 Silver Jubilee*. Melbourne: Chinese Association of Victoria.

——— (2003). "News August 2003". Wayback Machine. Chinese Association of Victoria, 2 August. https://tinyurl.com/mvjsxdr8.

——— (2020). "The Bulletin Newsletter June 2020". The Chinese Association of Victoria, June. https://tinyurl.com/ycy2t42b.

CAV, and Vincent Chow (2002). "President's Report". Wayback Machine. Chinese Association of Victoria, 22 September. https://tinyurl.com/4743j62j.

CFV (2021). "About Us". 澳大利亚墨尔本侨友社中文学校 Chinese Fellowship Chinese School in Melbourne, Australia. https://tinyurl.com/ywkvvanh.

——— (2018). "About Us". Chinese Fellowship of Victoria. Accessed 15 January 2022. http://english.chinesefellowship.org.au/about-us/.
——— (1996). *Aodaliya Weisheng qiao youshe er shi wu zhounian yinxi jinian tekan* 澳大利亞維省僑友社二十五週年銀禧紀念特刊 *(Chinese Fellowship of Victoria, Australia: 25th Anniversary Commerorative Journal)*. North Melbourne: Chinese Fellowship of Victoria.
——— (1975). "Newsletter April 1975". Chinese Fellowship of Victoria, April. State Library of Victoria.
——— (1974). "Newsletter August 1974". Chinese Fellowship of Victoria, August. State Library of Victoria.
——— (1975). "Newsletter August 1975". Chinese Fellowship of Victoria, August. State Library of Victoria.
——— (1997). "Newsletter August 1997". Chinese Fellowship of Victoria, August. State Library of Victoria.
——— (1975). "Newsletter February 1975". Chinese Fellowship of Victoria, February. State Library of Victoria.
——— (1999). "Newsletter February 1999". Chinese Fellowship of Victoria, February. State Library of Victoria.
——— (1984). "Newsletter January 1984". Chinese Fellowship of Victoria, January. State Library of Victoria.
——— (1975). "Newsletter July 1975". Chinese Fellowship of Victoria, July. State Library of Victoria.
——— (1975). "Newsletter June 1975". Chinese Fellowship of Victoria, June. State Library of Victoria.
——— (1987). "Newsletter June 1987". Chinese Fellowship of Victoria, June. State Library of Victoria.
——— (1989). "Newsletter June 1989". Chinese Fellowship of Victoria, June. State Library of Victoria.
——— (1984). "Newsletter March 1984". Chinese Fellowship of Victoria, March. State Library of Victoria.
——— (1989). "Newsletter March 1989". Chinese Fellowship of Victoria, March. State Library of Victoria.
——— (1975). "Newsletter May 1975". Chinese Fellowship of Victoria, May. State Library of Victoria.
——— (1984). "Newsletter May 1984". Chinese Fellowship of Victoria, May. State Library of Victoria.
——— (1990). "Newsletter May 1990". Chinese Fellowship of Victoria, May. State Library of Victoria.
——— (1974). "Newsletter November 1974". Chinese Fellowship of Victoria, November. State Library of Victoria.

Bibliography

——— (1975). "Newsletter November 1975". Chinese Fellowship of Victoria, November. State Library of Victoria.
——— (1986). "Newsletter November 1986". Chinese Fellowship of Victoria, November. State Library of Victoria.
——— (1990). "Newsletter November 1990". Chinese Fellowship of Victoria, November. State Library of Victoria.
——— (1994). "Newsletter November 1994". Chinese Fellowship of Victoria, November. State Library of Victoria.
——— (1996). "Newsletter November 1996". Chinese Fellowship of Victoria, November. State Library of Victoria.
——— (1975). "Newsletter October 1975". Chinese Fellowship of Victoria, October. State Library of Victoria.
——— (1991). "Newsletter October 1991". Chinese Fellowship of Victoria, October. State Library of Victoria.
——— (1974). "Newsletter September 1974". Chinese Fellowship of Victoria, September. State Library of Victoria.
——— (1975). "Newsletter September 1975". Chinese Fellowship of Victoria, September. State Library of Victoria.
CFV et al. (1989). "墨爾本各界團體聲援 (Melbourne Organisations from All Walks of Life Voice Support)". *Australian Chinese Daily*, 27 May.
Chang, Arthur Gar Lock and Ann Turner (1991). *Arthur Lock Chang Interviewed by Ann Turner*. Sound recording. National Library of Australia.
Chew, Franklin and Diana Giese (2000). *Franklin Chew Interviewed by Diana Giese in the Chinese Australian Oral History Partnership Collection*. Sound recording. Chinese Australian Oral History Partnership. TRC 4581. National Library of Australia.
Chin, Daryl N. and Diana Giese (1996). *Daryl Chin Interviewed by Diana Giese for the Post-War Chinese Australians Oral History Project*. Sound recording. Post-War Chinese Australians Oral History Project. Darwin. TRC 3540. National Library of Australia.
Chin, Ernie and Diana Giese (1993). *Ernie Chin Interviewed by Diana Giese for the Post-War Chinese Australians Oral History Project*. Sound recording. Post-War Chinese Australians Oral History Project. Darwin. TRC 3007. National Library of Australia.
Chin, Lee Lin, Michelle Rimmer, Bianco Zeng, Forest Lyn, Kianie Zeng, Shanice Cheung and Xue Feng Zhang (2018). "Members of Australia's Cantonese Speaking Community Are Concerned about the Declining Number of Second and Third Generation Migrants Learning to Speak Cantonese". *SBS News*. SBS TV, 19 May. https://tinyurl.com/3uh37brk.

Chinese Museum of Australia (1996). "The Chinese in Australia and Oceania International Conference". Chinese Museum of Australia, 21 September. Ms Acc17.032, Papers of Diana Giese, File 10. National Library of Australia.

"Chinese Youth League Monthly Tea Meetings", 26/08/1962 "NSW Chinese Workers' Association Volume 1". Item. Canberra, 1970 1953. 22, A6122, 2235. National Archives of Australia. https://tinyurl.com/5yh63w5t.

"Chinese Youth League of Australia – Volume 1". Item. Canberra, 1958 1944. A6122, 1914. National Archives of Australia. https://tinyurl.com/43u8p364.

"Chinese Youth League of Australia – Volume 2 [227pp]". Item. Canberra, 1962 1958. A6122, 1915. National Archives of Australia. https://tinyurl.com/5n6mfud5.

Ching-hwang, Yen (2016). *Ethnicities, Personalities and Politics in the Ethnic Chinese Worlds*. Singapore: World Scientific.

Chow, Benjamin and Diana Giese (1998). *Benjamin Ming Tung Chow Interviewed by Diana Giese for the Post-War Chinese Australians Oral History Project*. Post-War Chinese Australians Oral History Project. TRC 3707. National Library of Australia.

Chua, McAndrew (n.d.). "The Racial Politics of Public Health in 1910's Darwin Chinatown". *Journal of Northern Territory History*, no. 21): 59–78. https://doi.org/10.3316/informit.032944074798518.

Chung, Frank (2020). "'Asian Dog, You Brought Corona Here': Young Women Racially Abused, Spat on in Sydney Street". *news.com.au*, 31 March. https://tinyurl.com/yc42kkcv.

City of Melbourne Council (2023). "Successful Applicants 2023". Melbourne: Community Meals Subsidy Program. https://tinyurl.com/4y7crdpp.

——— (2024). "Successful Applicants 2024". Melbourne: Community Meals Subsidy Program. https://tinyurl.com/4y7crdpp.

Collins, Jock (2002). "Chinese Entrepreneurs: The Chinese Diaspora in Australia". *International Journal of Entrepreneurial Behavior & Research* 8, no. 1/2 (February): 113–33. https://doi.org/10.1108/13552550210423750.

Consumer Affairs Victoria (2020). *Search for an Incorporated Association*. https://tinyurl.com/382h3r5j.

Cooke, Karen (1984). "Reasonable Tones Carry the Message of Hate". *The Age*, 25 July.

"Correspondence – Subject – [Pauline] Hanson PART 2" (1996). Item. Canberra, September. M4439, 1 PART 2. National Archives of Australia.

"Correspondence – Subject – [Pauline] Hanson PART 3" (1996). Item. Canberra, September. M4439, 1 PART 3. National Archives of Australia.

Couchman, Sophie (2019). "Melbourne's See Yup Kuan Ti Temple: A Historical Overview". *Chinese Southern Diaspora Studies* 8: 50–81.

Bibliography

Cox, David R. (1987). *Immigration and Welfare: An Australian Perspective*. Sydney: Prentice Hall.
Craig, Terence Michael (1987). "The Australian League of Rights and Its Divisions". Manuscript.
Cunningham, Philip J. (2014). *Tiananmen Moon: Inside the Chinese Student Uprising of 1989*. Lanham: Rowman & Littlefield Publishers.
Curran, James (2022). *Australia's China Odyssey: From Euphoria to Fear*. Sydney: NewSouth Publishing.
CWA, ed. (1995). *Chung Wah Association, 1910–1995: 85th Anniversary*. Perth: Chung Wah Association.
——— (2010). *Chung Wah Association Centenary Celebration Souvenir Publication, 1910–2010*. Perth: Chung Wah Association.
——— (1984). "Chung Wah News April 1984". Chung Wah Association, April.
——— (1984). "Chung Wah News August 1984". Chung Wah Association, August.
——— (1984). "Chung Wah News June 1984". Chung Wah Association, June.
——— (1984). "Chung Wah News November 1984". Chung Wah Association, November.
——— (1984). "Chung Wah News October 1984". Chung Wah Association, October.
——— (1983). "Chung Wah News September 1983". Chung Wah Association, September.
CYL (1979). *40th Anniversary Chinese Youth League of Australia: Commemorative Bulletin*. Sydney: Chinese Youth League. https://tinyurl.com/yh45dx8u.
——— (2019). *80 週年紀念冊 Bashi Zhounian Jinian Ce (80th Anniversary Commemorative Edition)*. Sydney: Chinese Youth League.
——— (2005). "China Tour 2005". Wayback Machine. Chinese Youth League of Australia. https://tinyurl.com/2am6fkju.
——— (2005). "Consulate General's Visit". Wayback Machine. Chinese Youth League of Australia. https://tinyurl.com/4hywhxuz.
——— (1991). "CYL News August 1991". Chinese Youth League, August. National Library of Australia.
——— (1994). "CYL News May 1994". Chinese Youth League, May. National Library of Australia.
Damousi, Joy, Marilyn Lake, Henry Reynolds and Mark McKenna (2010). "Why Do We Get So Emotional about Anzac?" In *What's Wrong With Anzac?*, 94–109. Sydney: UNSW Press. http://www.jstor.org/stable/j.ctt5vkmx8.8.
Darian-Smith, Kate and Michael Cathcart (2004). *Stirring Australian Speeches: The Definitive Collection from Botany to Bali*. Melbourne: Melbourne University Press.

Davidson, Andrew P. and Kuah-Pearce Khun Eng (2008). "Introduction: Diasporic Memories and Identities". In *At Home in the Chinese Diaspora: Memories, Identities and Belongings*, edited by Kuah-Pearce Khun Eng and Andrew P. Davidson, 1–11. London: Palgrave Macmillan UK. https://doi.org/10.1057/9780230591622_1.

Deutchman, Iva Ellen (2000). "Pauline Hanson and the Rise and Fall of the Radical Right in Australia". *Patterns of Prejudice* 34, no. 1 (January): 49–62.

Dinjaski, Melanie (2020). "Coronavirus: Two Asian Women Target of Spitting Racial Attack in Marrickville, NSW Police Commissioner Mick Fuller". *9news.com.au*, 31 March. https://tinyurl.com/6urm94ds.

Dorling, Philip (2017). "Still Anti-Asian? Anti-Chinese? One Nation Policies on Asian Immigration and Multiculturalism". The Australia Institute, May. https://tinyurl.com/2xu6ma3x.

Douw, Leo (1999). "Introduction". In *Qiaoxiang Ties: Interdisciplinary Approaches to "Cultural Capitalism" in South China*, edited by Leo Douw, Michael R. Godley and Cen Huang, 22–44. London; New York: Kegan Paul International in association with International Institute for Asian Studies.

——— (1999). "The Chinese Sojourner Discourse". In *Qiaoxiang Ties: Interdisciplinary Approaches to "Cultural Capitalism" in South China*, edited by Leo Douw, Michael R. Godley and Cen Huang, 22–44. Kegan Paul International in association with International Institute for Asian Studies.

Edwards, Louise (2019). "Victims, Apologies, and the Chinese in Australia". *Journal of Chinese Overseas* 15, no. 1 (10 April): 62–88. https://tinyurl.com/mwvuh2nv.

Ellis, John Brant (n.d.). "Anti-Racism Rally and March through Melbourne, 8th December 1996". Acquisition: [1999.0081] "Papers of John Brant Ellis". University of Melbourne Archive. Accessed 9 January 2024.

"Eric Butler, National Director Australian League of Rights" (1972). Television. *Monday Conference*. Australia: Australian Broadcasting Corporation, 26 June.

Facebook (2020). "Hundreds Gather in Rundle Mall to Protest against Racial Violence against Asian Community". 11 July. https://tinyurl.com/38cbt72d.

Fang, Jason (2020). "我们是"吃了'六四'人血馒头"：澳洲学运领袖忆"六四"" "Wǒ men shì "chīle 'liùsì' rén xuè mántou": Àozhōu xué yùn l ǐ ngxiù yì "liùsì"" ("We Ate the Blood Buns of 'June 4th'": Australian Student Movement Leaders Recall 'June 4th'"). 9 June. Accessed 17 March 2021. https://tinyurl.com/5n6dvz2r

Farr, Malcolm (2017). "Hanson's 20-Year Conspiracy Theory". *news.com.au*, 14 March, sec. Leaders. https://tinyurl.com/5n977jja.

Farrelly, Paul J. (2018) *The Australia-China Council: The First Forty Years*. Canberra: Australia-China Council.

Bibliography

FCA (1992). "Chinese Community Bulletin August 1992". Federation of Chinese Associations, August. National Library of Australia.

——— (1992). "Chinese Community Bulletin October 1992". Federation of Chinese Associations, October. National Library of Australia.

——— (1992). "Chinese Community Bulletin September 1992". Federation of Chinese Associations, September. National Library of Australia.

——— (2021). "关于华联会历史 guanyu hualianhui lishi (About FCA's History)". 维省华联会 Federation of Victorian Community Associations. https://www.vicfca.org.au/vicfcahistory?lightbox=dataItem-juumat123.

——— (n.d.). "注册会员团体 zhuce huiyuan tuanti (Registered Member Organisations)". Federation of Chinese Associations – 维省华联会, https://www.vicfca.org.au/vicfcagroup.

FDA (2020). "Submission to the Senate Inquiry into Issues Facing Diaspora Communities in Australia". Falun Dafa Association of Australia.

FDC (2016). "Joint Statement of the Chinese Community in Australia on Protest against Maoist Concert". Federation for a Democratic China, 24 August. https://tinyurl.com/mspxrf3u.

Feng, Chongyi (2017). "Academic Chongyi Feng: Profits, Freedom and China's 'Soft Power' in Australia". *The Conversation*, 6 June. https://tinyurl.com/4x92bx29.

——— (2016). "Culture, Free Speech and Celebrating Mao Downunder". *The Conversation*, 24 August. https://tinyurl.com/3n4mdjmv.

——— (2011). "The Changing Political Identity of the 'Overseas Chinese' in Australia". *Cosmopolitan Civil Societies Journal* 3, no. 1: 121–38.

Feng, Tim (2020). "Response to Racial Abuse of Two Sisters in Marrickville". *acca.org.au*, 6 April. https://tinyurl.com/3ntr8hwu.

Fewsmith, Joseph (2001). *China since Tiananmen: The Politics of Transition*. Cambridge, UK: Cambridge University Press.

Fischer, Tim (1996). "Correspondence – Subject – [Pauline] Hanson". November. M4439, Canberra. National Archives of Australia.

Fitzgerald, John (2007). *Big White Lie: Chinese Australians in White Australia*. Sydney: UNSW Press.

——— (2000). "Diaspora and Discourse: Transnationalism and the Subject of Modern History". In *Re-Examining Chinese Transnationalism in Australia-New Zealand*, edited by Manying Ip, 13–24. Canberra: Centre for the Study of the Chinese Southern Diaspora, ANU.

——— (2021). "Eric Abetz's War on Chinese Australians Has Beijing Rubbing Its Hands". News. *Crikey*, 7 February. https://tinyurl.com/2zhepyp5.

Fitzgerald, Shirley (1997). *Red Tape, Gold Scissors: The Story of Sydney's Chinese*. State Library of New South Wales Press.

Fitzgerald, Stephen (2015). *Comrade Ambassador: Whitlam's Beijing Envoy*. Melbourne: Melbourne University Press.
Flowers, James and Diana Giese (2000). *James Flowers Interviewed by Diana Giese in the Chinese Australian Oral History Partnership Collection*. Sound recording. TRC 4550. National Library of Australia.
Fong, Darwina and Diana Giese (1992). *Darwina Fong Interviewed by Diana Giese in the Post-War Chinese Australians Oral History Project*. Sound recording. Post-War Chinese Australians Oral History Project.
Fong, William and Diana Giese (1993). *William Fong Interviewed by Diana Giese in the Post-War Chinese Australians Oral History Project*. Sound recording. Post-War Chinese Australians Oral History Project.
Fox, Vashti Jane (2022). "Fascism and Anti-Fascism in Perth in the 1980s". In *Histories of Fascism and Anti-Fascism in Australia*. Routledge.
Franklin, Matthew (1998). "PM Parries Questions on Hanson". *Courier Mail*, 15 May.
Freri, Mariana (2013). "Groups Oppose Racial Discrimination Act Change". NITV, 22 November. https://tinyurl.com/mracxd7c.
Fung, Edmund S.K. and Jie Chen (1996). *Changing Perceptions: The Attitudes of the PRC Chinese towards Australia and China, 1989–1996*. Australia-Asian Papers: No. 78. Centre for the Study of Australia-Asia Relations, Faculty of Asian and International Studies, Griffith University.
Galbally, Frank (1978). *Report of the Review of Post-Arrival Programs and Services for Migrants*. Canberra: Migrant Services and Programs.
Gao, Jia (2013). *Chinese Activism of a Different Kind: The Chinese Students' Campaign to Stay in Australia*. Social Sciences in Asia: Volume 37. Leiden: Brill.
——— (2001). "Chinese Students in Australia". In *The Australian People: An Encyclopedia of the Nation, Its People and Their Origins*, by James Jupp, 222–5. Cambridge; New York; Melbourne: Cambridge University Press.
———. (2006) "Migrant Transnationality and Its Evolving Nature: A Case Study of Mainland Chinese Migrants in Australia". *Journal of Chinese Overseas* 2, no. 2: 193–219.
——— (2017). "Rediscovering the New Gold Mountain: Chinese Immigration to Australia Since the Mid-1980s". In *Contemporary Chinese Diasporas*, edited by Min Zhou, 209–31. Singapore: Springer Singapore. https://tinyurl.com/ynubmz5p.
——— (2011). "Seeking Residency from the Courts: The Chinese Experience in the Post-White Australia Era". *Journal of Chinese Overseas* 7, no. 2: 187–210. https://doi.org/10.1163/179325411X595404.

Bibliography

Gardner, Nathan Daniel (2022). "All as One to One for All: Comparing Chinese Australian Responses to Racism during the "Hanson Debate" and COVID-19". *Journal of Chinese Overseas* 18, no. 1 (18 March): 1–30.

——— (2022). "United We Stood but Divided We Were: Chinese Australian Unity and the 1984 Immigration Debate". *History Australia* 19, no. 2 (3 April): 305–24. https://doi.org/10.1080/14490854.2022.2048038.

Gerathy, Sarah (2016). "Pauline Hanson Controversy: Chinese Community Campaigns against "Racist" Ideas". *ABC News*, 8 July. https://tinyurl.com/3u9azujr.

Gibson, Peter Charles (2022). *Made in Chinatown: Chinese Australian Furniture Factories, 1880–1930.* Sydney: Sydney University Press.

Giese, Diana (1997). *Astronauts, Lost Souls & Dragons: Voices of Today's Chinese Australians.* Brisbane: University of Queensland Press.

——— (1995). *Beyond Chinatown: Changing Perspectives on the Top End Chinese Experience.* Canberra: National Library of Australia.

——— (1999). *Chinese Australian Oral History Partnership.* Sound recording. National Library of Australia.

——— (1999). *Courage and Service: Chinese Australians and World War II.* Marrickville, NSW: Courage and Service Project.

——— (1990). "Papers of Diana Giese". Manuscript.

——— (1992). *Post-War Chinese Australians Oral History Project.* Sound recording. National Library of Australia.

Glascott, Joseph (1984). "Garden Site a Battleground". *Sydney Morning Herald*, 21 December.

Goodwin, Richard (1976). "Chinese Don't Want to Become a Sideshow for City Tourists". *The Age*, 19 January.

——— (1984). "'Too Many Asians' Immigration Policy Question". *Warrnambool Standard*, 19 March.

Goot, Murray and Ian Watson (2001). "One Nation's Electoral Support: Where Does It Come From, What Makes It Different and How Does It Fit?" *Australian Journal of Politics & History* 47, no. 2: 159–91. https://tinyurl.com/4ms5zmsf.

Grant, Bligh (2019). "Introduction". In *The Rise of Right-Populism: Pauline Hanson's One Nation and Australian Politics*, edited by Bligh Grant, Tod Moore and Tony Lynch, 1–25. Singapore: Springer.

Grant, Bligh, Tod Moore and Tony Lynch, eds (2019). *The Rise of Right-Populism: Pauline Hanson's One Nation and Australian Politics.* Singapore: Springer.

Grassby, Al (1973). *A Multi-Cultural Society for the Future.* Canberra: Australian Government Publishing Service.

——— (1976). "Commissioner for Community Relations: First Annual Report". Canberra: Office of the Commissioner for Community Relations.
Gries, Peter Hays (2004). *China's New Nationalism*. 1st ed. University of California Press.
Gurvich, Victoria (1998). "Liberal Pick Attacks One Nation". *The Age*, 7 May.
Hage, Ghassan (2012). *White Nation [electronic resource]: Fantasies of White Supremacy in a Multicultural Society*. Hoboken: Taylor & Francis.
——— (2000). *White Nation: Fantasies of White Supremacy in a Multicultural Society*. New York: Routledge.
Hamilton, Clive (2018). *Silent Invasion: China's Influence in Australia*. Melbourne: Hardie Grant Publishing.
——— (2018). "Why Do We Keep Turning a Blind Eye to Chinese Political Interference?" *The Conversation*, 4 April. https://tinyurl.com/9a8tcnrv.
Hamilton, John (2008). *Gallipoli Sniper: The Life of Billy Sing*. Sydney: Pan Macmillan Australia.
Harding, Harry (1995). "The Concept of 'Greater China': Themes, Variations and Reservations". In *Greater China: The Next Superpower?*, edited by David Shambaugh, 8–34. Studies on Contemporary China. New York: Oxford University Press.
Hartcher, Peter (2021). *Red Zone: China's Challenge and Australia's Future*. Melbourne: Schwartz Publishing.
Hartley, Anna (2019). "Chinese Neighbourhood Watch Groups Deny They Are Vigilantes". *ABC News*, 21 October. https://tinyurl.com/3xcnt7z5.
Hawke, Robert James Lee (1989). "Announcement on Chinese Students". Parliament House, Canberra.
——— (1989). "Speech by the Prime Minister: Memorial Ceremony for Those Killed in China", 2. Canberra.
Hearman, Vannessa (2023). "Australian News Photography and Contested Images of Famine in Indonesian-Occupied East Timor". *Australian Historical Studies* 54, no. 3 (3 July): 530–53. https://doi.org/10.1080/1031461X.2023.2189275.
Henderson, Gerard (1998). "It's a Myth That the Media Made One Nation". *The Age*, 14 July.
Higgins, Claire M. (2017). *Asylum by Boat: Origins of Australia's Refugee Policy*. Sydney: NewSouth Publishing.
Hokari, Minoru (2011). *Gurindji Journey: A Japanese Historian in the Outback*. Sydney: University of New South Wales Press.
Holstein, James and Jaber Gubrium (1995). *The Active Interview*. Thousand Oaks, California: SAGE Publications. https://doi.org/10.4135/9781412986120.

Bibliography

Howard, John (1997). "Address to the Chinese Australian Forum Chinese New Year Dinner". Speech, Sydney, NSW, 21 February. https://tinyurl.com/3c464tdn.

——— (1998). "Address to the Chinese Chamber of Commerce Golden Jubilee". Speech, Perth, WA, 24 July. https://tinyurl.com/yp3keatk.

——— (2001). "John Howard: 'But We Will Decide Who Comes to This Country and the Circumstances in Which They Come', Election Campaign Launch – 2001". Speakola, 28 October. https://speakola.com/political/john-howard-election-campaign-launch-2001.

——— (2013). *Lazarus Rising: A Personal and Political Autobiography*. Sydney: HarperCollins Publishers.

Howard, John Winston (1996). "Transcript of the Prime Minister the Hon John Howard MP Address to the Queensland Division of the Liberal Party State Council". 10. https://tinyurl.com/5nfdxb6e.

Huang, Jianli (2010). "Conceptualizing Chinese Migration and Chinese Overseas: The Contribution of Wang Gungwu". *Journal of Chinese Overseas* 6, no. 1: 1–21. https://doi.org/10.1163/179325410X491446.

Human Rights and Equal Opportunity Commission (1991). *Racist Violence: Report of the National Inquiry into Racist Violence in Australia*. Canberra: Australian Government Publishing Service.

Ibrahim, Yasmin (2016). "Tank Man, Media Memory and Yellow Duck Patrol: Remembering Tiananmen on Social Media". *Digital Journalism* 4, no. 5 (3 July): 582–96. https://doi.org/10.1080/21670811.2015.1063076.

ICEAA (2015). "LB 集团《和平颂》音乐晚会再创澳洲海外华人演艺高峰 LB Jituan 'Heping Song' Yinyue Wanhui Zai Chuang Aozhou Haiwai Huaren Yanyi Gaofeng (LB Group's 'Ode to Peace' Concert Hits a New Peak of Overseas Chinese Performing Arts)". Wayback Machine. *pc181.com*, 28 June. https://tinyurl.com/3cemwcjm.

——— (2016). "《光榮 夢想》ICEAAI爱西亚艺术团 'Guangrong Mengxiang' ICEAAI Ai Xiya Yishu Tuan ('Glory and Dream' ICEAAI Western and Asian Arts Appreciation Group)". Wayback Machine. *A China Media*, 15 August. https://tinyurl.com/yswes5uh.

——— (2016). "纪念毛泽东逝世四十周年音乐会《光荣梦想》声明 Jinian Mao Zedong Shishi Sishi Zhounian Yinyue Hui 'Guangrong Mengxiang' Shengming (Concert Commemorating the 40th Anniversary of Mao Zedong's Death 'Glory and Dream' Announcement)". News. yeeyi.com, 6 September. https://www.yeeyi.com/main/newsdetail/150663/?cityFilter=1.

ICECAV (2000). "The Bridge August 2000". Indo-China Ethnic Chinese Association of Victoria, August. State Library of Victoria.

――― (2002). "The Bridge August 2002". Indo-China Ethnic Chinese Association of Victoria, August. State Library of Victoria.
――― (1998). "The Bridge December 1998". Indo-China Ethnic Chinese Association of Victoria, December. State Library of Victoria.
――― (1999). "The Bridge February 1999". Indo-China Ethnic Chinese Association of Victoria, February. State Library of Victoria.
――― (2001). "The Bridge February 2001". Indo-China Ethnic Chinese Association of Victoria, February. State Library of Victoria.
――― (1998). "The Bridge January 1998". Indo-China Ethnic Chinese Association of Victoria, January. State Library of Victoria.
――― (1998). "The Bridge July 1998". Indo-China Ethnic Chinese Association of Victoria, July. State Library of Victoria.
――― (1999). "The Bridge July 1999". Indo-China Ethnic Chinese Association of Victoria, July. State Library of Victoria.
――― (2002). "The Bridge March 2002". Indo-China Ethnic Chinese Association of Victoria, March. State Library of Victoria.
――― (1998). "The Bridge May 1998". Indo-China Ethnic Chinese Association of Victoria, May. State Library of Victoria.
――― (1997). "The Bridge November 1997". Indo-China Ethnic Chinese Association of Victoria, November. State Library of Victoria.
――― (1992). 印支華人相濟會成立十週年紀念特刊 *Yinzhi Huaren Xiang Ji Hui Chengli Shi Zhounian Jinian Tekan Indo-China Ethnic Chinese Association of Victoria Commemorative Magazine, 1981–1991*. Melbourne: Indo-China Ethnic Chinese Association of Victoria.
"Immigration Restriction Bill" (1901). Melbourne: Commonwealth Hansard, 26 September. https://parlinfo.aph.gov.au/parlInfo/search/display/display.w3p;query=Id%3A%22hansard80%2Fhansardr80%2F1901-09-26%2F0017%22.
Ingham, Mike (2012). "Twenty Years on: Hong Kong Dissident Documentarians and the Tiananmen Factor". *Studies in Documentary Film* 6, no. 1 (21 May): 81–97. https://doi.org/10.1386/sdf.6.1.81_1.
Insiders (2022). Melbourne: Australian Broadcasting Corporation, 13 February. https://iview.abc.net.au/show/insiders/series/0/video/NC2209V003S00.
Interviewee 1 (2018). Researcher with Anonymous Interviewee 1. Interview by Researcher, 20 July.
Interviewee 2 (2018). Researcher with Anonymous Interviewee 2. Interview by Researcher, 24 August.
Interviewee 3 (2018). Researcher with Anonymous Interviewee 3. Interview by Researcher, 18 September.
Interviewee 4 (2018). Researcher with Anonymous Interviewee 4. Interview by Researcher, 24 September.

Bibliography

Interviewee 5 (2018). Researcher with Anonymous Interviewee 5. Interview by Researcher, 24 September.
Interviewee 6 (2018). Researcher with Anonymous Interviewee 6. Interview by Researcher, 25 September.
Interviewee 7 (2018). Researcher with Anonymous Interviewee 7. Interview by Researcher, 16 November.
Interviewee 8 (2019). Researcher with Anonymous Interviewee 8. Interview by Researcher, 12 July.
Interviewee 9 (2019). Researcher with Anonymous Interviewee 9. Interview by Researcher, 12 July.
Interviewee 10 (2019). Researcher with Anonymous Interviewee 10. Interview by Researcher, 13 July.
Izenberg, Gerald N. (2016). *Identity: The Necessity of a Modern Idea*. Intellectual History of the Modern Age. Philadelphia: University of Pennsylvania Press.
Jakubowicz, Andrew (1987). "Days of Our Lives: Multiculturalism, Mainstreaming and "Special" Broadcasting". *Media Information Australia*, no. 45 (August): 18–32.
——— (2014). "'Don't Mention It…': What Governments Want to Hear and Why about Multicultural Australia". *Cosmopolitan Civil Societies Journal* 6, no. 2: 1–24.
——— (2002). "White Noise: Australai's Struggle with Multiculturalism". In *Working Through Whiteness: International Perspectives*, edited by Cynthia Levine-Rasky, 107–25. Albany, US: State University of New York Press.
Jakubowicz, Andrew and Christina Ho (2013). *"For Those Who've Come across the Seas…": Australian Multicultural Theory, Policy and Practice*. Australian Scholarly Publishing.
Jayasuriya, Laksiri and Pookong Kee (1999). *The Asianisation of Australia?: Some Facts about the Myths*. Melbourne University Press.
Jayasuriya, Laksiri, David Walker and Jan Gothard (2003). "Introduction". In *Legacies of White Australia: Race, Culture and Nation*, edited by Laksiri Jayasuriya, David Walker and Jan Gothard, 1–7. Accessed 8 February 2022. https://search.informit.org/doi/10.3316/informit.320552821160680.
Jayasuriya, Laksiri, David Walker and Jan Gothard, eds (2003). *Legacies of White Australia: Race, Culture and Nation*. Perth: University of Western Australia Press.
Jesser, John (1979). "Some Tensions, but Bigoted Propaganda Failed, Grassby Says: Upsurge in Race-Hate Campaign". *Canberra Times*, 21 November. http://nla.gov.au/nla.news-article110968919.
——— (1979). "Upsurge in Race-Hate Campaign". *Canberra Times*, 21 November.

Job, Peter (2018). "The Evolving Narrative of Denial: The Fraser Government and the Timorese Genocide, 1975–1980". *Critical Asian Studies* 50, no. 3 (3 July): 442–66. https://doi.org/10.1080/14672715.2018.1489731.
Jupp, James (2007). *From White Australia to Woomera: The Story of Australian Immigration*. 2nd ed. Cambridge: Cambridge University Press.
––––– (2021). *The Australian People: An Encyclopedia of the Nation, Its People and Their Origins*. Cambridge; New York; Melbourne: Cambridge University Press, 2001.
KCS (n.d.). "About Us". Kong Chew Society. Accessed 7 August 2021. http://www.kongchewsociety.com.au/about-us/.
Keating, Paul (1995). "Tenth Anniversary Dinner of the Australian Chinese Forum". Speech, Sydney, NSW, 12 October. https://tinyurl.com/2fx8vyru.
Kee, Pookong (1988). *Chinese Immigrants in Australia: Construction of a Socio-Economic Profile*. IAESR Working Paper, no. 13/1988. Melbourne: Institute of Applied Economic & Social Research.
Kemp, Rod and Marion Stanton (2004). *Speaking for Australia: Parliamentary Speeches That Shaped the Nation*. Melbourne: Allen & Unwin.
Kendall, Timothy (2005). "Using the Past to Serve the Present". In *East by South: China in the Australasian Imagination*, edited by Charles Ferrall, Paul Millar and Keren Smith. Wellington, NZ: Victoria University Press.
Khatun, Samia (2019). *Australianama: The South Asian Odyssey in Australia*. Brisbane: University of Queensland Press.
Khoo, Tseen and Rodney Noonan (2011). "Wartime Fundraising by Chinese Australian Communities". *Australian Historical Studies* 42, no. 1 (March): 92–110. https://doi.org/10.1080/1031461X.2010.541472.
Kitching, Kimberley, ed. (2021). *Issues Facing Diaspora Communities in Australia*. Canberra: Senate Printing Unit.
Knibbs, G.H. (1908). "Official Year Book of the Commonwealth of Australia 1901–1907". Census. Official Year Book. Melbourne: Commonwealth Bureau of Census and Statistics.
––––– (1917). "Part II. – Birthplaces". Census. 1911 Census of the Commonwealth of Australia. Melbourne: Commonwealth Bureau of Census and Statistics.
––––– (1917). "Part VIII. – Non-European Races". Census. 1911 Census of the Commonwealth of Australia. Melbourne: Commonwealth Bureau of Census and Statistics.
Knox, David (2009). "Hey Hey It's Still Blackers". *TV Tonight*, September. Accessed 18 October 2018. https://tinyurl.com/tavb6hzp.
Kuah-Pearce, Khun Eng and Andrew P. Davidson, eds (2008). *At Home in the Chinese Diaspora*. London: Palgrave Macmillan UK. https://doi.org/10.1057/9780230591622.

Bibliography

Kuah-Pearce, Khun Eng and Evelyn Hu-Dehart (2006). "Introduction: The Chinese Diaspora and Voluntary Associations". In *Voluntary Organizations in the Chinese Diaspora*, edited by Khun Eng Kuah-Pearce and Evelyn Hu-Dehart, 1–28. Hong Kong: Hong Kong University Press. https://www.jstor.org/stable/j.ctt2jc01q.5.

Kuehn, Julia, Kam Louie and David M. Pomfret (2014). "China Rising: A View and Review of China's Diasporas since the 1980s". In *Diasporic Chineseness after the Rise of China: Communities and Cultural Production*, edited by Julia Kuehn, Kam Louie and David M. Pomfret, 1–16. Vancouver: UBC Press.

Kuhn, Philip A. (2008). *Chinese Among Others: Emigration in Modern Times*. Lanham: Rowman & Littlefield Publishers.

Kuo, Mei-fen (2013). *Making Chinese Australia: Urban Elites, Newspapers and the Formation of Chinese-Australian Identity, 1892–1912*. Monash Asia Series. Melbourne: Monash University Publishing.

Kuo, Mei-fen and Judith Brett (2013). *Unlocking the History of the Australasian Kuo Min Tang, 1911–2013*. Melbourne: Australian Scholarly Publishing.

Kwok, Jen Tsen (2017). "An Etymology of 'Asian Australian' Through Associational Histories Connecting Australia to Asia". *Journal of Australian Studies* 41, no. 3 (3 July): 351–66. https://doi.org/10.1080/14443058.2017.1346696.

――― (2006). "Asian Australian Citizenship as a Frame of Enactment in the Parliamentary 'First Speech'". *Journal of Intercultural Studies* 27, no. 1–2 (February): 187–211.

Kwok, Jen Tsen and Juliet Pietsch (2017). "The Political Representation of Asian-Australian Populations since the End of White Australia". *AAPI Nexus: Policy, Practice and Community* 15, no. 1–2: 109–36.

Lake, Marilyn and Henry Reynolds (2008). *Drawing the Global Colour Line: White Men's Countries and the International Challenge of Racial Equality*. Cambridge: Cambridge University Press.

Lake, Marilyn, Joy Damousi, Mark McKenna and Henry Reynolds (2010). *What's Wrong with ANZAC?: The Militarisation of Australian History*. 1st ed. Sydney: UNSW Press.

Lam, Felix (2014). "Peak Organisations ACCA, CASS & KSS Visit to Canberra over Senator Palmer's Offensive Insult". Australian Chinese Community Association, 29 August. https://tinyurl.com/4cecer5k.

Lam, Tac Tam and Diana Giese (1995). *Tac Tam Lam Interviewed by Diana Giese in the Post-War Chinese Australians Oral History Project*. Sound recording. TRC 3214. National Archives of Australia.

Leach, Michael, Geoff Stokes and Ian Ward, eds (2000). *The Rise and Fall of One Nation*. Brisbane: University of Queensland Press.

Lee, Francis (1984). "From the Asian Side of the Blainey Debate". *The Australian*, 5 October.

——— (2010). *Out of Bounds: Journey of a Migrant*. Sydney: Universe Books.

Lee, Wellington and Diana Giese (1998). *Wellington Lee Interviewed by Diana Giese for the Post-War Chinese Australians Oral History Project*. Sound recording. TRC 3699. National Library of Australia.

Leong, Maurice and Diana Giese (2000). *Maurice Leong Interviewed by Diana Giese for the Chinese Australian Oral History Partnership Collection*. Sound recording. Chinese Australian Oral History Partnership. TRC 4583. National Library of Australia.

Li, Peter S. (2005). "The Rise and Fall of Chinese Immigration to Canada: Newcomers from Hong Kong Special Administrative Region of China and Mainland China, 1980-2000". *International Migration* 43, no. 3 (June): 9-32. https://doi.org/10.1111/j.1468-2435.2005.00324.x.

Lim, Hong and Diana Giese (1996). *Hong Lim Interviewed by Diana Giese for the Post-War Chinese Australians Oral History Project*. Sound recording. TRC 3502. National Library of Australia.

Lim, Louisa (2014). *The People's Republic of Amnesia: Tiananmen Revisited*. Cary, US: Oxford University Press, Incorporated.

Ling, Chek (2011). "Move On, Move On! What It Is to Be Chinese in Australia Today". *Cosmopolitan Civil Societies: An Interdisciplinary Journal* 3, no. 1 (24 March). https://doi.org/10.5130/ccs.v3i1.1809.

Link, Perry (2010). "June Fourth: Memory and Ethics". In *The Impact of China's 1989 Tiananmen Massacre*, edited by Jean-Philippe Béja, 13-32. London: Taylor & Francis.

Lippmann, Lorna (1984). "Punch-up Threat on TV Denied". *Canberra Times*, 27 May 1974.

———. "Racist Propaganda and the Immigration Debate". In *Multicultural Australia Papers*, Vol. 33. Melbourne: Ecumenical Migration Centre.

Liu, Hong and Els van Dongen (2016). "China's Diaspora Policies as a New Mode of Transnational Governance". *Journal of Contemporary China* 25, no. 102 (November): 805-21. https://doi.org/10.1080/10670564.2016.1184894.

Lloyd Neubauer, Ian (2016). "Australia's Pauline Hanson Wins on Anti-Islam Ticket". *Aljazeera*, 11 July. https://tinyurl.com/mv6j832u.

Lopez, Mark (2000). *The Origins of Multiculturalism in Australian Politics 1945-1975*. 1st ed. Melbourne: Melbourne University Press.

Low, Angeline (2006). "The Roles and Contributions of Chinese Women Entrepreneurs in Community Organizations in Sydney". In *Voluntary Organizations in the Chinese Diaspora*, edited by Khun Eng Kuah-Pearce and Evelyn Hu-Dehart, 201-30. Hong Kong: Hong Kong University Press.

Bibliography

Loy-Wilson, Sophie (2017). *Australians in Shanghai: Race, Rights and Nation in Treaty Port China*. London: Routledge. https://doi.org/10.4324/9781315756998.
Macintyre, Stuart and Anna Clark (2004). *The History Wars*. Melbourne Univ. Publishing.
Mackie, Jamie (1997). "The Politics of Asian Immigration". In *Asians in Australia: Patterns of Migration and Settlement*, edited by James E. Coughlan and Deborah J. McNamara, 10–48. Melbourne: Macmillan Education Australia.
Manne, Robert (1998). *The Way We Live Now: The Controversies of the Nineties*. Melbourne: Text Publishing.
Markus, Andrew, James Jupp and Peter F. McDonald (2009). *Australia's Immigration Revolution*. Sydney: Allen & Unwin.
Markus, Andrew and M.C. Ricklefs (1985). *Surrender Australia? Essays in the Study and Uses of History: Geoffrey Blainey and Asian Immigration*. George Allen & Unwin.
Martínez, Julia (2015). "Chinese Politics in Darwin: Interconnections between the Wah On Society and the Kuo Min Tang". In *Chinese Australians*, edited by Sophie Couchman and Kate Bagnall, 240–66. Boston: Brill. https://tinyurl.com/ym334v7v.
Massola, James (2016). "Labor Senator Sam Dastyari Quits over Chinese Donations Scandal". *Sydney Morning Herald*, 7 September. https://tinyurl.com/57j86ka.
McGregor, Russell (2011). *Indifferent Inclusion: Aboriginal People and the Australian Nation*. Canberra: Aboriginal Studies Press.
McKay, Sandra (1998). "Kennett Promotes Asian Candidate". *The Age*, 7 April.
McNamara, Deborah J. and James E. Coughlan (1997). "Future Directions: Asian Immigration into the Twenty-First Century". In *Asians in Australia: Patterns of Migration and Settlement*, edited by James E. Coughlan and Deborah J. McNamara, 320–30. Melbourne: Macmillan Education Australia.
Mingjiang, Li (2019). "China Debates Soft Power: Implications for Chinese Foreign Policy". In *Chinese Scholars and Foreign Policy*, 44–62. London: Routledge.
Moran, Anthony (2017). *The Public Life of Australian Multiculturalism*. Cham: Springer International Publishing.
Morris, Barry and Gillian K. Cowlishaw, eds (1997). *Race Matters: Indigenous Australians and "our" Society*. Canberra: Aboriginal Studies Press.
Moss, Irene and Diana Giese (1997). *Irene Moss Interviewed by Diana Giese for the Post-War Chinese Australians Oral History Project*. Sound recording. Post-War Chinese Australians Oral History Project. TRC 3612. National Library of Australia.

Newman, Gerard (2011). "1998 Queensland Election (Current Issues Brief 2 1998–99)". Archived on Wayback Machine. Parliamentary Library, 10 August. https://tinyurl.com/4h648tuv.
Ng, Teddy and Andrea Chen (2014). "Xi Jinping Says World Has Nothing to Fear from Awakening of 'Peaceful Lion'". *South China Morning Post*, 28 March. https://tinyurl.com/4uh95zfd.
Ngan, Lucille Lok-Sun and Kwok-bun Chan (2012). *The Chinese Face in Australia: Multi-Generational Ethnicity among Australian-Born Chinese*. New York: Springer.
Northern Territory, ed. (1997). *Sweet & Sour: Experiences of Chinese Families in the Northern Territory*. Darwin: Museum and Art Gallery of the Northern Territory.
"NSW Chinese Workers' Association Volume 1". Item. Canberra, 1970 1953. A6122, 2235. National Archives of Australia. https://tinyurl.com/4hxchxhu.
NSW Fair Trading (2021). "Association Summary (ICEAA)". NSW Incorporated Associations Register. https://tinyurl.com/bd453rb6.
Nyíri, Pál (2004). "Expatriating in Patriotic?: The Discourse of 'New Migrants' in the People's Republic of China and Identity Construction among Recent Migrants from the PRC". In *State/Nation/Transnation: Perspectives on Transnationalism in the Asia Pacific*, edited by Katie Willis and Brenda S.A. Yeoh, 120–43. Florence, US: Taylor & Francis Group.
O'Connor, Beverley (2017). *Concerns over Beijing's Monitoring of Australian Chinese: An Interview with John Hugh*. Interview (Australian Broadcasting Corporation), 4 April. https://tinyurl.com/p6ntf963.
Office of the Commissioner for Community Relations (1978). "Commissioner for Community Relations: Annual Report". Annual Report. Canberra: Australian Human Rights Commission.
——— (1979). "Commissioner for Community Relations: Annual Report". Annual Report. Canberra: Australian Human Rights Commission.
——— (1980). "Commissioner for Community Relations: Annual Report". Annual Report. Canberra: Australian Human Rights Commission.
——— (1981). "Commissioner for Community Relations: Annual Report". Annual Report. Canberra: Australian Human Rights Commission.
Om, Jason (2019). "'We're Not Panda-Hugging Spies': What It's Like to Be a Chinese-Australian Voter". *ABC News*, 8 May. https://tinyurl.com/3m4rwusb.
O'Neil, Allan (2005). "More Cooperation and Less Conflict: Chinese-European Relationships in South Australia's Northern Territory". *Journal of Northern Territory History*, no. 16: 79–90.

Bibliography

O'Neill, J.P. (1971). "Bulletin 1. Summary of Population: Part 4. South Australia". Census. Census of Population and Housing, 30 June. Canberra: Commonwealth Bureau of Census and Statistics, 1972.
Overseas Chinese Culture, 海外風, no. 23 (August 1989).
Pan, Chengxin (2012). *Knowledge, Desire and Power in Global Politics: Western Representations of China's Rise*. Cheltenham, UK: Edward Elgar Publishing.
Pan, Qiuping (2018). "Ethnic Identity and Immigrant Organizations". *Journal of Chinese Overseas* 14, no. 1 (23 April): 22–53. https://tinyurl.com/42438jca.
Peel, Mark and Christina Twomey (2018). *A History of Australia*. 2nd ed. Palgrave Essential Histories. London: Palgrave.
Persian, Jayne (2017). *Beautiful Balts: From Displaced Persons to New Australians*. Sydney: NewSouth Publishing.
Pfitzner, Bernice and Diana Giese (1996). *Bernice Pfitzner Interviewed by Diana Giese for the Post-War Chinese Australians Oral History Project*. Sound recording. Post-War Chinese Australians Oral History Project. TRC 3490. National Library of Australia.
"Photographs of the Northern Territory, NT1912/1022 – NT1915/1028". Item. Canberra, 1925 1912. A3, ALBUM 1. National Archives of Australia. https://tinyurl.com/yzemunk9.
"Photographs of the Northern Territory, NT1915/1028 – NT1917/383". Item. Canberra, 1925 1912. A3, ALBUM 2. National Archives of Australia. https://tinyurl.com/3c88kj5x.
Piperoglou, Andonis (2018). "'Border Barbarisms', Albury 1902: Greeks and the Ambiguity of Whiteness". *Australian Journal of Politics & History* 64, no. 4: 529–43. https://doi.org/10.1111/ajph.12518.
"PM 12 November 1996 [Prime Minister's Daily Program; Petitions; Liberal Party Branch Correspondence; Letters of Support; Appointments; Conflicts of Interest; X-Rated Videos; Pauline Hanson; Soldiers Memorial]". Item. Canberra, 1996 1996. M4326, 140. National Archives of Australia.
"PM 16 December 1996" (1996). Papers. Canberra. M4326, 164. National Archives of Australia.
Povinelli, Elizabeth A. (2002). *The Cunning of Recognition: Indigenous Alterities and the Making of Australian Multiculturalism*. Politics, History, and Culture. Durham, NC. Duke University Press.
Prain, Michael (1975). "Chinatown Is Planned for the City". *The Sun*, 7 June.
Prior, Tom (1984). "Wills Man Likes Asians – in Asia". *The Sun*, 8 November.
Pua, Rogelia Pe- (1996). *Astronaut Families and Parachute Children: The Cycle of Migration between Hong Kong and Australia*. Australian Govt. Pub. Service.
QCF (1998). "QCF Media Contact Records". Queensland Chinese Forum. Member's Personal Papers.

––– (1998). "QCF Press Release: Liberal Party's Shabby Deal on Preferences". Queensland Chinese Forum, 8 May. Member's Personal Papers.
––– (2014). *Queensland Chinese Forum: Celebrating 20th Anniversary 1994-2014*. Fortitude Valley QLD: Queensland Chinese Forum.
Qi Jiazhen (2017). "吃了六四的人血馒头，我们更应该"不忘记、不恐惧、不冷淡、不堕落，不放弃"！Chīle Liùsì De Rén Xuè Mántou, Wǒ men Gèng Yīnggāi "Bù Wàngjì, Bù Kǒ ngjù, Bù Lěngdàn, Bù Duòluò, Bù Fàngqì"! (After Eating the Blood Buns of Victims of June 4th, We Should "Never Forget, Never Fear, Never Be Indifferent, Never Be Corrupted, and Never Give up"!). 独立中文笔会 *"Independent Chinese Pen Centre"*. Blog. 30 May. https://www.chinesepen.org/blog/archives/85931.
"Questions without Notice: Immigration" (1996). Canberra: Commonwealth Hansard, 8 October.
Ramsey, Alan (1996). "Hanson and a Question of Blame". *Sydney Morning Herald*, 16 November.
Rayner, Michelle (2008). "History Under Siege: Battles over the Past, Part 3, Australia". Text. *Radio National*, 2 April. https://tinyurl.com/298udrm8.
Razik, Naveen (2020). "'Race-Baiting McCarthyism': Eric Abetz Slammed for Asking Chinese Australians to Denounce Communist Party during Diaspora Inquiry". *SBS News*, 15 October. https://tinyurl.com/v973dry6.
Reeves, Keir and Tseen Khoo (2011). "Dragon Tails: Re-Interpreting Chinese Australian History". *Australian Historical Studies* 42, no. 1: 4–9.
Register (1918). "Chews V. Lees: A Chinese Wounded". 22 January.
Richards, Mike (1979). "A Foot in the Coalition Door". *Sydney Morning Herald*, 28 February.
Ricklefs, M.C. (1997). "The Asian Immigration Controversies of 1984–85, 1988–89 and 1996–97: A Historical Review". In *The Resurgence of Racism: Howard, Hanson and the Race Debate*, edited by Christine Winter and Geoffrey G. Gray, 39–61. Monash Publications in History 24. Melbourne: Monash University Publishing.
Rolls, Eric C. (1993). *Sojourners: The Epic Story of China's Centuries-Old Relationship with Australia: Flowers and the Wide Sea*. Brisbane: University of Queensland Press.
Ruptly (2016). "Australia: Chinese Protesters Rally against South China Sea Ruling in Melbourne". YouTube. *Ruptly News Watch*, 23 July. Accessed 7 October 2021. https://www.youtube.com/watch?v=jSeaPFxRyxA.
Ryan, Jan (1995). *Ancestors: Chinese in Colonial Australia*. South Fremantle: Fremantle Arts Centre.
––– (2003). *Chinese Women and the Global Village*. Brisbane: University of Queensland Press.

Bibliography

Said, Edward (2003). *Orientalism*. 5th ed. London: Penguin.

Sarib, Joe, Diana Giese and Daryl N. Chin (1997). *Joe Sarib Interviewed by Diana Giese with Daryl Chin for the Post-War Chinese Australians Oral History Project*. Sound recording. TRC 3665. National Library of Australia.

SBS Your Language (2016). "Mao Concert Press Conference". News, 26 August. https://tinyurl.com/sapyppcx.

Scalmer, Sean (2001). "From Contestation to Autonomy: The Staging and Framing of Anti-Hanson Contention". *Australian Journal of Politics and History* 47, no. 2 (1 June): 209–24.

———. (1999) "The Production of a Founding Event: The Case of Pauline Hanson's Maiden Parliamentary Speech". *Theory & Event* 3, no. 2. https://muse.jhu.edu/article/32548.

Scott, David (v). *"The Chinese Century?": The Challenge to Global Order*. Global Issues. London: Palgrave Macmillan.

Seccombe, Mike (2019). "From the Archives: Hawke Weeps As He Tells of Massacre". *Sydney Morning Herald*, 17 May. https://tinyurl.com/26efan8j.

Sewell, William H. (2005). *Logics of History: Social Theory and Social Transformation*. Chicago Studies in Practices of Meaning. Chicago: University of Chicago Press.

Sham-Ho, Helen and Diana Giese (1996). *Helen Sham-Ho Interviewed by Diana Giese in the Post-War Chinese Australians Oral History Project*. Sound recording. Post-War Chinese Australians Oral History Project. TRC 3514. National Library of Australia.

Sham-Ho, Helen, Jackie Huggins and Peter Read (2008). *Helen Sham-Ho Interviewed by Jackie Huggins and Peter Read in the Council for Aboriginal Reconciliation Collection*. Sound recording. Council for Aboriginal Reconciliation Collection. TRC 5961. National Library of Australia.

Shergold, Peter (1984). "Australian Immigration since 1973". In *The Great Immigration Debate*, edited by Frances Milne and Peter Shergold, 14–28. Sydney: Federation of Ethnic Communities' Councils of Australia.

Silverstein, Ben (2021). "'Throwing Mud' on Questions of Sovereignty: Race and Northern Arguments over White, Chinese, and Aboriginal Labour, 1905–12". *Australian Historical Studies*, 22 April, 1–20. https://tinyurl.com/49va7ta7.

Simon-Davies, Joanne and Chris McGann (2018). "Top 10 Countries of Birth for the Overseas-Born Population since 1901". Statistical Snapshot. Research Paper Series, 2018–19. Canberra: Parliamentary Library, Statistics and Mapping Division, 22 November.

Singer, Renata and Michael Liffman (1984). *The Immigration Debate in the Press, 1984*. rev. ed. Melbourne: Clearing House on Migration Issues.

Singh, Jasbeer, T. Sandhu and B. Singh (1987). *Australasian Who's Who*. 1st ed. Adelaide: Oriental Publications. https://tinyurl.com/2dtfu3eb.

So, Alvin Y. and Ludmilla Kwitko (1990). "The New Middle Class and the Democratic Movement in Hong Kong". *Journal of Contemporary Asia* 20, no. 3 (August): 384–98.

Soutphommasane, Tim, Maxine Beneba Clarke, Bindi Cole Chocka, Benjamin Law, Alice Pung and Christos Tsiolkas (2015). *I'm Not Racist but: 40 Years of the Racial Discrimination Act*. Sydney: NewSouth Publishing.

Stats, Katrina (2015). "Welcome to Australia? A Reappraisal of the Fraser Government's Approach to Refugees, 1975–83". *Australian Journal of International Affairs* 69, no. 1 (1 February): 69–87. https://tinyurl.com/mb5m4kjw.

Stone, John (1997). "Australian for Upset". *National Review* 49, no. 22 (24 November): 32–34.

Stone, Shane and Roger Steele (n.d.). "Progress of the Chinese Community of the Northern Territory". *Northern Perspective* 18, no. 1: 28–35. https://doi.org/10.3316/ielapa.960201915.

Stratton, Jon (1998). *Race Daze: Australia in Identity Crisis*. Pluto Press.

Stratton, Jon and Ien Ang (1998). "Multicultural Imagined Communities: Cultural Difference and Naitonal Identity in the USA and Australia". In *Multicultural States: Rethinking Difference and Identity*, edited by David Bennett, 135–62. London: Taylor & Francis Group. Accessed 8 February 2022. http://ebookcentral.proquest.com/lib/unimelb/detail.action?docID=165180.

STRB (1989). "「六·四屠殺」– 周月 澳各大城市紀念活動悼英魂 Liù·Sì Túshā' – Zhōu Yuè Ào Gè Dà Chéngshì Jìniàn Huódòng Dào Yīnghún (June 4th Massacre – One Month on, All Major Australian Cities Hold Memorial Events to Honour the Heroes)". *星島日報 (Sing Tao Daily)*, 5 July.

——— (1996). "國家黨侯選人犯眾怒掀巨波 Guojia Dang Hou Xuan Renfan Zhongnu Xian Ju Bo (National Party Candidate Provokes a Huge Wave of Public Anger)". *星島日報 (Sing Tao Daily)*, 15 February.

——— (1996). "大選關鍵時刻令何華德面紅尷尬 Daxuan Guanjian Shike Ling Hehuade Mianhong Ganga (Critical Election Moment Causes Red Face for Howard)". *星島日報 (Sing Tao Daily)*, 15 February.

——— (1996). "独立议员韩珍反移民轮，五华裔议员反应不同 Duli Yiyuan Hanzhen Fan Yimin Lun, Wu Huayi Yiyuan Fanying Butong (Independent MP Hanson Opposes Immigration, Five Chinese-Descendent MPs Respond in the Contrary)". *星島日報 (Sing Tao Daily)*, 24 September.

——— (1996). "紐省18華人社團商對策聯合各族裔抗種族主義 Niu Sheng 18 Huaren Shetuan Shang Duice Lianhe Ge Zu Yi Kang Zhongzu Zhuyi (18

Bibliography

NSW Chinese Community Groups Discuss Countermeasures to Unite All Ethnic Groups in the Fight against Racism)." 星岛日报 *(Sing Tao Daily)*, 16 October.

――― (1996). "韩珍反亚言论触发种族紧张，五位华裔议员联合声明谴责 Hanzhen Fan Ya Yanlun Chufa Zhongzu Jinzhang, Wu Wei Huayi Yiyuan Lianhe Shengming Qianze (Hanson's Anti-Asian Remarks Trigger Racial Tension, 5 Chinese-Descendent MPs Announce Joint Statement of Condemnation)". 星岛日报 *(Sing Tao Daily)*, 26 October.

――― (1996). "華裔社區勿再緘默，探行動阻種族主義 Huayi Shequwu Zai Jianmo, Tan Xingdong Zu Zhongzuzhuyi (The Chinese Community Should Not Remain Silent and Explore Ways to Stop Racism)". 星岛日报 *(Sing Tao Daily)*, 4 November.

――― (1996). "反種族歧視掀澎湃浪潮，三大城市本周有大集會 Fan Zhongzu Qishi Xian Pengpai Langchao, San Da Chengshi Ben Zhou You Da Jihui (Anti-Racism Actions Surge, Three Big Rallies in Three Bigs Cities This Week)". 星岛日报 *(Sing Tao Daily)*, 18 November.

――― (1996). "華裔韓越裔土著及工會代表慷慨激昂 Huáyì Hányuèyì Tǔzhù Jí Gōnghuì Dàibi ǎ o Kāngk ǎ iji'áng (Impassioned Chinese, Korean and Vietnamese Australians, Indigenous and Labor Party Representatives)". 星岛日报 *(Sing Tao Daily)*, 25 November.

Sun, Baoqiang (2017). "STOP "溫水煮青蛙"！STOP "Wenshui Zhu Qingwa"! (STOP "Boiling the Frog"!)". *Australian Values Alliance*. Blog. http://evebch.ava.org.au/2016/08/stop.html.

――― (2016). "孙宝强：澳洲之耻 文明之殇（特荐）Sūnbǎoqiáng: Àozhōu zhī ch ǐ wénmíng zhī shāng (tè jiàn) (Sun Baoqiang: Australia's Shame, Civilisation's Sorrow (Recommended))". August. https://tinyurl.com/yb2xnkcy.

Sun, Wanning (2016). "Chinese Language Media in Australia: Developments, Challenges and Opportunities". Australia-China Relations Institute.

――― (2020). "Response to "Red Flag: Waking Up to China's Challenge" by Peter Hartcher". *Pearls and Irritations*. Blog. 24 March. https://tinyurl.com/5abw5mnz.

――― (2020). "Submission to the Senate Inquiry into Issues Facing Diaspora Communities in Australia". https://tinyurl.com/22mb2dxx.

Sun, Wanning, John Fitzgerald and Jia Gao (2018). "From Multicultural Ethnic Migrants to the New Players of China's Public Diplomacy". In *China's Rise and the Chinese Overseas*, edited by Bernard P. Wong and Chee-Beng Tan, 55–74. Routledge Contemporary China Series 170. London: Routledge.

Sun, Wanning, Jia Gao, Audrey Yue and John Sinclair (2011). "The Chinese-Language Press in Australia: A Preliminary Scoping Study". *Media International Australia* 138, no. 1 (February): 137–48. https://doi.org/10.1177/1329878X1113800115.
Sydney Morning Herald (1979). "Anti-Asian Campaign in Perth". 3 December.
Sydney Morning Herald (1976). "Censored History – A Selection of the Thoughts of Eric Butler". 22 March.
Sydney Morning Herald (1984). "Immigration Issue Causes TV Audience Row". 16 June.
Sydney Morning Herald (1976). "Pushing a 'Cure-All' Gospel: League of Rights Has Strong Support". 22 March.
Sydney Morning Herald (1918). "Rival Chinese Factions". 22 January.
Sydney Morning Herald (1972). "The Grim Politics of Extremism". 28 February.
Sydney Morning Herald (1976). "We Seek to Influence Politicians". 22 March.
Sydney Today (2019). "力挺黄向墨！全澳128家华人社团联合发声：强烈抗议无良媒体及政客攻讦！Li Ting Huang Xiangmo! Quan Ao 128 Jia Huaren Shetuan Lianhe Fasheng: Qianglie Kangyi Wu Liang Meiti Ji Zhengke Gongjie! (Support Huang Xiangmo! Across Australia, 128 Chinese Community Groups Issue Joint Statement Strongly Protesting against Unscrupulous Media and Politicians!)". *Sydney Today*, 16 February. Accessed 13 October 2021. https://www.sydneytoday.com/content-101907675683025.
SYS (2004). 四邑特刊: *Seeyup Society 1854–2004 (Siyi Tekan "Seeyup Special Issue")*. Melbourne: Seeyup Society.
Syvret, Paul (1998). "Chinese Call for Libs to Be Put Last". *Financial Review*, 13 May.
Tan, Chee-Beng and Bernard P. Wong (2018). "Introduction: Contemporary China's Rise and the Chinese Overseas". In *China's Rise and the Chinese Overseas*, edited by Bernard P. Wong and Chee-Beng Tan, 1–12. Routledge Contemporary China Series 170. London: Routledge.
Tan, Su-Lin (2020). "Chinese-Australians Hunt White Men Who Hit Asian Delivery Rider". *South China Morning Post*, 7 July. https://tinyurl.com/58swvhar.
Tavan, Gwenda (2013). "Creating Multicultural Australia: Local, Global and Trans-National Contexts for the Creation of a Universal Admissions Scheme, 1945–1983". In *Wanted and Welcome? Policies for Highly Skilled Immigrants in Comparative Perspective*, edited by Triadafilos Triadafilopoulos, 39–59. New York: Springer.
——— (2005). *The Long, Slow Death of White Australia*. Melbourne: Scribe.
The Drum Wednesday April 8 (2020). *ABC News*. https://tinyurl.com/42ek54a9.

Bibliography

The Guardian (2014). "Cabinet Papers 1988–89: Bob Hawke Acted Alone in Offering Asylum to Chinese Students", 31 December. https://tinyurl.com/muxbhv5r.

Tianda Yanjiuyuan, ed. (2013). *Zhongguo Meng, Fu Xing Meng: Xi Jinping Dang Xuan Zhong Gong Zhong Yang Zong Shu Ji Quan Qiu Ping Lun Yu Bao Dao Xuan Ji*, 中国梦, 复兴梦: 习近平当选中共中央总书记全球评论与报道选辑 *(Chinese Dream, Revival Dream: Global Comments and Reports on Xi Jinping's Election as General Secretary of the CPC Central Committee)*. Hong Kong: Tianda Yanjiuyuan Chuban. https://tinyurl.com/55usz3um.

To, James Jiann Hua (2014). *Qiaowu: Extra-Territorial Policies for the Overseas Chinese*. Leiden: Brill. https://tinyurl.com/bccmewkw.

Tribune (1971). "Chinese Crew Wins in Stand for Human Rights". 24 February.

Tribune (1974). "Seaman's Official: 'Owners' Extortion'". 17 September.

Tsang, Henry and Diana Giese (1998). *Henry Tsang Interviewed by Diana Giese for the Post-War Chinese Australians Oral History Project*. Sound recording. TRC 3685. National Library of Australia.

Tsoulis, Eugenia (2013). "Hand in Hand: Indigenous Australia and Multiculturalism". In *"For Those Who've Come across the Seas…": Australian Multicultural Theory, Policy and Practice,* by Andrew Jakubowicz and Christina Ho, 249–50. Melbourne: Australian Scholarly Publishing.

UCT (1996). "從種族到文化：反種族歧視大集會 Cong Zhongzu Dao Wenhua: Fan Zhongzu Qishi Da Jihui (From Racism to Culture: Anti-Racial Discrimination Rallies)". 華聯時報 *(United Chinese Times)*, 28 November.

——— (1996). "為反擊種族歧視狂潮各華人群體籌備組堂 Wei Fanji Zhongzuqishi Kuangchao Ge Huaren Qunti Choubei Zu Tang (Chinese Groups Prepare to Organize a Counter-Attack on Racist Frenzy)". 華聯時報 *(United Chinese Times)*, 24 October.

Victorian Parliament (1984). *Chinatown Historic Precinct Act 1984*. http://www.legislation.vic.gov.au/.

Walsh, Kerry-Anne (2018). *Hoodwinked: How Pauline Hanson Fooled a Nation*. Sydney: Allen & Unwin.

Wang, Gungwu (1991). "Among Non-Chinese". *Daedalus* 120, no. 2 (Spring): 135–57.

——— (1981). *Community and Nation: Essays on Southeast Asia and the Chinese*. Southeast Asia Publications Series, no. 6. Sydney: Published for the Asian Studies Association of Australia by Heinemann Educational Books (Asia) Ltd and George Allen & Unwin.

——— (1995). "Greater China and the Chinese Overseas". In *Greater China: The Next Superpower?*, edited by David Shambaugh, 274–96. Studies on Contemporary China. New York: Oxford University Press.

Wen, Philip (2016). "Controversial Chairman Mao Tribute Concerts Sharpen Chinese Community Divide". *The Age*, 22 August. https://tinyurl.com/36z6fcbw.

——— (2016). "Divisive Mao Zedong Concerts in Sydney, Melbourne Cancelled". *Sydney Morning Herald*, 1 September. https://tinyurl.com/2nynzncr.

Wensen (2016). "一个红色幽灵在澳洲徘徊，华人社区暗流汹涌（特稿）Yige Hongse Youling Zai Aozhou Paihuai, Huaren Shequ Anliu Xiongyong (Te Gao) (A Red Ghost Haunts Australia and Is an Undercurrent of the Chinese Community (Special Feature))". *Australian Values Alliance*. Blog. 22 August. http://wensenw.blogspot.com.au/2016/08/blog-post_98.html.

——— (2016). "联盟，我以你为荣！Lianmeng, Wo Yi Ni Wei Rong! (Alliance, I Am Proud of You!)". *Australian Values Alliance*. Blog. 28 September. http://wensenw.blogspot.com.au/2016/09/blog-post_28.html.

——— (2017). "神圣的使命——守护澳洲价值！Shensheng de shiming – shouhu Aozhou jiazhi! (The Sacred Mission – Protect Australian Values!)". Blog. ava.org.au, April. http://evebch.ava.org.au/2017/04/blog-post_16.html.

Wesley, Michael (2007). *The Howard Paradox: Australian Diplomacy in Asia, 1996–2006*. Sydney: ABC Books.

"What Hawke's Ultimate Heart-on-Sleeve Moment Says about How He Engaged with the World" (2019). 17 May. https://tinyurl.com/mryv5w9x.

Wickens, Chas. H. (1924). "Part V. – Race". Census. 1921 Census of the Commonwealth of Australia. Melbourne: Commonwealth Bureau of Census and Statistics.

Windschuttle, Keith (2004). *The White Australia Policy*. Sydney: Macleay Press.

Winter, Christine and Geoffrey G. Gray, eds (1997). *The Resurgence of Racism: Howard, Hanson and the Race Debate*. Monash Publications in History 24. Melbourne: Monash University Publishing.

Wong, Bernard P. and Chee-Beng Tan, eds (2018). *China's Rise and the Chinese Overseas*. Routledge Contemporary China Series 170. London: Routledge.

Wong, Lok Yee Lotte (2018). "Melbourne Chinatown Redevelopment: The Unwritten Perspective from the Chinese Community". Honours Thesis, University of Melbourne. https://tinyurl.com/6d55e4e5.

Wong, Peter and Diana Giese (2001). *Peter Wong Interviewed by Diana Giese for the Chinese Australian Oral History Partnership Collection*. Sound recording. TRC 4701. National Library of Australia.

Wu, Siew-Mei (1995). "Maintenance of the Chinese Language in Australia". *Australian Review of Applied Linguistics* 18, no. 2 (1 January): 105–36. https://doi.org/10.1075/aral.18.2.06wu.

wxzun.com (2016). "澳洲华人社区需要正能量！《光荣梦想》音乐会邀请悉尼华人力压反对声音！Aozhou Huaren Shequ Xuyao Zheng Nengliang!

Bibliography

'Guangrong Mengxiang' Yinyue Hui Yaoqing Xini Huaren Li Ya Fandui Shengyin! (The Australian Chinese Community Needs Positive Energy! 'Glory and Dream' Concert Requests Sydney Chinese to Suppress Dissenting Voices!)". Defunct News Site. *wzxun.com*, 26 August. http://www.wzxun.com/detail/5363880.html.

Xu, Bin (2020). "Listening to Thunder in the Silence on Tiananmen: Politics and Ethics of the Memory of the June Fourth Movement". *China Information*, 9 September. 0920203X2095656. https://doi.org/10.1177/0920203X20956561.

Xu, Samantha Zhan and Wei Wang (2021). "Change and Continuity in Hurstville's Chinese Restaurants: An Ethnographic Linguistic Landscape Study in Sydney". *Linguistic Landscape. An International Journal* 7, no. 2 (16 June): 175–203. https://doi.org/10.1075/ll.20007.xu.

Yan, Qinghuang and Hongbo Zhou (2016). 南澳中華會館: 四十周年紀念特刊 *Nan'ao Zhonghua Huiguan: Si Shi Zhou Nian Jinian Tekan (CASA 40th Anniversary Commemorative Magazine): 1971–2011*. Black Forest: The Chinese Association of South Australia Inc.

Yang, William (1997). *Pauline Hanson Chasing Ethnic Fish and Chips down Oxford St [i.e. Street], Sydney Gay & Lesbian Mardi Gras, 1997*. Photograph. 3097590. National Library of Australia.

——— (1997). *The Era of Hanson, Sydney, 1997*. Photograph. 1771247. National Library of Australia.

——— (1997). *The Era of Hanson, Sydney, 1997*. Photograph. 248674. National Library of Australia.

Yao, Xiaofang and Paul Gruba (2020). "A Layered Investigation of Chinese in the Linguistic Landscape: A Case Study of Box Hill, Melbourne". *Australian Review of Applied Linguistics* 43, no. 3 (11 September): 302–36. https://doi.org/10.1075/aral.18049.yao.

Yee, Herbert S. (2011). *China's Rise – Threat or Opportunity?* London: Taylor & Francis Group.

Yen, Mavis Gock, Siaoman Yen and Richard Horsburgh (2022). *South Flows the Pearl: Chinese Australian Voices*. Sydney: Sydney University Press.

Ying Lu, R. Samaratunge and C.E. Hartel (2011). "Acculturation Strategies among Professional Chinese Immigrants in the Australian Workplace". *Asia Pacific Journal of Human Resources* 49, no. 1 (1 March): 71–87. https://tinyurl.com/bdf5je66..

Yong, C.F. (1977). *The New Gold Mountain: The Chinese in Australia, 1901–1921*. Adelaide: Raphael Arts.

Young, Edmund (1973). "Chinese Language Course". *Overseas Trading*, 14 December.

——— (1967). "Letters: Chinese in Australia". *The Bulletin*, 7 October.

——— (1973). "Letters: Chinese Suffer". *The Bulletin*, 25 August.
——— (1981). "Letters: Perkins' Views Racist". *The Bulletin*, 6 October.
Young, Katie and Gim Wah Yeo, eds (1986). *National Conference of the Australian Chinese Community Sydney, November 28–30, 1986*. Sydney: The Conference.
Young, W.M. (1868). "Report of the Condition of the Chinese Population in Victoria". Report. Melbourne: Houses of Parliament.
Yu, Haiqing (2020). "Chinese Australians' Take on Anti-Chinese Racism in Australia. Part 3 of a Series on Racism". *John Menadue: Pearls and Irritations*, 23 June. https://tinyurl.com/4rbuabtu.
Yuan, Ye (2016). "《光荣梦想》海外华人纪念毛泽东逝世四十周年大型文艺晚会即将举行 'Guangrong Mengxiang' Haiwai Huaren Jinian Mao Zedong Shishi Sishi Zhounian Daxing Wenyi Wanhui Jijian Juxing ('Glory and Dream': Overseas Chinese Will Hold a Concert to Commemorate the 40th Anniversary of the Death of Mao Zedong)". Social Media. *weibo.com*, 12 April. https://tinyurl.com/mza5af55.
Zhao, Dingxin (2001). *The Power of Tiananmen: State-Society Relations and the 1989 Beijing Student Movement*. Chicago: University of Chicago Press.
Zhao, Iris, Erin Handley and Michael Walsh (2020). "China Is Attacking Australia over Racism – but Ordinary People Are Getting Stuck in the Middle", 17 July. https://tinyurl.com/5ar3ufdk.
Zheng, Xiaogang (2017). "澳洲价值守护联盟:澳洲应该协助一个类如 ISIS 的'艺术'在墨尔本上演吗? Aozhou Yinggai Xiezhu Yige Lei Ru ISIS de 'Yishu' Zai Moerben Shangyan Ma? (Should Australia Support Staging ISIS-like 'Art' in Melbourne?)". *Australian Values Alliance*. Blog. ava.org.au, 1 February. http://evebch.ava.org.au/2017/02/isis.html.
——— (2017). "澳洲應該協助一個類如 ISIS 的'藝術'在墨爾本上演嗎? Aozhou Yinggai Xiezhu Yige Lei Ru ISIS de 'Yishu' Zai Moerben Shangyan Ma? (Should Australia Support Staging ISIS-like 'Art' in Melbourne?)". 民主中國陣線（民陣）Federation for a Democratic China (FDC), 6 February. https://tinyurl.com/2a97envh.
Zhou, Naaman (2017). "Chinese Ballet Show Draws Protests for 'Glorifying Red Army'". *The Guardian*, 17 February. https://tinyurl.com/bdfpvrp7.
冷眼 (Dispassionate View) (1996). "婆林·韓琳效應'的省思', 澳洲漢聲雜誌 Pólín·Hánlín Xiàoyìng 'De Xǐng Sī', Àozhōu Hàn Shēng Zázhì ('Reflections' on the Pauline Hanson Effect, Australian Chinese Voice Magazine)". *Chinese Culture Monthly*, December. National Library of Australia.
通天曉 (Know It All) (1994). "中國留學生「填表熱」/Migration Rush". *澳洲動態 Education & Living in Australia*, 11 March. National Library of Australia.

Appendix 1
Sample interview questions

Reproduced below is an example of the qualitative, theme-targeted interview questions. As the interviews were given anonymously, the reproduced example has had identifying features removed.

Interviews were conducted in person, digitally recorded, and lasted between two and four hours. They were targeted at the interviewees' personal experiences in community organisations during the historical episodes relevant to this study. Nevertheless, the interviews' conversational nature meant that discussion inevitably digressed to other facets of the interviewees' lives. Allowing interviewees to speak as they wished before returning to the main line of questions was treated as ceding some control to interviewees and considered part of the collaborative process.

Interview with X of the Chinese Youth League
Interview conducted on 25/09/2018
Interviewer: Nathan D. Gardner Molina

- The Chinese Youth League (CYL) has a long history. It has seen a lot of change during its lifetime – in Australia, the Chinese Australian community and even in itself. Can you describe what the CYL was like in the 1970s? What kinds of people were attracted to the CYL's

activities? Do you have any knowledge of what it was like for the CYL to operate within the context of the "White Australia" period?
- From the 1950s and into the 1970s, it also developed and delivered a political message. Evidently, the CYL was of considerable interest to ASIO during the Cold War for its communist leanings. Prominent figure from the Chinese Youth League, Arthur Locke, stated in an interview with Ann Turner that he was aware of ASIO's surveillance of the group and there exists evidence of this surveillance in the archives. What is your recollection of this surveillance issue? Did you ever personally feel this attention? Did this ease after Australia's recognition of China in 1972 or after Australia embraced multiculturalism around the same time? Has the political stance of the CYL changed over the years?
- Throughout the 1960s and the early 1970s, ASIO considered the CYL to be the most influential ethnic Chinese community organisation in Sydney, particularly through groups like the Australia China Friendship Society, the Chinese Seamen's Association and the Australian Chinese Workers Association. This influence is often depicted as a social-political one. Is this claim about influence accurate?
- During the 1970s, the Australasian Kuomintang was also active and offered similar cultural activities, but supported Taiwan/ROC's political ideology. Can you comment on the CYL's relationship with the KMT? Did the relationship between the CYL and the KMT have any impact on the local Chinese Australian community?
- As relations became normalised between Australia and China following Australia's recognition of the PRC, the CYL was one of the first community organisations to send delegations and tour groups (particularly comprised of youth) to China. Can you describe the significance of these trips? What were these trips like for their participants?
- You were XYZ of the CYL in 19XX and it seems to have been quite a busy year for you. This was not long after the immigration debate [Blainey debate] in 1984. What was the effect of this debate on Sydney's Chinese Australian communities? How did the CYL respond to this issue?

Appendix 1

- As the immigration debate wore on, you appeared on a televised debate on a current affairs program. As I understand there were other representatives of Chinese Australian communities there, as well as non-Chinese Australians/White Anglo-European Australians opposed to multiculturalism. Could you recount your participation in this program (what it was like; who approached who; did people participate equally, etc)? What do you think were the effects of this program after it went to air? Do you think the CYL was fairly and accurately portrayed in the program?
- 1986 was also the year of the National Conference of Chinese Australian community organisations in Sydney. Could you explain the CYL's involvement? What was the rationale behind the event? Were the intended objectives of the event achieved?
- You became XYZ in 20XX, which is another significant period. Pauline Hanson had just failed in her bid for the Australian Senate in November 2001. How had the CYL responded to Hanson's time in Parliament? How was Hanson's failure to be re-elected received by the CYL?
- This period has also been popularly referred to as the start of the Chinese century. Symbols of this include the Beijing Olympics, its growing economic power and China's assertiveness toward other nations in its neighbourhood. How did the CYL react to the rise of China? Did the CYL's historic political leanings toward the PRC influence its responses?
- In recent years, there have been certain developments that have put pressure on Chinese Australian communities. The return of Pauline Hanson, the push to change the *Racial Discrimination Act* (Section 18C) and recently Fraser Anning's maiden speech in Parliament have signalled that racism and restrictive immigration are political issues once again. How does the CYL respond to these issues? Are there any parallels you can see between now and other periods in Australian history?
- Anxieties about Chinese influence in Australia are also growing in media, political and (now with the publication of Clive Hamilton's book *Silent Invasion*) academic arenas. Chinese Australian communities are concerned that this is stoking a new wave of Sinophobia in Australia and that is negatively impacting on the lives

of Chinese Australians. Again, has the CYL responded to this issue and are there any similarities between now and other periods in Australian history? Considering such things as the continuing rise of China, the lurch to the right for many democratic countries and the history of Australian multiculturalism, how do you foresee this issue unfolding in the future?
- You said to me in an earlier phone conversation that you had a desire to do things for the community without chasing prominence and prestige. Can you elaborate on this: firstly, the personal duty people feel to serve the community; and secondly, the esteem that comes from being seen to serve the community?

Appendix 2

Profiles of prominent Chinese Australian community organisations encountered in the book

Appendix 2 provides a profile of the organisations that featured most prominently in this book. These organisations were fortunate to have a rich and diverse amount of their historical materials preserved in archives, libraries, digital databases and private collections. Often this was the case because institutions or individuals deemed these organisations important enough for their records to be preserved. Past and present members of organisations have also contributed to these records by giving interviews with historians or journalists. This appendix is neither an exhaustive list of the organisations that appeared in the book, nor an exhaustive list of the people who played important roles in these organisations and among Chinese Australian communities at large. It is nevertheless supplied for the reader's reference and to offer a glimpse of the diversity of Chinese Australian community organisations.

1. Australian Capital Territory Chinese Australian Association 堪培拉澳華會	
Formed	1988 in Canberra.
Years most active	1990 to mid-2000s.
Founding mission	Cultural maintenance and to promote integration of Chinese migrants into Australian society. To promote the interests of and to encourage greater cooperation between Chinese Australians in the ACT.
Member profile	Families with school-age children. Predominately Cantonese-speaking backgrounds.
Key people	Alice Chu – 朱盧婉貞 David Lee – 李騰謙 David Ng – 吳耀華 Peter Pan – 潘南強 Rita Wong-Brooks – 黄麗達
Key initiatives	• Creation of Cantonese language radio programs. • Educational and recreational tours of China and Hong Kong. • Assisted in the creation of sister-city relations between Canberra and Beijing.

Appendix 2

2. Australian Chinese Community Association 澳華公會	
Formed	1974 in Sydney.
Years most active	Mid-1970s to present.
Founding mission	Community welfare and cultural maintenance. Migration and settlement services. Greater cooperation and unity among Sydney's various Chinese Australian communities.
Member profile	At its founding, it was a cross-section of Sydney's contemporary Chinese Australian communities: locally born Chinese Australians of Cantonese-speaking backgrounds (and other Southern Chinese languages); recent business and professional migrants from Hong Kong; and some representatives of newly established refugee communities of ethnically Chinese from Southeast Asia. In later decades, ACCA has incorporated Chinese Australians with Malaysian and Singaporean backgrounds, as well as more recent migrants from Mainland China.
Key people	Benjamin Chow – 周明棟 Catherine Chung – 鐘綺薇 Kip Fong – 鄺紹翕 Stanley Hunt – 陳沛德 Kenneth Kwok – 郭家梁 Lawrence Lau – 劉國隆 Garry Leong – 梁子成 Angeline Leung – 歐陽英蘭
Key initiatives	• Settlement and social worker services for newly arrived refugees in the 1970s and 1980s. • Cantonese and Mandarin-language schools. • Creation of an aged care home for elderly Chinese Australians. • Various cultural festivities and community outreach programs.

3. Australian Chinese Forum/Chinese Australian Forum 澳華論壇	
Formed	1985 in Sydney (name changed in 1996).
Years most active	1985 to present.
Founding mission	To increase political awareness and participation among Chinese Australians. To promote multiculturalism and inter-ethnic understanding. To represent common Chinese Australian interests in the public domain.
Member profile	Well-educated, wealthy professionals and businesspeople. Many founding members were Hong Kong migrants and some born locally in Sydney or coming from other (former) Commonwealth territories.
Key people	(Luan) Thiam Ang Benjamin Chow – 周明棟 Francis Lee – 李潤輝 James Lee – 李齊平 Jon-Claire Lee Jason Yat-sen Li – 李逸仙 Irene Moss Tony Pun – 潘瑞亮 Helen Sham-Ho – 何沈慧霞
Key initiatives	• Anti-racism campaigns during the Blainey debate, Hanson debate, following proposed changes to Section 18C of the *Racial Discrimination Act*, and during the COVID-19 pandemic. These campaigns included public debates, media appearances and petitioning of state and federal governments. • Regular public forums about current affairs with politicians, government representatives and academics as guest speakers. • Information campaigns and support for Australia to become a republic during the 1999 referendum.

Appendix 2

4. Australian Chinese Workers Association 澳洲华人总工会	
Formed	2012 in Sydney.
Years most active	2010s to present.
Founding mission	Settlement, legal, employment and social support services. Youth leadership initiatives.
Member profile	University students and young professionals. Predominately young migrants from Mainland China.
Key people	David Chen/Chen Qingsong – 陈青松
Key initiatives	<ul><li>Campaign for the "Overseas Chinese Citizen Card".</li><li>Established a memorial for Chinese gold miners at Rookwood cemetery in New South Wales.</li><li>Research project: 澳大利亚华人社区发展报告 *The Report of the Development of Chinese Community in Australia 2018*.</li></ul>

5. Australian Council for the Promotion of the Peaceful Reunification of China 澳洲中国和平统一促进会	
Formed	2000 in Sydney.
Years most active	2000s to present.
Founding mission	To unite Chinese Australian communities and organisations behind the PRC's vision of reunification with Taiwan. To foster closer ties between Australia and the PRC through cultural exchanges and philanthropy.
Member profile	Migrants and expats from the PRC. Membership overlaps with many of the native place associations, business and cultural groups that have been created by migrants from the PRC in recent decades.
Key people	William Chiu – 邱维廉 Xiangmo Huang – 黄向墨
Key initiatives	• Various cultural and philanthropic programs. • Leadership and coordination of smaller community organisations to oppose views critical of the PRC.

Appendix 2

6. Australasian KMT 中國國民堂駐澳洲總支部	
Formed	In 1914, the Young China League reformed as the KMT in Melbourne. Other branches around Australia, New Zealand and the Pacific opened and were eventually consolidated as the Australasian KMT in 1923, headquartered in Sydney.
Years most active	1920s to 1960s.
Founding mission	To unite overseas Chinese in support for China's nationalist cause and ultimately the creation of a Chinese republic.
Member profile	19th-century Chinese migrants to Australia (mainly from Guangdong province) and their descendants who had established themselves in Australia's metropolitan areas and regional cities.
Key people	Eugene Seeto – 司徒惠初
Key initiatives	- Fundraising for local and international causes, especially for China during the Second World War. - Continued support for the ROC during the Cold War.

7. Australian Values Alliance 澳洲价值守护联盟	
Formed	2016 in Sydney.
Years most active	2016 to present.
Founding mission	To protect Australian society and democratic institutions from the political influence of the Chinese Communist Party.
Member profile	Mainly middle-aged or older professionals or businesspeople, some with political experience and others without. Most are emigrants from the Chinese mainland.
Key people	Chongyi Feng – 冯崇义 John Hugh – 胡煜明
Key initiatives	• Protests and political petitioning of events or lobbying it deems to be "communist propaganda" or examples of "PRC influence". • Support of politicians, academics and journalists who criticise the PRC. • Maintenance of a de-centralised, non-hierarchical organisational structure.

Appendix 2

8. Cathay Club/Cathay Community Association 國泰會	
Formed	1981 in Brisbane.
Years most active	Mid-1980s to today.
Founding mission	Social activities, cultural maintenance and community service.
Member profile	Founded by ethnic Chinese migrants from Papua New Guinea. Predominately middle-class professional and small business backgrounds.
Key people	Ken Cheung Peter Low
Key initiatives	• Settlement programs for Indochinese refugees in the Brisbane area during the 1980s. • Founding member organisation of the Queensland Chinese Forum. • Homecare services for the elderly. • Construction of the CCA community centre.

9. Chinese Association of South Australia 南澳中華會	
Formed	1971 in Adelaide.
Years most active	1970s to 2010s.
Founding mission	Community welfare and cultural maintenance. Sports and social activities.
Member profile	Young and middle-aged migrants, especially those with families. Students, academics, small-business owners and professionals. Many were new, well-educated migrants from Malaysia, Singapore and Hong Kong.
Key people	Ching-hwang Yen – 顏清湟 Edmund Young
Key initiatives	• Creation of Mandarin-language school and cultural events like the "Dragon Ball" and Dragon Boat racing. • Assistance for ethnic Chinese and Southeast Asian refugees settling in the Adelaide area. • Anti-racist campaigns including holding public forums and coordination with government bodies. • Campaign to have Mandarin taught at the South Australian Institute of Technology (now University of South Australia).

10. Chinese Australian Services Society/CASS/CASSCare 華人服務社	
Formed	1981 in Sydney. Later dropped the acronym and became known simply as "CASS", which then became the forerunner organisation to CASSCare.
Years most active	1980s to present.
Founding mission	Community welfare, cultural maintenance, social services.
Member profile	Originally migrant families of ethnic Chinese background (Mainland, Hong Kong, Malaysia, Singapore) with young children or elderly parents. Membership now extends into Korean, Indonesian and Vietnamese migrant communities.
Key people	Cecilia Fong – 方秀玲 Henry Pan – 潘南弘
Key initiatives	• Creation of multiple childcare sites across Sydney that use community languages (Mandarin, Cantonese, Indonesian and Korean). • Residential aged care. • Disability support services. • Public cultural displays and social activities for members.

11. Chinese Association of Victoria 维多利亚省中华协会	
Formed	1982 in Melbourne.
Years most active	1980s to present.
Founding mission	Cultural maintenance, community welfare, social and recreational activities.
Member profile	Mainly ethnic Chinese Malaysian and Singaporean migrants. Professionals and businesspeople with young families.
Key people	Frank Chew – 周呈恭 Vincent Chow – 周仲民 Chooi-Hon Ho – 何柯水凤 Chua Ka-sing – 蔡家声
Key initiatives	• Creation of a Mandarin-language school. • Construction of the CAV community centre. • Social activities for members and cultural performances in the community. • Educational and recreational tours of China and Hong Kong.

Appendix 2

12. Chinese Fellowship of Victoria 侨友社	
Formed	1971 in Melbourne.
Years most active	1970s to 2000s.
Founding mission	Cultural maintenance, community welfare and social services. To foster unity among Melbourne's Chinese communities and closer relations between Australia and China.
Member profile	Local Chinese Australian community of Cantonese-speaking backgrounds. Elderly and recent migrants from the Mainland. Students, blue- and white-collar workers, businesspeople and professionals.
Key people	Gim Wah Yeo – 楊錦華 Katie Young – 黃琚寧 Patrick Yuen – 袁錦亞
Key initiatives	• Creation of a Mandarin-language school and library. • Regular cultural displays and social activities for members. • Educational and recreational tours of China and Hong Kong. • Instrumental in organising two national conferences of Chinese Australian organisations in 1986 and 1989.

13. Chung Wah Association 中华会馆	
Formed	1909 in Perth.
Years most active	1910s to 1920s, then again from 1970s to present.
Founding mission	Originally a society for mutual assistance, settlement and social services. Since the multicultural turn in the 1970s, it has become dedicated to cultural maintenance, social and recreational activities and community welfare.
Member profile	Originally created by 19th- and early 20th-century Chinese migrants from Guangdong province and the Nanyang region (mostly Singapore) who worked a variety of manual trades or as merchants. In the late 20th century, membership reflected young professionals and families migrating from Hong Kong, Southeast Asia and steadily more members coming from the PRC in the 21st century.
Key people	Eric Tan – 陳繼志
Key initiatives	• Creation of clubhouse in the early 20th century. • Regular cultural performances and social activities for members. • Quarterly bilingual magazine from 2011 to present.

Appendix 2

14. Chung Wah Society 中華會	
Formed	1946 in Darwin.
Years most active	1970s to present.
Founding mission	Cultural maintenance, community service, social and recreational activities. To maintain Darwin's Chinese history.
Member profile	Predominately made up of the descendants of 19th- and early 20th-century Chinese emigrants from Southern China and the Nanyang region. Darwin's long-established Chin, Yuen and Tam families have a strong presence in the organisation. Members are local businesspeople and professionals.
Key people	Daryl Chin Roland Chin Adam Lowe Charles Tsang See-Kee – 會棠昭 Ray Yee
Key initiatives	• Reconstruction of the All Deities Temple. • Establishment of the NT Chinese Museum. • Dance troupe for cultural performances and social activities for members.

15. Chinese Youth League 侨青社	
Formed	In 1939 in Sydney, the Chinese Youth Dramatic Association reformed as the CYL in response to Japan's invasion of China.
Years most active	1940s to 1980s.
Founding mission	To support China's effort against Japan in the Second World War, the Communists in the Chinese Civil War, and then the PRC during the Cold War (CYL became less political late in the 20th century). To provide cultural maintenance, community welfare and social services for Chinese Australians as well as Chinese expats (especially sailors) in Sydney.
Member profile	Sydney's local Chinese Australians who came mainly from Cantonese-speaking backgrounds. Blue- and white-collar workers, students and small business owners.
Key people	Arthur Gar Locke – 鄭嘉樂 Tony Goh – 吳昌茂 Eddy Young – 楊廣釗 Peter Wong – 黃保榮
Key initiatives	• Fundraising for China and its Allies' war effort. • Supported industrial action taken by ethnic Chinese seafarers (for example, from Hong Kong and Singapore). Supported Maoist-aligned Australian unions like the Seamen's Union of Australia. • Creation of dance and theatre troupes as well as sports teams and competitions. • Cultural performances for the public and social activities for members.

Appendix 2

16. Federation of Chinese Associations 维省华人社团联合会	
Formed	1979 in Melbourne.
Years most active	1980s to 2000s. Became more active during the late 2010s.
Founding mission	To represent the common interests of Victoria's diverse Chinese Australian communities at state and national levels. To foster greater cooperation and unity among the member organisations.
Member profile	An umbrella organisation of community organisations from across Victoria. Membership was diverse: founding members were the pro-PRC CFV and the pro-ROC Chinese Youth Society. In the 2010s, member organisations exceeded 100 with most of them being native place associations created by Mainland emigres.
Key people	Peter Chan – 陳文山 Wellington Lee – 李錦球 Tsebin Tchen – 陳之彬 Gim Wah Yeo – 楊錦華
Key initiatives	• Instrumental in organising two national conferences of Chinese Australian organisations in 1986 and 1989. • Brought together different communities and organisations for joint annual Chinese New Year celebrations in Melbourne's Chinatown. • Raised funds for relief following natural disasters in China.

17. Indo-China Ethnic Chinese Association of Victoria 印支華人相相濟會	
Formed	1981 in Melbourne.
Years most active	1980s to 2000s.
Founding mission	Cultural maintenance, community welfare and social services.
Member profile	Ethnic Chinese migrants and refugees from Vietnam, Cambodia and Laos. Blue- and white-collar workers, young families.
Key people	Cuong Diep – 葉保強 Ngai Chung Cheng – 鄭毅中
Key initiatives	• Refugee and migrant settlement programs. • Community opposition to Hanson and Howard during the latter half of the 1990s. • Spearheaded a federation of Indochinese Chinese Australian community organisations. Advocated resisting PRC and ROC influence during the 1990s and 2000s. • Indochinese migration exhibit at the Melbourne Immigration Museum, *The Story of A Hoa*.

Appendix 2

18. Queensland Chinese Forum 昆士蘭華人論壇	
Formed	Formally constituted in 1994 in Brisbane. The precursor to QCF was the Council of Chinese Organisations of Queensland which had formed in response to the 1984 Blainey debate.
Years most active	1990s to 2010s.
Founding mission	To foster greater cooperation among Queensland's Chinese Australian communities and organisations and to represent their common interests at the state and national level.
Member profile	Founding member organisations included the Cathay Club, the Hong Kong Business & Professional Association and the Taiwan Friendship Association. Current organisations continue to represent Chinese Australian communities from various migrant backgrounds including China, Hong Kong, Papua New Guinea, Taiwan and Singapore, as well as locally born Chinese Australians.
Key people	Chek Ling Peter Low Tom Loy – 巫貴林 Bill Qui Michael Yau
Key initiatives	• Anti-racism media campaigns, especially during the Hanson debate. • Various philanthropic campaigns and cultural events.

19. See Yup Society 四邑會館	
Formed	1854 in Melbourne.
Years most active	1850s to 1920s. Became active again in the 1970s.
Founding mission	Community welfare and legal advocacy for Chinese emigrants from the See Yup region of Guangdong.
Member profile	As a See Yup native place association, its membership was derived from emigrants from the Tai Shan, Xin Hui, Kai Ping and Yin Ping districts of Guangdong province. Membership was overwhelmingly male (with or without families in China). Since the 1970s, SYS's membership has transformed to include families with young children or elderly parents – either locally born or from China.
Key people	Louis Ah Mouy – 雷亞妹 Maurice Leong Kwok Cheong – 梁國祥
Key initiatives	• The welfare and settlement of Chinese immigrants to Melbourne in the 19th and early 20th centuries. • Renovation of the See Yup Kuan Ti Temple and its return to active service. • Establishment of a Mandarin-language school and elderly care services. • Various philanthropic and charity initiatives in Victoria and Guangdong.

Index

89ers 142–170, 310, 312, 313; *see also* Tiananmen Massacre

Abetz, Eric 1, 272, 294, 305
ACT Chinese Australian Association (ACTCAA) 174, 244–247, 265, 269, 312
 and Hanson debate 206
 and the Tiananmen Massacre 149–151, 169
 connections with the PRC 245, 254
Australasian Kuomintang (AKMT) 37, 76, 82, 310
Australian Chinese Community Association (ACCA) 72, 73, 83–87, 88, 93, 95–100, 100, 127, 132, 156, 173, 264, 269, 285, 299, 310, 312
 and Blainey debate 107, 113
 and Hanson debate 210
 and the Tiananmen Massacre 147, 153
 "Australian Chinese Day" 257
 connections with the PRC 249, 250

Australian Chinese Forum (ACF) 113–117, 119, 122, 124, 128, 173, 213; *see also* Chinese Australian Forum (CAF)
 and Blainey debate 120
 and the Tiananmen Massacre 147, 151, 151
Australian Chinese Workers Association (ACWA) 273, 284–288, 306
Australian Security Intelligence Organisation (ASIO) 33, 67, 68, 76
Australian Values Alliance (AVA) 290–298, 306, 315

Barton, Edmund 37, 42
Blainey debate 103–138, 170, 201, 232, 307, 311

Campbell, Graeme 205
CASS (formerly known as the Chinese Australian Services Society) 167, 285

Chinese Association of South Australia (CASA) 54–58, 63, 88, 97–98, 118, 121, 122, 125, 132, 133, 166, 174, 311
and Blainey debate 109, 119, 120
and the Tiananmen Massacre 151, 169
Chinese Association of Victoria (CAV) 116, 133, 247–253, 269, 301, 315
and Hanson debate 206
and Blainey debate 300
Chinese Australian Forum (CAF) 204, 252, 260, 262, 263, 264, 299, 301, 301, 312, 314; see also Australian Chinese Forum (ACF)
and Hanson debate 204, 206, 216, 217–219, 232
Chinese Communist Party (CCP) 1, 4, 6, 60, 147, 172, 173, 174, 236, 238, 272, 282, 289, 291, 292, 294
and the Tiananmen Massacre 143, 145, 149, 312
Chinese Fellowship of Victoria (CFV) 58–62, 63, 67, 71, 74, 75, 77, 78, 79, 80, 81, 82, 86, 92, 118, 132, 279, 301, 305, 310
and Blainey debate 107–109, 113, 119, 120
and Hanson debate 206
and the Tiananmen Massacre 145, 146, 148, 151, 151
connections with the PRC 243, 269, 312
Chinese Youth League (CYL) 75–77, 79, 80, 82, 171, 310
and the Tiananmen Massacre 147
connections with the PRC 246, 269
Chung Wah Association (CWA) 35–40, 94, 309
and Blainey debate 107, 109, 113

Chung Wah Society (CWS) 40–45, 68, 131, 259, 309
Clark, Manning 125
COVID-19 299–304

diaspora 14, 81, 101, 148, 173, 173, 240, 252, 254, 282
Senate Inquiry into Issues Facing Diaspora Communities in Australia 271

English Language Intensive Courses for Overseas Students (ELICOS) 142
ethnic identity 12, 16, 83, 122, 256

Federation of Chinese Associations (FCA) 17, 70, 82, 171
and Hanson debate 210
and the Tiananmen Massacre 150
Fraser 29–31
Fraser government 131, 132

Hamilton, Clive 4–5, 275, 277, 282, 283, 305
Hanson, Pauline 240, 261, 302, 313
cross-community Chinese Australian response 209–215, 218, 219
Hanson debate 197–233
One Nation 199–200, 207, 208, 214, 215, 217, 221, 225, 227, 229–230
opposition to 227
Hartcher, Peter 1, 4, 276, 282, 305, 307, 318
Hawke, Bob 111, 116, 135, 139, 145, 152, 154, 155, 157
Hawke government 104, 107, 132, 168, 204
Howard, John 135, 136, 170, 199, 202, 203, 206, 210, 211, 218, 222, 226, 228, 228–231, 239, 240

Index

Howard government 168, 204, 219, 231
Howard paradox 253

immigration 7, 14, 25, 26, 27–31, 87, 94, 96, 104, 105, 111, 129, 132, 141, 168–168, 170, 197, 201, 203, 204, 263, 276
Indo-China Ethnic Chinese Association of Victoria (ICECAV) 62, 198, 206, 207–208, 278, 301, 314, 314
International Cultural Exchange Association (Australia) (ICEAA) 288–290

Keating, Paul 205, 225
Keating government 168, 203
Kuomintang (KMT) 60, 66

Morrison, Scott 300
multiculturalism 25–30, 51, 66, 70, 82, 100, 105, 112, 126, 129–130, 132, 135, 136–137, 170, 197, 198, 204, 223, 231, 232, 239, 240, 262, 262, 274, 303, 304, 309, 313, 317, 318

National Conference of the Australian Chinese Community 2, 103, 106, 118, 119, 122–129, 153, 210, 216, 311
National Front 90

patriotism 4, 60, 61, 63, 81, 82, 86, 145, 151, 172, 237, 238, 241, 242, 296
People's Liberation Army (PLA) 146, 147
People's Republic of China (PRC) 1, 4, 8, 60, 66, 74, 76, 77, 80, 100, 127, 141, 150, 166, 171, 210, 238–258, 269–270, 271–284, 307, 310, 312

qiáowù 242, 244, 247, 252, 254, 256, 258, 269, 282–288, 317
Queensland Chinese Forum (QCF) 198, 216–223, 301
and Blainey debate 216
and Hanson debate 216, 217, 232

Racial Discrimination Act 1975 29, 96, 99, 122
racism 5, 6, 29, 34, 57, 82, 85, 87–99, 100, 101, 106, 108, 109, 112, 129, 133, 134, 136, 137, 197, 198, 201, 206, 208, 211, 213, 214, 217, 218, 223, 225, 229, 231, 272, 276, 285, 294, 299, 299, 301, 304, 311, 315, 317
Australian media 66, 92–97, 100, 101, 109–112, 131, 199, 202, 223, 226, 227, 232, 251, 311
League of Rights 91, 311
Republic of China (ROC) 60, 60, 74, 82, 256, 257, 310; *see also* Taiwan
Ruddock, Philip 170

See Yup Society (SYS) 45–51, 61, 68, 243, 309

Taiwan 8, 61, 74, 75, 81, 127, 150, 210, 254, 269, 276, 310; *see also* Republic of China (ROC)
Tiananmen Massacre 139–174, 146, 149, 232, 243, 278, 312
transnational 14, 66, 78, 79, 81, 82, 101, 173, 273, 282, 283, 290, 310, 317

385

unity 2, 51, 61, 66, 77, 83, 85, 117–122, 126, 129, 137, 153, 156, 232, 282, 296, 307, 310, 311

White Australia policy 7, 9, 25, 27, 28, 37, 42, 50, 63, 65, 68, 69, 78, 84, 85, 86, 104, 129, 139, 197, 231, 264, 309, 313

Whitlam, Gough 28–30, 65

Whitlam government 25, 27, 84

Wong, Peter 157, 161, 221, 230

www.ingramcontent.com/pod-product-compliance
Lightning Source LLC
Chambersburg PA
CBHW061245230426
43662CB00021B/2434